Statistics and Public Policy

Statistics
and Public Policy

Edited by

BRUCE D. SPENCER

Department of Statistics
Northwestern University, Illinois, USA

CLARENDON PRESS · OXFORD
1997

Oxford University Press, Great Clarendon Street, Oxford OX2 6DP

Oxford New York

Athens Ayckland Bangkok Bogota Bombay Buenos Aires
Calcutta Cape Town Dar es Salaam Delhi Florence Hong Kong
Istanbul Karachi Kuala Lumpur Madras Madrid Melbourne
Mexico City Nairobi Paris Singapore Taipei Tokyo Toronto
and associated companies in
Berlin Ibadan

Oxford is a trade mark of Oxford University Press

Published in the United States
by Oxford University Press Inc., New York

A catalogue record for this book is available from the British Library

Library of Congress Cataloging in Publication Data
Statistics and public policy/edited by Bruce D. Spencer.

Includes bibliographical references and index.
1. Policy sciences–Methodology. 2. Social sciences–Statistical
services. I. Spencer, Bruce D.
H97.S763 1997   300'.1'5195–dc20   96-36204
ISBN 0 19 852341 6 (Hbk)

Typeset by Hewer Text Composition Services, Edinburgh
Printed in Great Britain by Biddles Ltd., Guildford, Surrey

Preface

The articles in this book explore uses of statistics in public affairs, such as AIDS diffusion, DNA fingerprinting, human rights, and national defense. Such uses of statistics have been a concern of a teacher and friend, Richard Savage, a person of strong heart and mind who has challenged many of us to think more widely and deeply. His work in the field is the inspiration for this collection of chapters.

Professor Savage began his statistical research in a part of mathematical statistics known as nonparametric statistics, with a particular interest in rank orders. His first published paper in 1953 was a review of the extant literature on the subject.[1] He made a number of important contributions to this field, among them the well-known Chernoff–Savage theorem[2] which he developed with Herman Chernoff, a contributor to this volume (chapter 1). Three decades after his first paper, Professor Savage was still publishing new and interesting results in this field.[3]

Professor Savage is one of a few mathematical statisticians of his generation who chose to pursue the application of statistical principles and concepts to problems of public policy. Some of his like-minded colleagues, such as William Kruskal, Lincoln Moses, and Frederick Mosteller, have a similar interest, and have contributed chapters to this volume (chapters 5 and 12). The development of Dr Savage's interests dates back to his days as a visiting faculty member at Stanford (1954–57). While at Stanford he served as statistical consultant to the Center for Advanced Study in the Behavioral Sciences. There he worked with James Coleman (see Chapter 10), Karl Deutsch,[4] and others. Later, he was asked to participate in the first National Research Council study of undercount in the U.S. census.[5] He returned to the Center for Advanced Study in the Behavioral Sciences as a Fellow in 1970. He also attended a conference led by Nathan Keyfitz (who wrote chapter 11 in this volume) at the East–West Institute in Hawaii, which explored the role of statistical thinking in demography. Professor Savage's long-term interest in statistics and public policy is reflected in his publications, in his teaching, and in his term as President of the American Statistical Association (1984).[6]

His presidential address to the American Statistical Association (ASA) reflected his public policy interests both as a professional statistician and as a citizen. He noted that

[The] ASA and most statisticians have attempted to avoid partisan politics or the advocate role. Nevertheless professional involvement in political issues—such as what style of government we should have, how the government should make budget choices, how we should maintain and promote liberty, and we can obtain peace—should be emphasized. In these partisan areas, there are opportunities for the statistician to work impartially to allow the decision-making process to be more enlightened .... Adversion of self-deception and consideration of all options are necessary for enlightenment in partisan decision making.[7]

Drawing on examples from the national statistical system, cost-benefit analysis, human rights, and defense, Professor Savage made suggestions of how statisticians can enhance the decision process in partisan affairs. The address struck responsive chords among his listeners and led to increased awareness of the roles of statistics in human rights (see chapter 2 by Thomas Jabine) and national defense (see chapter 3 by David Chu and Nancy Spruill) in particular.

A problem presented to me by Professor Savage—how much money should the government spend on the census—served as the beginning of my own research work. He had enough faith to let his students flounder around while finding their bearing, and he liked to challenge his students and teach them how to think. His curiosity, high academic standards, and his faith that the theory of mathematical statistics could apply to real-world problems influenced not only students, but also faculty and friends, such as Allan Sampson, Stephen Dresch, Stephen Fienberg, Leslie Kish, Philip Redfern, Allen Wallis (see chapters 9, 13, 4, 7, 8, and 6 respectively), and many others. He served as a generous advisor and mentor and directed 18 dissertations at Minnesota, Florida State and Yale.

Professor Savage served as Editor of the two flagship statistics journals in the U.S., the *Journal of the American Statistical Association* (1968) and the *Annals of Statistics* (1974–77). He delights in incisive comments and close reading, and those who do not take offense at his penetrating and honest comments—as well as many of those who do—value them highly.

This book was conceived of as a way to honor our teacher, colleague, and friend, Richard Savage. We thought that the best way to acknowledge his contributions to the field was to communicate and extend his influence to new groups of students. We wanted to show them that there were interesting problems in statistics and public policy that were accessible, important, and deserving attention. The mission for the authors was to write chapters exemplifying aspects of statistics with important connections to public issues. The chapters were to emphasize ideas rather than technical detail or generality. The hope is to stimulate further interest and research into statistics and public policy. If readers of the book take away an appreciation of statistics in public affairs, and if some are moved to explore new questions, this book will have been successful in its goals and will honor a great statistician the authors of the book have been privileged to know.

Preparation of this book was partially supported by the National Institute on Aging through grant RO1-AG10156. I am grateful to Juha Alho and Mary Mulry for critical comments. My deepest gratitude goes to my wife Donna for her patience and constructive criticism through all phases of this project.

Evanston
October 1996

Bruce D. Spencer

1 Savage, I. R. (1953). Bibliography of nonparametric statistics and related topics. *Journal of the American Statistical Association*, **48**, 844–906.
2 Chernoff, H. and Savage, I. R. (1958). Asymptotic normality and efficiency of certain nonparametric test statistics. *Annals of Mathematical Statistics*, **29**, 972–94.
3 Savage, I. R. (1980). Lehmann Alternatives. *Nonparametric Statistical Inference, Vol. I, II*, Budapest, 795–821. Colloquia Mathematica Societatis János Bolyai, 32, North-Holland, Amsterdam–New York, 1982.
4 Deutsch, K. and Savage, I. R. (1960). A statistical model of the gross analysis of transaction flows. *Econometrica*, **28**, 551–72.
5 *America's Uncounted People*. Division of Behavioral Sciences, National Research Council–National Academy of Sciences. Report of the Advisory Committee on Problems of Census Enumeration, 1971. Published by the National Academy of Sciences, May 1972.
6 It is interesting that in recent years there has appeared a strong relationship between statistics based on ranks and the properties of voting systems, which are of course fundamental to a democracy. See Saari, D. G. (1995). *Basic geometry of voting*. New York: Springer.
7 Savage, I. R. (1985). Hard–soft problems. *Journal of the American Statistical Association*, **80**, 1–7, p. 6.

Biographies

Herman Chernoff has been Professor of Statistics at Harvard University since 1984. Previously he served on the faculties of MIT (1974–84), Stanford (1952–75), the University of Illinois (1949–52), and the University of Chicago (1947–49). Dr Chernoff works in a variety of areas of theoretical statistics, including asymptotic theory, sequential analysis, and statistical analysis for pattern recognition and classification. He is a member of the American Academy of Arts and Sciences and the National Academy of Sciences, and received his B.S. in Mathematics from City College of New York in 1943 and his M.Sc. and Ph.D. in Applied Mathematics from Brown University in 1945 and 1948.

David S. C. Chu is Director of RAND's Washington Office and Associate Chairman of RAND's Research Staff. He served as Assistant Secrety of Defense (Program Analysis and Evaluation) from July 1988 until January 1993; he had earlier exercised similar responsibilities as Director, Program Analysis and Evaluation (1981–88). In these positions he advised the Secretary and Deputy Secretary of Defense on the allocation of the Department's resources, helping plan the forces and weapons systems that determine long-term defense capabilities. Prior to his Pentagon appointments, Dr Chu was the Assistant Director of the Congressional Budget Office for National Security and International Affairs (1978–81). He was educated at Yale, receiving his B.A. in Economics and Mathematics in 1964 and his Ph.D. in Economics in 1972.

James S. Coleman was a leading sociologist who was concerned with analysis of educational systems, theories of social change and collective action, and social networks. He was the author of the 1966 'Coleman Report' which was used to buttress arguments for achieving racial balance in public schools. Dr Coleman received a degree in chemical engineering from Purdue University in 1949 and a doctorate in sociology from Columbia University in 1955. He taught at the University of Chicago from 1956–59, went to Johns Hopkins University in 1959 to found and head its Department of Social Relations, and returned to the University of Chicago in 1973 for the remainder of his career until his death in 1994. He was a member of the National Academy of Sciences and the American Academy of Arts and Sciences, and received many other honors.

Stephen P. Dresch is a political economist and social commentator who has worked in academia and in government. From 1985–90 he was Dean and Professor in Economics and Business at Michigan Technological University. Following that he served as an elected member of the Michigan House of Representatives (1991–92). Professor Dresch has long-standing research interests in the economics of higher education, and has published numerous books, articles, and columns. He received his A.B. in Philosophy from Miami University (Ohio) in 1963 and his M.Phil. and Ph.D. in Economics from Yale University in 1996 and 1970.

Stephen E. Fienberg is Maurice Falk Professor of Statistics and Social Science, Carnegie Mellon University in Pittsburgh. He has served as Dean of the College of Humanities and Social Sciences at Carnegie Mellon and as Vice President for Academic Affairs at York University in Toronto. He has served as editor of the *Journal of the American Statistical Association* and was a founding co-editor of *Chance*. He has published extensively on statistical methods for the analysis of categorical data, and on aspects of sample surveys and randomized experiments. His research interests include the use of statistics in public policy and the law, surveys and experiments, and the role of statistical methods in census taking.

Thomas B. Jabine is an independent statistical consultant who specializes in sampling, survey research methods, statistical policy, and the use of statistics to monitor human rights. He was formerly Statistical Policy Expert for the Energy Information Administration, Chief Mathematical Statistician for the Social Security Administration, and Chief of the Statistical Research Division of the Bureau of the Census. He is a consultant to the past Chair of the American Statistical Association's Committee on Scientific Freedom and Human Rights.

Kenneth R. Janson is Executive Vice President, Chief Financial Officer, and Treasurer of D&N Financial Corporation, a banking company providing consumer and business products and services primarily in Michigan, U.S.A. Previously he held faculty appointments at Michigan State University and Michigan Technological University. Trained as an economist and accountant, Dr Janson holds M.S. and Ph.D. degrees from the University of Wisconsin at Madison and is a Certified Public Accountant.

Nathan Keyfitz is Professor Emeritus of Population and Sociology at Harvard University. He was born in Canada, studied at McGill University in Montreal and the University of Chicago, where he received the doctorate in 1952; since then he has taught at the University of Chicago, at the University of California at Berkeley, and has been at Harvard since 1972. He has been awarded eight honorary degrees from three countries, is a member of the National Academy of Sciences and the American Academy of Arts and Sciences, and in 1993 the Austrian Government awarded him its Medal for Science. He is the author of numerous articles and books, including *Applied Mathematical Demography* and *Introduction to the Mathematics of Population*.

Leslie Kish has been Professor of Sociology since 1960 (Emeritus since 1981) at the University of Michigan, where he has also been Senior Research Scientist at its Institute for Social Research. He has been teaching and doing research in the methods and applications of survey sampling at Michigan since 1947. He organized and directed the Sampling Program for Foreign Statisticians in 1961, with graduates practicing and teaching in 95 countries. He has been honored as the Henry Russel Lecturer (1981) at the University of Michigan, received an Honorary Doctorate in Statistics from the University of Bologna (at its 900th anniversary), is an Honorary Fellow of the Royal Statistical Society, and was President of the American Statistical Association. He is the author of numerous articles and books.

William H. Kruskal is Ernest deWitt Burton Distinguished Service Professor Emeritus at the University of Chicago, where he has been a faculty member since 1955. He chaired the Department of Statistics for six years, served as Dean of the University's Division of Social Sciences for nine, and later served as Dean Pro Tempore of the (now) Irving B. Harris Graduate School of Public Policy Studies. His many research interests include censuses and government statistics more generally, the meaning of ideas such as representative sampling, normality, and relative importance, as well as linear models and nonparametric statistics. He headed the Committee on National Statistics during its first six years, and has served as President of the American Statistical Association and the Institute for Mathematical Statistics.

Lincoln Moses taught statistics at Stanford University from 1952 to 1992 in an appointment equally divided between the Statistics Department and the School of Medicine. During his years at Stanford he occupied various academic dean positions, for ten years in all. For two and a half years, beginning in 1978, he headed the statistics area (Energy Information Administration) of the newly founded US Department of Energy. Upon returning to Stanford, he helped found, and for two years direct, the Undergraduate Program in Public Policy. During 1984–85 he chaired the Committee on National Statistics of the National Academy of Sciences/National Research Council. He is the author of numerous books and articles.

Frederick Mosteller is Roger I. Lee Professor of Mathematical Statistics Emeritus, Harvard University. He directs the Center for Evaluation of the Initiatives for Children Project at the American Academy of Arts and Sciences. His research work has been devoted to theoretical and applied statistics. He works in data analysis, meta-analysis, robust methods in health and medicine, and in social sciences, with some publications in sports statistics. At Harvard he has chaired the departments of Statistics, of Biostatistics, and of Health Policy and Management. He is the recipient of numerous awards and honors, and has written many influential books and papers.

Philip Redfern read mathematics at Cambridge where he was classed a Wrangler in the Mathematical Tripos Part 2 in 1942. He joined the UK Government Statistical Service in 1947 at the Central Statistical Office and completed his civil service career in 1982 as Deputy Director of the Office of Population Censuses and Surveys. There, he was involved in the planning and execution of the censuses of population of 1971 and 1981. In the mid-80's he carried out a study on behalf of the Statistical Office of the European Communities (Eurostat) into census practices in the different countries of the Community and in Canada and the US. This work led him to present a series of papers on censuses and population registers to meetings in Europe and North America.

Allan R. Sampson is Professor of Mathematics and Statistics and Acting Director of the Center for Statistics at the University of Pittsburgh, where he has been on the faculty since 1978. Prior to that he taught at Florida State University and was Manager of the Department of Biostatistics at Abbott Laboratories. His research interests include multivariate analysis, clinical trials, and reliability theory. Professor Sampson has worked with the U.S. Census Bureau, the American Statistical Association, and the Committee on National Statistics to improve disability statistics. He received his A.B. in Mathematics from UCLA in 1966 and his M.S. and Ph.D. in Statistics from Stanford in 1968 and 1970.

Sam L. Savage is a consulting professor of operations research at Stanford University, where he has developed a course on Operations Research in Spreadsheets. He received his Ph.D. in computer science from Yale University in 1973. After spending a year at General Motors Research Laboratory, he joined the faculty of the University of Chicago Graduate School of Business, with which he has been affiliated since 1974. In 1985 he led the development of a software package, What'sBest!, that couples linear programming to Lotus 1–2–3, and has recently published additional quantitative software tools for spreadsheets. Current areas of interest include stochastic information systems and petroleum prospect portfolio management.

Nancy L. Spruill is the Deputy Director for Acquisition Resources in the Office of the Under Secretary of Defense for Acquisition and Technology. Dr Spruill started her career in 1971 with the Center for Naval Analyses (CNA) as a technical staff analyst. She became a project director before leaving CNA for the Office of the Secretary of Defense in 1983, where she worked in a number of areas including force management and personnel and program analysis and evaluation. In 1993 Dr Spruill moved to Defense Mapping Agency. While there she was Acting Deputy Comptroller and the Chief, Programs and Analysis Division for the DMA Comptroller. Dr Spruill has been on her present assignment since 1995. She received a B.S. in Mathematics from University of Maryland and an M.S. and Ph.D. in Mathematical Statistics from George Washington University.

Stephen M. Stigler is the Ernest DeWitt Burton Distinguished Service Professor of Statistics and member of the Committee on the Conceptual Foundations of Science at the University of Chicago. He received his Ph.D. in statistics from the University of California at Berkeley. His research has included work in mathematical statistics, the application of statistics in the social and behavioral sciences, and the history of statistics and its applications. He is a member of the American Academy of Arts and Sciences and several professional societies; he has edited the *Journal of the American Statistical Association* and is Chairman of the Board of Trustees of the Center for Advanced Study in the Behavioral Sciences.

Allen Wallis has spent most of his career in universities, at Yale, Stanford, Columbia, Chicago, and Rochester. At Chicago he was Professor of Economics, Chairman of the Statistics Department and Dean of the Graduate School of Business. For the two decades 1962–82 he was Chancellor of the University of Rochester. Dr Wallis joined the State Department in July 1982 and served as Under Secretary for Economic Affairs until January 1989. He edited the *Journal of the American Statistical Association* from 1950 to 1959 and was President of the Association in 1965. He is the recipient of numerous honors, including five honorary doctor's degrees, the Wilks Medal from the American Statistical Association, and the Secretary of State's Distinguished Service Award. Since 1989 he has been a Resident Scholar at the American Enterprise Institute for Public Policy Research in Washington.

Contents

Contributors

Herman Chernoff, Department of Statistics, SC 713, Harvard University, Cambridge, MA 02138, USA.

David S. C. Chu: RAND, 1333 H Street, N.W., Washington, DC 20005, USA

Stephen P. Dresch: *The Kauth house*, 318 Cooper Avenue, Hancock, MI 49930, USA.

Stephen E. Fienberg: Department of Statistics, Carnegie Mellon University, Pittsburgh, PA 15213–3890, USA.

Thomas B. Jabine: 3231 Worthington Street, N.W., Washington, DC 20015–2362, USA.

Kenneth R. Janson: D&N Financial Corporation, 400 Quincy St, Hancock, MI 49930, USA

Nathan Keyfitz: 1580 Massachusetts Avenue, #7C, Cambridge, MA 02138, USA.

Leslie Kish: Institute for Social Research, University of Michigan, Ann Arbor, MI 48106–1248, USA.

William H. Kruskal: Statistics Department, University of Chicago, 5734 University Avenue, Chicago, IL 60637, USA.

Lincoln E. Moses: Statistics Department, Stanford University, Sequoia Hall, Stanford, CA 94305, USA.

Frederick Mosteller: Statistics Department, Harvard University Science Center, 1 Oxford Street, Room 604, Cambridge, MA 02138, USA.

Philip Redfern: 17 Fulwith Close, Harrogate, North Yorkshire, HG2 8HP, UK.

Allan R. Sampson: Mathematics and Statistics Department, University of Pittsburgh, Pittsburgh, PA 15260, USA.

Sam L. Savage: Department of Operations Research, Terman Engineering Center, Stanford University, Stanford, CA 94305–4022, USA.

Nancy L. Spruill: 123 North Park, Arlington, VA 22203, USA.

Stephen M. Stigler: Statistics Department, University of Chicago, 5734 University Avenue, Chicago, IL 60637, USA.

W. Allen Wallis: American Enterprise Institute, 1150 Seventeenth St., N.W., Washington DC 20036–4603, USA.

Introduction

Statistics – meaning statistical data, statistical methods, and statistical thinking – play important and fascinating roles in public issues. Yet these roles are unknown to statistics students and even professional statisticians. This book shows some ways in which statistics affect and are affected by public issues such as government policy- or decision-making, public administration, law, and public debate. The book describes examples of statistics in public policy areas as disparate as national defense, AIDS diffusion, DNA fingerprinting, human rights violations, scientific manpower, population registers and censuses, individuals with disabilities. Although readers of the book should have some prior statistical training – typically a minimum of half a year of undergraduate-level statistics – the emphasis is on ideas rather than technical detail or mathematical generality.

The book is written more from the statistical than the policy perspective, and is organized around three general statistical issues: statistics for describing a state of affairs, methods, and issues in data collection, and statistics for policy analysis, or what will happen if we do x.

The remainder of this introduction gives an overview of the articles in the book, and draws out some common themes. It also attempts to draw attention to some unanswered statistical questions.

PART I. USES OF STATISTICS FOR DESCRIPTION

Statistics are used in important ways for description and summarization in public affairs. In this part of the book, we illustrate some of these uses and ponder some questions that arise.

'Issues in DNA fingerprinting' by Herman Chernoff discusses the history and statistical issues involved in matching DNA samples, as in the well-known trial of O. J. Simpson. Issues include calculation of the odds that the match is due to chance, and courtroom interpretation of those odds. Chernoff notes that 'where well preserved biological specimens belonging to the guilty party are available, it is almost impossible for an innocent person to be falsely identified with an honest and careful analysis . . . To put it bluntly, a false identification is much more likely to be due to an error in labeling the biological specimens, or tampering with the evidence, or even to the existence of a hitherto unknown evil identical twin, than to a "false match" of the specimens.' He discusses the probabilistic models and assumptions used in calculating probabilities of matches, the interpretation of those probabilities in terms of weight of evidence and the use of Bayes theorem, and the so-called 'prosecutor's fallacy' and 'defense attorney's fallacy'. Chernoff discusses philosophical and pragmatic issues related to the logic of the probability calculations – even if the assumptions of no mislabeling or evidence tampering are granted, the probability calculations still are based on idealized assumptions that will not be completely true.

Thomas Jabine's article on 'The emerging field of human rights statistics' discusses statistics related to civil and political rights, and economic and social rights. He presents ten examples of human rights statistics, including: lynchings in the US, executions in the 'Dirty War' in Argentina between 1976 and 1983, persons with no health insurance, childhood immunizations, statistics used in monitoring human rights treaties, race and sex discrimination in housing and employment, numbers of land mines, and rape in the former Yugoslavia. These statistics are used for advocacy as well as enforcement purposes, and the sources of such statistics are important. Not surprisingly, governmental data are more prevalent for social-economic rights, and non-governmental sources (such as Amnesty International) supply more of the data on civil and political rights. Whether governmental data on civil and political rights can be trusted is one aspect of data quality discussed by Jabine. The field is just emerging and the problems are very difficult and very important.

In the area of national defense, statistical techniques served successfully in World War II to estimate German equipment production, in the 1970s to estimate manpower supply for the All Volunteer Force in the US, and currently for anti-submarine searches, signal processing, and inventory control. Yet, David Chu and Nancy Spruill, in 'Making defense decisions', note that statistical thinking is strikingly absent at the decision-making level in the US. They provide examples of how probabilistic thinking rather than deterministic thinking can improve other areas of defense, including intelligence, weapons choices, operational practices such as missile defenses, resource allocation, and cost estimation. They conclude that 'statistical inference from an organized data base directly applicable to the problem at hand has proved more effective than the traditional "anthropological" style of information gathering and inference'. This parallels Herman Chernoff's observation that DNA fingerprinting is 'incomparably better' than eyewitness identification by strangers, and accords with studies in other contexts such as college-admission processes (Dawes 1971) and psychological diagnosis and prediction more generally (Meehl 1965).

Many statisticians believe that their methods are impartial and bestow objectivity to scientific or policy issues, either through randomization or diligent statistical modeling. Stephen Fienberg, in 'Ethics, objectivity, and politics: statistics in a public policy context', argues that this impartiality is a myth, perpetuated in many statistics courses where problems are predefined and the statistician relies on outsiders to define variables, populations of study, and hypotheses of interest.

One of the most important questions for statisticians who work on data collection is *what data should they be collecting*? Margaret Martin recalls the time a government official from the Department of Health, Education and Welfare's Office of the Assistant Secretary for Planning and Evaluation (ASPE) – a non-statistician – 'had just been assigned to review the statistical agencies within the department to evaluate whether they were doing a good job or not. She was concerned about how to know what they *should* be doing. She looked at three major text books on statistics and, of course, there isn't word one about what statistics should be collected, only about how to compute them.' (Straf and Olkin 1994, p. 140) The report of the committee that was formed to guide ASPE (National Research Council 1976) suggested than 'an appropriate strategy has been to bring cost–benefit ideas to the decision-making process and proceed with extreme caution to avoid unjustified formal structures' (Savage 1985, p. 2). This is very difficult, because to understand the benefits from collecting and reporting data, one needs to know what would happen (or be expected to happen) if the data were not collected and reported versus if the data were collected and reported. At best, one sees half the picture – if data were not collected in the past, one may know what occurred in their absence, or if data were collected then one may know what occurred in their presence; thus, comparison of the effects of data versus no data cannot typically be based on direct observation and experience. In addition, the contexts in which data are used are so complicated that the roles of data are difficult to isolate (Boruch and Boe 1995). Assigning economic values to the outcomes is yet a further difficulty.

Data collection and statistical reporting can interfere with the system being measured, in substantial ways. This may be viewed as a corrupting effect, if unintentional, but sometimes it is intentional. For example, the educational leadership may decide to give systemwide tests to public school students, with the belief that parents will pay attention to the scores and put pressure on their local schools to improve their scores; this in turn may lead teachers to tilt their course content closer to what is measured on the test. What is measured and reported receives attention, and this may decrease attention to non-measured processes.

Once decisions have been made about exactly what topics are to be studied, definitions of the variables to be measured are critical, as Fienberg illustrates with examples of definitions of poverty and race and ethnicity. Another absolutely critical question for statisticians is how much precision or accuracy is needed in a government statistic (for example, the rate of inflation), yet here too statistical textbooks provide little help. Yes, the textbooks tell how to optimize precision if cost is specified (by someone else) or how to optimize cost if precision is specified, but where is there practical guidance on how to find the optimal balance between the two?

It is true that in principle decision theory (or cost–benefit analysis) can prescribe simultaneously the optimal cost and precision, but the theory is difficult to apply in practice. Statistical decision theory assumes that an action is to be made from a prespecified set of possible actions, there are a prespecified set of possible states of nature, the consequences of the action depend on the unknown state of nature, the preferences (or economic valuation) over actions under alternative states of nature are reflected by a loss function or utility function, and getting more information both incurs a cost and reduces uncertainty over the state of nature. In actuality, however, the actions and the possible states of nature may not be identified until after the data are collected – we sometimes do genuinely learn new, unexpected, things from data. Ascertainment of preferences is not only quite complex in practice but raises other difficult questions, for example *whose* preferences are to be considered? Should the statistician reflect his or her own preferences, or those of the head of the agency for whom the data are to be collected? If the latter, what if the decision maker is not trying to obtain 'truth' but wants the statistics to tell a particular story or to support a particular decision, one made before the data are collected? Nevertheless, loss functions have been constructed in some public policy contexts (see Spencer 1980).

Fienberg presents several detailed examples of these and related themes. At at time when the unemployment rate was holding constant, the Nixon White House pressured the Bureau of Labor Statistics to include in its monthly press briefings statistics on the numbers of people holding jobs because they were showing favorable trends. (Had the number of jobholders been declining, there would have been no such pressure.) This kind of selective effect can lead to an artificially rosy picture, desired by political incumbents, which is not an appropriate action for a statistical agency. Fienberg's discussion of quality control in the welfare system illustrates the tension between statistical uses for regulation and those for 'pure' information, as the regulatory uses lead to corrupt reporting practices and underemphasis on errors that lead to underpayments by the government. Similarly, statisticians who serve as expert witnesses in litigation risk their objectivity being compromised by the adversarial nature of the legal process. In the US, statistical agencies are currently within larger non-statistical agencies, and may face dilemmas when making forecasts. When a new program or policy is implemented, for example a program to reduce energy consumption, the future will depend to some extent on the success of the program. How much independence does the statistical agency have to predict that the new program will have some non-negligible probability of being unsuccessful? Political pressures also led to cancellation of important but politically controversial surveys of sexual behaviors and attitudes and surveys of infection rates and risky behaviors that could be used to increase our knowledge about the extent of the AIDS epidemic.

One other example discussed by Fienberg is the undercounting of minorities and other groups of people in the decennial census, and consequent perturbations in electoral districts and political representation. These are the among the most basic political concerns in a democracy. Census undercount occurs not only in the US, but also in other countries (as is discussed by Redfern in Chapter 8 in this volume). Politics and statistics meet or clash, depending on one's point of view, in several ways here. Perhaps the biggest question for the 1990 census undercount concerned how accurately we could estimate the error of an error estimate; i.e. how accurate is the estimate of undercount? If the estimates of undercount are very accurate, they should be used to adjust the census figures, otherwise not. The undercount estimates were based on a large sample survey, known as the Post-Enumeration Survey, or PES. The size of the PES sample played a role in limiting the accuracy of the undercount estimates, because sampling error was a major component of error in the PES. During the 1980s, the government decided to cut the size of the PES sample below its originally specified level, and this cut increased the error in the undercount estimates and made adjustment less likely. An open question is how large the PES sample size should have been, and what decision rules should be used to decide whether or not accuracy would be improved by adjustment of the census (Mulry and Spencer 1991).

Another kind of use of statistics centers on statistical concepts rather than on particular data. Public discourse inevitably involves vague and rather qualitative concepts, such as a population that is or is not economically well off. There are two levels to the vagueness. One is the definition for an individual to be well off; the other is how to move from concepts of individual status to a measurement for a society as a whole. Statistics are used to provide relevant information for these concepts; for example, the government estimates the income for samples of individuals, and it analyzes the income data to construct poverty indices to provide social measurements. The process of constructing statistics requires, however, that definitions be made. The definitions may be wanting in one or more respects (as Fienberg's article illustrates), but the specificity of the definition allows progress to be made by critiquing and improving the statistical definitions. This is a normal part of government statistics.

Some uses of statistical definitions are very subtle, involving concepts such as probable, significant, and normal (as used in the preceding sentence). William Kruskal and Stephen Stigler, in 'Normative terminology: "normal" in statistics and elsewhere', note that the word 'normal' is both remarkably useful and ambivalent. 'Normal' conveys at the same time a sense of the usual, the average, and the idea of a norm, or optimum goal. They explore this ambivalence through an historical review of the use of 'normal' in statistics, where it appears both as a distribution and as a set of linear equations that give the least-squares estimates, in medicine, and in the name of a school for training teachers, the normal school. The emergence of 'normal distribution' as a term is found to have taken place over several decades in the last half of the nineteenth century, while the origin of 'normal equations' can be identified with an isolated, puzzling use in 1822. (Mosteller and Youtz (1990) provide a complementary discussion of how 'probable', 'likely' etc. are used and interpreted.)

PART II. DATA COLLECTION FOR DESCRIPTION

In the US and other countries, the government collects vast amounts of data and produces myriad statistical reports from surveys and other data sources. It was not until the latter part of the 1930s and the early 1940s, however, that probability sampling really took root in US government statistical agencies (Duncan and Shelton 1978). Prior to this, European statisticians were wrestling with the relative merits of stratified probability sampling and non-random (purposive) sampling, and in a 1934 *Journal of the Royal Statistical Society* paper, Jerzy Neyman demonstrated the superiority of stratified probability sampling for large-scale government surveys. (In the same paper he also showed how to minimize the sampling variance of estimators of population means and totals from stratified random samples and, if that were not enough, reworked R. A. Fisher's concept of fiducial intervals into the now popular notion of confidence intervals.) Some personal observations about developments of statistics during this exciting period are provided in 'Statistics in Washington, 1935–1945' by W. Allen Wallis. Wallis observes that during the last half of the 1930s, there were spectacular developments in the field of statistics, both in theory and in practice, in both governmental and academic institutions . . . There never was a better time for a statistician to be alive than the last 60 years. Not yet anyway.

The major types of surveys currently conducted by and for the government in the US and elsewhere are reviewed by Leslie Kish in 'Periodic and rolling samples and censuses'. He compares the relative strengths and limitations of surveys, censuses, and population registers and which are best for meeting different needs. Although all of these data collection methods are used for studying change over time and variations in space (geography), the theory of sampling has been focused almost entirely on spatial aspects. For example, an arbitrary week is chosen to represent employment for monthly labor surveys, and every tenth year is designated for census estimates of income. Kish notes that just as surveys spread their samples geographically and cumulate them, so can we spread censuses over time. Instead of obtaining income measurements every tenth year from a fraction f of the households (as is done in the census 'long form'), we could instead take measurements every year from $f/10$ of the households. The data could be cumulated over time and would also give better resolution for years intermediate between censuses. This concept of a 'rolling census' for the long form is under consideration by the US Bureau of Census, and it is just one of a class of designs Kish proposes. By considering space- and time-variations on equal footing, Kish changes the way governmental sampling problems are traditionally framed. With this broader perspective, he introduces some basic kinds of sampling designs that exploit overlap, illustrates them with examples, and indicates their strengths and difficulties. The article points toward territory yet to be explored.

Censuses are facing severe problems from undercount and lack of public cooperation, as both Fienberg and Kish noted. One possible solution is to get rid of the census as we know it. Philip Redfern, in 'Numbering the people: issues of accuracy, privacy and open government', contrasts the advantages of a census versus that of a central address registry in which individuals are identified by a *personal number*. Redfern discusses the increasing problems faced by traditional censuses in many countries, including the US and UK. Undercount is prevalent, and difficult to either remove or accurately make adjustments for. Register-based censuses are used in the Nordic countries; a main limitation is the limited range of topics covered. Rolling samples (as discussed by Kish) can be used effectively to expand that range, however. Another problem of the register-based census is the vulnerability of administrative records systems to changes in laws affecting the availability of administrative records. Redfern argues that greater accuracy of public agencies' records improves the efficiency of government and confers benefits on its citizens including protection of their rights (quite apart from helping the production of statistics). Yet, concern over Big Brother is prevalent enough that people fear the government becoming too efficient; Redfern argues that such fears are based more on emotions than on facts. Whether or not the reader agrees that a register census is desirable, the issue remains that traditional censuses are becoming increasingly problematic, and some satisfactory alternative is needed.

In 'Surveying individuals with disabilities', Allan Sampson focuses on studies of a particular subpopulation with significant policy interest and discusses complexities that arise in obtaining survey data from individuals with disabilities. While some of the issues are typical of surveying rare populations, such as how to get sufficiently many individuals with disabilities in the sample, many of the concerns are unique to individuals with disabilities. Sampson pays particular attention to definitions, phrasing of questions, and reliability and validity of disability questions. Policy issues related to these concerns are examined, with particular attention given to the Americans with Disabilities Act (ADA).

Alternative definitions of disability lead to very different statistics. Although the ADA refers to disabilities, whether an individual has a disability depends on definition, and definitions are difficult to specify in legislation. Alternative survey definitions lead to large changes in the proportion of the population with a disability, effects far larger than sampling error. For example, the Disability Insurance Program of the US Social Security Administration was diving into bankruptcy – saved only by a reallocation of Social Security tax income – because the classification of an individual as disabled fluctuated enormously over time as political, bureaucratic, and economic situations changed; these changes reflected changes in definition rather than changes in the population. Commenting on the definition used by the Social Security Administration, its former Commissioner, Robert M. Ball, noted that

many aspects of disability are somewhat subjective. You can settle roughly 80 per cent of the cases quite easily. They are very clear-cut, either they are disabled or they are not. The 20 per cent depends on an evaluation, not only of the individual's mental or physical capacity, but their background, training, their previous work experience, and people that look very much the same in terms of physical and mental handicaps can come out somewhat differently if you look at functional disability as you should. I am not sure that you are ever going to be able to write an absolute definition that will control all the courts so they agree with what Congress has in mind (Subcommittee on Social Security, 1993, pp. 69–70).

Similarly, the cost of health care reform in the US depends to a significant extent on the cost of mental disability – and how it is defined. Sampson discusses alternative conceptual frameworks and how to evaluate them.

Another aspect of definitions is their impact on society and on the individuals who are categorized. Labeling individuals with a disability has sociological impact as well as ramifications for the individual, who may internalize the classification. This is related to the classification of a person as 'abnormal', a concept explored by Kruskal and Stigler. It is interesting as well that definitions may depend on the past values of statistics purporting to measure related characteristics. For example, poverty definitions change over time, and the threshold for an individual to be in poverty in an affluent country will be higher than the threshold in less affluent countries. Similarly, it is possible that the definition of disability may be relative, so that the proportion who are disabled is constrained to fall within limits at a point in time, and the definition is altered up or down until the measured proportion matches the target range. This situation might arise from a public desire to help those who need it, but at the same time not to help too many people (for reasons of cost among other things).

Existing theory of sample surveys is developed almost entirely from the goal of estimating characteristics of aggregates (populations) of individuals. James Coleman, in 'Constructed social networks in the study of diffusion', describes the needs for improvements to sampling theory to allow for estimation of relationships among individuals. Using the spread of sexually transmitted diseases such as AIDS as a motivating example, Coleman describes a standard model for the rate of spread of the disease as a function of two kinds of parameters, the probability of transmission given a contact between an infected and uninfected person, and the probability of a contact between any two people. The interpersonal contacts may be represented in terms of links between nodes (people) in a social network. Although these kinds of models are well-established in the stochastic process literature, there has been relatively little attention to the development of surveys to allow estimation of the parameters of the networks. A problem is that without some assumed structure, there are vastly too many parameters to estimate from a reasonably small fraction of the population. Coleman discusses the kinds of models that are needed to allow practical estimation of the relevant aspects of the network, and proposes some *ad hoc* methods to construct a 'pseudo' social network. The methods are implementable, but involve some implicit as well as explicit assumptions[1]. In addition to the modeling and estimation problems, measurement error presents a problem in that people misreport their relationships; for example, in the General Social Survey in the US males report three to four times as many opposite-sex sexual partners as do females (Smith 1992). It is a challenge for statisticians to try to improve on Coleman's methods, for example by developing appropriate models amenable to standard statistical estimation methods.

PART III. USES OF STATISTICS FOR POLICY ANALYSIS

Policy analysis includes many activities. Lincoln Moses and Frederick Mosteller (in this volume) note that

Progress in activities like medical care, education, and business grows largely from making change in the way things are done. We will call those 'policy changes'. Their many forms include: decisions to change, abandon, or begin regulatory measures; decisions to invest or divest; decisions to introduce, modify, or curtail services or product lines. The success of policy changes rests in large part on the availability and reliability of the information considered in making the decision.

Descriptive uses of statistics are discussed in Part I, and some sources of data (existing and needed) are discussed in Part II. In Part III we consider some other ways in which statistics are produced for policy analysis.

Statistical analysis for policy decisions occurs in the large and in the small. The former includes large-scale studies, often conducted under contract or by separate branches of an agency. Analysis in the small refers to analyses that an individual might perform, for example by constructing a spreadsheet with some existing data.

---

1. In some ways, his method is similar to the 'hot deck' method used to fill in for missing data in surveys.

Much of the role of statistics in policy analysis can be viewed as part of a forecasting problem: what would the future be like if we took action X or Y? Although forecasts of population size, or energy consumption, or the costs of health care, to give a few examples, can be used to indicate needs that policy-makers should address, forecasts of more complex matters seem completely beyond current capabilities. For example, Nathan Keyfitz (personal communication 1993) is concerned that very few statistics are available on the human capital of youth, including knowledge, initiative, discipline, health, and values. We do have some measures on academic accomplishment, delinquency, and drug use, but Keyfitz would note that these are partly a result and partly a cause of youth culture. Forecasts of the human capital of the next generation (children of today's youth) seem impossibly difficult. The result of the lack of measurement of human capital of youth, and lack of forecasts for the future, is that such characteristics are not in the forefront of public attention. Keyfitz has written that 'in a statistics-minded people like ours what is not measured is thought not to exist, and certainly not to be important'.

Keyfitz's article, 'Why forecasts fail and policies are often frustrated', poses some difficult questions in forecasting the effects of policy changes. He presents a number of examples to show that, although short-term effects can perhaps be satisfactorily predicted by relatively simple statistical models, longer-range effects typically cannot. The reason is that the causal processes are complex and involve various feedbacks. To develop appropriate causal models will involve insights from many disciplines. Lacking models to predict how policy interventions will cause changes, how can we forecast the effects of policy changes?

In 'Experimentation: just do it!' Lincoln Moses and Frederick Mosteller explain how useful and feasible experimentation can be for predicting the effects of policy changes. As Keyfitz makes clear, the alternative (non-experimental) methods for forecasting the effects of policies tend to be inadequate. Also, incremental improvements tend to be more achievable than large ones, and the best technology is needed for their evaluation. With a variety of examples from medical care, education, criminal justice, and many other fields, Moses and Mosteller show that experimentation is more feasible than widely believed. They provide guidance on how to do experiments, and they discuss specific ways to broaden the use of randomized experiments. These include large but simple randomized experiments instead of more complex designs with fewer subjects, dividing institutions into smaller equivalent systems ('firms') which form control groups for each other, modern methods of research synthesis to consolidate information from multiple experiments, and more effective reporting of experiments in publications. They urge expanded use of systematic experimentation in policy formulation, and they include valuable guidance for statisticians, teachers of policy, and teachers of statistics.

Stephen Dresch and Kenneth Janson illustrate the use of simulation to check on the trustworthiness of models that are used to support policy formation. They share with Keyfitz the concerns that 'when [social] and statistical science is foiled by the complexities of phenomena . . . superficial and misleading analyses rationalize unwise and ill-considered policy actions'. In 'Talents, rewards and professional choice: a general equilibrium analysis', they explore an important case study to show how misleading policy conclusions can arise from an incorrect analytical model. The policy question is whether the government should provide increased financial support for science and engineering education. Although problems of measurement error and model specification prohibit a full and realistic study of the issue, government policy-makers have relied on simpler analyses to justify their decisions. Can those analyses be trusted? Dresch and Janson note as key aspects of the real process that individuals have different kinds of talents, that different occupations reward individuals differently, depending on the individual's mix of talents, and that individuals prefer to maximize their rewards. Government intervention can be interpreted as changing the structure of rewards offered by different occupations. Based on these observations, Dresch and Janson construct a model of the labor market, a model that is so simple that they call it a 'caricature' but that is more complex than the standard models in that it reflects the key aspects of the process of occupational choice. They carry out simulations under this model with two purposes in mind. First, they can explore the effects of policy actions, although the model is so simple that these effects can be taken only qualitatively. Second, and more important, they can use the simulation results to indicate what data would be collected by observational (i.e. non-experimental) studies of the process in the real world. Comparing inferences based on such 'realistically observable data' to the 'truth' (which is known in the simulation model), they show that there are substantial biases in the usual empirical analyses of real data on these processes. In particular, estimates of the economic returns to higher education are severely inflated, and Dresch and Janson question the government's rationale for setting the levels of support for science and engineering education. The general approach used by Dresch and Janson seems widely applicable.

Analyses in the small are the prime concern of Sam Savage in his article 'Statistical analysis for the masses'. This is quite important, as the corporate and other databases grow more rapidly than the availability of competent statisticians to analyze the data. Savage reports the unhappy observation that graduates of basic statistics courses fail to understand the most basic concepts, such as probability distributions, distributions of averages being more concentrated than those of single observations, and that the expectation of a nonlinear function of a random variate is not equal to the function of the expected value of the variate. One may expect errors in inference when such people, let alone those with less training in statistics, conduct statistical analysis. Savage discusses the need for spreadsheets to include tools that are both easy to use and that enhance correct interpretation of statistics. Although spreadsheets already include tools for graphical display and point estimation (for example means, standard deviations, and regressions), the tools do not adequately facilitate understanding of variability or nonlinearity of systems. An example is that the average output of a system is typically not the output corresponding to the average input. The emphasis would be on codifying important concepts of statistics into tools that are easy to use, even if the underlying technology is not well understood by the users. Given the wide use of spreadsheets and similar non-specialized software for analyzing data, such tools could bring about widespread improvements in data analyses that are actually conducted. Planning and developing such tools is an open area for development.

An example of a tool Savage would like to see more widely available is the means for assessing the uncertainty of forecasts. For example, the one thing about most forecasts that is certain is that they will be at least somewhat in error. There is substantial theory to show how decision-makers can use estimates of forecast uncertainty to hedge against forecast errors and appropriate courses of action. Yet, obtaining estimates of the uncertainty of forecasts is a problem not just for analyses in the small but for large-scale studies as well.

Although a probability distribution is a preferred means for representing uncertainty, usual government forecasts are not accompanied by probabilities or by intervals with specified probabilities of encompassing the future values. One reason for this is the difficulty of producing the underlying statistical analyses. Even the Office of the Actuary of the US Social Security Administration, which must by law produce forecasts of the hundreds of billions of dollars per year of income and outflow, lacks the staff to produce such probabilistic analyses. (These forecasts are important, as they affect the laws stipulating what the social security tax rates ('FICA') will be.) One way around this problem of lack of analytic resources is to develop simplified stochastic models that can be used to produce probabilistic forecasts, as described by Alho and Spencer (in press). Assessment of the uncertainty of forecasts and government statistics more generally is an important and difficult task.

The problems and examples in this book are serious, important, and too little studied in statistics courses and programs. We hope the reader will have fun learning about the issues in statistics and public policy, and that some readers will be stimulated to contribute towards resolving them. This book is written with the student in mind, although in this difficult area we are all students.

REFERENCES

Alho, J. M. and Spencer, B. D. The practical specification of the expected error of population forecasts. *Journal of Official Statistics*. (In press.)

Boruch, R. F. and Boe, E. (1996). *On 'Good, Certain, and Easy Government': the policy use of statistical data and reports*. Graduate School of Education, University of Pennsylvania.

Dawes, R. M. (1971). A case study of graduate admissions: Application of three principles of human decision making. *American Psychologist*, **26**, 180–8. Reprinted in W. B. Fairley and F. Mosteller, *Statistics and public policy*, Addison-Wesley, Reading, MA. 1977.

Duncan, J. W. and Shelton, W. C. (1978). *Revolution in United States Government Statistics 1926–1976*, US Department of Commerce, Washington, DC.

Meehl, P. E. (1965). Seer over sign: The first good example. *Journal of Experimental Research in Personality*, **1**, 27–32.

Mosteller, F. and Youtz, C. (1990). Quantifying probabilistic expressions. *Statistical Science*, **5**, 2–34 (with discussion).

Mulry, M. H. and Spencer, B. D. (1991). Total error in PES estimates of population: The Dress Rehearsal Census of 1988. *Journal of the American Statistical Association*, **86**, 839–54 (with discussion 855–63).

National Research Council (1976). *Setting Statistical Priorities*. Report of the Panel on Methodology for Statistical Priorities of the Committee on National Statistics. National Academy of Sciences, Washington, DC.

Savage, I. R. (1985), Hard–soft problems. *Journal of the American Statistical Association*, **80**, 1–7.

Smith, T. W. (1992). A methodological analysis of the sexual behavior questions on the General Social Surveys. *Journal of Official Statistics*, **8**, 309–22.

Spencer B.D. (1980). *Benefit–cost analysis of data used to allocate funds*. Springer, New York.

Straf, M. and Olkin, I. (1994). A conversation with Margaret Martin. *Statistical Science*, **9**, 127–45.

Part I
Uses of statistics for description

1 Issues in DNA fingerprinting[1]

HERMAN CHERNOFF

INTRODUCTION

The use of blood types for identification of parents and criminals began to be replaced in 1985 by the much more powerful technology of *DNA profiling*, popularly referred to as *DNA fingerprinting* (Jeffreys *et al.* 1985). Since then the use of this method in court has been questioned, and it has been the subject of numerous discussions in legal and scientific journals.

We have a technical tool, with a power orders of magnitude greater than what was available earlier. It is incomparably better than eyewitness identification by strangers which is often admitted as evidence. Still the resulting evidence has on occasion been discarded by judges because expert witnesses for the defense denied that the claimed odds of many billions to one were reliable (Kaye 1993, p.118).

It is likely that in the near future most courts will admit such evidence, and the technology will be refined, but the debate about applicability will continue for some time. One important saving grace of the current situation is that DNA profiling is extremely effective in screening out innocent suspects. Where well preserved biological specimens belonging to the guilty party are available, it is almost impossible for an innocent person to be falsely identified with an honest and careful analysis. Thus, when the technology is applicable, innocent suspects are likely to be recognized quickly, saving them considerable pain and eliminating false leads in police searches. The method has been used successfully to establish the innocence of prisoners who were convicted of rape years before DNA profiles became widely available (Kaye 1993, p.115).

There are several issues which are not easy to resolve. Some of these stem from the adversarial nature of the legal system where it is the function of a lawyer to present the best possible case for his client. It is not the lawyer's function to give a balanced view of the evidence. Rather, the defense must seek to create doubts, sound or otherwise, among the judges about the admissibility, and among jurors about the weight, of the evidence presented by the prosecution. In an area where arguments are seldom quantified, probabilistic reasoning is not well understood, and the underlying models used by statistical analysts are approximations; odds of billions to one are easy to criticize. The result is often unnecessary confusion, which a good defense lawyer can exploit.

To put it bluntly, a false identification is much more likely to be due to an error in labeling the biological specimens, or tampering with the evidence, or even to the

1. This chapter is based on research supported in part by ONR contract N00014–91–J1005 and NSF contract DMS-9104990.

existence of a hitherto unknown evil identical twin, than to a 'false match' of the specimens.

Although the courts and technology will probably arrive at a moderately sensible and stable equilibrium in the treatment of DNA profiles within the next few years, the history is a reflection of the uneasy tension derived from the use of expert witnesses in legal matters involving the combined professions of law, some branch of science or technology, and statistics. It may be that a discussion of the history and the issues will contribute enough clarity to help reduce somewhat the trauma, in putting into practical legal use the next technological breakthrough, for establishing relevant matters of fact.

DNA ANALYSIS

The power of DNA analysis derives from the stability of the DNA molecule, and the uniqueness, except in the case of identical twins, of an individual's DNA. With the exception of sperm cells in men and egg cells in women, the nucleus of each living cell in the human body carries 23 distinct pairs of *chromosomes*. The sperm and egg cells each carry only one set of 23 chromosomes. Of each pair of chromosomes, one comes from the father's sperm and one from the mother's egg. Each of the 46 chromosomes is a molecule consisting of a long strand of DNA in the form of two intertwined substrands.

The chromosomes are duplicated in the process of cell reproduction, and parts of each pair are combined to form a single chromosome in egg and sperm production. Because the chromosomes carry the essential instructions for cell function, this duplication process is almost error free, and changes, called *mutations*, rarely survive. Some surviving mutations lead to apparent changes in appearance, but others, at certain sites or *loci* of the chromosomes, seem to have no effect. Certain loci are much more predisposed than others to tolerate mutations, and these are highly *polymorphic* giving rise, in the population, to many distinct forms called *alleles*, which are detectable in the laboratory. Inasmuch as they seem to have no apparent function, these *silent* polymorphisms do not affect mating behavior.

One laboratory technique cuts out a section of each of a chromosome pair at a certain locus and effectively weighs the sections to distinguish the various alleles. The result is a column with two crude rectangular shadows or bands. The locations of the bands in the column are subject to measurement error and are called *band weights*. Sometimes only one band appears. This may be because the subject is *homozygous* (identical alleles) or two bands *coalesce* because the weights are so similar, or one band weight is off scale, or the specimen has degraded. The results for the forensic specimen and the suspect are compared in adjacent columns, visually or by machine. A match is declared if the bands for the two specimens line up closely enough.

If there are 30 alleles for a locus such as D12S79, and each individual has two chromosomes for this locus, there are $465 = 30(31)/2$, not necessarily uniformly distributed, possible variations. The number of possibilities becomes enormous if several different loci are used.

There are other established methods of discriminating between alleles. Each is associated with advantages and disadvantages. These involve costs, errors in measurement, difficulties with forensic specimens which may be degraded and in small quantities, and contamination with extraneous DNA. One such promising procedure is the use of PCR (polymerase chain reaction) which multiplies enormously the amount of DNA material from a portion of a specimen. It is said to have the ability to provide as much DNA as necessary from a single nucleated cell. It is quick and economical. It is also easily contaminated, and forensic experience with it is limited at present. There are several available techniques for determining alleles with PCR.

STATISTICAL CONSIDERATIONS

Statistical considerations enter primarily in two ways. Because the match decisions for band weights are subject to measurement error, some allowance must be made. Even assuming no errors in measurement, the presence of a match must be evaluated for its weight of evidence in favor of the hypothesis that the two specimens are from the same individual.

Let us ignore the error in measurement problem until later. A typical calculation follows. Supposing that the forensic specimen comes from a guilty party; what is the chance that an innocent suspect will provide a match with the two measurements ordinarily derived from the forensic specimen at a given locus? If the distribution of weights in the population assigns probabilities p_1 and p_2 to the observed forensic band weights (which we will assume here are different) then the probability that a randomly selected innocent subject will lead to a match is calculated, using statistical independence assumptions, to be $2p_1p_2$. If p_1 and p_2 are about 0.05 each, this product is 0.005. Moreover, if we obtain matching in four independent probes with comparable discriminating power, we will have observed an event with probability of the order of magnitude of one in a billion.

As we shall see, this calculation is subject to criticism. Moreover, the probability calculated here does *not* purport to be the probability that the suspect or an identical twin was responsible for the forensic specimen. The evidence is most easily assessed in terms of Bayes' theorem. Let G and I represent the alternative hypotheses that the suspect is and is not responsible for the forensic specimen. Allowing for the possibility that the forensic specimen might have been left by an innocent party, the notation of G and I for guilt and innocence is slightly misleading, but mnemonically helpful. Let E be the evidence observed and we may have $E = M$ for *match* and $E = D$ for different or *non-matching*.

The approach using Bayes' theorem requires some *prior probabilities* $P(G)$ and $P(I) = 1 - P(G)$ which will depend on the juror's evaluation of other information. Then $P(G)/P(I)$ is called the juror's *prior odds* in favor of G. We introduce the *posterior probabilities* $P(G|E)$ and $P(I|E)$ and the *posterior odds* $P(G|E)/P(I|E)$ which represent the juror's probabilities and odds *given the evidence E*. Finally the *likelihood ratio* is $P(E|G)/P(E|I)$, the ratio of the probabilities of the evidence given the hypotheses.

Bayes' theorem states that the *posterior odds is equal to the prior odds multiplied by the likelihood ratio.* Thus

$$\frac{P(G|E)}{P(I|E)} = \frac{P(G)}{P(I)} \times \frac{P(E|G)}{P(E|I)} .$$

In other words the likelihood ratio is a factor by which the juror's prior odds is converted to his or her posterior odds. In our problem we assume that if $E = D$ (non-match), then $P(D|G)$ is small while $P(D|I)$ will be quite close to one. In that case, a non-match will multiply the prior odds by a very small number and tend to overwhelm, in favor of I, any prior evidence. On the other hand if $E = M$, then $P(M|G)$ is close to 1 while $P(M|I)$ is the small number we indicated previously to be about one in a billion or 10^{-9}. Then the likelihood ratio is huge and the prior odds will be multiplied by a large number supporting a large increase of the posterior odds over the prior odds. For example if the prior odds were 1/4, or 1 for G to 4 for I, a match with $P(M|I) = 10^{-9}$ would give posterior odds of about 250 million to 1, and the posterior probability of I, $P(I|M)$ would be approximately 4×10^{-9} and not the same as $P(M|I)$ or 10^{-9}.

For the benefit of readers not accustomed to statistical reasoning and Bayes' theorem, an example which might lend some additional perspective is a simplified version of that of HIV testing with an instrument which never gives a false negative, but gives false positives 5% of the time (for disease-free subjects) on a population with 1% infected. Many individuals who tested positive thought that they were infected and some felt that their probability of being infected was 0.95. By Bayes' theorem the posterior odds of infection given the evidence was the prior odds times the likelihood ratio or $(0.01/0.99) \times 1.0/(0.05) \approx 0.202$. This means that the posterior probability of infection is close to 0.20 and not 0.95. In other words, while $P(+|\text{disease-free}) = 0.05$, $P(\text{disease-free}|+) \approx 0.80$. Note that the assumed *prevalence rate* in the population, 0.01, analogous to the prior probability of G in our forensic example, is extremely important here.

In our forensic example above the distinction between $P(I|M) = 4 \times 10^{-9}$ and $P(M|I) = 10^{-9}$ seems unimportant since either number is overwhelming. Any scientific problem in drawing conclusions must come from questions about how the probability 10^{-9} was calculated in the first place. However, there also exists the practical problem of how to present such evidence to a judge or jury so that it is meaningful.

In this context, attention has been drawn by Thompson and Schumann (1987) to the 'prosecutor's fallacy' and the 'defense attorney's fallacy'. The court is primarily interested in $P(I|M)$ or $P(G|M) = 1 - P(I|M)$. The 'prosecutor's fallacy') is to confuse $P(M|I)$ with $P(I|M)$. The HIV example shows that the distinction may sometimes be important. The 'defense attorney's fallacy' is to argue if $P(M|I) = 10^{-5}$, that we live in a city of 10^{6} people and thus there are about 10 people who match and so $P(G|M) = 1/10$. Implicitly the defense attorney is suggesting that prior to the evidence of matching, everyone in the city is equally likely to be the source of the forensic specimen and the prior odds should be $1/10^{6} = 10^{-6}$. If the suspect were there because there were other signs of guilt, the juror has a right to believe, on the basis of these other signs, that the prior odds ought to be substantially greater than one in a million.

LEGAL CONSIDERATIONS

One of the first uses of DNA profiling, described in Wambaugh (1989) came up in a village in England where two 15-year-old girls were raped and murdered three years apart. The DNA analysis of semen found on these two bodies determined that one perpetrator had been involved in both cases. The plan, to test every man of ages between 17 and 34 within a few miles of the village, failed to reveal a match because the perpetrator convinced an acquaintance to substitute his own blood sample for the perpetrator's. When that evasion was uncovered, the perpetrator confessed.

Although a subsequent test revealed a match, it is ironic that that evidence was unnecessary, because the perpetrator, convinced of the accuracy of the test and admissibility of the evidence, confessed. Because several thousand men were tested, the appropriate version of the defense attorney's fallacy would have been relevant, reducing the effect of the evidence on the posterior odds of guilt in this case.

The immediate reaction to the introduction of DNA profiles in legal circles was one of enthusiasm for a major breakthrough. This was tempered by warnings, described by Thompson and Ford (1989), against the premature introduction in court of this approach, before the tests had been adequately validated and debated in the scientific literature, leading to general acceptance in the scientific community. Attention was drawn to another method, protein gel electrophoresis, similar in some aspects to DNA profiling, but lacking its highly polymorphic property. Its use had become routine, but was subsequently ruled inadmissible in California and Michigan after serious doubts were raised about its reliability. This development raised havoc in law courts because the method had provided important evidence in a large number of cases.

Certain safeguards have been generally accepted by the courts to deal with expert testimony in general, and testimony involving novel technological developments in particular. In response certain safeguards have been generally accepted. The most frequently cited rule for determining the *admissibility* of a novel scientific technique is the Frye rule (Kaye 1993, p.104). Under this rule the judge must decide that the 'thing from which the deduction is made must be sufficiently established to have gained general acceptance in the particular field in which it belongs'. Courts have noted that the particular procedure need not be 'unanimously endorsed' by the scientific community, but must be 'generally accepted as reliable'. The use is questionable if there is no pool of experts which would permit the opposing side to find experts who can critically examine the validity of an opponent's scientific evidence. Under the Frye rule it is not necessary to reopen the issue of admissibility in each case, but considerations of *weight of evidence* may have to be considered by individual courts.

The frustration with the delay between the development and acceptance of new technology has led some jurisdictions to apply a more liberal approach for admissibility. Rule 702 of the Federal and Uniform Rules of Evidence requires only relevance, in that qualified scientific testimony should assist in understanding the evidence or to determine a fact in issue. On the other hand, Rule 403, which applies to all evidence, scientific and non-scientific alike, provides that 'evidence may be excluded if probative value is substantially outweighed by the danger of unfair prejudice, confusion of the issues, or misleading the jury'. This rule has concerned courts faced with probabilities of 1 out of several hundred billion for fear that jurors may be overly impressed by such numbers and give them undue weight and deference (Kaye 1993, p.118). This does not mention some, possibly well placed, cynical skepticism about the meaning of such numbers.

A recent decision by the Supreme Court (Kaye 1993, p.105) has established the precedence of the Federal Rules of Evidence over the Frye rule for Federal cases. Here, as in many judicial opinions, the term *scientific validity* tends to appear in a somewhat circular way.

PROBLEMS

The warnings against premature use of DNA profiles were well founded. By 1989, enough questions were raised that the scientific and legal communities solicited a report by the National Research Council (NRC) of the National Academy of Sciences. Unfortunately this report (Committee on DNA Technology in Forensic Inference 1992) has received considerable criticism and has not quite served as well as intended to settle the issues.

Three commercial firms, Lifecodes, Cellmark, and Cetus, as well as the FBI and many state agencies have been involved in providing forensic analysis. One of the difficulties at the beginning was the lack of a pool of qualified experts for use by the defense. That was partly due to the fact that expertise was required in three distinct areas. Laboratory scientists could testify about the technology. Academic geneticists and statisticians could testify about probability. Neither of these two groups have much contact with specialists in forensic science, where one must learn to deal with degraded specimens that are not obtained from well run scientific laboratories. Some of the expert witnesses were not very expert in any of these fields. Also troublesome was the fact that many of the experts for the prosecution represented the commercial laboratories doing the analysis and had some incentive to build up their business by claiming how effective their techniques were. Moreover there was little significant statistical expertize in these laboratories.

A particularly difficult point was that the commercial laboratories were reluctant to share their techniques and proprietary data, mostly derived from opportunistic rather than random samples, with potential competitors. How could a defense expert criticize a calculation based on estimates of certain probabilities derived from unspecified models and unavailable studies of the distribution of polymorphisms in the population? Geisser (1990) tells of a defense lawyer who cleverly used this reluctance to provide the data to have the evidence ruled inadmissible.

In addition Geisser states that the FBI was also reluctant to cooperate with scientists requesting data. which led to the embarrassment of the FBI of having a scientific publication point out the difficulty of accessing the data on the basis of which their estimates were calculated. Finally some of the scientists acting as expert witnesses for the defense claimed harassment on the part of authorities ranging from interference in scientific publications to questions about visa status (Kolata 1991).

In 1989, the Castro case in New York attracted a good deal of attention. Highly qualified experts for both sides were brought in from all parts of the country and they produced 2000 pages of testimony. In this case, an error in laboratory work left the issue of probability estimates moot. This case was subsequently the illustrative example of Berry (1991) where it was pointed out that Lifecodes had apparently underestimated the measurement error in their procedures. The measurement error determines a standard deviation for the difference of the measured band weights of an allele for two specimens from the same individual. Two band weights are said to match if their difference is less than k estimated standard deviations of the difference. Over time Lifecodes changed k from 2 to 3. But in the Castro case, even though one of the differences was 3.66 standard deviations, Lifecodes decided to call it a match. By underestimating the measurement error, and consequently the standard deviation of the difference, the people at Lifecodes put themselves in the embarrassing position of stretching the criterion in order to claim a match, thereby destroying a pretense at objectivity.

It was hoped that the NRC report would establish a clear-cut explanation of how, when and where DNA profile analysis could be used, and that this report would be accepted by the scientific community. Instead it gave rise to considerable criticism (Aldhous 1993). In response to this criticism, the NRC is planning to produce a second report to clarify ambiguous wordings and issues on which they may have left chinks in the armor against wily defense lawyers and prosecutors.

RECOMMENDATIONS OF THE NRC REPORT

The main issues addressed by the NRC report were quality control in a rapidly evolving technology, objectivity and scientific standards. To deal with another major issue, the weight of evidence, the *ceiling principle* was proposed as a conservative method for dealing with the calculation of the probability of a match $P(M|I)$.

Some recommendations involve precautions for dealing with new developments and future standards. These include publication, accreditation, and the use of data to be gathered by sampling the population for blood specimens, which should be stored for further analysis as new techniques develop. For current methods, recognized as fundamentally sound, open availability of data and laboratory records were stressed.

One problematic recommendation was 'Prosecutors and defense counsel should not oversell DNA evidence. Presentations that suggest to a judge or jury that DNA typing is infallible are rarely justified and should be avoided.' Another follows the *ceiling principle*, to be described later. 'Until ceiling frequencies can be estimated from appropriate population studies . . . The testing laboratory should then calculate an estimated population frequency . . . provided that population studies have been carried out in at least three major "races" (e.g. Caucasians, Blacks, Hispanics, Asians, and Native Americans) and that statistical evaluation of HW equilibrium and linkage disequilibrium has been carried out . . .' The report does not say what to do if the tests reject equilibrium. The concepts of HW and linkage equilibrium will be discussed in the section on the ceiling principle.

CRITICISM OF THE NRC REPORT

A newspaper article published just before the NRC report was made public claimed that the report recommended that DNA evidence be barred from the courts (Kaye 1993, p.103). In response, Victor McKusick, chairman of the NRC committee, held a press conference stating that the report 'approved of the forensic use of DNA substantially as it is now practiced'. In a book review, Lewontin (1992) quotes several portions of the report which seem to be less than wholehearted in support of current practice. It is his contention that it is in the nature of NRC reports to be unanimous, and so reports should be expected 'to contain contradictory compromises among contending interests'. The portion of the recommendations that warns against the infallibility of DNA typing seems to be an example of such a compromise. While everyone may agree that low-quality analysis might lead to misleading conclusions, this sentence, vague as it is, could conceivably be used as a wedge to break open an otherwise tight prosecutor's case.

Lewontin quotes several other portions of the text of the NRC report. One example is 'The current laboratory procedure for detecting DNA variation . . . is *fundamentally* sound. [emphasis added].' Thus this sentence can be regarded as less than a ringing endorsement. Another example consists of three portions: 'It is now clear that DNA typing methods are a most powerful adjunct to forensic science for personal identification and have immense benefit to the public' and later 'DNA typing is capable, *in principle*, of an extremely low inherent rate of false results [emphasis added]' and these are followed by 'The committee recognizes that standardization of practices in forensic laboratories in general is more problematic than in other laboratory settings; stated succinctly, forensic scientists have little or no control over the nature, condition, form, or amount of sample with which they must work.' It isn't clear that these passages are as self-defeating or damning as Lewontin suggests, but they do present difficulties for judges in individual courts.

In my opinion the really important issue is that of quality control which was well addressed by the report. There is no way that the report could, without sounding tentative, point out that we have an immensely powerful tool that needs a great deal of care and expertise to be applied properly. However, the issue which is the source of the most criticism in the scientific literature is the ceiling principle for the calculation of $P(M|I)$. Here the criticism comes from both the right and the left if I may use these politically loaded terms to represent conservative and not conservative, in the sense of favoring or not favoring the suspect. On one hand Cohen (1992) demonstrates that there are possible circumstances where the principle is not conservative. On the other hand, it is attacked as being unnecessarily conservative as well as illogical.

What is the potential harm of being too conservative? Then the prior odds are multiplied by a much smaller number than is appropriate to calculate the posterior odds of G to I. Starting with a prior of $1/10$ a likelihood ratio of 10^5 in place of 10^8 would result in a posterior of 10 000 to 1 in place of 10 million to one. There is still no problem in going from the evidence M to G, the hypothesis that the specimens, allegedly from the crime scene and from the suspect, are from the same source. When one considers the apparently common practice of tampering with the evidence, or the possibility of an accidental mislabeling of the specimens, or in the case of PCR, the contamination of the specimens, the weak link, if any, is in going from that hypothesis G to actual guilt.

To be sure, there may be exceptional cases where the likelihood ratio is not so compelling. Typically such cases are those which don't follow the usual routine and demand real expertise for proper analysis. The NRC emphasis on quality control and training and certification for expert witnesses is needed to deal with those cases which seem to appear with surprising frequency, considering the adjective exceptional.

THE CEILING PRINCIPLE

A fundamental result in genetics (Weir 1990) involves a large population in which there are k possible alleles at a certain locus in proportions $p_1, p_2, \ldots, p_k$. After one generation of *random mating* within the population, these proportions will not change much, and the proportion of the population which have the ith and jth alleles will be approximately $2p_i p_j$ for $i \neq j$ and p_i^2 for $i = j$. This corresponds to the statement that for a randomly selected offspring, each of the two alleles he or she inherits are independently selected with probabilities p_i for $i = 1, 2, \ldots, k$. Such a population is said to be in *Hardy–Weinberg (HW) equilibrium*. The assumption of random mating is most likely to be accepted for those loci for which the polymorphisms are silent.

If we deal with a stable population which has few people coming in or out for several generations, and a locus whose alleles have no outwardly observable distinct manifestations, one might expect HW equilibrium to hold. Most populations that are sampled to estimate the p_i are not of the type described above. For example US Hispanics represent mixtures of quite separate subgroups, some of which may be thought of as relatively homogeneous. We show, with a simple artificial example, what can happen with such heterogeneous populations when we do not have random mating. If three alleles 1, 2, 3 appear with frequencies (0.3, 0.5, 0.2) in one subgroup and with frequencies (0.5, 0.1, 0.4) in a second subgroup of equal size, the combined group will have frequencies (0.4, 0.3, 0.3). Assuming HW equilibrium within each subgroup and no mating across these two subgroups, the frequency of offspring with alleles (1,2) would be $(0.3)(0.5) + (0.5)(0.1) = 0.20$. Treating the combined group as though it were in HW equilibrium, we would calculate the wrong result $2(0.4)(0.3) = 0.24$.

In the formation of the egg and the sperm, a pair of the parent's chromosomes may undergo a process where each chromosome may break into several relatively large pieces which recombine with complementary pieces of the other. The *recombination* takes place so that the egg or sperm has one complete set of 23 chromosomes, but each of these may have sections from each of the originating pair. Thus, for example, each chromosome of the sperm may carry part of the chromosomes originating from each of the father's parents. Alleles of two loci that are close to each other on a chromosome are likely to be *linked* in the sense that if one appears in the egg or sperm, the other is very likely to accompany it. For loci that are far apart on a given chromosome, there tends to be practically no such linkage.

For loci on different chromosomes there is believed to be no such linkage. It follows that for a stable population with random mating the alleles of loci on different chromosomes are statistically independent. This is called *linkage equilibrium* and permits one to multiply probabilities of events involving loci on different chromosomes to obtain resulting probabilities for the occurrence of all the events. Neither HW equilibrium nor linkage equilibrium is expected to obtain for populations consisting of several different subgroups, among which there is not much mixing, i.e. where random mating does not apply. The existence of such subgroups is referred to as *population substructure*.

If HW and linkage equilibrium are assumed, the probability of a random individual matching a given profile may be calculated as the product of terms $2p_{i1}p_{i2}$ where p_{i1} and p_{i2} are the relative frequencies of observed alleles i_1 and i_2 of the ith locus in the *heterozygous* case where these alleles are different, or of terms p_i^2 where p_i is the probability of the observed allele i in the *homozygous* case where both chromosomes have the same allele i. The practice of assuming HW and linkage equilibrium when there is population substructure will lead to incorrect estimation of $P(M|I)$. However, experiments based on artificially combining various groups have consistently shown relatively minor effects due to assuming independence when substructure exists. For this reason it is conjectured that a test for lack of HW equilibrium will have very little *power* (ability to reject the hypothesis of equilibrium) without very large sample sizes. Lack of power is correlated with a relatively minor effect on the calculation of $P(M|I)$.

Considering the lack of power of the test, it should be remarked that various investigations had no difficulty in detecting lack of equilibrium by observing more homozygous cases than expected. Others, for example Devlin *et al.* (1990) have attributed that effect to coalescence and measurement error.

When only one band appears for the specimen, there are other possible explanations besides homozygosity and coalescence. One is that one weight was so small or large that it was offscale for the measuring instrument and did not appear. The other involves degraded specimens. To deal with the first explanation the NRC report recommends replacing p_i^2 by $2p_i$ which is considerably more conservative.

Several treatments of the measurement error problem are referred to by the terms *floating bins* and *fixed bins*. We will describe the fixed-bin approach used by the FBI. The possible observations on band weight are divided up into cells or nonoverlapping bins. Several populations including Caucasians, Hispanics and Blacks are sampled separately. For each population sampled and each locus used, a histogram is formed to estimate the frequency distribution of band weights, i.e. the proportion of the measurements that fall into each of the bins.

The band weights of a forensic specimen and a suspect are declared to match if the difference in the observations is small enough, i.e. less than 5% of the average weight. Weir and Gaut (1993) state that in studies conducted by the South Carolina Law Enforcement Division (SLED) DNA laboratory, corresponding bands, from a blood sample and a vaginal swab (containing epithelial cells) from each of a sample of a women, never differ by more than 5.6% of their average band weight. Consequently, at SLED a wider matching interval is used than at the FBI, and a non-match is declared when the difference in corresponding bands exceeds 5.6% of the average length. In both laboratories, when a non-match is declared, the suspect is cleared. If the suspect is not cleared on any of the loci tested, a match is declared and a probability $P(M|I)$ is calculated and associated with the event of a match.

According to the ceiling principle, the estimate of $P(M|I)$ is then a product of terms of the form $2p_{i1}p_{i2}$ for heterozygous cases at the ith locus and of the form $2p_i$ for apparent homozygous cases. The value of the p corresponding to a band weight for a locus depends on the position of the interval $e(1 \pm 0.05)$ where e is the band weight of the forensic specimen. If this interval lies within one of the fixed bins, use a conservative estimate of the probability of falling in the fixed bin as p. If the interval overlaps two or more of the fixed bins, the NRC report recommends adding the estimated probabilities of the overlapped fixed bins (I assume here that they mean to have a conservative estimate of the probability of falling in any one of the overlapped fixed bins).

This proposal was criticized by Weir and Gaut (1993) among others who argue that one should only consider the maximum of the probabilities for the overlapped fixed bins. Since the fixed bins are usually considerably wider than $2(0.05)e$, then either one or two bins are overlapped. A fixed bin may contain several alleles, each of which contributes some part of the probability of falling in that bin. If most of the probability corresponding to each of two neighboring bins is concentrated on alleles close to the common boundary, then the NRC proposal is essential for an interval overlapping these bins. Weir (personal communication) argues that a study of the data in the FBI samples indicates that this contingency does not arise.

The ceiling principle involves estimating each bin probability by an appropriate upper bound. This is to be selected by sampling various data bases. 'Random samples of 100 persons should be drawn from each of 15–20 populations, each representing a group relatively homogeneous genetically; the largest frequency in any of these populations or 5% whichever is larger, should be taken as the ceiling frequency . . . The goal is not to ensure that the ethnic background of every particular defendant is represented, but rather to define the range of allele frequency variation.' The report also adds an interim suggestion while the samples are being collected of (1) using 10% in place of 5%, (2) using upper 95% confidence bounds on the bin frequencies for the separate racial groups studied to date, and (3) indicating how rare matches are by mentioning the total number of profiles in the combined data bases on the assumption that none of them match the forensic specimen.

PROBABILITY MODEL

Ideally we wish to see which of the possible perpetrators lead to a match with the forensic specimen. In general it is not possible to identify and assemble such a group. Even in the original case cited (Wambaugh 1989) the group tested did not include potential perpetrators who were older than 34 or from outside the local area. However, one may ask how rare is this matching profile.

The natural method for making a quantitative evaluation is to construct a *relevant* probability model from which a reasonable, or at least a conservative, estimate of $P(M|I)$ could be calculated. Our discussion suggests a model where the suspect is selected at random from a *reference population* of possible perpetrators, and $P(M|I)$ would be the proportion of that population which has matching profiles. But, as indicated above, not enough is ordinarily known about the profiles of that population to be useful.

One conservative approach is to find a substantial population in which the forensic profile or the alleles of that profile are very common. Then we might ask what is the probability that our suspect is a randomly selected innocent individual, from that population, who happens to have a profile matching that of the forensic specimen. Another conservative approach is to propose the population from which the suspect comes and to estimate $P(M|I)$ as the probability of finding a matching profile from that population.

The last method is conservative in the following sense. Without looking at the suspect's profile, the expectation of the log of the probability of a match with someone of an arbitrary population is no greater than that with someone of the suspect's population. However, the suspect is a member of several populations. For example we could take all his close relatives including his siblings if he has any. That population may be difficult to use because the relatives may be unwilling to be profiled, and besides there may be no such relatives who are possible suspects.

It may be that the suspect is a member of a relatively homogeneous group on which there exists data and for which geneticists may feel satisfied that the loci considered are such that there is every reason to expect genetic equilibrium among the loci studied. That would constitute a reasonable group to use to provide a conservative estimate of $P(M|I)$ using independence.

The NRC report attempts to bypass the reference population issue by sampling a substantial number of relatively homogeneous populations to see how much allele frequencies vary among these, and to replace estimated frequencies by upper bounds independent of the particular population.

To return to the population of relatives, one might construct a hypothetical infinite population of possible siblings of the suspect. That would provide a very conservative estimate of $P(M|I)$ based on HW and linkage equilibrium, and every locus where the suspect is heterozygous would provide a factor a little smaller than 4 (Weir and Hill 1993). Then four loci could contribute a likelihood ratio of no greater than $4^4 = 256$. To achieve more impressive likelihood ratios it will be necessary to use more loci. Such a scheme was proposed by Belin (personal communication). One advantage of such a scheme is that HW and linkage equilibrium is more likely to be accepted in this context by geneticists. Another is that estimates of matching probabilities at individual loci, from empirical data cumulated from siblings, would not be sensitive to the populations from which the samples were drawn or even how the samples were drawn.

The last proposal involves a hypothetical reference population. To apply HW and linkage equilibrium in other populations, we are more or less forced to invoke a hypothetical infinite population from which the individuals in our sample and the suspect are drawn. The reason is that once we have matching on four or five loci, in a population of a few billion, our individual has been almost certainly uniquely identified, in which case we are almost sure to have matching on the other loci. In other words, for finite populations, independence breaks down for events involving matching at several loci. However, this breakdown is not a basis for critics of DNA profiling to cite as evidence favoring the defense. For homogeneous subpopulations most geneticists seem willing to accept HW and linkage equilibrium as a reasonable model, at least for loci in different chromosomes.

What I have attempted in this section, is to point out some fundamental problems in defining a suitable quantitative measure of $P(M|I)$ and to suggest that the NRC approach is very conservative even though it invokes HW and linkage equilibrium.

CRITICISMS OF THE CEILING PRINCIPLE

Cohen (1992) has demonstrated, with an artificial counter-example, that the NRC claim that their approach is conservative, even in the presence of substructure, does not hold up and can fail badly. His example depends on lack of linkage equilibrium within the subpopulations. However, experiments carried out which created substructure in samples by combining data from different real populations, tend to reveal little effect from assuming independence (Devlin et al. 1993).

The NRC report has received criticism from those who feel that the ceiling principle is too conservative. It is argued that science demands a good estimate and not an overly conservative estimate. But for the decision makers, the issues are guilt or innocence, and the point of the DNA evidence is to establish whether or not it is reasonable to believe that the suspect was almost surely the source of the forensic specimen. Whether a $P(M|I) = 10^{-4}$ or 10^{-8} is usually irrelevant, because judges, when sampled, regard probabilities from 0.75 to 0.95 as 'beyond a reasonable doubt' (Gastwirth 1988).

Another argument (Weir and Gaut 1993) is that the ceiling principle suggests using probabilities of exclusive events which don't add up to 1. This violates the laws of probability. As an undergraduate, my school mates and I played a game, the object of which was logically to derive a given statement from $1 = 2$ as quickly as possible. That this is possible is the reason that applied mathematicians must check their models for coherence, existence and uniqueness before engaging in complex analysis. But the calculation using the above violation of probability is simple and transparent and is clearly dedicated to provide a conservative estimate of $P(M|I)$ in applications where the effect of substructure is expected to be minor. The danger of serious errors, other than conservatism, from the application of the ceiling principle, is negligible under treatment by experts.

There are arguments (Devlin *et al.* 1993) based on the data collected and experiments with those data that indicate that the ceiling principle is unnecessarily conservative. These arguments are persuasive, but they are based on a few experiments and limited data. It is claimed that overly conservative estimates require the use of many loci, and this increases the probability of the other error, i.e. that of incorrectly declaring a mismatch. But, that deficiency can easily be countered by increasing slightly the width of the interval of bandweights used to declare a match. As a result the use of additional loci might be a little less effective than expected by a naive analysis based on the original intervals. However, using more loci provides more information and can be used to reduce both the probability of declaring a match inappropriately and of declaring a mismatch inappropriately.

Devlin *et al.* (1993) claim that the plan to sample 100 individuals from each of a dozen populations is not a good experimental design and will force unduly conservative estimates. Finally (Kaye 1993, p.172) the choices of 5% and 10% 'rest on an unarticulated balancing of competing policies'. But with four loci the 10% figure is still adequate to obtain enormous likelihood ratios. With fewer than 5% of the population at a locus, the estimate of that proportion in samples of 100 could fluctuate wildly. No sharp analysis is required to see that these choices are adequate, if not optimal, for a conservative, yet effective approach.

PHILOSOPHY OF SCIENCE

A major shortcoming in the argument that the effect of assuming independence is minor is that the evidence is based on a few experiments with a limited number of data sets with few subjects, and often with opportunistic samples consisting of subjects who were readily available. One is inclined to believe that these results will generalize widely, but such an inclination is not proof.

Scientists typically do not deal with problems demanding near certainty even though lawyers may feel that the scientific method gives clear and definitive results. The reality is somewhat different. Scientists perform experiments suggested by partly baked hypotheses, conjectures and models to gather data, the analysis of which lead to better baked hypotheses and sharper experiments. At the end of a series of such experiments, a murky mess of ideas will gradually have given way to a clearer concept and more or less definitive experiments which can be replicated, and which need little statistical analysis to be understood and to be used for further increments in knowledge.

In the process the statistician often finds it convenient, in establishing the presence of certain effects, to set up null hypotheses which deny the presence of such effects and can be definitively rejected. But it is rarely the case that the statistician or scientists can set up a sharply stated hypothesis which is broadly applicable and get evidence that establishes it definitely. Failure to reject such a hypothesis is rarely the same as establishing it.

The hypothesis that one can apply independence in calculating $P(M|I)$ carries a great deal of baggage, and if stated so sharply will certainly be rejected with enough data. What is more relevant would be a measure of how much error the use of this hypothesis will introduce into the estimation of $P(M|I)$. We have some data on this issue for some cases, but we do not have as much basis to generalize as we would have if we confined attention to siblings or near relatives.

There is another difficulty with standard statistical practice. In the sequential process of refining hypotheses and experiments it is customary to use 95% or 99% confidence limits. One may be concerned with the meaning of a statement that one is 95% confident that $P(M|I) \leqslant 10^{-12}$. While such a statement is not made, even the conservative procedures suggested by the NRC report depend on the use of 95% confidence bounds.

Matching on four or five loci should be more than enough evidence to establish G. That will become clearer as growing data banks determine the frequency with which unrelated individuals match on two, three, four and five loci. In the meantime, scientific proof, where science has a capital S, will not be sufficient to convince defense experts who refuse to accept a model applying independence. But before long the scientific literature will be pretty much in agreement on the strength of DNA evidence, just as it is on the claim that cigarette smoking causes lung cancer, while cigarette company executives feel free to doubt that in testimony before Congress.

DNA EVIDENCE IN COURT

At first DNA evidence was accepted without question. As defense lawyers brought in expert witnesses, often with limited expertise, who questioned the quality and analysis, many courts excluded some or all aspects of the DNA evidence. While some courts insisted on quantitative evidence, others refuse to accept 'statistical' evidence. One issue was the subjective nature of the decision to declare a match, which gave rise in some courts to a desire to automate that process.

The NRC report attempted to put the entire matter in perspective. As a result, enterprising lawyers found openings in some vague language and some of the criticism of the report. For example, Weir (1993), in testifying for the prosecution, rejected HW equilibrium at two loci on two of three population data sets tested. The defense lawyer convinced the judge that the NRC instructions implied that both data sets should be excluded and that the remaining data set did not suffice for NRC standards, and the DNA evidence should be inadmissible. A more reasonable interpretation would have been merely to eliminate the data at the involved loci-population pairs.

In reaction to the controversy about the NRC report, in disregard of the fact that many, if not most of the criticisms were directed toward the *excessive conservatism*, a number of courts chose not to admit DNA testimony (Kaye

1993, p.148). Recently the decisions are beginning to move toward admitting DNA profile evidence and allowing the use of quantitative conclusions. The Minnesota Supreme Court decided to admit quantitative evidence after being faced with a threat by the state legislature to legislate its admissibility (Zack 1994) and the New York Court of Appeals (Fisher 1994) made a decision in favor of admitting DNA evidence.

In the meantime the NRC is in the process of preparing another report, presumably to correct some minor errors and to clarify the points on which the previous report was vague.

PRESENTING THE EVIDENCE

A major argument against admissibility of quantitative evidence has been the fear that juries would not understand and would be unduly influenced by such numbers. It has been suggested that some judges automatically *tune out* when numbers are discussed and therefore prefer more qualitative statements.

If a number is demanded, then there is a problem with declaring a probability of 10^{-12} in a world with 5 billion people. My suspicion is that rather than being unduly influenced to believe in guilt, the jury is liable to be skeptical of the result or unsure of how to interpret it. Certainly the defense lawyer could easily counteract any undue influence by pointing out the weakness of the chain of evidence from G to guilt. In the meantime the prosecution has a problem of showing how such numbers can be derived from samples of a few hundred subjects. A table of random digits could be the source of a tutorial on how probabilities of 10^{-12} are easily attained and, while events of such low probabilities will occur, we should be surprised to see them repeated.

The principle of calculating posterior odds from prior odds and the likelihood ratio seems simple enough to me, now that I am an experienced statistician. Geisser (1990), a devoted Bayesian, is convinced that such analysis would not be appreciated by most juries and judges. Simple tables showing what proportion of siblings match on one, two, . . . loci can help indicate forcefully to juries the strength of the evidence.

In summary, part of the function of the expert witness for the prosecution should be the design of a proper presentation of the evidence to inform the judge and jury of what the evidence does and does not mean.

CONCLUSIONS

There continues to be controversy about the force of evidence of matching DNA profiles. I predict that that controversy will diminish as courts realize that with proper quality control and real expertise, the current methods are ordinarily quite adequate to establish matching for legal purposes. It may take a few years for the experts to learn to deal with the few places where the NRC opened a door for clever defense lawyers.

It has been claimed that in a few years, we will have readily available direct sequencing methods which will describe the loci precisely without measurement error, and thereby eliminate the controversy. Those advances will be useful, but they will not dispose of the basic philosophical issues. The experts who argue that the numbers presented are meaningless because the models don't hold will be able to argue that point just as forcefully in the future.

What is liable to be more convincing, now as well as in the future, is the point essentially made by Wooley and Harmon (1992). The prosecutor can ask 'Why, if you think the suspect is innocent, you do not investigate another locus which is extremely likely to establish his innocence?'

From the point of view of when new methods of scientific evidence should be admitted, the legal profession is wise in not requiring unanimity among experts because such unanimity is difficult to deliver in fields as tenuous as science. On the other hand it is clear that the legal profession should move quickly to enhance the debate and analysis necessary to clarify the pros and cons of important new innovations. The debate tends to carry on long after the main issues are understood.

At about the time this manuscript was completed, O. J. Simpson was accused of murdering his wife and Mr Goldman. Supposedly DNA evidence was one of the factors that led to the decision to prosecute. Somehow the DNA evidence turned out to have surprising little impact on the outcome of the long drawn out and widely reported trial which ended with an acquittal. Several impressions arose from my irregular following of this trial. One was that the police forensic work was sloppy, and that the police, who testified that they did not regard Simpson as a suspect when they went to his house, were not reliable. I would not be surprised if it turned out that the jury, many of whose members were from the inner city, shared my skepticism and felt that the DNA evidence, which could easily be tampered with, could not be used to determine the outcome of the trial. I tend to regard this trial as a powerful endorsement of the recommendations of the need for quality control in the report of the National Research Council.

This chapter has neglected the privacy and ethical issues in DNA profiling which are important and which have been treated in the NRC report.

ACKNOWLEDGEMENTS

I wish to thank D. Balding, J. L. Gastwirth, K. Lange, R. C. Lewontin, and B. S. Weir for helpful discussions and D. H. Kaye for his article from which I borrowed much.

REFERENCES

Aldhous, P. (1993). Geneticists attack NRC report as scientifically flawed. *Science*, **259**, 755–6.

Berry, D. A. (1991). Inferences using DNA profiling in forensic identification and paternity cases. (with discussion) *Statistical Science*, **6**, 175–205.

Cohen, J. E. (1992). The ceiling principle is not always conservative in assigning genotypes for forensic DNA testing. *American Journal of Human Genetics*, **51**, 1165–8.

Committee on DNA Technology in Forensic Inference (1992). *DNA technology in forensic science*. National Academy Press, Washington, DC.

Devlin, B., Risch, N. and Roeder, K. (1990). No excess of homozygosity at loci used for DNA fingerprinting. *Science*, **249**, 1416–20.

Devlin, B., Risch, N., and Roeder, K. (1993). Statistical evaluation of DNA fingerprinting: a critique of the NRC's report. *Science*, **259**, 748–9.

Fisher, I. (1994). Ruling allows DNA testing as evidence. *The New York Times*, March 30, **B1**.

Gastwirth, J. L. (1988). *Statistical reasoning in law and public policy*, Vol. 2. Academic Press, Boston.

Geisser, S. (1990). Some remarks on DNA fingerprinting. *Chance: new directions for statistics and computing*, **3**, 8–9.

Jeffreys, A. J., Wilson, V., and Thein, S. L. (1985). Individual-specific 'fingerprints' of human DNA. *Nature*, **316**, 76–9.

Kaye, D. H. (1993). DNA evidence: probability, population genetics and the courts. *Harvard Journal of Law and Technology*, **7**, 101–72.

Kolata, G. (1991). Critic of genetic fingerprint testing tells of pressure to withdraw paper. *The New York Times*, December 20, A16.

Lewontin, R. C. (1992). The dream of the human genome. *The New York Review*, May 28, 31–40.

Thompson, W. C. and Ford, S. (1989). DNA typing: acceptance and weight of the new genetic identification tests. *Virginia Law Review*, **75**, 45–108.

Thompson, W. C. and Schumann, E. L. (1987). Interpretation of statistical evidence in court trials; the prosecutor's fallacy and the defense attorney's fallacy. *Law and Human Behavior*, **11**, 167–87.

Wambaugh, J. (1989). *The blooding*. Perigord Press, New York.

Weir, B. S. (1990). *Genetic data analysis: methods for discrete population genetic data*. Sinnauer, Sunderland, MA.

Weir, B. S. (1993). DNA fingerprinting report. *Science*, **260**, 473.

Weir, B. S. and Gaut, B. S. (1993). Matching and binning DNA fragments in forensic science. *Jurimetrics*, **34**, 9–19.

Weir, B. S. and Hill, W. G. (1993). Population genetics of DNA profiles. *Journal of the Forensic Science Society*, **33**(4), 218–25.

Wooley, J. and Harmon, R. P. (1992). The forensic DNA brouhaha: science or debate. *American Journal of Human Genetics*, **51**, 1164–5.

Zack, M. (1994). Use of DNA evidence widened. *Star Tribune*, April 30, A1.

2 The emerging field of human rights statistics

THOMAS B. JABINE[1]

> The scientific–statistical analysis of human rights appears at first unnecessary and harmful. One murder for political ends is too many; one starved child for political ends is too much. Nevertheless, there is an emerging field of human rights statistics. And a bit of thought can justify the need for the statistics.
>
> I. Richard Savage (1985)

The theme for this chapter is from Richard Savage's Presidential Address to the American Statistical Association at its 1984 annual meeting in Philadelphia. In his discussion of 'Hard–Soft Problems' he identified several possible areas of applied statistics, which he labelled 'partisan areas' where he believed there were '. . . opportunities for the statistician to work impartially to allow the decision-making process to be more enlightened'. One of the areas was human rights.

Savage's appeal to statisticians to use their skills and experience in partisan areas came at an opportune time. In 1979, largely in response to the disappearance of Carlos Noriega, the director of the Argentine statistical office, during the period of 'disappearances' and other human rights violations under that country's repressive political regime, the American Statistical Association established an Ad Hoc Committee on Scientific Freedom and Human Rights. Initially the committee (which was made a continuing committee in 1982) pursued only casework – inquiries and representations to governments and other actions on behalf of fellow statisticians whose rights had been violated.

It soon became clear, however, that statisticians might also be able to contribute to the protection and promotion of human rights by using the tools of their profession to improve quantitative procedures for assessing and monitoring the status of human rights in different places and over time. Initially, the committee met some resistance to the revision of its charter to include this kind of activity. Questions were raised as to whether it was appropriate for a professional or scientific society to concern itself with a politically controversial subject like human rights. Savage's address was undoubtedly an important factor in overcoming such concerns and making it possible for the committee to expand the scope of its activities.

My goal in this chapter is to persuade more statisticians, especially those who are drawn to applied work, to consider human rights as an area in which to apply their professional knowledge and skills. Because human rights is a broad concept, it is

1. The author wishes to thank David L. Banks, Herbert F. Spirer and Louise Spirer for helpful comments on early drafts of this chapter.

necessary to begin with a brief discussion of what the concept represents. I then give several examples of how human rights statistics have been and are being used to monitor and study human rights issues. A discussion of some features of human rights statistics that are common to many of the examples follows. At the end of the chapter I provide some recommended sources of information for those who may want to learn more.

WHAT ARE HUMAN RIGHTS?

The concept of individual rights, in a general sense, is fairly old, but the concept of human rights has emerged largely in the second half of this century. The term can have different interpretations for different persons and societies. However, since most countries of the world have subscribed to the Universal Declaration of Human Rights,[2] that declaration is a good place to seek broadly accepted definitions of different types of human rights. The definitions of specific rights in the Universal Declaration are couched in broad, some might even say vague, terms. Somewhat more specific definitions are provided in a subsequent series of international human rights treaties, including, for example, the International Covenant on Civil and Political Rights, the International Covenant on Economic, Social and Cultural Rights and the International Convention on the Elimination of All Forms of Racial Discrimination.

The first two treaties named above illustrate the existence of two broad classes of rights: *civil and political rights*, such as rights of persons against the imposition of torture or arbitrary detention and rights to freedom of expression and peaceful assembly; and *economic and social rights*, such as adequate nutrition, housing, medical care and education. Generally speaking, it isn't too difficult to recognize a violation of a civil or political right. It's harder to say what constitutes a violation of an economic or social right. How should adequate nutrition or housing be defined? Should the definition be absolute or should it vary according to the economic resources available to each country? The treaties that cover economic and social rights call for 'progressive realization' of these rights, to the maximum permitted by each country's available resources.

An important feature of each of the human rights treaties is a non-discrimination provision that the same rights will be enjoyed by all. For example, Article 2 of the Universal Declaration states, in part (United Nations 1985a):

Everyone is entitled to all the rights and freedoms set forth in this Declaration, without distinction of any kind, such as race, colour, sex, language, religion, political or other opinion, national or social origin, property, birth or other status.

---

2. Technically, United Nations members are bound by Article 55 of the United Nations Charter, which says that the United Nations shall promote '. . . universal respect for, and observance of human rights and fundamental freedoms for all without distinction as to race, sex, language, or religion'. The Universal Declaration of Human Rights, adopted by the General Assembly in 1948, was an authoritative statement of the meaning of Article 55. For further detail on the legal significance of the Universal Declaration see Forsythe (1983).

Monitoring compliance with this provision requires analyses of relevant data that are disaggregated into appropriate categories for each of these variables. In the United States, for example, since the passage of new civil rights laws in the 1960s, many statisticians have been called upon to analyze data to determine the extent of racial discrimination in voting, employment, access to housing, jury selection and application of the death penalty.

SOME EXAMPLES OF HUMAN RIGHTS STATISTICS

Moving quickly from the general to the specific, I now present ten examples of human rights statistics.

Example 1: Lynchings in the United States

The first example pre-dates the Universal Declaration of Human Rights. Lynching, hanging of persons by mobs without due process of law, often preceded by torture and mutilation, was common in the United States in the post-Civil War era and continued into the first four decades of this century. Most of the victims were black. Periodic statistics on lynchings were first compiled by the *New York Post* in 1885 and subsequently by the Tuskegee Institute. Victims were classified by race, date of execution, jurisdiction, location and the alleged offense of the victim, such as 'insults to white persons'. The statistics, released annually, received wide attention in the media. Although legislative response to the problem was slow in coming, the numbers gradually declined. Nearly 2000 blacks were lynched in the two decades from 1890 to 1909. The number fell to 875 between 1910 and 1929 and to 146 between 1930 and 1949 (Ploski and Williams 1983).

Example 2: 'No-name' burials in Argentina

During the 'Dirty War' in Argentina between 1976 and 1983, many persons perceived as enemies by the oppressive military regime were seized by government or paramilitary forces and subsequently tortured and executed. Such persons were known as the 'disappeared'; there was no accounting to their families or society.

Under the subsequent Alfonsin Government an attempt was made to account for the victims and identify the oppressors. As part of this accounting, the Secretary of Human Rights initiated a survey of cemeteries in the Province of Buenos Aires. Under the direction of Clyde Collins Snow, a forensic pathologist, data were collected on the number of 'no-name' burials, or burials of unidentified persons, in these cemeteries. The analysis covered the period of the Dirty War and the years that immediately preceded and followed it, as a control. Through the use of hypothesis testing and other formal methods of analysis the investigators conclusively demonstrated that most of the unidentified bodies that were buried in the cemeteries surveyed during the period of the Dirty War must have been those of the disappeared (Snow and Bihurriet 1992).

Example 3: One-third of a nation

In his second inaugural address, in 1937, Franklin D. Roosevelt presented, in rough statistical terms, what he viewed as the challenge to American democracy:

. . . In this nation I see tens of millions of its citizens – a substantial part of its whole population – who at this very moment are denied the greater part of what the very lowest standards of today call the necessities of life.

I see millions of families trying to live on incomes so meager that the pall of family disaster hangs over them day by day.

and at the end of the passage:

I see one-third of a nation ill-housed, ill-clad, ill-nourished. (United States Senate 1989)

It would be interesting to know what sources of data were consulted in developing these rough estimates; this was before the days of official poverty statistics and a regular, well-established program of income and expenditure surveys. Even if widely accepted minimum standards for adequate housing, clothing and nutrition had existed at the time, which they did not, the estimates that one-third of the population was below the standard in each category could have been substantially wide of the mark in either direction. Nevertheless, Roosevelt's dramatic statement made large numbers of people more aware than they had been of the plight of the poor in the United States. It was widely repeated and, indeed, may have provided part of the motivation for the subsequent development of statistical programs that provide a much sounder basis for monitoring the status of economic and social rights in the United States. Would a dry presentation of whatever data might have been available at the time, accompanied by the kinds of caveats that many of us might consider appropriate, have been as effective?

Example 4: Persons with no health insurance

The International Covenant on Economic, Social and Cultural Rights calls for countries that have ratified it to take steps toward '. . . the creation of conditions which would assure to all medical service and medical attention in the event of sickness' (United Nations 1985b, Article 12). In the United States (which has not yet ratified the covenant, but may in the future), an important indicator of access to basic health care services is whether or not a person, individually or as a family member, is covered by some form of health insurance. In discussions of the complex issues of health care reform, one principle on which many persons can agree is that, sooner or later, all persons should be covered by insurance that assures access to basic health care services. Most other industrialized countries have universal coverage, the United States does not.

One sees many different estimates of the proportion of the US population not covered by health insurance. Differences among estimates arise from several sources. Some estimates relate to persons uninsured at a particular point in time, others to persons not covered during all or some part of a specified time period, such as the past year. Some of the differences are the result of sampling error and some reflect measurement error – respondents to surveys misunderstood the question or were unable to answer it correctly. Some of the most vulnerable groups of the population, like homeless persons and migrant workers, may not have been covered by the surveys on which estimates are based.

One can also question the adequacy of the proportion of uninsured as an indicator of access to health care services. Some persons who cannot afford private health insurance, such as those covered by Medicaid, may have access that could be considered adequate by most definitions; some who are insured may have policies that don't provide coverage of all basic services and may not be able to afford services that are not covered. The proportion of uninsured is not a perfect measure of the underlying human right, but it is a useful indicator and one that anyone who has ever lacked health insurance coverage or been threatened with loss of coverage can relate to in a very personal way.

Example 5: Childhood immunizations

Immunization can provide relatively low cost protection from childhood diseases, some of them potentially life-threatening. Statistics on immunization rates show that the United States is lagging well behind many other countries. One of the goals adopted by the Department of Health and Human Services for the year 2000 is immunization of 90 per cent of all 2-year-olds (United States Department of Health and Human Services 1990). In a recent UNICEF report (1993), data on immunization rates for 1990–91 were not even available for the United States; rates for 1-year-old children shown for several other countries, such as Finland, Costa Rica, Poland and Cuba were above 90 per cent. US data for 1985 and earlier years show that immunization rates for the white population have consistently exceeded those for other races and that rates in central cites are below those for the rest of the population (Institute of Medicine 1993, p. 72).

In the debates on health care reform, and even before they began, the relatively poor record of the US on childhood immunization has received wide attention and various measures have been proposed to improve it. Improvement is not just a matter of national pride; it should not be difficult to show that the human and economic costs of not immunizing preschool children are higher than the costs of doing it. There are several statistical measurement issues associated with the collection of data on immunization; better data are needed on a regular basis to formulate an action program and to monitor its effects. In 1994, the National Center for Health Statistics initiated a large-scale four-year survey program of random-digit dialing telephone surveys, supplemented by field interviews with a sample of households without telephones, to collect the data on childhood immunizations needed to track progress toward the year 2000 goal.

Example 6: Monitoring international human rights treaties

In a preceding section, I noted that there are several international human rights treaties that impose obligations on the countries that ratify them to ensure the realization of specified rights by everyone. Seven of these treaties have formal reporting requirements. Under the International Covenant for Civil and Political Rights, for example, each country is required to file an initial report and subsequent reports at five-year intervals to the United Nations, describing legal and administrative means by which persons are assured enjoyment of the rights covered by the treaty. The reporting guidelines call for statistical information on several topics relevant to the specific rights included in the Covenant (Pocar 1991).

The reports are reviewed and discussed in public sessions by the UN Committee on Human Rights. There is an optional protocol to the Covenant which allows citizens of countries that have subscribed to it to appeal directly to the UN for redress of specific violations if they have exhausted the possibilities in their own countries. However, the main effects of the reporting system are achieved through moral persuasion and education. At the international level, violations by specific countries become more exposed to public view, even if not covered in a country's own report. At the national level, human rights advocacy groups have the opportunity (to a greater or lesser degree, depending on their government's policies for release and dissemination of its reports to the United Nations) to review and criticize their government's self-evaluation of its human rights performance.

Of the treaties requiring periodic reports to the United Nations, the United States has so far ratified only three: the International Covenant on Civil and Political Rights (1992), the International Convention on the Elimination of All Forms of Racial Discrimination (1994), and the Convention against Torture and Other Cruel, Inhuman or Degrading Treatment or Punishment (1994), but it may ratify others soon. Its first report under the International Covenant on Civil and Political Rights was due in September 1993, but was not submitted to the United Nations until July 1994 and was not made public until September 1994. Persons outside the government were not invited or allowed to participate directly in the preparation of the report. However, some statisticians, working through the Science and Human Rights Program of the American Association for the Advancement of Science, submitted suggestions about suitable sources of relevant data for inclusion in the report to the State Department official responsible for its preparation.

Following the release of the report, an evaluation of its statistical content found that there was very limited use of data. Most of the data that were included were part of a general demographic and socioeconomic profile of the U.S. and were not directly relevant to specific articles of the Covenant. When data were included, their presentation sometimes failed to meet ordinary standards of relevance, clarity, and attribution (Jabine, Lynch, and Spirer 1995).

With additional United States reports to the United Nations expected over the next several years, there should be many opportunities for statisticians to evaluate and provide feedback on the relevance, completeness, quality and interpretation of statistical data in the reports and perhaps eventually to assist in their preparation.

Example 7: The El Mozote massacre

In December 1981 troops of the Government of El Salvador killed well over 500 men, women and children of all ages in El Mozote and surrounding villages in the remote province of Morazán, on the pretext that the local residents had been cooperating with guerrilla forces operating in the area. Was it important to know the number of persons killed? At the time, it was. Late in the same month, the US Congress amended the Foreign Assistance Act of 1961 to require that, in order to continue foreign aid to El Salvador, the President would have to certify to Congress by 29 January 1982 that the Government of El Salvador was making progress in bringing to an end the indiscriminate torture and murder of Salvadorian citizens by elements of its armed forces.

Some reports of the massacre reached Washington, but the precise facts were hard to ascertain from a distance and administration spokespersons disputed the reports. President Reagan made the certification and aid continued. Subsequently, Congress required periodic certifications of progress for aid to continue and a numbers game began, with the State Department developing its time series data mainly on the basis of press and embassy reports and with local and international human rights organizations developing their own data series, showing much higher numbers of killings and other rights violations. It was at this time that members of the American Statistical Association's Committee on Scientific Freedom and Human Rights came to believe that the Committee's mission should be expanded beyond 'casework' to allow statisticians, as Richard Savage (1985) put it, '. . . to work impartially to allow the decision-making process to be more enlightened'.

The full story of what happened at El Mozote only emerged much later. The State Department denied in 1982 that there had been a massacre, but in July 1993, following an investigation by a Salvadorian 'Truth Commission', a Secretary of State's Panel concluded that one had indeed occurred and that US statements on the case had been wrong. A detailed account of what happened in El Salvador and in Washington is told in gripping fashion in a 1993 *New Yorker* article by Mark Danner.

Example 8: Housing market and employment audits

Most measures of discrimination by race, gender and other characteristics are indirect. There are abundant data showing, for example, that blacks and Hispanics in the United States have lower incomes than whites, whether measured by means, percentiles, indices of dissimilarity or other statistics. But what factors explain these differences? To what extent are they the consequence of direct discrimination against racial and ethnic groups? Statistical techniques can be used to try to adjust for the effects of education and other variables for which data are available but there can be no certainty about the appropriateness of the statistical techniques or the reasons for residual differences.

However, more direct measures of some types of discrimination can be obtained by using statistically designed experiments. In 1977 the US Department of Housing and Urban Development (1979) sponsored an extensive study, covering a sample of 40 metropolitan areas, in which black and white customers, matched on socioeconomic characteristics, visited realtors to inquire about housing that had been advertised for rental or purchase. One focus of the study was on 'steering', the practice of sending clients in different racial groups to different areas. The study report concluded that 70 per cent of the whites and blacks seeking rental housing and 90 per cent of those seeking to buy houses were steered to separate neighborhoods. With somewhat less frequency, more direct kinds of discrimination were observed.

Similar techniques have been used in numerous experiments. More recent surveys of housing discrimination conducted by the Department of Housing and Urban Development continue to show substantial discrimination against blacks and Hispanics. A recent study that sent pairs of equally qualified white and black applicants to apply for entry-level jobs found that 28 per cent of the white applicants were offered jobs, compared with 18 per cent of the black applicants (Wessel 1991). In a study sponsored by the American Association of Retired Persons, job résumés representing equally qualified younger and older job seekers were mailed to a large number of companies and employment agencies. Based on the responses, the investigators concluded that 'Older applicants are likely to confront age discrimination one of every four times they apply for available jobs.' (Lewis 1994).

Example 9: Landmines

Landmines kill or maim thousands of people each year, mostly in less developed countries where they have been widely used in internal and external conflicts. They are cheap to produce and costly to remove or disable. They do not distinguish between combatants and civilians. In some areas they have made it all but impossible for refugees from civil wars to return to their homes and work their lands. A recent report on the use of landmines in Cambodia provides an order of magnitude estimate that 1 of every 236 persons in the country is an amputee due to a landmine explosion (Asia Watch and Physicians for Human Rights 1991, p. 59).

The 1980 Landmines Protocol, an international treaty aimed at stopping landmine use against civilians, has proved almost completely ineffective. It is currently being formally evaluated at a United Nations treaty review conference. Several organizations that advocate a complete ban on the production and use of landmines gathered information in an attempt to document their huge social costs. The Vietnam Veterans of America Foundation coordinated a systematic effort to compile existing data and gather additional information on the consequences of landmine use as it affects refugee movement and resettlement; development and post-conflict reconstruction; medical, rehabilitative and psychological costs; mine clearance and mine awareness costs; and the environment. Particular attention was on four countries with severe problems: Afghanistan, Cambodia, Mozambique and the former Yugoslavia. Developing a framework for the analysis and finding and presenting the data to fit it posed tough challenges to statisticians and others participating in this effort (Roberts and Williams 1995).

Example 10: An investigation of rape in the former Yugoslavia

Early in 1993, at the request of the United Nations, a team of experts, including four medical specialists, undertook a two-week mission . . . to investigate reports concerning the widespread occurrence of rape and, in particular, allegations received that rape was being used in a 'systematic' way, especially in Bosnia and Herzegovina (United Nations 1993). Given the limited time available, the sensitivity of the subject, the lack of a central source of information and the difficulties of travel in wartime conditions, how could the team collect and analyze sufficient reliable data to provide a clear picture of the scale of the problem? How could they present the data in a manner that would withstand questions raised by the governments that would be held accountable for failing to control this basic violation of women's rights?

The team collected data from hospitals and medical centers on pregnancy rates, birth rates, abortion rates, sexually transmitted diseases and the number of pregnancies reportedly due to rape. They also interviewed and received direct testimonies of rape from individual victims and eye-witnesses to rape.

The key to the effectiveness of their mission was in the manner in which they analyzed and presented their findings. With the assistance of a statistical consultant with whom they were in frequent contact by telephone, the team quickly decided that it would not be possible for them to estimate the total number of rape victims, as members of the media and others had attempted to do. Instead, they carefully presented the factual data that they had gathered and described their relevance as evidence of large-scale rape. Where they used estimation procedures, the assumptions were clearly laid out. For example, the team had documented 119 cases of pregnancy resulting from rape. There have been medical studies suggesting that of every 100 incidents of rape, one results in pregnancy. On this basis, the team suggested that these 119 cases might represent roughly 12,000 incidents of rape. Recognizing that this estimate would be very sensitive to moderate variations in the 1 in 100 pregnancy rate, the team stated in its report that '. . . this figure . . . may only serve as a guide to the general scale of the problem' (United Nations 1993, pp. 67–68).

One of the conclusions reached by the team was that:

Rape of women including minors has occurred on a large scale. While the team of experts has found victims among all ethnic groups involved in the conflict, the majority of the rapes that they have documented had been committed by Serb forces against Muslim women from Bosnia and Herzegovina. (United Nations 1993, p.73)

Because of the careful manner in which the team presented the methods they used to collect and analyze data and because they refrained from presenting conclusions that they were unable to back up, their report, which appears as an annex to the report of a Special Rapporteur of the United Nations Commission on Human Rights, might well be regarded as a model for investigators who undertake to collect data on human rights violations under similar conditions.

HUMAN RIGHTS STATISTICS:
SOME GENERAL OBSERVATIONS

In this diverse set of examples there are some common threads. In this section, I make some observations about uses, sources, quality and effective presentation of human rights statistics.

Uses of data

We can distinguish between uses of human rights data for *advocacy* purposes and uses for *enforcement* of individual human rights. The line of demarcation is not always sharp; many kinds of data can serve both purposes. The data on lynchings described in Example 1 were compiled and published to support advocacy, which eventually succeeded, of specific legislation aimed at ending this gross violation of human rights, which was directed primarily at blacks. The data about landmines described in Example 9 are being assembled by advocates of a more effective international ban on the manufacture and use of landmines.

The housing discrimination audits that were described in Example 8 were undertaken to support and plan enforcement activities. The Department of Housing and Urban Development uses these audits to guide and monitor the effectiveness of its efforts to enforce laws that prohibit discrimination in access to housing. Since the data are publicly available, they can also be used by advocacy groups who are not satisfied with the enforcement efforts of the department.

Statistics are routinely used by both sides in legal proceedings brought by individuals who allege racial or gender discrimination in hiring and promotion by employers. Statisticians are often called upon to serve as expert witnesses in such cases. Their analyses are tend to be complex and controversial (see, for example, Dempster 1988).

One could argue that the statistics included in mandatory reports to the United Nations by countries that have ratified international human rights treaties are intended to be used for enforcement of specific human rights covered by the treaties. The reports are reviewed by UN committees which then make recommendations to the countries on how to improve their human rights policies and practices. However, some people who are directly involved in the United Nations human rights reporting and monitoring system or have examined it from the outside have come to the conclusion that its most effective use is to publicize violations and failures to make progress, thus empowering human rights advocacy groups in each country to exert pressure on their own governments to do better.

Another way of thinking about the uses of human rights statistics is that their underlying purpose is to make it possible for interested parties to *monitor* the status of specific human rights, observing changes over time and identifying discrimination in the treatment of different groups of the population. Many of the examples in the preceding section include this element. At least for the next several years, data on the proportion of the population without health insurance coverage (Example 4) will be needed to determine how well our health care system is succeeding in providing the right to basic health care for all persons. A large survey program has been initiated to monitor progress in achieving US goals to improve rates of childhood immunization (Example 5). During the late 1970s and early 1980s, the US administration was required by Congress to compile information about the extent of politically motivated killing and other rights violations in El Salvador and to certify that improvements were occurring if it wished to continue military and economic assistance to that country (Example 7).

Types and sources of data

There are both similarities and sharp contrasts between the types and sources of statistics suitable for monitoring economic and social rights and those that can be used to monitor and track violations of civil and political rights. For the latter, the emphasis is on counting events that constitute violations of the rights of specific persons, for example, instances of torture or unlawful detention. Some economic and social rights are defined with sufficient clarity so that violations can be identified. For example, the International Covenant on Economic, Social and Cultural Rights states that 'Primary education shall be compulsory and available free to all' (United Nations 1985b). But the definitions of most economic and social rights lack the specificity needed to permit unambiguous identification of violations. The same covenant, for example, speaks of '. . . the right of everyone to the enjoyment of the highest attainable standard of physical and mental health'.

In monitoring economic and social rights, therefore, the emphasis tends to be on statistical indicators that do not provide direct measures of violations but may suggest where violations can be found. In order to serve this purpose well, indicators must be disaggregated, that is, presented separately for population subgroups defined by gender, race, religion, geographic location and other classifiers. Race and religion present a special problem. In several countries, laws or policies prevent the collection, by government agencies at least, of data classified by race, ethnic origin or religion, so that alternative means of identifying vulnerable minorities must be devised.

The International Covenant on Economic, Social and Cultural Rights recognizes that not all economic and social human rights can be fully realized immediately. It calls for progressive realization of these rights to the extent permitted by each country's resources. Hence time series of the relevant indicators are required to determine whether a country is making genuine efforts toward progressive realization.

Disaggregation and time series data are, of course, also important for statistics of violations of civil and political rights. As a practical matter, we know that violations of these more clearly defined human rights occur and will not cease entirely simply because a country has ratified the International Covenant on Civil and Political Rights. What is important is to be able to determine whether violations affect some population subgroups disproportionately and whether the situation is improving.

The two major categories of human rights also offer a contrast with respect to the amount of data available and the sources of the data. Virtually all governments collect and publish extensive data on topics relevant to economic and social rights, such as education, health, nutrition, housing and employment. As Savage (1985) put it, '. . . the statistical description of human rights is already well established in the areas of food, health, education, and employment'. Data are collected through censuses and sample surveys and can also be derived from records developed for administrative programs related, for example, to education, taxation and social welfare. Although access to such data varies by country, many of the official data on these topics can be acquired and used by non-governmental organizations and individuals.

Official government data relating to violations of civil and political rights are much harder to find. Violations of these rights reflect unfavorably on governments that have ratified the relevant covenant; asking them to report to the United Nations about such violations asks them to imperil their images in the community of nations and among their own citizens, assuming that the reports are available to the latter. Even so, official statistics can provide some relevant information. As noted in Example 6, a group of statisticians provided information to the State Department about sources of data, largely from the Justice Department's Bureau of Justice Statistics, that might be useful in reporting to the United Nations under the Covenant on Civil and Political Rights.

Nevertheless, useful information on violations of civil and political rights is more likely to come from non-governmental sources. At the international level, Amnesty International, a widely respected human rights advocacy organization, issues periodic reports covering violations in all countries, plus numerous special reports on civil and political rights in countries where rights violations are especially common or serious. Although these reports are largely non-quantitative, some analysts and researchers have used them to construct standards-based subjective ratings of civil and political human rights performance by country (see, for example, Poe 1990).

For data on specific violations, however, the front-line troops are national human rights advocacy organizations that collect information about violations in their own countries from individuals who have been victimized or from their relatives and friends. The primary concern of such groups is to assist the victims, but as a by-product they produce counts of violations for which they have documented accounts. Their counts are unlikely to be complete, but can be used to place lower bounds on the occurrence of various kinds of human rights abuses, such as governmental use of torture and illegal detention. These incomplete counts are useful because they document the existence of serious human rights violations which should not be occurring at all and help to identify the population groups most affected. In countries with repressive governments, the work of these human rights monitors has frequently made them and those who report information to them the victims of violations, including torture and death.

Relevant data on violations of human rights may come from unexpected sources. Samuelson and Spirer (1992) suggest that much can be learned simply by observing what kinds of data are not available or are presented in a distorted manner. They report, for example, that the USSR '. . . stopped publication of infant mortality data in the 1970s, when the rates, which had been decreasing steadily, began to increase'. In 1968, the government of South Africa stopped publishing data on the racial distribution of cases of kwashiorkor, a serious disease of infants and children resulting from malnutrition. Data published prior to 1968 had shown that the rate for African South Africans was over 300 times the rate for white South Africans. As noted in Example 2, investigators in Argentina were able to develop information about state-sanctioned killings of 'enemies of the regime' from cemetery records. Wechsler (1987) tells a fascinating story of how investigators in Brazil were able to develop an archive with documentation of human rights abuses by the country's military judicial system from records of trials held in Brazilian military courts from 1964 through 1979.

However, it is possible that such sources of information may be harder to find as repressive regimes become more sophisticated and devise ways to cover their tracks. As suggested recently by Morehead (1993), producer of the BBC series *Human Rights, Human Wrongs*, a decline in the number of known prisoners of conscience may simply be an indication that 'It has become easier for governments to "disappear" their critics rather than risk the embarrassing publicity of holding them in prison.' The interpretation of time series data on, for example, political executions is difficult. Does a decline mean that the regime is becoming less oppressive or does it mean that a campaign of terror has succeeded in stifling all overt opposition to the regime?

Data quality

The elements of data quality are generally taken to include relevance, timeliness and accuracy or reliability. The literature on data quality, particularly in the field of survey research, is extensive (see, for example, Groves 1989; Biemer *et al.* 1991) and the quality of human rights statistics could easily be the subject of another article. I will limit myself to a few observations.

Some human rights advocates express the view that official statistics are totally unreliable and that non-governmental organizations should rely only on data that they themselves collect to monitor the status of the rights that are of concern to them. Government data are certainly never error free and their quality varies greatly from country to country. In the United States, for example, we know that some of the most vulnerable sectors of society, such as homeless persons or migratory workers and their families are not adequately represented in censuses and surveys.

Nevertheless, I believe that total abstinence from the use of official data is a counter-productive strategy for those who are interested in economic and social rights. In spite of their defects, official data can often be used effectively to monitor economic and social rights. Statistical agencies in the United States and many other countries provide, along with the data, detailed information on how the data were collected and what their limitations are. Like all data users, those who are using the data for human rights monitoring and advocacy should read the fine print and understand the strengths and weaknesses of the data before they analyze them and present their findings. Then, if they use the official data in statistically sound ways, it will be difficult for governments to argue that their conclusions are based on faulty data. The report of the United Nations team of medical experts investigating rape in the former Yugoslavia (Example 10) demonstrates the effectiveness of this policy.

Another argument for using official statistics to the extent feasible is that the costs of collecting useful and reliable demographic, social and economic data are great. Few private organizations have the resources to conduct periodic censuses or surveys themselves, but with modest resources they can acquire and make good use of government data.

Human rights analysts, particularly in the field of civil and political rights, often lack precise data and are forced to rely on 'order of magnitude' estimates of numbers needed for advocacy purposes. Many of the numbers cited in the ten examples fall in this category, including especially those relating to amputees from landmine accidents in Cambodia (Example 9) and rape in the former Yugoslavia (Example 10). Such estimates need not, and of course should not, be created from whole cloth; Mosteller (1977) provides an excellent discussion of order of magnitude estimation techniques that make the best use of available data and subject-matter expertise. To maintain credibility, human rights advocates must act responsibly in presenting and using order-of-magnitude estimates. A 1993 report on landmines by Human Rights Watch and Physicians for Human Rights provides an excellent illustration of responsible and effective use of such estimates.

Effective presentation

Effective uses of human rights statistics for advocacy and enforcement require that the data be presented clearly to non-statisticians, whether they are members of committees that monitor international human rights treaties, judges presiding over trials of discrimination suits, legislative bodies or members of the general public. Effective presentation begins with the choice of what data to present. Policy-makers, the media and the public can give only limited attention to any particular issue. The World Health Organization (1981), in a publication on the selection of indicators to monitor progress in meeting goals for providing adequate health care to all, suggested that '. . . it is particularly important to select a small number of national indicators that have social and political punch in the sense that people and policy makers will be incited to action by them'.

Several of our ten examples of human rights statistics illustrate the effectiveness of 'indicators with punch'. We can look at the lynching data as being not only the direct measure of a specific, particularly abhorrent abuse of human rights, but also as an easily understood indicator that effectively called attention to a general pattern of racism. In the United States today, the proportion of persons lacking health insurance coverage is an effective indicator of the failure of the health care system to provide basic health care services to all. All of us can relate to the plight of families facing financial ruin because of illnesses or injuries requiring treatment and care not covered by insurance. Childhood immunization rates are another effective indicator of the provision of health care services. Unfavorable comparisons of United States' rates with those of other countries provide a strong incentive for action. The devastating effects of landmines are dramatically shown by the estimate cited in Example 9 that about 1 of every 236 persons in Cambodia is an amputee due to a mine explosion.[3]

The technical resources available to assist statisticians in presenting data effectively are such that there is really no excuse for poor quality of presentation. This is not just a matter of computer graphics and multicolor displays, in fact, some of the available software, if not used with discretion, can violate principles for effective use of graphics that have been developed through empirical work and experimental research by Tufte (1983, 1990), Cleveland (1985, 1994) and others. We see increasingly effective presentations of data aimed at non-statisticians both by statistical agencies, such as the Census Bureau in its *Statistical Brief* series, and by non-governmental advocacy groups, such as the Children's Defense Fund in its annual reports on *The State of America's Children*.

Good choices of indicators and technical proficiency are necessary but not sufficient. The other essential element for effective presentation is integrity. If human rights statistics are being used in adversarial legal or enforcement proceedings, each party can be sure that the data it presents will be subjected to careful scrutiny by the other parties involved and that weaknesses in the data and their interpretation are likely to be exposed and attacked. The same is true for statistics used for human rights advocacy.

Danner's 1993 article on the El Mozote massacre provides an illuminating description of the weaknesses in the data presented by the Reagan Administration to Congress in January 1982 and of the Administration's attacks on the data presented by organizations like Americas Watch that opposed the certification which was required to continue United States aid to the Government of El Salvador. Some argued that the alleged number of persons killed (from 700 to 1000) must have been overstated, because the population of the canton of El Mozote at the time was only about 300 and there were survivors, ignoring press reports that the killing had taken place in several hamlets. The facts of the El Mozote massacre were not firmly established until much later; at the time the Administration's certification of improvement in human rights in El Salvador was accepted and Congress permitted aid to continue.

Principles of statistical integrity, in addition to calling for avoidance of intentionally deceptive practices, require that statisticians provide as much information about the sources and limitations of their data as is compatible with the form of their release, provide references to additional background information, and supply forthright answers, to the best of their ability, to any questions that may arise. United States statistical agencies and reputable survey research firms have adopted and documented these principles (see, for example, Gonzalez *et al.* 1975) and do a reasonably good job of following them. Following them is clearly the best long-run policy for persons who use statistics to argue in support of human rights.

---

3. Estimates like this one cannot be very precise. In a recent report citing this estimate (Human Rights Watch and Physicians for Human Rights 1993, p.126) it was footnoted as follows: 'Because of the difficulty in compiling complete statistics, this figure, like those cited below, is an estimate based on initial research . . . the ratios given here are believed to be correct as orders of magnitude.'

As noted in Example 3, Franklin D. Roosevelt's characterization of one-third of a nation as 'ill-housed, ill-clad, ill-nourished' dramatically called attention to the plight of the poor and no doubt helped to enlist support for some of the Government's programs designed to counter the effects of the Great Depression. However, given the subsequent growth in the quantity and quality of socioeconomic data since the 1930s and the growing numeracy of the media and the public, it is unlikely that such a broad statement would be allowed to pass unchallenged today. Indicators with 'punch' continue to be useful for advocacy, but must be carefully developed from the best available data, used with full awareness of all of their limitations.

LEARNING MORE ABOUT STATISTICS AND HUMAN RIGHTS

Let's suppose that you are not afraid of working with messy data (most real-world data are messy to some degree) and you have some interest in applying your statistical skills to human rights issues. How do you learn more about human rights and possible areas of statistical application?

Like anyone doing applied statistics, you will need to learn more about the substantive field of application. For general background on human rights, you might want to look at *Human rights in the world community: issues and action*, edited by Claude and Weston (1989), or *Human rights and world politics*, by Forsythe (1983).

Turning to publications that focus directly on the use of statistics to monitor and analyze human rights issues, there are two fairly recent items. *Human rights and statistics: getting the record straight*, edited by Richard Claude and the present author (Jabine and Claude 1992), is a collection of papers about the issues associated with the collection and use of human rights statistics. It includes several of the references cited in this chapter, including the paper by Samuelson and Spirer on 'Use of incomplete and distorted data in inference about human rights violation' and the paper by Snow and Bihurriet, 'An epidemiology of homicide: *Ningún Nombre* burials in the Province of Buenos Aires from 1970 to 1984'. If you are interested in getting some hands-on experience with human rights data, the final chapter of the book, 'A guide to human rights data sources', provides a listing, with information about content and means of access, of 29 data bases that contain quantitative information on human rights and related topics.

Data analysis for monitoring human rights, by Herbert and Louise Spirer (1994), is a manual designed for classroom or self-study training of human rights advocates who have little or no background in statistics. It includes examples and exercises, most of them based on real data. If you are trained as a statistician, you will already be familiar with the basic methods presented, but the many examples illustrating various kinds of applications make the manual well worth looking at.

Many human rights organizations need statisticians with special expertise, especially in the collection, processing, analysis and presentation of survey data. If you have such expertise and would like to do *pro bono* consulting with such groups, the American Association for the Advancement of Science, in collaboration with the American Statistical Association and the Electronic Information Privacy Center, has compiled a registry of persons who can provide assistance. They can be contacted for more information at the AAAS Human Rights Consulting Service in Information Management, 1333 H Street NW, Washington DC 20005, (USA telephone 202/326-6790 or e-mail: emunoz#aaas.org). For Internet users, information about the registry can be found on the World Wide Web at http://www.aaas.org/spp/dspp/shr/shr.htm. [Note: the final period is not part of the address.].

The Committee on Scientific Freedom and Human Rights of the American Statistical Association periodically issues an informative newsletter that covers new applications of human rights statistics as well as actions on behalf of statisticians throughout the world whose rights have been violated. If you would like to receive the newsletter by e-mail, send a message to 76221.1602@compuserve.com.

The great Indian statistician, P. C. Mahalanobis, said in 1956, in his presidential address to the Third Pakistan Statistical Conference, 'Statistics must have a clearly defined purpose, one aspect of which is scientific advance and the other, human welfare and national development.' All of these purposes can be served by working with human rights statistics.

REFERENCES

Asia Watch and Physicians for Human Rights (1991). *Landmines in Cambodia: the coward's war*. Human Rights Watch, New York.

Biemer, P., Groves, R., Lyberg, L., Mathiowetz, N., and Sudman, S. (ed.) (1991). *Measurement errors in surveys*. Wiley, New York.

Claude, R. P. and Weston, B. H. (ed.) (1989). *Human rights in the world community: issues and action*. University of Pennsylvania Press.

Cleveland, W. S. (1985). *The elements of graphing data*. Wadsworth and Brooks/Cole, Pacific Grove, CA.

Cleveland, W. S. (1994). *Visualizing data*. Hobart, Summit, NJ.

Committee on Monitoring Access to Personal Health Care Services, Institute of Medicine (1993). *Access to health care in America*. National Academy Press, Washington.

Danner, M. (1993). A reporter at large: the truth of El Mozote. *The New Yorker*, **69**, (41), 50–133.

Dempster, A. P. (1988). Employment discrimination and statistical science (with comments and rejoinder). *Statistical Science*, **3**, 149–95.

Gonzalez, M. E., Ogus, J. L., Shapiro, G., and Tepping, B. J. (1975). Standards for discussion and presentation of errors in survey and census data. *Journal of the American Statistical Association*, **70**, (351,pt.II), 5–21.

Groves, R. (1989). *Survey errors and survey costs*. Wiley, New York.

Human Rights Watch and Physicians for Human Rights (1993). *Landmines: a deadly legacy*. Human Rights Watch, New York.

Forsythe, D. P. (1983). *Human rights and world politics*. University of Nebraska Press.

Jabine, T. B. and Claude, R. P. (ed.) (1992). *Human rights and statistics: getting the record straight*. University of Pennsylvania Press.

Jabine, T. B. Lynch, J. P. and Spirer, P. F. (1995). Statistics in an international human rights treaty report. In *American Statistical Association 1995 Proceedings of the Governments Statistics Section*, pp. 77–86. Washington, DC.: American Statistical Association.

Lewis, R. (1994). For whom the job bell *doesn't* toll. *AAARP Bulletin*, **35**, (2).

Morehead, C. (1993). Where have all the prisoners gone? *Index on Censorship*, **22**, (10), 4.

Mosteller, F. (1977). Assessing unknown numbers: Order of magnitude estimation. In *Statistics and Public Policy*, (ed. W. B. Fairley and F. Mosteller), pp. 163–84. Addison-Wesley, Reading, MA.

Ploski, H. and Williams, J. (1983). *The Negro almanac: a reference work on the Afro-American*. Wiley, New York.

Pocar, F. (1991). The International Covenant on Civil and Political Rights. In *Manual on human rights reporting*, United Nations Centre on Human Rights, pp. 79–125. United Nations, New York.

Poe, S. C. (1990). Human rights and U. S. foreign aid: a review of quantitative studies and suggestions for future research. *Human Rights Quarterly*, **12**, 499–512.

Roberts, S. and Williams, J. (1995). *After the guns fall silent: the enduring legacy of landmines*. Vietnam Veterans of American Foundation, Washington, DC.

Samuelson, D. A. and Spirer, H. F. (1992). Use of incomplete and distorted data in inference about human rights violations. In *Human rights and statistics: getting the record straight*, (ed. T. B. Jabine and R. P. Claude), pp. 62–77. University of Pennsylvania Press.

Savage, I. R. (1985). Hard–soft problems. *Journal of the American Statistical Association*, **80**, 1–7.

Snow, C. C. and Bihurriet, M. J. (1992). An epidemiology of homicide: *Ningún nombre* burials in the Province of Buenos Aires from 1970 to 1984. In *Human rights and statistics: getting the record straight*, (ed. T. B. Jabine and R. P. Claude), pp. 328–63. University of Pennsylvania Press.

Spirer, H. F. and Spirer, L. (1994). *Data analysis for monitoring human rights*. American Association for the Advancement of Science, Washington.

Tufte, E. R. (1983). *The visual display of quantitative information*. Graphics Press, Cheshire, CT.

Tufte, E. R. (1990). *Envisioning information*. Graphics Press, Cheshire, CT.

United Nations (1985a). Universal Declaration of Human Rights. In *The International Bill of Human Rights*. United Nations, New York.

United Nations (1985b). The International Covenant on Economic, Social and Cultural Rights. In *The International Bill of Human Rights*. United Nations, New York.

United Nations (1993). Report of the team of experts on their mission to investigate allegations of rape in the territory of the former Yugoslavia from 12 to 23 January 1991. Annex II in *Situation of human rights in the territory of the former Yugoslavia*. Economic and Social Council, Commission on Human Rights, Forty-ninth session, agenda item 27.

United Nations Children's Fund (1993). *The state of the world's children, 1993*. Oxford University Press.

United States Department of Health and Human Services (1990). *Healthy people 2000: national health promotion and disease prevention objectives*, Conference edition. Public Health Service, Washington.

United States Department of Housing and Urban Development (1979). *Measuring racial discrimination*. US Government Printing Office, Washington.

United States Senate, Joint Congressional Committee on Inaugural Ceremonies (1989). *Inaugural addresses of the Presidents of the United States from George Washington 1789 to George Bush 1989*. US Government Printing Office, Washington.

Weschler, L. (1987). A reporter at large (Brasil: *Nunca mais*), parts I and II. *The New Yorker*, May 25 and June 1.

Wessel, D. (1991). Racial bias against black job seekers remains pervasive, broad study finds. *Wall Street Journal*, May 15.

World Health Organization (1981). *The development of indicators for monitoring progress towards health for all by the year 2000*. World Health Organization, Geneva.

3 Making defense decisions: what role might a statistical perspective play?[1]

DAVID S. C. CHU AND NANCY L. SPRUILL

INTRODUCTION

Despite the vast amount of data that informs decision making in the American defense community, there is surprisingly little statistical thinking at the decision-making level. Reflecting the concern about the absence of a statistical perspective, the Committee on National Statistics recently organized a workshop on the matter (Rolph and Steffey 1994).

Statistical techniques are none the less widely used in the US Department of Defense, principally at the working level, and mostly involving tactical use of data, specific engineering and scientific problems, or support activities. Thus, for example, statistical techniques are used in anti-submarine search processes, to help with signal processing, and to calculate inventory levels.

Reflecting the restricted role of statistics in decision making, very few of the civil service positions in the Department of Defense call for a statistician[2] – and even fewer in the ranks of the military services. This contrasts sharply with the significant role that statisticians play in other agencies of the federal government. The agencies concerned with economic, social welfare, and health issues especially come to mind as ones where statisticians play a prominent role advising the decision-making process.

The absence of a statistical perspective in defense decision-making, this chapter argues, reflects and reinforces a deterministic perspective on the making of choices – a perspective that is at variance with the reality of the world with which defense decision makers must deal. Decision making could be substantially improved if a statistical perspective and additional statistical techniques were brought to bear.

The present-day absence of a statistical perspective at senior decision-making levels is odd, because statistics played a significant role in World War II and the years immediately afterward, as the next section illustrates. But there is now a long list of defense problems where the quality of decision making would be measurably enhanced by the use of established statistical techniques (these are discussed in the third section). In the final section it is argued that ultimately if the leadership of the Defense Department takes a probabilistic view of the information available to it

1. The opinions expressed here do not necessarily reflect the views of RAND or the Department of Defense.

2. In 1992, 272 of the approximately 800 000 civilian positions in the Department of Defense were classified as statisticians (see Rolph and Steffey 1994).

and of the choices it must make, the extensive employment of useful statistical techniques will soon follow.

THE HISTORICAL CONTEXT

One of the great intellectual events of World War II was the development of operations research as a discipline applying sophisticated analytic tools to the real-world problems of military decision makers. As is well known, statistical techniques figure prominently in the tool kit of the operations research analyst. Indeed, Morse and Kimball (1970, p. 7) assert: 'the most important single mathematical tool of operations research is probability and statistical theory'.

Indicative of the powerful role that statistical techniques played in the decision making of the period is the classic report by Ruggles and Brodie (1947) on the estimation of German war production – an essential ingredient in intelligence estimates of Germany's ability to continue prosecuting the war. Markings and serial numbers from captured German equipment were used to estimate total production, using an implicit set of techniques later formalized by Goodman (1952, 1954). When actual production data became available after the war, Ruggles and Brodie (1947, p. 91) observed that 'the techniques of analyzing markings on enemy equipment was superior to the more abstract methods of intelligence such as reconciling widely divergent prisoner of war reports, basing production estimates on pre-war capabilities or projecting production trends based on estimates of the degree of utilization of resources in the enemy country'. Statistical inference from an organized data base directly applicable to the problem at hand proved more effective than the traditional 'anthropological' style of information gathering and inference. Despite the powerful lesson of the Ruggles–Brodie result, statistical inference is still much less frequently applied to higher-level problems than the statistics community might recommend.

While operations research techniques spread throughout the Department of Defense in the post-World War II years, they were principally employed in 'applied' problems and did not generally influence senior decision making. Even the advent of systems analysis in the McNamara Pentagon of the 1960s emphasized quantitative analysis rather than statistical techniques *per se*. The absence of a statistical perspective in decision making reflected the then current practice of the automobile industry from which McNamara came – as well as the limited role of statistics in the economics of the day. Indeed, one of the applied areas in which statistics came to play a major role was logistics, paralleling industrial practice, including the estimation of failure rates and the management of maintenance processes and inventory stockage levels.

Statistical analysis did play a significant role helping implement the All Volunteer Force in the early 1970s, however. The decision to move from conscripts to volunteers as the basis for filling the ranks of America's military required setting compensation levels that would attract and retain the necessary number and quality of military personnel without bankrupting the treasury in the process. That this was not a trivial problem from either the analytic or political perspective can be seen in the early failures to set compensation levels properly, with almost disastrous results for military recruiting and the near failure of the volunteer concept. At the nadir in 1978, the military managed to fill its recruiting goal for non-prior service male enlistees only by accepting approximately half its accessions from the ranks of high school dropouts, and in reaction Congress began mandating minimum recruit quality standards. By this time, a small army of economists armed with increasingly sophisticated econometric techniques, and aided by survey instruments of growing sophistication, was producing a much firmer basis for setting compensation policy (see, for example, Bowman *et al.* 1986). They employed observational and survey data (but only rarely randomized experiments) to estimate supply functions. These described the propensity of American youth to volunteer and remain in service relative to the level and type of compensation offered (among many factors, including individual background characteristics that were separately used in other statistical studies to predict who was most likely to succeed in the military, and used to guide recruiting policy). Their work undergirded the decisions of the late 1970s and early 1980s, increasing compensation in ways that the Department of Defense could afford, with the result that today the American military enjoys the highest personnel quality in its history, and the All Volunteer Force not only boasts the support of its own uniformed leadership (who had once been highly skeptical, if not fundamentally opposed), but the admiration of other nations.

WHAT OTHER DEFENSE DECISIONS MIGHT BENEFIT FROM STATISTICAL HELP?

The role that statistical analysis played in helping estimate German armaments production in the 1940s and make a success of the All Volunteer Force in the 1970s could equally well be emulated in other areas of defense: intelligence, resource allocation, cost estimation, weapons choices, and operational practices. A few words on each serves to outline why statistical analysis could help decision makers, and the issues that might be considered, before we turn in the final section to discussing how an expanded role for statistical analysis in decision making might be achieved.

Intelligence

If there is a single element of American defense decision making characterized by a deterministic view of the world it is intelligence. One of the centerpiece documents of the intelligence community is the National Intelligence Estimate. By design, it is intended to produce a consensus position on the issue addressed. (To be fair, it should be noted that minority views are permitted.) For planning purposes a consensus position is of great value. But for decision making it may obscure more than it reveals, especially if there is a significant probability that 'secondary' possibilities might occur. That is information of considerable value to decision makers.

To illustrate, consider the results of a series of exercises conducted by RAND researchers Roger Molander and Peter Wilson (1993). Given the name 'Day After . . .' exercises, they seek to compare pre-event decision making with the information and capabilities decision makers wish they would have had, given how events actually turn out in the exercise. Consistently, decision makers confronted with a 'before' scenario with one intelligence 'prediction', who then encounter a different reality, wish for 'better' intelligence. For example, in future scenarios involving North Korea, estimating the number of nuclear weapons North Korea might possess and where they might be stored is critical to formulating a proposed course of action. In the 'Day After . . .' exercises decision makers focus on these parameters. *Ex ante* discussion tends to accept deterministic values – with often disappointing results *ex post*, leading to a consistent recommendation that intelligence be 'improved'. Surely a part of what decision makers have in mind is an intelligence estimate that acquaints them with the *range* of possibilities, and attempts to estimate (or at least characterize) what the intelligence community believes is the probability mass associated with the important alternatives – most especially, the alternatives that would frustrate the course of action they are contemplating. Even an 'equal ignorance' uniform distribution over the range of important alternatives would significantly affect the decision-making process, when compared to one that emphasizes a point estimate.

The current focus of the intelligence community on producing a consensus position for a single value or description of the situation might therefore usefully be replaced by producing a consensus distribution describing the alternative possibilites. This would formalize what is often true of current estimate documents, in which some decision makers find great value in reading the footnotes with their dissenting opinions – because these describe alternatives, who believes in them, and why, thus allowing the decision maker to construct implicitly his or her own distribution.

A further advantage of creating a consensus distribution is that it separates values in the debate from a description of the potential alternative outcomes and their likelihood. In actual debates the recommendations offered to decision makers usually reflect both an implicit distribution of potential outcomes in the mind of the adviser, as well as how that adviser values the outcomes. The decision maker, of course, will want to apply his or her own values, and would be better served if the recommendations separated the adviser's values from the adviser's view of the distribution of outcomes. Focusing debate on establishing a consensus distribution would help achieve this objective.

Resource allocation

The ultimate purpose of resource allocation decisions in the Department of Defense is to ensure that the military forces the country might need now and in the future are available to the President. What forces might be needed, of course, requires some view of how the future might unfold – 'scenarios', to use the jargon of the Department.

For much of the Cold War the most demanding scenario involved possible conflict with the Soviet Union. It was usually argued that forces capable of dealing successfully with the Soviets could also deal successfully with other contingencies as 'lesser included cases'. In this situation, size became the principal criterion for shaping the military forces of the United States.

With the end of the Cold War, the future against which the Department of Defense must plan is much less certain. Will the United States again face a major power that fundamentally threatens its interests and those of its close friends? Will it face only limited challenges? How likely is something in between – military problems that still require substantial forces, perhaps very different in character one from another, and thus in the types of forces each requires?

This is clearly a situation where techniques for decision making under uncertainty are especially helpful. Indeed, merely acknowledging the extent of the uncertainty might lead to a very different principal criterion for the shaping of US military forces: that they must hedge against the range of possibilities that might occur, taking due account of the time that the United States would have to prepare for the particular event. Such a decision-making paradigm would emphasize the diversity of force structure, and how quickly the surviving force structure could serve as a basis for building larger structures, should the need arise. In contrast, most of the post-Cold War thinking about the shaping of the American military has continued to emphasize its size, whether it is the 'Base Force' of the Bush Administration, or the Bottom Up Review of the Clinton Administration.

Cost estimation

The popular debate over the process of estimating costs for major defense programs tends to compare the actual cost of the program with the predicted cost, with great emphasis placed in choosing as the benchmark predicted cost the 'cost' in the contract that is signed with the prime contractor.

A statistician would not be surprised that contract costs systematically underestimate actual costs, if only because initial contracts are typically awarded by a competitive process in which cost is often a decisive element (the 'low bid'). Moreover, costs in a contract are frequently targets the contractor is encouraged to meet through innovative action; the Department of Defense believes that without such innovative action actual costs would be higher. While the record of defense cost estimation compares favorably with that of other large, complex undertakings (notwithstanding popular impressions to the contrary) (President's Blue Ribbon Commission 1986), it is still the case that development estimates for major weapon systems in recent decades underestimated actual costs by approximately 20 per cent, with estimates for production contracts (not surprisingly) proving somewhat more accurate (see Drezner 1992).

Many events influence the actual costs of a program, including both events of a character one can anticipate in advance (for example, that there will be test failures of some kind that will delay the completion of development, leading to added costs relative to a 'no failure' case), and events whose character one cannot anticipate (for example, physical performance anomalies outside the envelope of known results). In principle, the distribution of the former can be estimated, or at least postulated based on past experience. Were such a distribution employed (or, more appropriately, a series of distributions[3] for the major components of cost), a distribution of anticipated cost outcomes would be created for decision makers to consider. Specific point estimates of cost, including the contractor's, could then be considered not in terms of whether they were likely to be 'right' or 'wrong', but in terms of where in the distribution they fell. Obviously, point estimates falling in the extreme tails of the distribution would be discounted by prudent decision makers.

Just such a procedure was employed to estimate the development costs of the F-22 aircraft for the United States Air Force. Using data from past tactical aircraft development programs a distribution of development costs for the F-22 could be estimated. Such a distribution, of course, only captures the 'known unknowns' (for example, the variance in the length of the testing program), not the 'unknown unknowns' (for example, new flight principles). The Defense Acquisition Board meeting to approve F-22 development used this distribution to consider competing claims about likely development costs. Because this distribution was available with which to judge competing claims, a proposal to use an estimate that would have fallen in the extreme lower tail of the distribution was rejected, and an estimate closer to the center selected. The budget provisions for F-22 development were revised accordingly. (Subsequent events validated this decision.)

That the traditional approach to the debate of cost estimates is not likely soon to be abandoned, however, is illustrated by the recent introduction in the 104th Congress of the 'DoD Acquisition Management Reform Act'.[4] The bill would reward contractors who come in 'below' the budget, and punish contractors and programs who run 'over' budget. The backers of the bill seem oblivious to the possibility that such legislation might merely change the point in the cost distribution that's offered as the budget estimate, without changing the distribution itself, i.e. without changing the actual cost performance. While greater budget honesty is to be applauded (and was in fact one objective in the F-22 example), improved cost performance – changing the underlying cost distribution – would be a superior objective for statutory action. It is not clear how provisions of the sort proposed will change the underlying cost distribution; it is clear that, other things being equal, they provide an incentive to pick a conservative point in the distribution to advertise as the 'cost' of the program, in order to secure the rewards (or at least avoid the penalties) promised by the legislation.

Weapons choices

Tests provide an important element of information used in making decisions about weapon systems, including which alternative design to pursue, and whether to buy any new system at all. 'Fly before you buy' exemplifies the former, operational

---

3. The distributions tend to be asymmetric with the mode less than the median. Examples include the triangular distribution (see Book 1995).

4. S. 646 and H.R. 1368.

testing of early production models the latter. In recent years Congress has taken especial interest in operational testing, creating an independent office for its oversight, and adding a requirement for live fire testing.

Much like the demands placed on the intelligence community, and the perspective taken of cost estimates, the interest in operational test results exhibits a decidedly deterministic flavor. The implicit perspective is that a system should either 'pass' or 'fail' the test. A combination of budget limitations, aversion to extensive testing, and, again, a deterministic view of the world leads the executive branch to propose only a limited number of test replications. Thus, statistical confidence in the test results may be poor, although in practice little attention is paid to this issue.

Indicative of the deterministic view is the frequent setting of test standards against an absolute norm, rather than as a test of the hypothesis that the new system is sufficiently better than the extant system so as to warrant the expenditure of public funds. As a result, in two recent cases standards were inadvertently set in such a manner that it was either practically (or in another case theoretically) impossible to pass them![5]

However limited the funds for testing itself, even more limited are the funds for test design. Thus, for example, even when repeated tests are undertaken, little if any thought is given to 'learning' on the part of the testers, such that observations taken in the first run are not independent of observations in the next run. To cite a typical situation, pilots attacking a target on the first pass, when they are unfamiliar with the terrain and the appearance of the target, will typically perform less well than in subsequent passes. Basing one's estimate of weapons performance on the results of repeated passes with the same pilots will overestimate performance in combat (when the pilot often will get only one pass).

Moreover, in a continued reflection of the 'pass/fail' deterministic perspective, when tests are performed it is often insisted that they be 'all up', even if the expense involved might be better devoted to obtaining high-confidence results by repeated tests of only part of the system. This is a problem especially posed by the original live fire testing legislation, which was read by some as requiring tests that would involve destruction of entire articles (for example, to test vehicle vulnerability to anti-armor rounds, aircraft vulnerability to anti-aircraft weapons, ship vulnerability to torpedoes). While it might be financially viable to sacrifice enough ground vehicles to obtain confidence in the results, that is not typically feasible for aircraft or ships. (Indeed, for ships it was early conceded to be infeasible and that the available funds would be much better spent on testing key components, as subsequent legislation has recognized.)

Operational practices

There remain many important opportunities to bring a statistical perspective to the sorts of issues that led originally to the development of operations research. One example is the design of missile defenses. Clearly any successful defense will require

---

5. SINCGARS, an Army radio, and ASPJ, a Navy aircraft jammer, respectively.

layers of defending elements, since the objective of most defenses will be to reduce the attacking vehicles that reach the target to zero. The success of the overall defense is not only a function of the excellence of each layer, but also of the relationship of the failure modes among defensive layers. A system in which the failure modes are independent (or, better yet, negatively correlated) may produce better overall results than one whose failure modes are similar, even if each layer of the latter performs better.[6]

The value of the statistical perspective, of course, is to focus attention on outcomes outside the central tendency of the distribution. It is these outcomes that produce the 'surprises' that could lead to military defeat. By requiring consideration of the distribution of possible outcomes, the statistical adviser prepares the decision maker for the full reality of the world he or she actually faces.

WHAT IS NEEDED TO IMPART A STATISTICAL PERSPECTIVE IN DEFENSE DECISION MAKING?

That statistics might usefully play a larger role in defense decision making is hardly a novel proposition. For example, Hunter (1984) demonstrated how Bayesian analysis could be profitably employed by military and political analysts.

Likewise, the lack of statistical advice has been noted before. Indeed, Savage in his 1984 speech to the annual meeting of the American Statistical Association lamented the lack of interaction between statisticians and defense analysts, and with decision makers. He challenged all to change the situation, emphasizing the need to introduce the 'concept of uncertainty and measurement of variability' into strategic discussion. He noted that this would take 'skill and hard work but . . . will add much realism'. (Savage 1985, p.1)

The profession responded to his challenge. In 1988, the Association formed an Ad Hoc Committee on Statistics and Security. Its purpose is to strengthen the statistical component of work on international security, and especially to include major sources of chance variation when making strategic security decisions. In 1994, the Association made the committee permanent (renaming it the Committee on National and International Security).

Returning to the subject on which he had worked so productively in the early years of his career, Ruggles applied his World War II 'numbers racket' technique to arms control verification in a presentation to the Association meetings (Session on Statistics and National Security, August 1990). Ruggles concluded that factory marking analysis can provide a cost-effective and reliable method for monitoring compliance with arms limitation and reduction treaties.

At the private urging of influential statisticians, who were following up on Savage's challenge, the Department of Defense asked the Committee on National Statistics and the Committee on Applied and Theoretical Statistics of the National Academy of Sciences to convene a workshop on statistical modeling, simulation, and operational testing of weapons systems. The workshop (Rolph and Steffey

---

6. We owe this example to David Vaughan of RAND.

1994) led to a panel study by the Committee on National Statistics, the purpose of which is to improve the effectiveness and efficiency of testing and evaluating weapon systems – a key component of the defense acquisition process. Convened at the specific request of the Department of Defense Director of Operational Test and Evaluation, the panel will identify where, and assess how, alternative statistical methods could improve the operational testing and evaluation that supports decision making on defense systems. As part of its work, the panel will consider whether, and to what extent, technical criteria and organizational and legal requirements for testing and evaluation constrain optimal decision making. Presumably, among its subjects will be the tendency of statutes to require the Secretary of Defense to 'certify' that a particular system has met a certain standard, or that its costs will fall below a certain threshold. Such certifications embody a deterministic view of the world that is the antithesis of the statistical perspective.

The reinfusion of statistics in defense decision making has started, but much remains to be done. As but one example, for many years the principal scientific advisory body to the Department of Defense, the Defense Science Board, contained not a single statistician, and the situation in the similar boards advising the individual military departments was not much better.

Ultimately, of course, there is only so much that the statistical community itself can do to persuade decision makers of the value of a statistical perspective in making public policy choices. It will take interest in hearing about a statistical perspective by the political leaders of the Department of Defense, and its most senior civil servants, before statistics and statisticians are likely to play a significant role. It will take a commitment by those leaders to follow good statistical practices, especially when the results run counter to tradition or intuition, before a statistical perspective can be expected to flourish.

Such interest and such leadership are unlikely to arise, however, without repeated examples of how statistics and the statistical perspective can make a difference – examples that only the thoughtful practicing statistician can offer. It is one of the lasting burdens of the estrangement that arose between the military and intellectual communities in the later Cold War years that so few examples are available. New examples will require hard work, for the statistical community to learn the institutional specifics of defense issues, and for the defense community to improve its (rusty) statistical tools, so it can grasp the import of the statisticians' advice. That this anthology invited a commentary on the issue is a good sign that perhaps we are ready to make a new beginning.

REFERENCES

Book, S. A. (1995). Do not sum 'most likely' cost estimates. *Proceedings of the International Society of Parametric Analysts*, 17th Annual Conference, San Diego, California, 30 May to 2 June 1995, pp. Risk 16–Risk 41.

Bowman, W., Little, R., and Sicilia, G. T. (ed.) (1986). *The All-Volunteer Force after a decade: retrospect and prospect*; Pergamon-Brassey International Defense Publishers.

Drezner, J. A., *et al.* (1992). *An analysis of weapon system cost growth*, RAND, MR-291-AF.

Goodman, L. A. (1952). Serial number analysis. *Journal of the American Statistical Association*, **47**, 622–34.

Goodman, L. A. (1954). Some practical techniques in serial number analysis. *Journal of the American Statistical Association*, **49**, 97–112.

Hunter, D. E. (1984). *Political military applications of Bayesian analysis, methodological issues* (a Westview replica edition): Westview Press, Boulder, CO.

Molander, R. and Wilson, P. (1993). '*The day after . . .*' study: nuclear proliferation in the post Cold War world. *RAND Report*, Vol. 1–3, MR-266-AF, MR-253-AF, MR-226-AF.

Morse, P. M. and Kimball, G. E. (1970). *Methods of operations research*. Peninsula Publishing, Los Altos, CA.

President's Blue Ribbon Commission on Defense Management (1986). *A quest for excellence*, Appendix A, June 1986, pp. 61–2.

Rolph, J. E. and Steffey, D. L. (1994). *Statistical issues in defense analysis and testing, summary of a workshop*. National Academy Press, Washington DC.

Ruggles, R. and Brodie, H. (1947). An empirical approach to economic intelligence in World War II. *Journal of the American Statistical Association*, **42**, 72–91.

Savage, I. R. (1985). Hard-soft problems. *Journal of the American Statistical Association*, **80**, (389), 1–7.

4 Ethics, objectivity, and politics: statistics in a public policy context

STEPHEN E. FIENBERG

INTRODUCTION

For decades, statisticians have perpetrated a myth: that the methods they use impart objectivity to the scientific or policy issue they are used to elucidate, either through the randomization at treatment, the random selection of subjects from some appropriate population, or through the careful application of statistical models and the assessment of their fit. We have looked back to those who laid the groundwork for an identifiable field of statistics, people such as Francis Galton, Karl Pearson, R. A. Fisher, and Francis Walker, and have described them as dispassionate scientists who brought the formalism of statistical thinking to areas of application such as biology or government data gathering and thereby overcame the biased and unscientific approach of others. But quality statistical methodology often serves as a thin veneer layered over scientific investigations that are far from objective or policy neutral. This was as true for our statistical forebears as it is in the modern statistical world. Thus, we often neglect to note the extent to which the social eugenics movement influenced Galton, Pearson, and Fisher (see, for example, MacKenzie 1981; Porter 1986), or racism affected Walker's leadership of the decennial census (see Anderson 1987). To a large extent this may not matter at all, but I believe that there are contexts where it does.

A few examples may suffice to make the issue clearer. Consider Fisher's 1918 formulation of the intraclass correlation coefficient, a tool he intended to be used in the study of heredity (for details see Bennett 1983). The same paper included Fisher's first articulation of the analysis of variance, one of his greatest technical contributions. For me, such contributions to mathematical statistics and genetic contributions can stand on their own, unfettered by the eugenics views that often served as their stimulus. We can judge their value as technical tools in isolation from the social context that led to their creation, and knowledge that Fisher was an ardent eugenicist doesn't affect the way *we* use the tools he developed, although it may have influenced how Fisher used them to some extent. But the case of Karl Pearson is more complex, and the dividing line between his eugenics efforts and his statistical ones is far less clear. For example, Pearson co-founded *Biometrika* largely to provide an outlet for the publication of statistical work linked to eugenics. How we are to judge his *views* on spurious correlation and causation, as opposed to the phenomena more broadly, in the end must link to the context in which they were expressed. For scientists working at the interface between statistics and other fields, such as Galton, Pearson, Fisher, and Walker, the subtleties of the political and social context of their work often matter far more than we tend to acknowledge. Bulmer *et al.* (1991) make this point quite forcefully in discussing the social reformist origins and influences of the social surveys from 1880 through 1940. How statisticians do and should deal with such political and social influences, especially in the context of public policy and national statistics programs, is the topic of this chapter.

This chapter represents an elaboration on themes first developed in Fienberg (1989*a*). Many of the topics I discuss and the examples I use are what Savage (1985) has described as hard–soft problems. Moreover, Savage has worked on and thought hard about aspects of such major public policy issues such as the accuracy of the decennial census (see Savage and Windham 1973; Savage 1980, 1982). For me, as for Savage, immersion in these problems occurred as part of committee and panel activities at the National Research Council (NRC) and especially its Committee on National Statistics (CNSTAT).

My personal experiences suggest to me that statisticians need to be aware that values and political pressures influence scientists' choice of problems and often the statistical methods they use. Once we acknowledge this, I believe we need to cope with the reality that values and political circumstances imply. Some colleagues believe that the influence of social values and political pressures is negligible in areas studied by statistics students. I think not; especially if our students attempt to analyze data to answer real scientific or policy questions. For example, we might even develop professional mechanisms to help our colleagues recognize unreasonable pressure and resist it, or we might try to analyze statistically the types and contexts in which this pressure is encountered as well as the ways with which it is dealt. The remainder of this chapter focuses on a series of problem areas where substantial political pressures have imperiled the collection and dissemination of quality statistical information of material importance. In the following two sections I list a number of these problems. And then I examine four problems in detail (updating the accounts in Fienberg 1989*a*).

THE POLITICAL CONTEXT OF SETTING STATISTICAL PRIORITIES

In Fienberg (1989*a*) I began by noting that the national statistical establishment in the United States (which for me includes the federal statistical agencies as well as the statistical infrastructures found in university, business, and industrial settings) had survived almost eight years of budgetary pressure and occasional political hostility. Many statistical activities were substantially strengthened during this period while others suffered. But overall the national statistical enterprise was in a reasonable position to provide quality statistical data for policy purposes and public information, as the new administration of President George Bush assumed control of the executive branch in January 1989. While most of the credit for this state of affairs should be given to the professionals in the statistical agencies and to those of our colleagues who have worked with them on specific projects, this does not change the fact that national statistical data always have and continue to be permeated with extratechnical issues and values.

The setting of statistical priorities, especially in the context of a hostile political environment, reemerged once again in 1995, as the new Republican majority in Congress sought to reduce federal government expenditures in substantial ways. At the time of writing major changes in statistical programs are again in the air, including major alterations to the decennial census (Anderson and Fienberg, 1996), and the real question in the minds of many is the extent to which statistical priorities may be driven by social and political goals. For many readers this issue is certainly not new (see Hauser 1973; Savage 1985). As Alonso and Starr (1987) noted:

Official statistics do not merely hold a mirror to reality. They reflect presuppositions and theories about the nature of society . . . Lest there be any confusion, we should emphasize that to say official statistics are entangled with politics and social life is not to say that they are 'politicized' in the sense of being corrupt. In some circumstances they may be corrupt, but that is not our point . . . Our point, rather, is that political judgments are implicit in the choice of what to measure, how to measure it, and how to present and interpret the results.

These choices are embraced in the context of setting government statistical priorities (see, for example, the 1976 report of the Committee on National Statistics Panel which Savage chaired, as well as Savage (1976)). If we view these issues within the scope of statistics, then we cannot hope to separate or insulate statistics from politics. Savage attempted to provide a far more narrowly sculpted concept of priority setting, and he argued that one should consider the priority-setting devices that yielded plans in specific areas as a formal set of statistical tools. I believe that it wasn't so much that he expected the formal results to be taken seriously, but rather that the process of trying to place the problem of priority setting in a formal context would help organize our thinking about it. Kruskal (1989) makes a strong case for attempting to separate technical statistical issues and citizenly or political values, even though I believe that both he and Savage agree with me that the task is, in the end, an impossible one.

Today, as in the past, American society faces a large number of basically social–political issues that can clearly be illuminated by statistical information, for example the measurement of poverty (see Citro and Michael (1995) and the discussion in the following section). Yet there are multiple perspectives on any of these issues and most individual statistical data sets will reflect, to a greater or lesser extent, political and social perspectives whether or not we openly admit it and no matter how much care is exerted by the statisticians involved.

EXAMPLES OF POLITICAL PRESSURE
IN STATISTICAL SETTINGS

Having stated my basic thesis, I would like to illustrate it by means of a series of anecdotes. I argue by example for at least two reasons. First, no one to date has done any systematic thinking on these issues and thus it is not clear how to carry out a careful empirically based investigation (cf. Dawes 1989). Second, the examples are vivid and I hope that they will stimulate readers to think about the issues of politics and statistics. My examples have been clearly chosen to illustrate instances where I think that political pressure and intervention has been harmful to the quality of national statistical data.

The anecdotes that follow should be viewed in the context of a federal statistical system that has a number of mechanisms to protect it from political interference. One of the best known of these is the Office of Management and Budget (OMB) Circular on the Compilation, Release, and Evaluation of Principal Economic Indicators. There are also instances where such intervention has taken place but has, in retrospect, produced reasonable or even positive results. For example, in his memoir, *An American life*, Jeb Stuart Magruder (1976, p. 102) relays the following story:

One battle was with the Bureau of Labor Statistics (BLS), which puts out the monthly figures on employment. These figures had traditionally been put in terms of the unemployment rate, which in 1970 was holding steady at about six per cent. At the same time, while the unemployment rate was constant, the number of people holding jobs was at an all-time high, and getting higher each month . . . We saw no reason why BLS couldn't stress the positive fact – a record number of jobs – at its monthly briefings, but BLS did not agree. I spoke with its director, Geoffrey Moore, several times. I tried persuasion, and when that didn't work I finally told him, 'Look, Mr Haldeman says this is what the President wants. If you want to argue with Mr Haldeman, fine. But if not, change your style.'

The BLS changed its style . . . It was a small victory, one achieved after a great deal of pushing; it seemed to us outrageous that a bureau of the Labor Department should defy a reasonable request by the President.

Janet Norwood, a former Commissioner of BLS, has suggested that Magruder's recollection is not quite correct but it may well be that, as long as he and others perceive it to be correct, the perception of the intrusion of politics on statistics (however minor) is reinforced. While the political context of BLS's releases cannot and should not be ignored, neither should BLS be driven by external pressures and demands, for then we can expect to see the willful distortion of statistical information in a form most statisticians would find reprehensible. But, in the end, statistical theory doesn't tell us what kinds of data to collect or what variables to report; these matters are largely the province of other scientists or policymakers.

Federal statistical agencies in the United States have long prided themselves on their independence and their ability to produce data in a neutral fashion. I am reminded of a meeting several years ago where one of the speakers commented that 'government statistical data should be valueless'. Actually he meant value-free, and when pressed he was unwilling to admit that the wording of questions in a survey or the definition of a variable inevitably reflects a perspective that is almost certain to have a political or societal component. For example, the national unemployment rate, produced by the BLS based on data from the Current Population Survey (CPS), is based on an activity concept of work. It is constructed from a battery of questions designed to exclude all of those not considered to be in the labor force (either employed or unemployed but looking for work) from both the numerator and denominator of the rate. While this approach makes considerable sense, it clearly reflects a societal attitude towards unemployment and the need to search for work, i.e. the basic measure reflects social values. Starting from a different social perspective we might easily be led to use a different battery of questions and come up with what is in effect a different definition of the unemployment rate. Even the recent major revision to the CPS (see Plewes 1994) did not change this structure in any substantial way.

The revisions to the CPS were, however, substantial. They included the implementation of a number of recommendations going back to the Levitan Commission report from the 1970s (National Commission on Employment and Unemployment Statistics 1979), and included a totally revamped questionnaire which reduced the presuppositions about women as homemakers, and thus uncompensated members of the labor force. The revised questionnaire and procedures resulted in an approximate increase in the overall unemployment rate of about 0.5 per cent, a change that would have been politically explosive had the survey changes not been carried out with enormous professional care.

Despite the fact that national data cannot be value-free, I believe that most federal statistical agencies do an excellent job in insulating their data from unnecessary political aspects, including the political views of those working for the agencies. Yet, even when they succeed in their political 'neutrality', their data collection efforts occur in the context of a mandate that comes from the political arena, i.e. from Congress or from politically appointed federal administrators. I would argue that statisticians who collect data mandated by others can, at best, attempt to remain 'disinterested' and impartial, but they certainly cannot uncouple their efforts from societal values and perspectives. Moreover, once produced, statistical data 'enter the political fray on behalf of social interests' (Prewitt 1987, p. 262) and thus the statistician's job does not end with the production of impartial reports or data summaries.

The OMB definition of poverty is linked to a specific Bureau of the Census statistical series dating back to the early 1960s, and the annual production of data on families in poverty. Who is naive enough to believe that such data will not be used for partisan political purposes? Thus, when the Census Bureau released the 1993 poverty figures based on data from the CPS, administration officials and reporters were quick to note that the poverty rate had risen even though the increase over 1992 was not statistically significant (DeParle 1994). Are we well served by the lack of alternatives to this admittedly flawed definition (for example it does not include in-kind benefits from government transfer programs such as food stamps or the negative impact of the increase in Social Security taxes) and the absence of empirical estimates to go with them? A recent panel of the Committee on National Statistics suggested not. It attempted to choose among alternative concepts of what we mean by poverty and how various sources of income and expenditures should be represented in it, while recognizing that 'there is no scientific basis by which one concept can be indisputably preferred to another' (Citro and Michael 1995, p.3). In the end the panel made a choice, and it also recommended using data from the newer Survey of Income and Program Participation rather than the CPS. The panel was immediately accused of being unscientific by one of its own members who wrote a dissenting view as part of the report, because it exercised choice where technical statistical tools were of little guidance. Yet not changing the measure that has been in use since the 1960s is also a political choice, but one whose shortcomings are well documented by the panel. This is an example of statistical priority setting, and in my view those on the panel were acting responsibly, by recognizing quite clearly the social and political context of its recommendations, while at the same time understanding the need and justification for change.

Yet another illustration relates to OMB Statistical Policy Directive No. 15 on race and ethnicity categories for statistical and administration reporting issued in 1977. While this Directive was intended to standardize reporting practices and to support the need for data by various federal civil rights and other compliance agencies, the classification scheme has in turn been written into laws. As a consequence the data collected under the mandate of the directive has become a mechanism for enforcing laws such as the Voting Rights Act and those affecting affirmative action programs. The Statistical Policy office in OMB is currently considering a revision to the directive and various population groups that fit somehow under the ethnic/racial label are vying for their 'own categories'. Government bureaucrats representing the civil rights agencies tend to argue for no change. This leads the statistical system into the midst of a political thicket from which it is difficult to disentangle the clearly statistical components. Evinger (1995) provides a status report on the revision process.

This might be all well and good but for the ambiguity of the definitions and the very notion that everyone neatly fits into one and only one of the five basic categories: American Indian or Alaskan Native, Asian or Pacific Islander, Black, Hispanic, and White. For detailed definitions see Table 1. Empirical evidence suggests otherwise (see Edmonston et al. 1996), and the use of a sixth category, other, is only of partial assistance. Scientists have difficulty providing biological bases for identifying racial or ethnic membership and we are still left with the legacy from bygone eras when people were identified by how they looked to others, e.g. by the color of their skin.

With the increasing use of self-identification, the effects of the OMB classification scheme on statistical data collection are even more problematic. There is an inherent uncertainty associated with any such classification scheme and the implication of such uncertainty for policy purposes needs to be understood. Much of this has been rather openly discussed recently, as statisticians in OMB and elsewhere have considered possible changes in racial and ethnic categories (Anderson and Fienberg 1995; Edmonston et al. 1995; Evinger 1995). Clearly the process is at least as much political as it is statistical, and the outcome is less than obvious. In the meantime, the racial and ethnic data collected in the decennial census, by our national surveys, and in most of our day-to-day activities, are based on the OMB scheme.

Table 1   Racial and ethnic categories currently used for federal statistics and program administrative reporting (from OMB Statistical Directive 15, 1977)

American Indian or Alaskan Native	A person having origins in any of the original peoples of North America, and who maintains cultural identification through tribal affiliations or community recognition
Asian or Pacific Islander	A person having origins in any of the original peoples of the Far East, Southeast Asia, the Indian subcontinent, or the Pacific Islands. This area includes, for example, China, India, Japan, Korea, the Philippine Islands, and Samoa
Black	A person having origins in any of the black racial groups of Africa
Hispanic	A person of Mexican, Puerto Rican, Cuban, Central or South American, or other Spanish culture or origin, regardless of race
White	A person having origins in any of the original peoples of Europe, North Africa, or the Middle East

As we noted, much public policy is based on the use of the official OMB racial/ethnic categories. In fact, in two of the four examples in the next section of this chapter, on the differential undercount in the census and on Title VII employment discrimination litigation, we deal with policy issues that are shaped by the specific racial/ethnic categories used in decennial census data.

FOUR DETAILED EXAMPLES

The following subsections describe four problem areas where substantial political pressures have imperiled the collection and dissemination of quality statistical information of material importance: quality control and the welfare system, underenumeration and the decennial census, the extent and consequences of the AIDS epidemic, and employment discrimination litigation. The discussion of underenumeration and the decennial census is the most extensive both because of my familiarity with the issues and because of its potential implications for national statistics.

Quality control in family assistance programs

During the 1960s the federal government initiated a series of family assistance programs to be administered by the states with federal financial support and oversight. The three principal programs (Aid to Families with Dependent Children, Food Stamps, and Medicaid) serve related purposes and overlapping populations. For each a special quality control (QC) system was established by the federal government to address concerns about ineligibility, fraud, and abuse. A major review of these QC programs was carried out by a CNSTAT panel chaired by John Neter and the following material is based in part upon its reports (see Affholter and Kramer 1987; Kramer 1988).

While there is a shared concept of a quality control system within the statistical community, this concept is not always well understood outside. The QC structure for family assistance programs has, from the outset, focused on only a small part of what most statisticians would include in a complete system. Specifically they deal with the accuracy of eligibility and benefit determinations by the states. Each month, state officials take samples from two universes of cases: active cases (units receiving benefits) and negative cases (units denied benefits and terminations). These samples are used to calculate various error rates in the program administration and are then re-evaluated by federal agencies to establish substantial monetary sanctions against states with poor QC performance.

These systems as described would not in and of themselves be problematic in the context of the present discussion, except for the fact that they use statistical concepts and methods to achieve potentially conflicting objectives, i.e. political objectives as well as quality control ones. The political and punitive aspects of the QC systems have prevented the implementation of broad-based quality improvement by overriding technical judgment in several areas. For example, the current system basically ignores the differential precision of the estimated error rates produced by different states. As a consequence, the risk of oversanction or undersanction due to sampling error alone varies from state to state, and these variations are often substantial. Moreover, QC programs at the state level are placed in the position of trying to achieve two conflicting set of goals: the first is a statistical goal focusing on system improvement; the second is a regulatory goal of ensuring accountability for payment accuracy. Using one data collection system to achieve both goals creates considerable problems; the political pressure to achieve the regulatory goal compromises the statistical goal, often severely. This point comes up again and again in different agencies and with different data systems. Few politicians and administrators recognize the need to protect statistical data from regulatory uses (see the related discussion in Fienberg 1994a). In addition, the sanction system is based only on overpayment errors rather than on overpayment and underpayment errors as well as improper denials. This choice of sanction system serves to reinforce the focus on a specific form of regulation and not on overall quality improvement, and was made despite statistical advice on the need for a more comprehensive system. The administrative response to the panel's strong recommendation to revamp the financial accountability of the state QC programs by including all sources of payment inaccuracy was slow to come, and has since been overtaken by various initiatives to completely devolve the welfare programs to the states with no controls or oversights.

An interesting sidelight that arose in the CNSTAT panel review of these programs was the controversy over the use of two-phase regression estimators for the state error rates in the three programs. Whether one supports the use of this particular estimator (that had been originally recommended for use to the federal agencies by Westat, a non-government survey and statistical consulting company) depends heavily on how one chooses to view the accuracy of the error estimates in the state and federal reviews. Different perspectives are rooted in fundamentally different assumptions that are not immediately verifiable from the statistical design of the sampling procedures or from the data themselves. The panel proposed a set of changes which would do away with the two-stage evaluation system and thereby sidestepped the resolution of a basically unresolvable statistical dispute. This is an example of what Spencer and Moses (1990) describe as data problem involving *ambiguous preferences*.

In many ways the impingement of political pressure on the QC programs for family assistance programs was subtle and in other ways it was quite overt. One need only look at the financial stakes to understand why statistical integrity might easily get lost in the shuffle. Moreover, with the current moves toward a different kind of welfare reform, with all authority and resources transferred to the states, the panel's efforts will likely have little impact.

Underenumeration and the decennial census

Concerns about the accuracy of the census counts in the United States have existed almost as long as the census itself. In volume 2 of the *Journal of the American Statistical Association*, General Francis A. Walker (1890), Superintendent of the US Censuses of 1870 and 1880, wrote about the undercount of Blacks in the 1870 census and he elicited one of the earliest statistical proposals for adjustment for the undercount from H. A. Newton and H. S. Pritchett, both of whom used the method of least-squares to fit a third-degree polynomial to census data for 1790 to 1880 and then measured the undercount for 1870 as a residual from the fitted curve (see Stigler (1988) for further details).

Writing about the census undercount over a decade ago, Savage (1982) noted:

Currently, a subject of broad interest is the size of the census undercount, the consequences of the undercount in apportionment of the House of Representatives, and in allocation of funds, the correction of undercount, and the reduction of undercount. It is not clear if these issues have technically adequate and ethically acceptable solutions.

He went on to describe the two quantitative techniques that had been used to estimate the undercount at a national level: demographic analysis and the dual-system or capture–recapture technique. Demographic analysis combines birth, death, immigration, and emigration records with other administrative records to carry forward the population from one census to the next, deriving an estimate of the overall population size, and thus the undercount. The methodology can be used to provide population and undercount figures by age, race, and sex, but only at a national level. Demographic analysis cannot be used to provide reliable state, regional, and local estimates, principally because of the absence of accurate data on migration. In the dual-system estimation approach, those included in the census are matched with a second source (for example a random sample of the population) and this information is used to produce an estimate of those missed in both sources and thus an estimate of the undercount in the original census. This technique can be used directly at the national level as well as at state and sub-state levels. For further details on the implementation of the dual-system methodology in the 1990 census and its statistical accuracy, see Hogan (1993) and Mulry and Spencer (1993), as well as the other articles that appeared in the special section of the September 1993 issue of *Journal of the American Statistical Association.*

Substantial controversy surrounded the sub-national undercount estimates that emanated from the 1980 Census Bureau effort to measure the differential under-count (for example, see Ericksen and Kadane 1985; Freedman and Navidi 1986). Savage (1982) expressed his doubts about whether the Bureau should have adjusted in 1980: '[If] nothing else, the essay should make clear that reduction of the undercount or modification of the census to reduce the effect of the undercount are complex, difficult tasks that we are not prepared to carry out. So my solution is more research.' The story of undercount and the 1990 census was in part a response to the call for more research and how the results of that research were received.

In 1982, while the dispute over adjusting the 1980 census still raged, the Census Bureau launched a major research program to improve the methodology used for census adjustment and it commissioned CNSTAT to establish a Panel on Decennial Census Methodology, whose charge included the review of the census undercount research program. The panel's 1985 report (Citro and Cohen 1985) outlined the basic issues that needed to be addressed in the adjustment research program. Subsequently, the panel reviewed the proposed methodology developed by the Census Bureau staff for adjustment in 1990, and its implementation in two separate pretests. This methodology was based on a newly designed post-enumeration survey and the use of dual-systems estimation, and was designed to overcome problems with the dual-systems approach used in the 1980 census. In October 1987, the Department of Commerce, in which the Bureau of the Census is located, announced that the 1990 Census would not be adjusted for the differential undercount. A March 1988 congressional hearing provided documentation on the deliberations at the Bureau prior to the announcement and substantiates the charges of political interference:

- There was virtually complete agreement among the statisticians in the Under-count Research Staff and others in the Statistical Standards and Methodology Division that the adjustment methodology had been successfully implemented in the Los Angeles Census Pretest and 'that adjustment was technically sound and feasible'.
- In May 1987, the Bureau's Undercount Steering Committee recommended proceeding with plans for adjustment, and Census Director John Keane made the decision to proceed with appropriate plans.
- The Bureau's plans were overruled by political officials in the Commerce Department.

It is beyond doubt that those perceived most likely to benefit from the decision not to plan for adjustment are the Republicans, whose administration made the decision in opposition to professional statistical advice. Even though Census Director John Keane was a political appointee of the Republican administration he appears to have resisted pressure to take a politically expedient position on adjustment. It was therefore especially disconcerting to many of those who had closely followed the planning activities for possible adjustment that the Republican administration attempted to put a scientific gloss over what had become an intensely political decision.

In October 1988, the Commerce Department decision was challenged in a new lawsuit brought by the City of New York and other state, county, and local governments. The trial was scheduled to take place in July 1989 but at the last minute a settlement was reached in which the October 1987 decision was withdrawn and the Department of Commerce agreed to conduct a post-enumeration survey (PES) of smaller scale than was originally planned, but one which might still allow the Census Bureau to implement an adjustment for the differential undercount, and to make a decision on adjustment in July 1991. Only later was the size of the PES to become a matter of concern when some statisticians critical of adjustment claimed that the data were too sparse for the purposes. Cutting the size of the PES sample size greatly increased the likely odds of not adjusting, because the estimates of the undercount would be less likely to pass a 'test of hypothesis of no differential undercount'. The cut involved minimal savings relative to the size of the overall census budget and was requested in the litigation settlement negotiations by lawyers from the Justice Department. There was no proposal for a reduced-sized PES by statisticians at the Bureau of the Census nor was there any discussion of the matter in advance by Bureau statisticians or its statistical advisory committee. In retrospect, we can now recognize that cutting the sample size was an important political act.

In Fienberg (1989a), I noted that the story about politics and the 1990 census was not over, and more than five years later it is still making headlines. The 1990 census took place on schedule, and in June 1990 the Census Bureau went into the field with its revamped PES based on a sample of over 5000 census blocks and the residents of over 165 000 households. In the spring of 1991, Bureau statisticians applied the dual-system methodology to produce a set of adjusted counts for the entire nation, and set in motion an elaborate evaluation process. Based on the results of this process, the new Bureau Director, Barbara Bryant, concluded that the adjusted counts were superior to those based solely on the regular enumeration process and she recommended to the Secretary of Commerce that the adjusted counts be adopted as the official census figures. On July 15, 1991, Commerce Secretary Robert A. Mosbacher announced that the results of the 1990 census would not be adjusted to correct for what he acknowledged as an undercount of approximately 5 million people. Choldin (1994) describes in detail aspects of the taking of the 1990 census and the process leading up to the decision not to adjust.

Following Secretary Mosbacher's announcement, New York City immediately re-initiated its lawsuit over adjustment and a trial was ultimately held in a federal district court in May 1992. The trial lasted three weeks and it consisted primarily of testimony from a large number of expert statistical witnesses – nine for the plaintiffs and five for the defense. For a more detailed description of the statistical issues at trial, we refer the reader to Fienberg (1992, 1994b), and a 1993 quartet of articles in *Jurimetrics* by Fienberg, Rolph, Wachter, and Freedman, as well as to a lengthy 1995 exchange in *Statistical Science* involving Breiman, Freedman, Wachter, Belin, Rolph, Ericksen, Kadane, and myself, among others. Eleven months later, the judge issued an opinion ruling in favor of the Department of Commerce, but on relatively narrow grounds. Because the decision not to adjust came under the Administrative Procedures Act, plaintiffs had to demonstrate that the decision was 'arbitrary and capricious'. The judge found the plaintiffs' case failed to meet this standard, but he went on to note that they 'made a powerful case that discretion would have been more wisely employed in favor of adjustment. Indeed, were this court called upon to decide this issue *de novo*, I would probably order the adjustment.'

New York City and the other plaintiffs appealed this judgment, arguing that the district court erred in applying an arbitrary and capricious standard of review, and that the case should be remanded for reconsideration under a constitutional claim of equal representation according to the Fifth and Four-teenth Amendments. Had the appellate court simply responded positively to this request, most observers would have been surprised. But in its August 1994 decision the appellate court went even further, not only overturning the original decision but also arguing that, at the original trial, the plaintiffs carried their burden of proof, showing that the Secretary of Commerce, in his refusal to adjust the census based on the PES, failed to make 'an effort to achieve equality as nearly as practicable'.

This time the States of Oklahoma and Wisconsin, intervenors in the litigation (Wisconsin was a potential loser of a congressional seat were adjustment mandated), appealed the decision to the Supreme Court, along with the federal government. The Court heard oral arguments in the matter in January 1996. With surprising speed, the Court rendered its decision in a unanimous opinion issued on March 20, 1996, holding that the decision the Secretary of Commerce not to adjust the census results 'conformed to applicable constitutional and statutory provisions' and 'was not subject to heightened scrutiny.' The Court thus reversed the circuit court decision and in effect decreed that the unadjusted census counts would remain the official numbers for 1990. While this ended the political and legal debate for 1990, the decision by the Supreme Court came essentially at the same time as the Census Bureau announced its plans for the 2000 census, plans which involve both sampling for non-response follow-up and a form of adjustment similar to that in dispute for 1990 (for further details on both the Supreme Court deliberations and the plans for the 2000 census, see Anderson and Fienberg 1996). The debate over the methodology continues in the US Congress, but as before largely on political rather than statistical grounds.

The extent and consequences of the AIDS epidemic

Acquired Immune Deficiency Syndrome (AIDS) is the medical description for the final stages of a series of diseases caused by a human retrovirus known as HIV. This virus attacks the immune system, damaging its ability to fight other diseases. In 1981, the Centers for Disease Control (CDC), the lead federal agency for monitoring the outbreak and spread of infectious diseases, received reports of a number of cases of previously healthy male homosexuals with severely compromised immune systems. This previously unidentified disease was sub sequently labeled AIDS and the CDC became the lead agency tracking the spread of the AIDS epidemic.

The term AIDS is typically used to denote various forms of HIV infection even though progression from one stage to the next is not automatic. A relatively large group of individuals possess the HIV virus (the first stage), and a much smaller group of those infected have gone on to develop AIDS Related Complex (ARC) while even fewer have actually suffered from AIDS itself. The HIV virus is known to be transmitted through sexual contact, exposure to blood and blood products, and from mother to child during the prenatal period, but information on rates of transmission is poor at best (Curran *et al.* 1988; Auerbach *et al.* 1994). The population groups exhibiting the greatest incidence of AIDS are homosexual men, intravenous drug abusers (and their offspring), and hemophiliacs.

While the CDC has the principal responsibility for collection of data on AIDS, it has retained a rather narrow focus and other federal government agencies have begun to gather data on various aspects of the AIDS epidemic and its impact on individuals and families, the health care system, the economy, and society more broadly. I noted (Fienberg 1989*a*) that we knew so little about the transmission and development of the disease that the uncertainty associated with any forecasts was often as large as the forecasts themselves. As an illustration, I pointed to a 1988 revision of the New York City Health Department estimate of the number of people in New York City infected by HIV from 400 000 to 200 000, which triggered a renewed debate over the accuracy of the figures being used to set local and national policies with respect to AIDS (see 'Halving of estimate on AIDS is raising doubts in New York', *New York Times*, July 22, 1988). The revised figures were based heavily on data from the Kinsey survey of sexual behavior (conducted about 40 years ago) whose statistical quality is questionable at best (see Cochran *et al.* 1953), and data from San Francisco on infection among homosexual and bisexual men. The AIDS figures for New York City were revised again less than a month later (see 'New York again revises its Aids virus estimate', *New York Times*, August 11, 1988) to somewhere between '149,000 and 226,000' on the basis of a range in the estimate of the number of infected homosexual and bisexual men! Since that time our knowledge has become only marginally better.

To address the basic issue of population-based infection rates, the National Center for Health Statistics (NCHS) developed plans for a national household seroprevalence survey (NHSS) of HIV infection (Weeks *et al.* 1989). The pilot test of this survey was originally scheduled for Washington, DC, but, when local health officials publicly raised concerns about the survey on the grounds related to the confidentiality of the respondents, politically appointed officials at CDC, which is NCHS's parent organization, canceled the test. In part, they feared that the public debate would affect data collection in CDC's non-probability sample of 'sentinel hospitals and other surveillance programs' (see the description in Stoto 1989) and Turner et al. (1989). But such data known to be subject to extreme non-response biases (see Hull et al. 1988) and thus many statisticians, including the present author, viewed the sentinel programs as of marginal quality and value at best, with or without additional non-response.

The pilot test for NHSS was later implemented in Allegheny County, Pennsylvania, although in a less elaborate form. In particular, NCHS decided to make the responses anonymous (as opposed to confidential), thus eliminating the possibility of linking them to other records and thereby eliminating some potential uses of the data such as the possibility of quality control follow-ups. Cooperation by the local health department helped to ensure that the pilot was a success. The screening response rate for occupied households was 95 per cent, and, for those containing an eligible sample person, 85 per cent gave a blood sample and completed the questionnaire. Thus the overall response rate was 81 per cent (Research Triangle Institute 1989). Encouraged by these results, NCHS proceeded to design and conduct a larger and more elaborate pretest in Dallas, Texas. In addition to the main survey, which this time included oversampling in strata with high expected HIV prevalence, there was a second component that involved recontacts with a sample of refusals. The pretest, like the Pittsburgh pilot, was conducted as a completely anonymous survey. Again the results were impressive. Participation rates were as high as in Pittsburgh: the screening response rate for occupied households was 98 per cent, and, for those containing an eligible sample person, 84 per cent gave a blood sample and completed the questionnaire. Thus the overall response rate was 84 per cent (Horvitz et al. 1990). The non-response follow-up component provided data that were used to construct separate logistic regression models for men and women that allowed informative adjustments for non-response (Massey et al. 1990).

NCHS and CDC then assembled an advisory group of statistical experts to review the results of the pilot and pretest, and virtually all of its members praised the initial efforts and recommended that NCHS proceed with a national survey. During these discussions, officials from CDC asked about how the proposed NHSS compared with CDC's non-probability sentinel hospital and other surveillance programs. Members of the advisory committee were quite clear in noting that CDC's ongoing efforts were simply an *ad hoc* collection of observational programs (for example samples of convenience at selected medical centers in selected cities) and were not capable of doing what the NHSS would do, namely provide accurate and reliable information for estimating the prevalence of HIV infection in the United States. Shortly thereafter, CDC announced that it did not plan to implement the NHSS because of non-response problems that would yield biased results. Since the publicly stated reason for cancelation cited appeared to ignore the evidence presented from the pilot and pretest and the advice of the special advisory committee, one can only speculate on what the real reason was.

In parallel to the efforts at NCHS to mount a national seroprevalence survey, researchers were trying to launch various other data collection efforts related to AIDS, including studies of sexual attitudes and behavior (see Turner *et al.* (1989) for an excellent description of what is needed and why). Most of what we 'know' in the behavioral area continues to be 'fake-lore' on sexuality based on bad data and bad data collection practices. In 1989, the funding of the proposed survey was approved by the National Institutes of Health but the Office of Management and Budget withheld approval of the survey questionnaire because of the complaints from several congressmen and senators who branded the survey as 'pornographic' (Dannemeyer 1989). Yet the social and moral dimensions of problems surrounding the AIDS epidemic are critical to an understanding of what statistical data to collect and how to interpret them. As Mary Grace Kovar has pointed out, there is also the epidemic of fear – one which is less visible than the AIDS epidemic itself, but whose social impact may be greater. The ability of federal agencies and university-based researchers to gather such social, behavioral, and attitudinal information is heavily influenced by the social and political attitudes of administration officials. Unfortunately to many of them, AIDS remains a social threat concentrated among some of the most undesirable groups in society.

Given the seeming extent of the AIDS epidemic, it is rather surprising that such data were not collected several years ago. Why was it so difficult to mount reliable data collection efforts about HIV infection and its potential causes? The answer that many people gave to this question in the late 1980s was political pressure within the executive branch to conform to the original Reagan administration position that the spread of AIDS was not a serious matter for most Americans. Because of the linkage of AIDS with intravenous drug usage, aspects of statistical measurement were also bound up in that administration's 'war on drugs'. (Booth 1988). Although federal research funds for medical research on AIDS increased dramatically following the change in administration in 1988, prejudice and political pressure with regard to the collection of statistical information remained. For example, in 1991, Senator Jesse Helms argued that the proposed sex survey was not intended to stop the spread of AIDS, but to compile supposedly scientific evidence that homosexuality is 'just another normal lifestyle'. A committee of the Institute of Medicine at the National Academy of Sciences reported (Auerbach *et al.* 1994):

Serious gaps remain in the information available on the prevalence of behaviors that put people at risk for HIV. Nationally representative data on sexual and substance-using behaviors are still unavailable, so it is impossible to estimate with any accuracy how many people are indeed at risk for HIV infection from any particular behaviors. Nor is it known to what extent individuals engage in multiple risk behaviors. Until these kinds of data exist, it will be difficult to monitor the epidemic and to design and target truly effective HIV interventions.

Shortly thereafter, the National Opinion Research Center released the results of its long-delayed survey on American sexual behavior conducted in 1992 with financial support from several private foundations (Gagnon *et al.* 1994*a*, *b*). And, much to most people's surprise, the results suggest far less high-risk sexual behavior and fewer homosexual relationships than were expected.

Title VII employment discrimination litigation

This example is basically different from the preceding ones in that it is linked to national statistics in quite a different way from the decennial census or quality control for family assistance programs. The focus of my concern here is the involvement of statisticians as expert witnesses for parties in employment discrimination litigation. The two links with the other examples are the extratechnical considerations for statisticians testifying in such adversarial proceedings and yet another CNSTAT study, by its Panel on Statistical Assessments as Evidence in the Courts (see Fienberg 1989*b*).

As the CNSTAT panel reports, there was a remarkable growth in the use of statisticians as expert witnesses during the late 1970s and early 1980s, especially in connection with litigation brought under Title VII of the Civil Rights Act of 1964, a federal statute which states that it is an unlawful employment practice for an employer to 'fail or refuse to hire or discharge any individual, or otherwise to discriminate against any individual with respect to his compensation, terms, conditions, or privileges of employment, because of such individual's race, color, religion, sex, or natural origin'. Much of the evidence used in Title VII cases, especially those involving class actions, is statistical in nature and it has become typical for both plaintiffs and defendants to hire expert witnesses to present statistical evidence in support of or in opposition to a claim of employment discrimination. The statistical data in these cases tend to consist of employer records on applications and former and present employees, as well as labor market 'availability' data often drawn from national sources, such as the Bureau of Labor Statistics, and state and local labor statistics offices.

In the typical Title VII case, the plaintiff's expert uses a data base and presents an analysis supportive of the plaintiff, followed by a rebuttal by the defendant's expert who often presents a somewhat different data base and often a dramatically different statistical analysis. For example, the plaintiff's expert may use multiple regression analysis and five predictors to argue that men and women similarly situated received different levels of compensation while the defendant's expert uses reverse regression and seven variables to reach an opposite conclusion (for a discussion of the rationale for these two different analytical stances see Conway and Roberts (1986) and Dempster (1988). The ensuing battle of the experts often turns the statisticians into advocates and invokes forms of political and social pressure on them in a fashion that is analogous to that which I have discussed in a government context above.

What becomes clear from an examination of actual Title VII cases (see Fienberg 1989*b*) is that the very nature of the adversarial system draws the expert witness away from neutrality and objectivity. The process begins with the briefing of the expert by counsel who invariably presents the facts of the case from the perspective of the client. Moreover, access to various types of data, for example company employment files, is often a function of the party with whom the expert is working.

As an expert's involvement with a case grows, so too may friendship with counsel. Fisher (1986) reminds us that 'Particularly because lawyers play by rules that go beyond those of academic fair play, it becomes insidiously easy to see only the apparent unfairness of the other side while overlooking that of one's own side. Continuing to regard oneself as objective, one can slip little by little from true objectivity.'

Addressing the broad range of litigation areas involving statistical testimony, Meier (1986) describes these extratechnical dimensions of the statistician as expert witness quite well:

As we have just seen, the professional integrity of the expert witness and, through him, of the profession that he represents is not well protected by the courts and hardly at all by counsel. But before we assume too readily that simple morality and personal ethics will be an adequate substitute, we should reflect for a bit on . . . corrupting influences . . . First, there is the fact that the expert witness is playing someone else's game and, inevitably, has to accept the rules as he finds them. His instructor in these matters is, of course, his client's counsel, and the witness is ill-equipped to resist the role of adversary when his lawyer thrusts it upon him . . . Among the most difficult of the corrupting influences to deal with is what I call aggrandizement. In Title VII cases . . . the Supreme Court has placed the statistician in the key role. Long ignored and treated with contempt in literature and in the courts, the statistician has been elevated to Olympian levels . . . He will be tempted to ignore or minimize those qualifications that he might emphasize in an academic setting, he may fail to emphasize schools of thought other than his own, and he may lay claim to overly broad scope for the inferences he draws.

Meier goes on to describe a host of other additional influences added by the adversarial system including bribery, flattery, co-option, and personal views. Meier also advocates the use of personal and professional codes as a way to defend the integrity of statistical testimony.

A reviewer of an early draft of Fienberg (1989a) correctly pointed out that we should not simply view the statistician as an innocent noble soul corrupted by immoral or at least amoral lawyers. Rather we must recognize that some statisticians are fully aware that they are being hired as expert witnesses because their testimony will help win the case and they exploit this situation by securing high fees for their services. While we should not condemn such professional colleagues, we should also not regard them as totally innocent of co-option. It is for this reason that Meier and others argue for professionally adopted ethical standards regarding expert testimony.

That these issues extend far beyond the area of Title VII employment discrimination litigation is quite clear to anyone who has been involved as a consultant or an expert witness in the legal arena. For several quite different illustrations of how statisticians take markedly different and polarized perspectives, see: (1) the exchange among Fienberg (1993), Rolph (1993), Freedman (1993), and Wachter (1993), who were 4 of the 14 testifying statistical experts in the New York City census adjustment trial; (2) the related exchange between Breiman (1994) and Freeman and Wachter (1994) on the one hand and Belin and Rolph (1994) and Ericksen et al. (1994) on the the the other; and (3) the paper by Freedman and Zeisel (1988), on statistical proof of cancer causation and environmental issues, which is followed by extensive comments from others and which grew out of a law suit involving DDT contamination that was ultimately settled out of court. The CNSTAT panel report reviews two other major areas involving statistical testimony, antitrust litigation, and environmental issues, as well as touching upon such areas as taxation and identification evidence in criminal cases.

In addition to the use of personal and professional codes of conduct as methods to insulate statisticians from the distortion of professional standards and practice in the legal setting, other mechanisms can be invoked such as the use of court-appointed experts. The report of the Panel on Statistical Assessments as Evidence in the Courts devotes considerable attention to this issue. None the less, the ethical issues surrounding the role of statisticians as expert witnesses are worthy of much greater attention by the statistical profession.

SOME LESSONS

The basic themes of this chapter have been three-fold. First, virtually all of what we might label as national statistics, whether produced by federal government agencies or by those in universities or the private sector, will reflect political and social perspectives and values. Second, despite the fact that national data cannot be value-free, I believe that most federal statistical agencies do an excellent job in insulating their data from unnecessary political aspects. Third, there are a series of problem areas where substantial statistical pressures have imperiled the collection and dissemination of quality statistical information of material importance. The four major illustrations in this chapter have been quality control and the welfare system, underenumeration and the decennial census, the extent and consequences of the AIDS epidemic, and Title VII employment discrimination litigation. It is my view that statisticians need to be aware that this pressure exists and to develop professional mechanisms to help our colleagues recognize unreasonable pressure and resist it.

The theme that relevant national statistical data cannot be value-free is not a new one, as I noted at the outset, but the recognition of this perspective from within the statistical community is not widespread. A shared understanding of the issues I have tried to raise in this chapter should help to strengthen rather than undercut the quality of national statistics programs. Writing in a related context, the sociologist Stanley Lieberson noted (Lieberson 1988): 'It is perfectly appropriate at any and all times to ask about the social underpinnings of knowledge, but that is not the same thing as asking whether the knowledge is valid – at least valid under the broad criteria of what the society is able to define as "true" in its current state of affairs.' He goes on to note that 'we are all too willing to allow socially and politically relevant subjects to be studied in the form in which the society states the questions, rather than by the way that our knowledge tells us to approach the problem'.

An area not dealt with explicitly in the paper, but in which the linkages between politics and statistics are clear, is forecasting (or projections). Considerable judgment is exercised in deciding what aspects of the future will be like the past, or the rate at which changes will take place. Projections sometimes appear to avoid judgments by saying, in effect, *if* the following trends continue, here is what will happen and the choice of scenarios in turn focuses attention on some matters and not on others. The diversity of scenarios may inspire confidence that the future will actually fall within the range of alternative projections or forecasts, but the probability of such an event is rarely pondered let alone known. Draper (1995) describes an example of such circumstances in the context of forecasting the price of oil, where the actual outcome lay wholly outside the range of possibilities considered. Part of the problem is that the best guesses about the future are often to the effect that government policies (for example to reduce energy consumption) will be ineffective, and thus the only scenarios that will yield realistic forecasts are those that assume that policies won't work. Another example that comes to mind relates to forecasts on the likely size of the AIDS epidemic (another issue raised in the discussion of Draper's paper). When statistical agencies are part of larger government policy organizations, they may not have the independence to publish forecasts which say that administration policies won't work. On the other hand, some forecasts will not be made because they may well be effective in influencing behavior and thus help to produce the forecasted result, for example the occurrence of a deep economic recession.

What remains for us as statisticians is to learn how to recognize the overt forms of political and social pressure that may subvert the production of quality statistical data of relevance to the problems such as in the examples discussed earlier in this chapter. In the context of government statistical agencies we need both strong professional leadership that is capable of protecting the agencies from unreasonable political interference as well as congressional mandates that make clear the responsibilities for statistical quality and aspects of independence that are vested in the agencies. Professional statistical organizations have a special role to play in support of our colleagues in the government sector as they develop and enhance codes of ethics for professional statisticians. They can also monitor activities in the government statistics domain and thereby provide support for statisticians and agencies that appear to be the targets of unreasonable political pressure and interference. They might even try to analyze statistically the types and contexts in which this pressure is encountered and the ways with which it is dealt.

Finally, I note that the issues of political pressure and the quality of statistical data extend far beyond what is usually taken to be the domain of national statistics in the United States. The example of the battle of experts in the context of Title VII discrimination litigation was chosen to be illustrative and to provide an indirect link to the American federal statistics scene. The issues here are, in a real sense, universal; they are not simply American and not restricted to activities of national statistical agencies. The purity of the mathematical formulation of statistical ideas often vanishes once we actually measure phenomena in the real world and attempt to set our analyses into an interpretive context. But this does not mean that statisticians should abandon statistical principles in such contexts, but rather the reverse (see, for example Spencer 1985; Spencer and Moses 1990).

ACKNOWLEDGEMENTS

An earlier version of this chapter appeared in the *Journal of Official Statistics* and that material has undergone major revision, editing, and updating. The theme remains the same but some of the examples have been altered somewhat and some have been updated substantially. A few are totally new. This revision was partially supported by a grant from the Russell Sage Foundation to Carnegie Mellon University.

REFERENCES

Affholter, D. P. and Kramer, F. D. (ed.) (1987). *Rethinking quality control: a new system for the Food Stamp Program.* Committee on National Statistics, National Research Council, National Academy Press, Washington, DC.

Alonso, W. and Starr, P. (ed.) (1987). *The politics of numbers.* Russell Sage Foundation, New York.

Anderson, M. J. (1987). *The American Census: a social history.* Yale University Press, New Haven, CT.

Anderson, M. J. and Fienberg, S. E. (1995). Black, white, and shades of gray (and brown and yellow). *Chance,* **8**, (1), 15–18.

Anderson, M. J. and Fienberg, S. E. (1996). An adjusted census in 1990? The Supreme Court decides. *Chance,* **9**, (3) (in press).

Auerbach, J. D., Wypijewska, C., and Brodie, H. K. H. (ed.) (1994). *AIDS and behavior: an integrated approach.* National Academy Press, Washington, DC.

Belin, T. R. and Rolph, J. E. (1994). Can we reach consensus on adjustment? (with discussion). *Statistical Science,* **1**, 3–39.

Bennett, J. M. (1983). *Natural selection, heredity, and eugenics. Including selected correspondence of R. A. Fisher with Leonard Darwin and others.* Clarendon Press, Oxford.

Booth, W. (1988). War breaks out over drug research agency. *Science,* **241**, 648–50.

Breiman, L. (1994). The 1991 Census adjustment: undercount or bad data? (with discussion). *Statistical Science,* **9**, 486–508.

Bulmer, M., Bales, K., and Sklar, K. K. (ed.) (1991). *The social survey in historical perspective, 1880–1940.* Cambridge University Press, New York.

Choldin, H. M. (1994). *Looking for the last per cent: the controversy over census undercounts.* Rutgers University Press, New Brunswick, NJ.

Citro, C. F. and Cohen, M. L. (ed.) (1985). *The Bicentennial Census. New directions for methodology in 1990.* Committee on National Statistics, National Research Council, National Academy Press, Washington, DC.

Citro, C. F. and Michael, R. T. (1995). *Measuring poverty: a new approach,* report of the Panel on Poverty and Family Assistance: concepts, information needs, and measurement methods. Committee on National Statistics, National Academy Press, Washington, DC.

Cochran, W. G., Mosteller, F., and Tukey, J. W. (1953). Statistical problems of the Kinsey Report. *Journal of the American Statistical Association,* **48**, 673–716.

Conway, D. A. and Roberts, H. V. (1986). Regression analysis in employment discrimination cases (with discussion). In *Statistics and the law,* (ed. M. H. DeGroot, S. E. Fienberg, and J. B. Kadane) pp. 107–95. Wiley, New York.

Curran, J. W., Jaffe, H. W., Hardy, A. M., Morgan, W. M., Selik, R. M., and Donero, T. J. (1988). Epidemiology of HIV infection and AIDS in the United States. *Science,* **239**, 610–16.

Dannemeyer, W. E. (1989). Proposed 'Sex Survey'. *Science*, **244**, 1530.

Dawes, R. (1989). Probabilistic versus causal thinking. In *Thinking clearly about psychology: essays in honor of Paul Everett Meehl*, (ed. D. Cicchetti and W. Grove), pp. 235–64. University of Minnesota Press, Minneapolis, MN.

Dempster, A. P. (1988). Employment discrimination and statistical science (with discussion). *Statistical Science*, **3**, 149–95.

DeParle, J. (1994). Census report sees income in decline and more poverty. *New York Times*, 7 October, p. 1.

Draper, D. (1995). Assessment and propagation of model uncertainty (with discussion). *Journal of the Royal Statistical Society (B)*, **57**, 45–97.

Edmonston, B., Goldstein, J., and Tamayo-Lott, J. (1996). *Spotlight on heterogeneity: an assessment of the federal standards for race and ethnicity classification*. National Academy Press, Washington, DC. (In press.)

Ericksen, E. P., Fienberg, S. E., and Kadane, J. B. (1994). Comment on Breiman and on Freedman and Wachter. *Statistical Science*, **9**, 511–15.

Ericksen, E. P. and Kadane, J. B. (1985). Estimating the population in a census year: 1980 and beyond (with discussion). *Journal of the American Statistical Association*, **80**, 98–131.

Evinger, S. (1995). OMB review of federal racial and ethnic categories. *Chance*, **8**, (1), 7–14.

Fienberg, S. E. (1989a). Political pressure and statistical quality: an American perspective in producing relevant national data. *Journal of Official Statistics*, **5**, 207–21.

Fienberg, S. E. (ed.) (1989b). *The evolving role of statistical assessments as evidence in the courts*. (Committee on National Statistics and the Committee on Research on Law Enforcement and the Administration of Justice, National Research Council.) Springer, New York.

Fienberg, S. E. (1992). An adjusted census in 1990? The trial. *Chance*, **5**, (3–4), 28–38.

Fienberg, S. E. (1993). The New York City census adjustment trial: witness for the plaintiffs. *Jurimetrics*, **34**, 65–83.

Fienberg, S. E. (1994a). Conflict between the needs for access and demands for confidentiality. *Journal of Official Statistics*, **10**, 115–32.

Fienberg, S. E. (1994b). Ethical and modelling considerations in correcting the results of the 1990 Decennial Census. In *Ethics in modelling*, (ed. W. A. Wallace), pp. 104–44, Pergamon, New York.

Fisher, F. M. (1986). Statisticians, econometricians, and adversary proceedings. *Journal of the American Statistical Association*, **81**, 277–86.

Fisher, R. A. (1918). The correlation between relatives on the supposition of Mendelian inheritance. *Transactions of the Royal Society of Edinburgh*, **52**, 399–433.

Freedman, D. A. (1993). Adjusting the census of 1990. *Jurimetrics*, **34**, 99–106.

Freedman, D. and Navidi, W. C. (1986). Regression models and adjusting the 1980 census (with discussion). *Statistical Science*, **1**, 3–39.

Freedman, D. and Wachter, K. (1994). Heterogeneity and census adjustment for the intercensal base (with discussion). *Statistical Science*, **9**, 476–85.

Freedman, D. and Zeisel, H. (1988). From mouse to man: the quantitative assessments of cancer risks (with discussion). *Statistical Science*, **3**, 3–56.

Gagnon, J. H., Lauman, E. O., Michael, R. T., and Kolata, G. (1994a). *Sex in America: a definitive survey*. Little, Brown, New York.

Gagnon, J. H., Lauman, E. O., Michael, R. T., and Michaels, S. (1994b). *The social organization of sexuality*. University of Chicago Press.

Hauser, P.M. (1973). Statistics and politics. *American Statistician*, **27**, 68–71.

Hogan, H. (1993). The 1990 post-enumeration survey: operations and results. *Journal of the American Statistical Association*, **88**, 1047–60.

Hogan, H. and Wolter, K. (1988). Measuring accuracy in a post-enumeration survey. *Survey Methodology*, **14**, 99–116.

Horvitz, D. G., Weeks, M. F., Visscher, W., Folsom, R. E., Hurley, P. L., Wright, R. A., Massey, J. T., and Ezzati, T. M. (1990). A report of the findings of the National Household Seroprevalence Survey Feasibility Study. *Proceedings of the Survey Research Section*, pp. 150–9. American Statistical Association, Alexandria, VA.

Hull, H. F., Bettinger, C. J., Gallalier, M. M., Keller, N. M., Wilson, J., and Mertz, G. J. (1988). Comparison of HIV-antibody prevalence in patients consenting to and declining HIV-antibody testing in an STD clinic. *Journal of the American Medical Association*, **260**, 935–8.

Kramer, F. D. (ed.) (1988). *From quality control to quality improvement in AFDC and Medicaid*. Committee on National Statistics, National Research Council, National Academy Press, Washington, DC.

Kruskal, W. (1989). The statistician as citizen. Paper presented at ASA Sesquicentennial Session, Joint Statistical Meetings, New Orleans, August, 1988.

Lieberson, S. (1988). Asking too much, expecting too little. *Sociological Perspectives*, **31**, 379–97.

MacKenzie, D. A. (1981). *Statistics in Britain, 1865–1930. The social construction of scientific knowledge*. Edinburgh University Press.

Magruder, J. S. (1976). *An American life*. Atheneum, New York.

Massey, J. T., Ezzati, T. M., and Folsom, R. E. (1990). Statistical issues in measuring the prevalence of HIV infection in a household survey. *Proceedings of the Survey Research Section*, pp. 160–9. American Statistical Association, Alexandria, VA.

Meier, P. (1986). Damned liars and expert witnesses. *Journal of the American Statistical Association*, **81**, 269–76.

Mulry, M. H. and Spencer, B. D. (1993). Accuracy of the 1990 Census and undercount adjustments. *Journal of the American Statistical Association*, **88**, 1080–91.

National Commission on Employment and Unemployment Statistics (1979). *Counting the labor force*. US Government Printing Office, Washington, DC.

Panel on Methodology for Statistical Priorities. (1976). *Setting statistical priorities*. Committee on National Statistics, National Academy of Sciences, Washington, DC.

Plewes, T. J. (1994). Federal agencies introduce redesigned Current Population Survey. *Chance*, **7**, (1), 35–9.

Porter, T. M. (1986). *The rise of statistical thinking, 1820–1900*. Princeton University Press.

Prewitt, K. (1987). Public statistics and democratic politics. In *The politics of numbers*, (ed. W. Alonso and P. Starr), pp. 261–74. Russell Sage Foundation, New York.

Research Triangle Institute (1989). National Household Seroprevalence Survey: pilot study report. Report submitted to the National Center for Health Statistics.

Rolph, J. E. (1993). The census adjustment trial: reflections of a witness for the plaintiffs. *Jurimetrics*, **34**, 85–98.

Savage, I. R. (1976). Setting statistical priorities. *Statistical Reporter*, **No. 77–3**, 77–81.

Savage, I. R. (1980). Modifying census counts. *Conference on census undercount*, pp. 62–75. US Dept. of Commerce, Bureau of the Census, Washington, DC.

Savage, I. R. (1982). Who counts? (with discussion). *American Statistician*, **36**, 195–207.

Savage, I. R. (1984). Some problems with social statistical systems. *Amstat News*, July–August, 25–6.

Savage, I. R. (1985) Hard–soft problems (Presidential address). *Journal of the American Statistical Association*, **80**, 1–7.

Savage, I. R. and Windham, B. M. (1973). The importance of bias removal in official use of United States census counts. *Statistics Report*, M265. Florida State University, Department of Statistics.

Seltzer, W. (1994). Politics and statistics: independence, dependence, or interaction. *Working Paper, No. 6*. Department for Economic and Social Information and Policy Analysis, United Nations, New York.

Spencer, B. D. (1985). Optimal data quality. *Journal of the American Statistical Association*, **80**, 564–73.

Spencer, B. D. and Moses, L. E. (1990). Needed data expenditure for an ambiguous decision problem. *Journal of the American Statistical Association*, **85**, 1099–104.

Stigler, S. M. (1988). The centenary of JASA. *Journal of the American Statistical Association*, **83**, 583–7.

Stoto, M. A. (1989). Statistics for the AIDS epidemic. *Chance*, **2**, (2), 9, 52.

Turner, C. F., Miller, H. G., and Moses, L. E. (ed.) (1989). *AIDS. Sexual behavior and intravenous drug use*. National Academy Press, Washington, DC.

Wachter, K. (1993). The census adjustment trial: an exchange. *Jurimetrics*, **34**, 107–15.

Walker, F. A. (1890). Statistics of the colored race in the United States. *Publications [later Journal] of the American Statistical Association*, **2**, 91–106.

Weeks, M. F., Horvitz, D. G., Hurley, P. L., and Wright, R. A. (1989). Designing a household survey to estimate HIV prevalence: an interim report on the feasibility study of the National Seroprevalence Survey. Paper presented at the Fifth Conference on Health Research Methods, Keystone, Colorado, May 4, 1989.

5 Normative terminology: 'normal' in statistics and elsewhere

WILLIAM H. KRUSKAL AND STEPHEN M. STIGLER

The word 'normal' is ubiquitous in modern science, as it is in modern journalism, education, psychology, sports, law, indeed in all arenas where description must encompass a range, and where judgments are given verbal expression. It is a remarkably useful word; it conveys a sense of the usual, the average, while at the same time expressing the idea of a norm, or optimum goal. This ambivalence is frequently acknowledged by placing 'normal' in quotation marks, as in the following examples of headlines:

> Hawthorne had 'normal' interests
> PROVIDENCE, R.I. (AP) – Novelist
> Nathaniel Hawthorne took a 'normal'
> interest in the shape of girls' legs and
> enjoyed a smoke or drink with friends,
> according to a Brown University professor.
> *Wisconsin State Journal*, 28 November 1976

> Israeli relations 'normal' for
> first time, Egyptian says
> UPI story in the *Chicago Tribune*, 28 October 1981

> A 'normal' coup in Guatemala
> *Chicago Tribune*, Editorial 26 March 1982

The use of quotation marks indicates either irony or special usage.

The appeal of 'normal' as a term seems to stem from its two almost contradictory meanings – it is in this respect a rare one-word oxymoron. If an object can be called normal, it is at once in that comfortable class of the usual, the average, the everyday, and it is the norm, the model, the ideal. There have been times when political philosophies have exalted the everyday, the 'common man', as the ideal, and times when normal has been derided as a state of banal mediocrity. In medicine, physiology traditionally combines the two senses and admits only two possibilities, normal and pathological. Thomas Kuhn's concept of 'normal science' implies both the usual workaday practice of scientists and a strict adherence to an established scientific paradigm (Kuhn 1962). And in statistics, 'normal' has at times been used in at least three senses: to describe the usual, to denote an unattainable ideal, and a third that blends the first two – as an asymptotically 'normal' limit, the 'usual case' in a mathematical sense but still not fully attainable – a limit that almost seems a goal in a normative sense.

The relationships between the first two meanings, the usual and the ideal, and the role of the contrast between normal and abnormal in nineteenth-century European intellectual history, form a major part of Ian Hacking's 1990 book *The Taming of Chance*. Hacking traces the conceptual role of 'normal' in philosophy, social thought, and statistics, with specific emphasis on Comte, Broussais, Durkheim, and Galton. Hacking's thoughtful philosophical analysis is nicely complementary to our emphasis on the earlier history and more detailed discussion of the development in statistics. In particular, we treat normal equations and normal schools.

NORMAL IN STATISTICS

The normal distribution

In science, multiple discoveries have been found to be the rule (Merton 1973, p. 356), but multiple independent appearances of the same terminology for the same scientific object must surely be the exception. Yet this is exactly what happened with the appearance of the word 'normal' as descriptive of the probability curve $\varphi(x) = (1 / \sqrt{2\pi}) e^{-x^2/2}$ by Charles S. Peirce (1873), by Francis Galton (1877), and by Wilhelm Lexis (1877). Such multiplicity of naming – in three countries and two languages – is remarkable, and surely signals a widespread simultaneously evolving conceptual understanding in the 1870s: of populations of people, of measurements, and of their similarities. Merton (1992) discusses another instance of multiple terminological innovation, with the appearances of the name 'scientist' from 1834 on.

To be sure, 'normal' is not the only name that has been attached to this curve: 'Gaussian' is a prime competitor, after Carl Friedrich Gauss, who studied the curve in 1809 (but could not be said to have introduced it; see Stigler (1980*b*) for a detailed investigation of the introduction of *that* name). Nor is 'normal' the only possibility that could have evolved to serve the same role: 'standard' might be seen as a potential competitor or alternative, having some of the same connotations. Indeed, in 1838 De Morgan proposed this as name, writing that he would be 'calling it in the future the *standard law of the facility of error*' (De Morgan 1838, p. 143, his italics), but that usage was not adopted, even by De Morgan in his later works (for example De Morgan 1849).

In modern times the appellation 'standard' has become attached to only a particular case of the normal distribution. The 'standard' normal distribution is the probability density given by the curve $\varphi(x)$ above, but with expectation zero and standard deviation one. ('Standardized' is used more generally to refer to the rescaling of any distribution or data set to have mean zero and standard deviation one.) If the random variable X has the distribution $\varphi(x)$, then the family of distributions of $Y = \mu + \sigma X$, where μ is a constant and σ a non-negative constant, is the family of normal distributions (including the singular cases where $\sigma = 0$). Language may be used a bit loosely for convenience; thus one says that Y is normally distributed if there are constants μ and σ such that this equation holds, where X has a standard normal distribution. The notion of what is the 'standard' normal distribution has changed over time. Until the time of Karl Pearson the standard (though not so termed) was effectively taken to be the normal distribution $(1 / \sqrt{\pi})$ e^{x^2}; with standard deviation $1/\sqrt{2}$. More recently, the version $e^{-\pi x^2}$, with standard deviation $1/\sqrt{(2\pi)}$ and unit normalizing constant, has been proposed (Stigler 1982).

Conflicting claims and attributions

Terminology is seldom superficial; it can be key to the adoption of new ideas, or at the least it can signal their arrival (Kruskal 1978). And because of this, terminology itself can be subject to conflicting claims of priority. There have, in fact, been multiple attributions for introduction of the name 'normal'. One of the most widely reported arose in papers by Karl Pearson, where usage as early as 1893 was followed by passages in 1904–6 and in 1920 that seem to claim the term as his own:

> . . . my custom of terming the curve the Gauss–Laplacian or *normal* curve saves us from proportioning the merit of discovery between the two great astronomer mathematicians.
>
> Pearson (1904–6, p. 189, his italics)

> Many years ago I called the Laplace–Gaussian curve the *normal* curve, which name, while it avoids an international question of priority, has the disadvantage of leading people to believe that all other distributions of frequency are in one sense or another 'abnormal'.
>
> Pearson (1920, his italics)

Pearson did refer to 'the normal probability curve' in his earliest statistical publication (Pearson 1893); in this and other early references he made no mention of explicit antecedent usage. At times Pearson did write normatively of the normal distribution (Pearson and Lee 1903. p. 367), but most often he did not:

> I can only recognize the occurrence of the normal curve – the Laplacian curve of errors – as a very abnormal phenomenon. It is roughly approximated to in certain distributions; for this reason, and on account of its beautiful simplicity, we may, perhaps, use it as a first approximation, particularly in theoretical investigations.
>
> Pearson (1901, p. 111)

There are other, more recent, blurred attributions. Maistrov (1974, p. 148) says (without documentation) that the term comes from Henri Poincaré. The earliest use of 'normal' by Poincaré of which we know was, however, in lecture notes prepared and distributed in 1893–4, where he said

> Je dirai, pour abréger, que la loi de probabilité est *normale*, lorsque la valeur de la probabilité est représentée par cette intégrale.
>
> Poincaré (1896, p. 76)

A set of the mimeoed original notes as distributed in 1894 in Paris can be found in the Irving Fisher Papers at Yale University Library, where the phrase is slightly different: 'Lorsqu'une loi d'écarts est exprimée par cette integrale nous disons que la probabilité est normale'. In this and later mentions of normality, Poincaré, like Pearson, gave no references to antecedent usage.

The second recent attribution appears in a paper by Hilts (1973), who gives Francis Galton as the creator of 'normal' in his 1889 *Natural inheritance*. It is true that Galton used the term in that book, and he also made no reference to earlier usages. But closer examination shows that none of these c. 1890 uses was independent of earlier uses, and of the three – Pearson, Poincaré, Galton – only Galton played an independent role in the introduction of the term, well before 1889. In fact, his apparently independent introduction of 'normal' goes back to 1877.

The naming of the curve

The curve $\varphi(x)$ acquired the name 'normal' rather gradually. From the curve's earliest appearance as a probability distribution (De Moivre 1733; Pearson 1920; Stigler 1986a), to its linkage with the theory of errors and the method of least squares (Adrain 1808; Gauss 1809; Laplace 1810; Stigler 1986a), $\varphi(x)$ was considered solely as a mathematical object: arising as an approximation to a binomial distribution (De Moivre 1733, 1738), as an approximation to a beta distribution (Laplace 1774; Stigler 1986b), as a solution to a differential equation (Gauss 1809), or in the context of a central limit theorem (Laplace 1810). Logically, we would expect the name 'normal' to be applied only after empirical and theoretical studies had shown that it or indistinguishably similar distributions occurred often in nature, and more, that a diversity of distributions occurred naturally of which this one was not only the most usual but also (to lend support to the normative sense of 'normal'), the most-favored or ideal state of affairs. It was only gradually over the nineteenth century that such evidence was gathered.

Comparisons of the empirical distribution of observational errors with one form of the curve $\varphi(x)$ were published by Bessel as early as 1818 (Stigler 1986a, pp. 202–4), but even at mid-century appreciation of the distribution of measurements had not converged to common acceptance of $\varphi(x)$ as an empirical law. One interesting indication of how $\varphi(x)$ was viewed occurs in the correspondence of Augustus De Morgan. As we have noted, De Morgan was no stranger to $\varphi(x)$; he had proposed the name 'the standard law of facility of error' in 1838. But in 1849, perhaps while preparing lectures on least squares for his classes at University College London, De Morgan sought the views of England's foremost astronomer.

On 9 October 1849, De Morgan wrote to the Astronomer Royal, George B. Airy, asking his opinion about the distribution of errors of observation. De Morgan's query was phrased so as to not prejudge the answer:

My dear Sir,
I wish you would give me the integral of all your associations on this point.
In a large number of observations, of a fairly good class, T being the true result, and α very

small, experience does it (as Dickens says[1]) that the number of observations lying between T and T + α, T + α and T + 2α, etc. is for some steps, pretty much of one order of magnitude – but that after a time, the numbers of observations which fall in the successive α-intervals diminish rapidly. So that, positives and negatives being equally likely, and OA the positive error which it would be justifiable to shoot a man for supporting the possibility of, the curve of error would be something like this

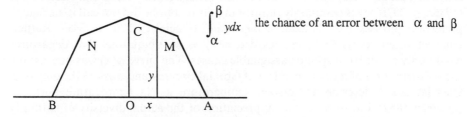 $\int_{\alpha}^{\beta} y dx$ the chance of an error between α and β

Now supposing you were drawing a diagram for an elementary work, just putting down what suggested itself – what should you draw?

* * *

Yours truly
A. De Morgan
7 Camden Street
Oct 9/49

Airy was a brilliant mathematician and his position as Director of the Royal Observatory afforded him extensive experience with observational data. He replied the very next day:

Royal Observatory Greenwich
1849 October 10

My dear Sir
In respect of the chance-curve of observations, my notions are as follows.

I am a devoted admirer of theory, hypothesis, formula, and every other emanation of pure intellect which keeps erring man straight among the stumbling-blocks and quagmires of matter-of-fact observations. I should therefore construct the desired curve by a formula, and (to show my disinterestedness) I recommend you to do what I never did myself, vis. to graphicize e^{-ct^2}. It will surely produce something very much like what you want, with the addition of two tails very much like the fine whipcord at the end of a four-in-hand persuader, with this difference however in effect, that whereas said whipcord is persuasively important, your two tails will be for probability unimportant.

* * *

Yours very truly
G. B. Airy

---

1. De Morgan is presumably quoting Mrs Micawber here, who was herself quoting her father, in Charles Dickens's novel *David Copperfield* ('experientia does it—as papa used to say', in Chapter 11). That novel was in the process of its first publication (serially in monthly parts) when De Morgan wrote his letter in October 1849; chapter 11 was published in Part 4, issued in August 1849. Bartlett (1992, p. 470) notes that the phrase was a play on the Latin 'Experientia docet' [experience teaches], a quotation attributed to Tacitus, *Histories*, bk V, Ch. 6, although Tacitus actually wrote 'experientia docuit' [experience has taught].

Airy had a reputation for being a hard taskmaster, although probably not so hard as might be suggested by his familiar reference to the similarity between the distribution's tails and a whip.

How, then did the 'standard law of facility of error' evolve into the 'normal' law? Quetelet (1844, 1846, 1869, 1870) had provided a mass of evidence that $\varphi(x)$; (or rather a binomial distribution that did not differ sensibly from $\varphi(x)$; see Stigler (1986a, p. 207ff.) was commonly fulfilled in nature, but he did not call it 'normale', preferring phrases like 'la courbe *binomiale*' (Quetelet 1870, p. 341). Rather, Quetelet often seems to have regarded $\varphi(x)$ as so ubiquitous that departures would only result from specific assignable causes. The curve $\varphi(x)$ was not just the usual distribution of measurements, but (special circumstances aside) the only one. Quetelet could describe an average temperature as 'la température normale' (Quetelet 1852), but he lacked an appreciation of the actual diversity of naturally occurring distributions, a background against which $\varphi(x)$ could be judged 'normale'. The first signs of what might be called a 'convergence toward normality' seem to have occurred, oddly enough, in American work.

An initial hint is found in Benjamin Peirce's 1852 paper on a criterion for the rejection of doubtful observations. The rejection of a measurement as 'doubtful' certainly represents a value judgment, a decision that it departs too much from some norm of acceptability, and we might well expect that an author discussing this topic would be drawn into using 'normal'. Benjamin Peirce nearly was, for, in discussing his criterion for judging when errors are so large as to be inconsistent with the hypothesis that they arose from the probability curve $\varphi(x)$, he wrote

In almost every true series of observations, some are found. which differ so much from the others as to indicate some abnormal source of error not contemplated in the theoretical discussions, . . .

B. Peirce (1852)

To the best of our knowledge, the first individual to take the further, complementary, step from abnormal to normal was Peirce's son, Charles Sanders Peirce. In a report published in 1873 C. S. Peirce referred to $\varphi(x)$ as 'the normal least-squares curve' (C. S. Peirce 1873). Peirce's use of the term may have only been a variation on 'usual' or 'ordinary', but this 'normal' terminology seems to have attracted an imitator in his father! Four years later, Benjamin Peirce, again on the subject of his criterion, was to write

There being given certain observations, of which the greater portion is to be regarded as normal and subject to the ordinary law of error adopted in the method of least squares, while a smaller unknown portion is abnormal and subject to some obscure source of error, to ascertain the most probable hypothesis as to the partition of the observations into normal and abnormal.

B. Peirce (1878, dated November 1877)

In commentary following Peirce's paper, Charles Schott emphasized that large errors could arise from an accumulation of small ones, 'and as such they may be regarded as *normal* (even if quite large), . . .' (Schott 1878, dated November 1877, his italics).

At this same time, and apparently quite independently, the same usage was developing in Europe. In 1877 (the foreword is dated May 1877) Wilhelm Lexis published his *Theorie der Massenerscheinungen*, in which he fitted the curve $\varphi(x)$ to distributions of deaths by age for several populations. He found a good fit for the higher ages, but there was generally an excess of deaths in the younger ages, well over that given by the fitted curve. (A version of Lexis's graph can be found in Stigler (1986a, p. 224).) Lexis referred to this excess of deaths as 'premature' ('vorzeitige'), and called those deaths, of the young as well as the old, that corresponded to the fitted curve $\varphi(x)$ the 'normalen' Sterbefälle (his quotation marks) or the 'normal group' ('Normalgruppe') (Lexis 1877, pp. 45ff.). The age corresponding to the center of the fitted curve was the 'Normalalter'. In a similar analysis in French in 1880 these terms became 'le groupe normal' and the 'Âge normal' (Lexis 1880), and in 1879 Perozzo described Lexis's work in Italian, using the phrases 'gruppo normale' and 'età normale' (Perozzo 1879). Lexis seems not to have called the curve itself 'normal', although this slight terminological step from the fitted group to the fitting curve would have seemed a natural one. About this time and apparently independently of the Peirces and Lexis, Francis Galton was slowly taking the same normal step.

It would be hard, perhaps impossible, to show that any nineteenth-century writer wrote more, thought more, or was more convinced of the ubiquity of the curve $\varphi(x)$ than Francis Galton. His belief in the ubiquity of this curve and his development of topics related to it exceeded even that of Quetelet. For over half a century Galton wrote widely on this topic, and he used a considerable variety of names for $\varphi(x)$, from the traditional ('the law of error', 'the exponential distribution', 'the mathematical law of deviation') to the more innovative ('law of statistical constancy', 'exponic hillock', 'exponic mountain'), and, of course, the 'normal' law. The earliest use of 'normal' in this sense that we have found in Galton's work was in a paper he read in February 1877 to the Royal Institution, four months before the date of Lexis's preface. Writing on 'Typical laws of heredity', Galton noted that the 'produce of peas of the same class deviated normally on either side of their own mean weight', and described a distribution similar to $\varphi(x)$ thus: '. . . It is perfectly normal in shape . . .' (Galton 1877). The term appears off and on, almost casually, in Galton's papers and books, apparently as a variation on 'usual' or 'ordinary' but with stronger connotations of desirability.

If there is a single point in Galton's work where 'normal' graduates from being only one of many alternative adjectives to being a special name, a recognition of its transition from casual to systematic usage, it would seem to be an 1885 paper presented to the Jubilee of the London Statistical Society. There he wrote, 'It is usually found that a series of observed values are "normally" variable, that is to say that they conform with sufficient exactitude for ordinary purposes, to the series of values calculated from the *à priori* reasonings of the law of Frequency of Error.' (Galton 1885, his punctuation). In this same paper he headed a table of the integral of $\varphi(x)$ 'Normal Curve of Distribution of Error.' Galton's 1889 *Natural inheritance* (particularly Chapter 5, 'Normal variability') served to further disseminate and confirm this terminology, and it is reasonable to surmise that Karl Pearson's study of *Natural inheritance* in 1889 (E. Pearson 1965) was his first encounter with the name 'normal'. Even as the name was taking hold in Galton's mind, there is at least one of his papers of that time in which he might well have used 'normal' but did not (Galton 1889*b*).

Had Galton, by 1885, read Lexis? Could his use of 'normal' as a name have been inspired by Lexis's 'Normalgruppe', perhaps subconsciously in a moment of cryptomnesia (Merton 1973, p. 402), or was it done independently, a Mertonian multiple? What evidence exists gives no reason to doubt that Galton's elevation of the term from adjective to name was only a natural consequence of his accumulating empirical research and a growing conviction that $\varphi(x)$ was a 'normal' state: both desirable (as evidence that the measurements were from a homogeneous population) and common. Lexis's work was first brought to public attention in England by Edgeworth in *his* 1885 paper read to the Jubilee of the Statistical Society. Edgeworth did not, however, specifically mention the 'Normalgruppe' in this paper, and since Galton's note was submitted prior to the meeting, it is doubtful that Edgeworth's paper had an influence on the preparation of Galton's. We have found no evidence, either in published work or unpublished correspondence, to indicate that Galton or any other English statistician had encountered Lexis's work prior to the spring of 1885; indeed John Venn, a frequent correspondent of Galton's, only noticed Lexis's work in 1887 (Venn 1888, p. 441).

The use of 'normal' to describe $\varphi(x)$ did not become universally widespread immediately after 1885. Even Galton himself occasionally used other terms at later times (such as 'law of frequency' in 1892 (Galton 1892, p. 28)), although his use of 'normal' did tend to increase in the years after 1885. Edgeworth used an imaginative, and sometimes bewildering, variety of terms for $\varphi(x)$ (he usually preferred 'Probability-Curve'), but we do find him writing, in 1887:

If we have been deceived by the appearance of Discordance . . ., and the facility-curve was really a normal Probability-Curve, yet we shall have lost little by taking the Median instead of the Arithmetic Mean.

Edgeworth (1887*a*)

The bullets successively fired from each gun being supposed to deviate according to the normal *Law of Error* . . . [italics in original]

Edgeworth (1887*b*, p. 30)

. . . when the law of discharge for the enemy's cannon is the normal one above described, when the registering flags arrange themselves in a Probability Curve.

Edgeworth (1887*b*, p. 54),

. . . the law . . . is not the normal symmetrical Law of Error . . .

Edgeworth (1887b, p. 55).

In an 1888 paper, Edgeworth drifted toward normality and back again:

. . . the law of error [used several times] . . . according to the normal law of error . . . The normal law of fluctuation . . . to obey the normal law of error . . . to comply very accurately with the typical law . . . the law of error [used several more times] . . . probability-curve . . .

Edgeworth (1888)

John Venn referred to $\varphi(x)$ as 'the exponential law' in the third edition of his *Logic of chance* (1888, but with preface dated December 1887), but by the next spring he was writing 'the law of dispersion here corresponds pretty closely to the normal one known as the binomial or exponential law'. (Venn 1889, p. 146, read April 24, 1888).

Karl Pearson adopted 'normal' from the beginning of his statistical work, as we have noted, and as his influence spread, the use of the name did too. It was used by the more applied statisticians in France (Julin 1921; Darmois 1928; March 1930), by Kapteyn (1903) in Holland, by Arne Fisher (1917) in Denmark, by Niceforo (1931) in Italy, by Czuber (1921, although not in earlier works) in Central Europe, and by Charlier (1931) in Sweden. Surprisingly, many of the more theoretical French probabilists preferred the Germanic 'loi de Gauss' (Bertrand 1888; Poincaré 1896; Laurent 1908; Borel 1909), although 'loi-limite de Laplace' can also be found (Fréchet and Halbwachs 1924).

In some statistical work, the normal distribution has engendered a peak of emotion, almost mythological. A well-known panegyric by Galton (expressed in terms of one of Galton's synonyms) begins:

I know of scarcely anything so apt to impress the imagination as the wonderful form of cosmic order expressed by the 'Law of Frequency of Error.' The law would have been personified by the Greeks and deified, if they had known it. It reigns with serenity and in complete self-effacement amidst the wildest confusion.

Galton (1889a, p. 66)

More recently, the late W. J. Youden, a creative chemist and statistician whose hobby was typography, printed on his calling card and elsewhere (see Wallis and Roberts 1956, p. 359) the following graphic in words:

THE
NORMAL
LAW OF ERROR
STANDS OUT IN THE
EXPERIENCE OF MANKIND
AS ONE OF THE BROADEST
GENERALIZATIONS OF NATURAL
PHILOSOPHY ◆ IT SERVES AS THE
GUIDING INSTRUMENT IN RESEARCHES
IN THE PHYSICAL AND SOCIAL SCIENCES AND
IN MEDICINE AGRICULTURE AND ENGINEERING ◆
IT IS AN INDISPENSABLE TOOL FOR THE ANALYSIS AND THE
INTERPRETATION OF THE BASIC DATA OBTAINED BY OBSERVATION AND EXPERIMENT

Galton and Youden, if their oratory seems a bit excessive, were unlikely to be led far astray. But others naively followed along in over-worship; for a criticism of such worship, see the fine book review by Pridmore (1974).

Normal equations

The expression 'normal equations' is standard in discussions of the method of least squares. The normal equations are simultaneous linear equations whose solution delivers the least squares estimates of the unknown coefficients. The term 'normal equations' was – as far as we know – introduced by Gauss in an 1822 expository paper; he provided no motive or explanation for the expression.

Why did Gauss use 'normal equations' ('Normalgleichungen' in the original)? Five possibilities come to mind but none dominates. First, the method of least squares may be geometrically understood as projecting orthogonally the observation vector to a manifold described by a given set of spanning vectors; a common descriptive phrase is 'dropping a normal' or 'dropping the normal'. Call the spanning vectors x_1, x_2, etc. and suppose for simplicity that they form a basis. Let X be the matrix whose ith column is x_i so that $X'b$ is the manifold of linear combinations of the given x_i's. The method of least squares estimates the expectation of Y (the observation vector) as a function of $X'b$ by dropping the normal from Y to that manifold. An easy way of writing down the normal equations is to take the inner products of x_i and $Y - X'b$. These must be zero by orthogonality, permitting the solution for b. It is natural to call the equations the 'normal equations' since they deliver an important vector normal to the manifold. (For a fine account of the underlying geometry see Herr (1983).) The connection between least squares and dealing with the normal to the manifold is immediate – normals minimize distance and its square.

The difficulty is that Gauss, so far as we can see, did not give that motivation – or any other. Nor did anyone else in the extensive literature we have examined give the above geometrical interpretation until relatively recent times. This geometric formulation of the problem itself, specifically the interpretation of the estimates as arising from an orthogonal projection, was a long time in entering the least squares literature, and we have not been able to trace its entry in a way that satisfies us. It has been a statistical commonplace for only some 40 or 50 years, if that. W. E. Deming was clearly aware of the geometry when he used the name in 1931, although there and in his 1943 book he seems to put more stress on justifying the name by the form of the equations: 'these equations are really normal – i.e. they are not only symmetric, but the quadratic form of the coefficients is positive definite' (Deming 1943, p. 58). This algebraic usage was common at the time; Deming cites Bôcher (1907, p. 150) as his source for it.

The geometric approach was given sharper explication by Bartlett in 1934. (Caution: do not conflate the geometric approach to least squares, a relatively simple matter, with R. A. Fisher's dazzling geometric approach to multivariate distribution theory (see Fisher 1915).

Yet it seems likely that the great Gauss must have known the geometric formulation. He dealt with much more difficult objects, for example curved surfaces, and used the term 'normal (line)' in his work on differential geometry. In addition, there were analytical geometry textbooks of the day that gave formulae for normal projections in two and three dimensions, although the descriptor 'normal' was little used compared to versions of 'perpendicular' (for example a letter from Gauss to Schumacher, January 6, 1842) and 'senkrecht'. The latter is infrequent – an example is in Biot (1817, p. 42). Even in 1873, in a geometric explanation of least squares, Laurent used 'perpendiculaires' (Laurent 1873, p. 253). Thoughtful speculation that Gauss might well have had the geometric interpretation in mind is given by van der Waerden (1977, pp. 86–7) (see also Schneider 1981 pp. 3, 4, 171 n. 29).

Second, Gauss may have used 'normal equations' simply as a variation for 'representative equations' – representative of various sets of equations that would determine the unknowns, albeit a particularly well-selected representative set. Anders Hald has pointed out to us that in Article 174 of his *Theoria motus* (Gauss 1809), Gauss twice refers to a 'normal position' ('positiones normales' in Latin) to mean the position of a heavenly body computed from a 'judiciously selected' set of observations of the position. The selected set would be chosen based on subjective criteria that were in line with geometric or mechanical intuition, but they would not be mathematically derived. It is as if one would fit a straight line to a collection of points by subjectively selecting two points with relatively extreme values of the abscissa whose ordinates were thought to be reliably determined. It would be a plausible but in no rigorous sense optimal determination. Here, as in 1822, Gauss gave no explanation for the term 'normal'.

A third possibility – we mention it only to strike it down – is that the normal equations were so-called because of relationships between the method of least squares and the normal distribution. That can hardly be, because, as we have seen, the term 'normal distribution' was not introduced until the 1870s, some time after 'normal equations' was an established term. We mention in passing that the least squares literature contains confusions about relationships between least squares and the normal distribution. There is no necessary connection between the two, although there are interesting contingent connections.

Fourth is the other canonical meaning of 'normal', as a norm or goal. Gauss may have meant by 'normal equations' those leading the way to good results or describing a norm. That would surprise us, but Gauss is silent and it is not impossible.

Fifth, Gauss may not have had any special denotation or connotation in mind, but simply wanted a verbal tag for convenience, just as a kennel may provide a name, say 'Spot', for a dog for sale, and the purchaser carries it along for simplicity. This is possible, we think, but it would also be a bit surprising since Gauss was sensitive to words and names; philology was one of his many interests (Dunnington 1955, pp. 237–8). In the other direction, an 1801 footnote in Gauss's *Disquisitiones arithmeticae* (p. 217 of the 1966 English translation) is a warning not to worry about his two-fold use of 'properly' in a number-theory context:

We select here the terms *properly* and *improperly* because there are no others more suitable. We want to warn the reader not to look for any connection between this usage and that of article 157 because there is none.

This is an example of solicitude toward readers.

We note also Gauss's use of 'Norm' in the usual sense for complex numbers $||z||$ (see Gauss 1832, pp. 541–3). The *OED*, second edition, gives as its earliest citation for the term 'norm' Gauss (1832), but we do not fully trust the *OED* in the normal context, for it tracks 'normal school' back only to the École Normale without any mention of the earlier use in Vienna, discussed below.

Explanations by others

Surprisingly few of the publications we examined seem concerned with rationales for the evocative term 'normal equations'. But of course some were. For example, an influential exposition of Gauss's work by the astronomer J. F. Encke (1832–4) had not used any name for them, but the astronomer J. W. L. Glaisher, commenting in 1874 (p. 318) on Encke called the equations the 'final equations'. Glaisher then says they 'are sometimes called the *normal* equations, but the name does not appear very felicitous. The only objection to the word *final* is that Encke terms *Endgleichungen* the equations from which x, y, z, . . . are immediately determined. [Glaisher's italics]' ('Immediately determined' here means stemming from the easy solution of a triangular set of equations following a particular procedure worked out by Gauss.) Later, in the continuation of Glaisher's paper (1880, pp. 600, 604; 1881, p. 19) Glaisher drops or forgets his view that 'normal' is infelicitous and uses 'normal equations' without comment. Ironically, in his 1874 paper Glaisher (1874, pp. 317–18) gave what he described as a geometrical interpretation of the method of least squares for the case of three linear parameters, but the geometry he discussed (murkily) was that of the ellipsoidal contours of the distribution of the estimates and the relationship of their probable errors to the axes of that ellipsoid, rather than recognizing them as arising by a projection from a higher-dimensional space.

Less helpful are such explanations as that by Leland (1921, p. 28): 'These are called the *Normal Equations*, as they are the same in number as the unknown quantities, and, therefore, may be solved simultaneously to determine the latter.' Of course there are huge numbers of sets of equations with that number; in addition, having the right cardinality is hardly enough for the least squares estimators.

A somewhat better but still wanting explanation was given by Rainsford (1958, p. 42): 'The term normal equations is applied to a system of linear equations in which there is the same number of equations as unknowns and the coefficients are symmetrical about the diagonal of the system.' So: correct cardinality plus symmetry. Yet that is not enough, for there still are lots of linear equations with those properties that do not deliver the least squares estimators. In general, the added requirement of idempotence does the trick.

'The normal equation for . . .'

A related small terminological tangle is the apparent desire of some authors to look at individual equations among the normal equations and to give them special links with individual linear parameters. Thus Chauvenet (1868, p. 512) says

the 'normal equation in x' is so called because it is the equation which determines the most probable value of x when the other variables are reduced to zero, or when x is the only unknown quantity; and so of the others.

If we read 'minimum sum of squared residuals' for 'most probable value', this is uninterestingly true when 'x is the only unknown quantity' for then there is but a single normal equation. Otherwise it is not clear what 'reduced to zero' means. If the other linear parameters are assumed zero, the quoted statement is wrong in general. Other writers have committed the same lapse, including William Woolsey Johnson (1892, p. 95), Merriman (1877a, p. 276), and Simon Newcomb (1906, p. 71). Even Gauss was tempted (see Gauss to Schumacher letter 843, July 21, 1843, p. 141 of Gerardy's (1969) *Nachträge*).

Finally, we return briefly to Glaisher's liking for the term 'final equations' as against 'normal equations', even though Encke had earlier appropriated 'final' for another meaning. These three texts provide pats on the back for 'final', but without scholarly reference to Encke: T. W. Wright (1884, p. 141) and Charles L. Crandall (1902, p. 7; 1907, p. 219).

Figure 1 shows a dot for each book or article we found published between 1821 and 1901 that discusses least squares. The publication dots are separated along two lines: those that call the normal equations just that, and those that give some other name or no name to them. Any interpretation of this figure is necessarily tentative, because the sampling of texts, which started with the list in Merriman (1877*b*), is not really structured. And not all the usages were clearly on one side or the other: J. F. Encke's 1832–4 article in the *Berliner Astronomisches Jahrbuch* was important and forms a central part of an 1888 compilation of Encke's publications. The editor of that 1888 volume was Harry Gravelius, who added a table of contents that mentions the normal equations three times. Yet when one turns to the cited pages the term 'Bedingungsgleichungen' is found!

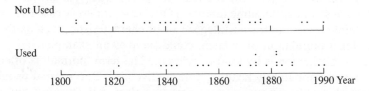

Fig. 1. The use, or non-use of 'normal equations' in 50 nineteenth-century writings where these equations appear. Gauss's introduction of the term corresponds to the lonely left-most dot on the lower of the two lines. Note the abrupt end in 1876 to a long sequence of works that did not use the term 'normal equations'; only in 1891 did non-use return. That period is just the time when 'normal' as a distribution was in the process of introduction. We do not want to make too much of that because of our informal sampling.

NORMALITY IN MEDICINE

Use of the term 'normal' in medical contexts is frequent, many-sided, and often confusing. Our brief review of medical normality is intended to provide counter-point for our primary statistical discussion, especially in the tension between normality as a goal and normality as something commonly found. No study of this could approach completeness; at least one writer traces the desirable/commonly found ambiguity back to Plato (Smith 1947; Benson 1972). We will take the relationship of what *is* to what *ought to be* as of abiding concern. This concern is nicely illustrated in a passage from George Bernard Shaw, exhibiting a case of normal meaning ideal and *not* common. Shaw wrote (1914, vii) of an ophthalmologist that 'He tested my eyesight one evening, and informed me that it was quite uninteresting to him because it was "normal". I naturally took this to mean that it was like everybody else's; but he rejected this construction as paradoxical, and hastened to explain to me that I was an exceptional and highly fortunate person optically, "normal" sight conferring the power of seeing things accurately, and being enjoyed by only about ten per cent of the population, the remaining ninety per cent being abnormal.'

Distinctions

The use of 'normal' in the medical literature in susceptible to classification in many ways. First, 'normal' may refer to a *single point*, number or unit, for example the little arrow on a fever thermometer; or 'normal' may refer to a *range* or some other aspect of a distribution, for example the statement that normal systolic blood pressure for healthy white males of age 30 lies between (or should lie between!) 110 and 145 mm Hg. This distinction, like most, is murky, for a normal temperature is rarely thought of as literally a point; *some* interval, if small, is kept in mind as we squint at the thermometer. Traditional, naive young parents with a first child may take the arrow over-literally, but that does not last long. In fact the breadth of observed values can be surprising. For example Eugene Du Bois (1948, p. 4) gives A. L. Ivy's temperature measurements of 276 healthy medical students; the symmetric central 95 per cent interval ($\bar{x} \pm 2s$) was 97.3 to 98.9 °F. (Using quantiles gives almost the same interval.) Of course not *every* case has an interval of uncertainty. A mode for an integer-valued characteristic, such as that of two children for a population of women, could serve as an example.

A second distinction is by kind of referent. The term 'normal' is often used of people to mean apparently healthy, a normative idea. But 'normal people' might mean something like average with respect to a class, à la Quetelet, and that may have very different implications. Consider, for example, normal urine (Hawk 1923), normal perverts (Karpman 1954; a pervert who leads an outwardly normal life), the normally ill child (van Eys 1979; used to comfort seriously ill children and their families). Then again, 'normal' may refer to the distribution of some kind of measurement regarded as a Gaussian random variable. Nearly always this usage is really one of 'approximately normal', 'approximately Gaussian'.

A major ambiguity for ideas like normal temperature, normal blood pressure, etc. is that of specification of the population. Typically one does not have a probability or otherwise structured sample from a frame; rather, one has a convenient set of measurements for, say, patients in the gastrointestinal clinic of a hospital during 1987, or blood pressure measurements for customers of a life insurance company. 'Normal' may refer to the correct mirroring of a population by a sample, as in 'epidemiologically acceptable normal population sample'. (Abrams *et al.* 1969).

A third distinction is that of normal as the ideal or goal, and normal as the everyday or usual. This is a difficult but important distinction; difficult because in many, but by no means all cases, the goal is to lie near the middle of an observed distribution. For seven, no less, meanings of 'normal' see Murphy (1972). Offer and Sabshin (1966, p. 97) present four approaches: normality as (1) health, (2) utopia, (3) average, and (4) process, where time is incorporated in terms of development, evolution, progression, etc. Some authors stress the everyday sense of normality, others the ideal. For example, King (1945) argues vigorously that normal should mean functioning in accord with design. His analysis, however, is weak in its instructions for describing design.

A relevant example, in the spirit of G. B. Shaw's quoted earlier, is that of numbers of teeth with defects in adults. The norm (in the goal sense) is surely zero, but the normal in the sense of normal range might be something like 5 to 20. Another example comes from a Letter to the Editor (Mower 1988) about physical attractiveness,

I, too, harbor fantasies of being inarguably . . . appealing in my physical appearance, the belle of the world ball. Like most of us, alas, I fall under the (pun intended) bell curve of normal, imperfect attractiveness.

A variant is to take as normal that value of a characteristic (say weight or blood pressure) leading to longest predicted life (Kayser 1962, p. 457). Here the tension between norm and description is manifest, especially for blood pressure measurements, where many physicians argued for ideals of blood pressure considerably lower than the pressures typically found. See, for example Robinson and Brucer (1939, pp. 413, 438, 440), Robinson (1940), and Master et al. (1950, p. 1467). For critiques, see Treloar (1940) and especially Knapp (1983). It is easy to see why there has grown up a philosophically oriented literature on normality and on associated questions like what is health? what is disease? See for example Canguilhem (1978; 1989), King (1954), Murphy (1972), and Hacking (1990). Smith (1947) covers the philosophical spectrum from Plato to 'My Darling Clementine'.

Psychiatry has an understandably unusual difficulty with concepts of health and illness, and thus with concepts of normality. One scholarly psychiatric book is simply called *Normality* (Offer and Sabshin 1966). Horton (1971) gives an interesting criticism of Offer and Sabshin, together with a description of an opinion survey (the subjects are psychiatric residents and patients) about 'typical normal' people.

Perhaps the most frequent use of 'normal' in medicine is for an interval on a numerical characteristic: temperature, blood pressure, weight, etc. Here there is great variability in nomenclature and structure. 'Normal range', 'cut-off points', 'standard ranges', and 'clinical limits' are some of the variant proposed terms. No one of these semantic variations really resolves the essential, and perhaps inherent, ambiguity of concept. The technical statistical structures where these terms arise also vary widely. Back in the 1920s, the entire range of a sample was often considered the normal range without consideration of sampling procedure, especially sample size. In a usual notation, $\bar{x} \pm \lambda s$ has been widely used, but with λ ranging from 0.2 to 3. Upper and lower sample 2.5 per cent points have been often used, as has $\bar{x} \pm \lambda s$ for the logarithm, transformed back. Several authors write in terms of tolerance intervals, a construct that seems to us on the over-subtle side in the medical setting, with its many difficulties. (for example Albert and Harris 1987, pp. 54–5).

One sometimes sees confusion, or at least commingling, of the idea of a normal (Gaussian) distribution with normal in either the usual or the goal senses. For example, Krause et al. (1975, p. 321) write that:

If a laboratory result falls near the center of the normal range, no problem is usually encountered in assuming 'normality' for the measured biological constituent.

For other examples see Offer and Sabshin (1966, pp. 105–8).

Medicine recapitulating statistics

Many papers in the literature on normality in medicine raise statistical eyebrows. In a way, the history of this literature recapitulates the development of statistical theory, but after a long lag. In particular, many discussions of something like normal range are silent about non-healthy people, an omission exactly like inattention to alternative hypotheses in significance testing frameworks. There are, however, some reasonable-to-excellent expositions, which include more detail about historical development than we are able to present. These estimable discussions include Mainland (1952), Oldham (1968), Elveback *et al.* (1970), Murphy (1972), Galen and Gambino (1975), and Martin *et al.* (1975).

Joint consideration of two or more characteristics

It is of great potential importance to consider jointly two or more characteristics; this is another way in which the medical literature partly recapitulates that of statistical theory. There are, of course, some treatments of joint distributions, notably by Galen and Gambino (1975), Healy (1979), and Albert and Harris (1987), and to be sure, most physicians in their clinical practice at least implicitly use joint distribution ideas (for example in not sounding the medical alarm bell after one anomalous test result in the midst of generally 'normal' readings.) No doubt the steady exploration of so-called expert systems in medicine will fold in joint distribution ideas. A related theme is that of warning against premature dichotomization. For example, Elveback (1972) strongly argues for reporting of estimated population quantiles.

Stratification, adjustment, etc.

As in other statistical settings, there has been wide discussion of allowing (or not) for covariate-like quantities. To what extent should we stratify, or adjust (which may have many meanings) or regress on age, sex, geography, ethnicity, etc. Some, such as Williams *et al.* (1978) and Leonard and Westlake (1978), argue for great adjustment or narrow strata, perhaps down to the individual patient, comparing characteristics when in good health and when ill. At the other extreme, some argue (Steinbach 1964) for a minimum of stratification or adjustment. Much depends of course on internal measurement variability versus variability among individuals in the population. And specification of the population is rarely simple.

Why normality concepts?

If there are many inherent difficulties, and no magic resolution to them, a fact that cannot have escaped medical authors, why is there such widespread interest among physicians in normal values of quantitative characteristics? Presumably the primary concern is with diagnosis and therapy for individual patients. Oldham (1968, pp. 185–8) gives two others: (a) normal values are useful as standards of comparison in public health analyses of groups, for example, workers in a particular industry; (b) the concept is useful in the elucidation of the nature of normality itself, thus helping to study biological questions. As Oldham says (p. 188) sets of data which have been exhaustingly sieved to ensure that they contain no individuals with recognizable disabilities [can] throw light on evolutionary, genetic and general biological questions.

Note the similarity here to traditional Shewhart discussions of process control and assignable causes. We are, however, skeptical; in part because surely everyone has some recognizable disability if looked at carefully enough. (If not, the person would be recognizably a miraculously healthy freak: a paradox!) Darrah (1939) argues in a psychiatric context that normal people are exceedingly rare, if they exist at all. Ryle (1947) gives a similar discussion, but instead of (b) above he gives its complement: to advance knowledge by looking at the more extreme variations! See also Canguilhem (1978, pp. 166–7; 1989, pp. 267–9).

Fox (1977, p. 11) points out that almost everyone in our 'society can be regarded as in some way "sick".' She quotes I. K. Zola, in part as follows:

Such data as these give an unexpected statistical picture of illness. Instead of it being a relatively infrequent or abnormal phenomenon, the empirical reality may be that illness, defined as the presence of clinically serious symptoms, is the statistical norm

Finally, we express mild surprise to have run across so few papers that treat non-quantitative variables: skin color, cardiac sounds, palpability, perhaps smells.

NORMAL SCHOOLS

The term 'normal school' generally means a training school for teachers,[2] yet the term's history has complexities that illuminate the ambiguities in 'normal' as used of the normal distribution and as used in other scientific contexts.

Many colleagues, if asked about the history of normal schools, think first of l'École Normale, whose prototype was established in Paris by Joseph Lakanal in 1794. That school was created as a model (that is, an exemplar) for instruction during the revolutionary period; indeed, that initial creation was to be the first of many and was sometimes known at the time as les Écoles Normales, although no

---

2. We have run across the following variant meanings, some based on undocumented, perhaps fanciful, etymologies:

A normal school is a school that provides teachers with 'rules for teaching'.
Butts and Cremin (1953, p. 286)

A normal school trains teachers to teach normal children.
From a conversation.

As a second meaning, after the teacher training institution one: another meaning is in contradistinction to special schools (for disadvantaged children).
(*Brockhaus* 1971, p.552)

A teacher-training school that is a model for other teacher-training schools . . . said of the École Normale Supérieure.
(*Encyclopedia Britannica*, Micropedia, 15th edition, 1985 printing)

second school followed. Laplace and Lagrange were among its instructors. Laplace presented the earliest version of his *Essai philosophique sur les probabilités* in lectures there, lectures that made no reference to the normal distribution under any name, although the subsequent version (1814) is famous for giving an entirely verbal description of the formula for the normal density (the constant *e* is 'that number whose hyperbolic logarithm is unity', an explanation that must have mystified its intended audience of non-mathematicians.) The initial École Normale enjoyed only a very brief life, to be followed by re-establishment as l'École Normale Supérieure about 1810 (Dupuy 1895; Allain 1891; Jeannin 1963). The term 'normal school' in fact goes back to 1765, and (to our knowledge) the first actual establishment of a school called a Normal School was in Vienna in 1771 (Melton 1982, p. 385; 1988, pp. 203–4). Its initial head, and the apparent coiner of the title 'Normalschule', was Joseph Messmer, then rector of the St Stephan Stadtschule in Vienna.

Messmer's view was that a normal school should primarily be an exemplary school for *children*, a school exhibiting stringent educational norms as a model. At the same time it would serve as a training facility for teachers – all this in an educational context of few schools, few good teachers, and increasing pressures for expanding education. Two vigorous monarchs, Frederic II of Prussia and Maria Theresa of Austria, had come to power in 1740, religious and national rivalries were intertwined, and education ('but not too much') was regarded by many as a significant source of strength.

The establishment of facilities for training teachers as such has a considerable earlier history. For example, in central Europe, teacher training schools existed as early as 1695 in Stettin and 1696 in Halle. They were generally called seminars (for example, the Halle school was called the Seminarium Selectum Praeceptorum) and, although they included practical teaching experience, they were not generally contiguous to the schools for children. The twin concepts of (1) a model school providing a norm and (2) an associated teacher training program were growing and becoming explicit during the eighteenth century. An important figure in this development was Johann Ignaz Felbiger. Felbiger began, with Catholic church support, to turn these ideas into reality in Silesia, especially near the town of Sagan (Krömer 1966; Melton 1982). There were short training seminars for young teachers, who would then – at least in principle – return to their homes and spread the development in a snowball-like way.

It appears that Felbiger and Messmer were in communication, and when Messmer responded in 1768 to an official request for an Austrian school reform plan, his proposal was to establish normal or model schools for children, and that they were to be associated with teacher-training facilities. Messmer turned out to be a poor administrator, and in 1774 Felbiger accepted Maria Theresa's invitation to come to Vienna with broad educational responsibilities, including administration of the Vienna Normal School. Messmer presumably returned to private life, not the last individual to be rejected from the normal for exceeding his limits. For a description of some of the other ways in which Maria Theresa affected the intellectual history of statistics, including statistics in national administration, education generally, and population counts, see Zarkovich (1990, pp. 22–4).

It appears that the name 'Normalschule' came from Messmer (although we do not have ironclad documentation on this) and was wildly successful. The name quickly spread to other parts of Europe and was picked up by Lakanal in Paris after the revolution. By that time, 'normal school' was coming to mean a training school for *teachers*, whether or not there was an associated school for children. Evidently the connotations of the word 'normal' were so attractive and powerful that the teachers in effect took it away from the children and appropriated it for adults.

But where did Messmer get the term 'normal'? So far as we know it had not been used by other enterprising pedagogues earlier. (The term 'Musterschule', model school, did have some currency, but was quickly displaced by 'Normalschule'.) 'Normal' of course had a history of use in non-educational contexts. For example, 'Normaljahr' was used in 1648 at the Peace of Westphalia, ending the Thirty Years War, to describe the earlier state of affairs (essentially as that on January 1, 1624), the conditions of state to be taken as normal and continuing, restoring the prewar status of established religion and property ownership. Again, in a public health context, there is the Viennese 'Sanitäts-Normative' of 1770.

We do not know how or why Messmer adopted the glorious term 'normal'. An attractive hypothesis is that the word was a term of art in calligraphy of the time, for Messmer was a noted and accomplished penman and penmanship was of great importance; indeed Messmer tutored young aristocrats in Maria Theresa's court in penmanship and other subjects (see von Helfert 1860, p. 133) Is it not plausible that model handwriting pages might have been called 'norms'? So far, alas, we have not found any support for that hypothesis. The books on calligraphy we have examined seldom use the word 'norm' or closely related words. The hypothesis might still hold if there were a local, transient school of handwriting for which 'norm' was a key word, but we have not found it. A possible channel is Delitsch (1928, see especially pp. 216, 220, 260, 283.)

The name 'Normal School' of course quickly spread over the world. In the United States of America by 1890 there were very roughly about 175 normal schools, and even several towns named 'Normal' after the school that gave the town its raison d'être. (Gray 1887, p. 422) (see also Butts and Cremin 1953, p. 450). Semantic fashions, and values of connotation, have their own lives, and, in the USA at least, by the end of World War II 'normal school' began to sound old-fashioned. That, joined with an increasing post-secondary student population, and the universal desire for glowing titles, has led by now to incorporation of most normal schools into state university or college systems. The Parisian École Normale Supérieure, however, retains its exalted status and tradition, but we do not think that it trains many teachers of children. The subsequent decline in the use of 'normal school' might be in part explained by overuse and boredom.

PUBLIC MATTERS

We have focused, rather narrowly, on the appearance of 'normal' in the terminology of statistics, medicine, and education. This history has of course a parallel and scarcely independent counterpart in the literature of science, journalism, and law, and more conspicuously in the realm of public discourse and public policy. For example, two of the three headlines quoted at the start relate to foreign affairs. It is interesting to speculate on the nature of the undoubted correlation between these developments: has the appearance of 'normal' in statistics and other scientific terminology been a reflection of its growing use in the public discussion? Or has the reverse been true, with the scientific usage inspiring the acceptance of and emphasis on the term in public discussion, with 'normal' being thus accorded a more precise connotation than would be the case without this adoption by social and physical scientists? We believe that, as is frequently the case in matters involving correlation, there is no unidirection causality, that both hypotheses hold and indeed have reinforced each other.

In some instances, the effect of public discussion on terminology has apparently been direct. While Karl Pearson did not christen the normal distribution, he played a crucial role in spreading the use of that name, and the reason he gave for the choice was explicitly grounded in the foreign policy concerns of the first decades of the century: an attempt to ease international tensions by using the diplomatically neutral term 'normal' rather than 'Gaussian' or 'Laplacian'. Exterior influences on other statistical usage were less direct and probably weaker. Gauss was a consummate mathematician, but his work on astronomy and geophysical surveys was intertwined with road-building, railroads, navigation, and other such important public matters. These may not have furnished Gauss's primary motivation, but he was certainly aware of the public uses of mathematics and the discourse surrounding it. It is interesting that the limited statistical study of the acceptance of 'normal equation' we reported above suggests that despite its eminent Gaussian pedigree it did not achieve popularity until the 1870s, in the same era that the normal name for the normal distribution arose. This suggests a connection, perhaps a growing awareness in mathematics of the increasing social use of the term, as documented by Hacking (1990).

The use of 'normal' in medicine, on the other hand, has always developed with a view towards public acceptance. Current analyses and debates about medical systems that bring to wide public attention concepts of normality in health could be traced back to the Sanitäts-Normative of 1770. A related study of probability semantics is by Kong et al. (1986).

Although the term 'normal school' itself has almost vanished, discussions of schools to train teachers are of immense current public interest. Current dialogue about education contains many semantic parts (equality, intelligence, home versus school influence, etc.) that can be seen as derivative of 'normality', even if that term does not play as central a role as it once did.

The influence of scientific normality upon the articulation of public policy is more speculative. The case is perhaps weakened by the fact, as we noted, that the appeal of 'normal' in foreign policy predates scientific uses, going back at least to the 1648 Peace of Westphalia. Still, the attention it receives (as opposed to several alternatives, such as common, usual, ordinary, or typical) must be due in part to a greater sense of precision it connotes. We need look no further than the most recent newspapers for reinforcement of this view; a headline from the October 18, 1994 issue of the New York Times reads:

Belfast Learns To Cope With Normality Of A Full Cease-Fire.

The story's text says that 'normalcy comes in small ways', like not always checking for explosives in the undercarriage of a car. No synonym would have captured the same idea!

Language, however, is an everchanging sea. In 1920, Warren Harding's speechwriter Judson Welliver evoked a powerful political response by appealing for a move 'back to normalcy'. In 1994, the Speaker-designate of the U-S House of Representatives could report (in the *New York Times*, 10 November 1994) having been told that 'the use of the word normal is politically incorrect'. A psychoanalyst can write 'I have suggested the term "adjustment neurosis" to clarify what we mean by "normal" in any culture'. (Fine 1979). Tides of usage of this sort have affected statistical usage as well, with one generation rebelling against the term as inspiring too facile an assumption of normality, while the next concocts ingenious transformations for ensuring that the assumption holds, a mathematical self-fulfilling prophecy. Yet the force of 'normal' – the delicious ambiguity it brings to both scientific and public discussion with its embodiment of both the usual and the ideal – seem to ensure that when it recedes it will not be for long. The forceful use of 'normal' has continued for over two centuries, and will likely do so for the next two. That this would be true seems, well, only normal.

ACKNOWLEDGEMENTS

We are most grateful to Robert Kass for his research assistance on normality in medicine. Our discussion of normal schools draws heavily on James Melton's work, and we do not generally repeat his extensive documentation. Mr P. S. Laurie, Royal Greenwich Observatory Archivist, graciously supplied copies of the Airy–De Morgan correspondence in Fall 1976. We are grateful to many colleagues for their advice and comments; in particular we thank George Barnard, Maurice Bartlett, John Bibby, K. R. Biermann, John Boyer, Lila Elveback, James Gustafson, Anders Hald, Lester King, E. Knobloch, James Melton, Robert K. Merton, Uta C. Merzbach, Peter Meyer, Frederick Mosteller, E. S. Pearson, Susan Shott, and B. van der Waerden.

REFERENCES

Abrams, M. E. *et al.* (1969) Oral glucose tolerance and related factors in a normal population sample. *British Medical Journal*, **1**, 595–8 (part II).

Adrain, R. (1808) Research concerning the probabilities of the errors which happen in making observations, etc. *The Analyst; or Mathematical Museum*, **1** (4), 93–109. (Probably published 1809 (see Stigler 1978); reprinted in Stigler (1980a, Vol, 1).

Airy, G. B. and De Morgan, A. (1849) Correspondence, October 9 and 10, 1849. Royal Greenwich Observatory Archives (Herstmonceux Castle), Section 2, RGOMS 998, (Pure Mathematics and Miscellaneous Science 1849 and 1850). The original of De Morgan's letter is at the University of London Library.

Albert, A. and Harris, E. (1987) *Multivariate interpretation of clinical laboratory data.* Dekker, New York.

Allain, E. (1891) *L'Oeuvre scolaire de la Révolution/1789–1802/Études critiques et documents inédits.* Firmin-Didot, Paris.

Bartlett, J. (1992) *Familiar quotations*, 16th edn, (ed. J. Kaplan). Little, Brown, New York.

Bartlett, M. (1934) The vector representation of a sample. *Proceedings of the Cambridge Philosophical Society*, **30**, 327–40.

Benson, E. (1972) The concept of the normal range. *Human Pathology*, **32**, 152–5.

Bertrand, J. (1888) *Calcul des probabilités.* Gauthier-Villars, Paris.

Biot, J. B. (1817) *Versuch einer analytischen Geometrie.* Riegle and Wiessner, Nürnberg. (Translated into German by J. T. Ahrens.)

Bôcher, M. (1907) *Higher algebra.* Macmillan, New York.

Borel, É. (1909) *Éléments de la théorie des probabilités.* Hermann, Paris.

Butts, R. F. and Cremin, L. A. (1953) *A history of education in American culture.* Henry Holt, New York.

Canguilhem, G. (1978, 1989) *The normal and the pathological.* D. Reidel, Boston; reprinted 1989 by Zone Books, New York. (Translated by C. R. Fawcett with R. S. Cohen). (For a clear review see Smith, R., (1990) *Annals of Science*, **47**, 199–201.)

Charlier, C. V. L. (1951) Gauthier-Villars, Paris.

Chauvenet, W. (1868) *A treatise on the method of least squares.* Lippincott, Philadelphia.

Crandall, C. L. (1902) *Notes upon least squares and geodesy.* Andrus & Church, Ithaca, NY.

Crandall, C. L. (1907) *Text-book on geodesy and least squares.* Wiley, New York.

Czuber, E. (1921) *Die Statistischen Forschungsmethoden.* L. W. Seidel, Vienna.

Darmois, G. (1921) *Statistique mathématique.* Oxtave Dion, Paris.

Darrah, L. W. (1939) The difficulties of being 'normal'. *Journal of Nervous and Mental Disease*, **90**, 730–7.

Delitsch, H. (1928) *Geschichte der Abendländischen Schreibschriftformen.* Hiersemann, Leipzig.

Deming, W. E. (1931) The application of least squares. *Philosophical Magazine*, **11**, 146–58.

Deming, W. E. (1943) *The adjustment of data.* Wiley, New York.

De Moivre, A. (1733) *Approximatio ad Summam Terminorum Binomii $a + bl^n$ in Seriem expansi.* (Photographically reprinted in 1926 in *Isis*, **8**, 671–83.)

De Moivre, A. (1738) *The doctrine of chances*, 2nd ed. Woodfall, London.

De Morgan, A. (1838) *An essay on probabilities, and on their application to life contingencies and insurance offices.* Longman, Orme, Brown, Green & Longmans, and John Taylor, London.

De Morgan, A. (1849) *Theory of probabilities.* (Article prepared for *Encyclopædia Metropolitana* (1845) and subsequently issued separately.) John Joseph Griffin, London.

Du Bois, E. (1948) *Fever and the regulation of body temperature.* Charles C. Thomas, Springfield, IL.

Dunnington, G. W. (1955) *Carl Friedrich Gauss, Titan of science: a study of his life and work.* Hafner, New York.

Dupuy, P. (1895) l'École Normale de l'an III. In *Le Centenaire de l'École Normale, 1795–1895.* Hachette, Paris.

Edgeworth, F. Y. (1885) Methods of statistics. *Jubilee Volume of the [Royal] Statistical Society* 181–217.

Edgeworth, F. Y. (1887a). The choice of means. *Philosophical Magazine*, **24**, 268–71.

Edgeworth, F. Y. (1887b). *Metretike: or the method of measuring probability and utility.* Temple, London.

Edgeworth, F. Y. (1888). The mathematical theory of banking. *Journal of the Royal Statistical Society*, **51**, 113–27.

Elveback, L. R., *et al.* (1970). Health, normality, and the ghost of Gauss. *Journal of the American Medical Association*, **211**, 69–75.

Elveback, L. R. (1972). A discussion of some estimation problems encountered in establishing 'normal values'. *Clinically oriented documentation of laboratory data*, (ed. E. R. Gabrieli). New York.

Encke, J. F. (1832–4). Über die Methode der kleinsten Quadrate. Published in three parts in the *Berliner Astronomisches Jahrbuch für 1834* (1832, pp. 249–312), *für 1835* (1833, pp. 253–320), and *für 1836* (1834, pp. 253–308).

Encke, J. F. (1888). *Gesammelte mathematische und astronomische Abhandlungen von J. F. Encke'* (ed. Gravelius). Ferd. Dümmlers, Berlin.

Fine, R. (1979). *A history of psychoanalysis*. Columbia University Press, New York. (As quoted by A. Storr in the *New York Times Book Review*, 5 August 1979, p. 3.)

Fisher, A. (1917). *The mathematical theory of probabilities and its application to frequency curves and statistical methods*. Macmillan, New York.

Fisher, R. A. (1915). Frequency distribution of the values of the correlation coefficient in samples from an indefinitely large population. *Biometrika*, **10**, 507–21.

Fox, R. C. (1977). The medicalization and demedicalization of American society. *Daedalus*, **106**, 9–22.

Fréchet, M. and Halbwachs, M. (1924). *Le calcul des probabilités a portée de tous*. Dunod, Paris.

Galen, R. S. and Gambino, R. (1975). *Beyond normality*. Wiley, New York.

Galton, F. (1877). Typical laws of heredity. *Nature*, **15**, 492–5, 512–14, 532–3. (Also published in *Proceedings of the Royal Institution of Great Britain*, **8**, 282–301.

Galton, F. (1885). The application of a graphic method to fallible measures. *Jubilee Volume of the [Royal] Statistical Society*, 262–5. Discussion 266–71.

Galton, F. (1889a). *Natural inheritance*. Macmillan, London.

Galton, F. (1889b). [Presidential address]. *Journal of the Anthropological Institute*, **18**, 401–19.

Galton, F. (1892). *Finger prints*. Macmillan, London.

Gauss, C. F. (1801). *Disquisitiones arithmeticae*. (Translated 1966 by A. A. Clarke. Yale University Press, New Haven, CT.)

Gauss, C. F. (1809). *Theoria motus corporum coelestium*. Perthes and Besser, Hamburg.

Gauss, Herr Hofrath und Ritter [Carl Friedrich] (1822). Anwendung der Wahrscheinlichkeitsrechnung auf eine Aufgabe der practischen Geometrie. *Astronomische Nachrichten*, **1/6**, columns 81–6.

Gauss, C. F. (1832). 'Theorie der Biquadratischen Reste' II Abk. pp. 541–3.

Gauss, C. F. (1887). *Abhandlungen zur Methode der kleinsten Quadrate von Carl Friedrich Gauss*, (transl. A. Börsch and P. Simon). Reprinted 1964, Physica, Würzburg.

Gerardy, T. (1969). *Nachträge zum Briefwechsel zwischen Carl Friedrich Gauss und Heinrich Christian Schumacher*. Niedersächsische Staats-und Universitätsbibliothek, Göttingen.

Glaisher, J. W. L. (1874). On the solution of the equations in the method of least squares. *Monthly Notices of the Royal Astronomical Society*, **34**, 311–34.

Glaisher, J. W. L. (1879–80). On the method of least squares. *Monthly Notices of the Royal Astronomical Society*, **40**, 600–13. (There is also an addition on pp. 18–23 of **41** (1880–1).)

Gray, T. J. (1887). Methods of instruction in the normal schools of the United States. *Proceedings of the National Education Association*, **26**, 472–80, discussion 481–3.

Hacking, I. (1990). *The taming of chance*. Cambridge University Press.

Hawk, P. B. (1923). *Physiological chemistry*, 8th edn. Blakiston Division, New York.

Healy, M. J. R. (1979). Does medical statistics exist? *BIAS*, **6**, 137–82.

Herr, D. G. (1980). On the history of the use of geometry in the general linear model. *American Statistician*, **34**, 43–7. (See also Herr, D. G. (1983). Geometry in statistics. In *Encyclopedia of Statistical Sciences*, vol. **3**, (ed. S. Kotz and N. L. Johnson), pp. 408–19.)

Hilts, V. (1973). Statistics and social science. In *Foundations of scientific method: the nineteenth century*, (ed. R. N. Giere and R. S. Westfall), pp. 206–33. Indiana University Press, Bloomington.

Horton, P. C. (1971). Normality – toward a meaningful construct. *Comprehensive Psychiatry*, **12**, 54–66.

Jeannin, P. (1963). *École Normale Supérieure*, chapter headed 'Enfances'. Office Français de Diffusion Artistique et Littéraire, Paris.

Johnson, W. W. (1892). *The theory of errors and the method of least squares*. Wiley, New York.

Julin, A. (1921). *Principes de statistique théorique et appliquée*. Marcel Rivière, Paris.

Kapteyn, A. C. (1903). *Skew frequency curves in biology and statistics*. Noordhoff, Groningen.

Karpman, B. (1954). *The sexual offender and his offenses*. Julian Press, New York.

Kayser, Ch. (1962). Le maintien de l'équilibre pondéral. *Acta neurovegetativa*, **24**, 457–91.

King, C. D. (1945). The meaning of normal. *Yale Journal of Biology and Medicine*, **17**, 493–501.

King, L. (1954). What is disease? *Philosophy of Science*, **3**, 193–203.

Knapp, T. R. (1983). A methodological critique of the 'ideal weight' concept. *Journal of the American Medical Association*, **250**, 506–10.

Kong, A., Barnett, G. O., Mosteller, F., and Youtz, C. (1986). How medical professionals evaluate expressions of probability. *New England Journal of Medicine*, **315**, 740–4.

Krause, R. O., *et al.* (1975). The impact of laboratory error on the normal range: a Bayesian model. *Clinical Chemistry*, **21**, 321–4.

Krömer, U. (1966). *Johann Ignaz von Felbiger/Leben und Werk*. Herder, Freiburg.

Kruskal, W. H. (1978). Formulas, numbers, words: statistics in prose. *The American Scholar*, **47**, 223–9.

Kuhn, T. S. (1962). *The structure of scientific revolutions*. University of Chicago Press.

Laplace, P. S. (1774). Mémoire sur la probabilité des causes par les évènements. *Mémoires de mathématique et de physique, présentés à l'Académie Royale des Sciences, par divers savans, & lû dans ses assemblées*, **6**, 621–56. (Translated in Stigler (1986b).)

Laplace, P. S. (1810). Mémoire sur les approximations des formules qui sont fonctions de très-grands nombres, et sur leur application aux probabilités. *Mémoires de la classe des sciences mathématiques et physiques de l'Institut de France, Année 1809*, pp. 353–415, supplement pp. 559–65.

Laurent, H. (1873). *Traité du calcul des probabilités*. Gauthier-Villars, Paris.

Laurent, H. (1908). *Statistique mathématique*. Octave Dion, Paris.

Leland, O. M. (1921). *Practical least squares*. McGraw Hill, New York.

Leonard, J. V. and Westlake, A. J. (1978). The derivation of reference ranges adjusted for age, sex and other variables. *Clinica Chimica Acta*, **82**, 271–9.

Lexis, W. (1877). *Theorie der Massenerscheinungen in der menschlichen Gesellschaft*. Wagner, Freiburg.

Lexis, W. (1880). Sur les moyennes normales appliquées aux mouvements de la population et sur la vie normale. *Annales de Demographie Internationale*, **4**, 481–97.

Mainland, D. (1952). *Elementary medical statistics*. Saunders, Philadelphia.

Maistrov, L. E. (1974). *Probability theory: a historical sketch*. Academic, New York.

March, L. (1930). *Les principes de la méthode statistique*. Félix Alcan, Paris.

Martin, H. F., (1975). *Normal values in clinical chemistry*. Dekker, New York.

Master, A. M., *et al.* (1950). The normal blood pressure range and its clinical implications. *Journal of the American Medical Association*, **143**, 1464–70.

Melton, J. van H. (1982). *Pedagogues and princes: reform absolutism, popular education, and the dialectics of authority in eighteenth century Prussia and Austria.* Ph.D. dissertation, University of Chicago.

Melton, J. van H. (1988). *Absolutism and the eighteenth-century origins of compulsory education in Prussia and Austria.* Cambridge University Press.

Merriman, M. (1877a). *Elements of the method of least squares.* Macmillan, London.

Merriman, M. (1877b). A list of writings related to the method of least squares. With historical and critical notes. *Transactions of the Connecticut Academy of Arts and Sciences,* **4**, 151–232.

Merton, R. K. (1973). *The sociology of science,* (ed. N. Storer). University of Chicago Press.

Merton, R. K. (1992). The multiple origins and epicine character of the word *Scientist.*

Mower, R. (1988). 'Plastic Surgery', Letter to the editor, *New York Times,* 20 July, p. C8.

Murphy, E. A. (1972). The normal, and the perils of the sylleptic argument. *Perspectives in Biology and Medicine,* summer 1972.

Newcomb, S. (1906). *A compendium of spherical astronomy.* (Reprinted 1960 Dover, New York.)

Niceforo, A. (1931). *Il metodo statistico,* nuova edizione. Messinai Principato.

Offer, D. and Sabshin, M. (1966). *Normality: theoretical and clinical concepts of mental health.* Basic Books, New York.

Oldham, P. D. (1968). *Measurement in medicine.* Lippincott, Philadelphia.

Pearson, E. (1965). Some incidents in the early history of biometry and statistics, 1890–94. *Biometrika,* **52**, 3–18. (Reprinted 1970 in *Studies in the history of statistics and probability,* (ed. E. S. Pearson and M. G. Kendall). Hafner, Darien, CT.)

Pearson, K. (1893). A symmetrical frequency curves. *Nature,* **48**, 615–16.

Pearson, K. (1901). On some applications of the theory of chance to racial differentiation. From the work of W. R. Macdonell, M.A., LL. D., and Cicely D. Fawcett, B. Sc. *Philosophical Magazine,* (6th series), **1**, 110–24.

Pearson, K. (1904–6). 'Das Fehlergesetz und seine Verallgemeinerungen durch Fechner und Pearson.' A rejoinder. *Biometrika,* **4**, 169–212.

Pearson, K. (1920). Notes on the history of correlation. *Biometrika,* **13**, 25–45. (Reprinted 1970 in *Studies in the history of statistics and probability,* (ed. E. S. Pearson and M. G. Kendall). Hafner, Darien, CT.)

Pearson, K. (1924). Historical notes on the origin of the normal curve of errors. *Biometrika,* **16**, 402–4. (See also letter in *Nature* (1926). p. 631.)

Pearson, K. and Lee, A. (1903). On the laws of inheritance in man. I Inheritance of physical characters. *Biometrika,* **2**, 357–462.

Peirce, B. (1852). Criterion for the rejection of doubtful observations. *The Astronomical Journal,* **2**, 161–63. (Reprinted in Stigler (1980a), vol. 2.)

Peirce, B. (1878). On Peirce's criterion. *Proceedings of the American Academy of Arts and Sciences,* **13**, 348–9. (Reprinted in Stigler (1980a), vol. 2.)

Peirce, C. S. (1873). On the theory of errors of observations. Of the *Report of the Superintendent of the U. S. Coast Survey for the year ending June 1870,* appendix No. 21, pp. 200–24 and plate 27. (Reprinted in Stigler (1980a), vol. 2.)

Perozzo, L. (1879). Distribuzione dei morti per età. *Annali di Statistica,* ser. 2, **5**, 75–93.

Poincaré, H. (1896). *Calcul des probabilités. Leçons professées pendant le deuxième semestre 1893–1894.* Gauthier-Villars, Paris.

Pridmore, W. A. (1974). Review of *Statistics in small doses,* by Winifred M. Castle (Edinburgh: Churchill Livingston 1972). *Journal of the Royal Statistical Society, (A),* **137**, 623–4.

Quetelet, A. (1844). *Recherches statistiques*. Hayez, Brussels.

Quetelet, A. (1846). *Letters à S.A.R. Le Duc Régnant de Saxe-Cobourg et Gotha, sur la theorie des probabilités, appliquée aux sciences morales et politiques*. Hayez, Brussels. (Translated 1849 as *Letters addressed to H. R. H. the Grand Duke of Saxe Coburg and Gotha, on the theory of probabilities as applied to the moral and political sciences*. Layton, London.

Quetelet, A. (1852). Sur quelques propriétés curieuses que présentent les résultats d'une serie d'observations, faites dans la vue de déterminer une constante, lorsque les chances de rencontrer des écarts en plus et en moins sont égales et independantés les unes des autres. *Bulletins de l'Académie Royale des Sciences, des Lettres et dès Beaux-arts de Belgique*, **19**, 303–17.

Quetelet, A. (1869). *Physique sociale, ou essai sur le développement des facultés de l'homme*, 2 volumes. Muquardt, Brussels.

Quetelet, A. (1870). *Anthropométrie*. Muquardt, Brussels.

Rainsford, H. F. (1958). *Survey: adjustment and least squares*. Frederick Ungar, New York.

Robinson, S. C. (1940). Hypotension: the ideal normal blood pressure. *New England Journal of Medicine*, **223**, 407–6.

Robinson, S. C. and Brucer, M. (1939). Range of normal blood pressure: statistical and clinical study of 11,383 persons. *Archives of Internal Medicine*, **64**, 409–44.

Ryle, JA. (1947). The meaning of normal. *Lancet* Jan, 4, 1947, 1–5. Reprinted in *Concepts of medicine*. (ed. B. Lush) 1961. Pergamon Press, New York, pp. 137–149.

Schneider, Ivo (1981). Die Arbeiten von Gauss im Rahmen der Wahrscheinlichkeitsrechnung: Methode der kleinsten Quadrate und Versicherungswesen. In *Carl Friedrich Gauss (1777–1855)*, (ed. I. Schneider), pp. 143–72. Minerva, Munich.

Schott, C. (1878). On Peirce's criterion [remarks]. *Proceedings of the American Academy of Arts and Sciences*, **13**, 350–1. (Reprinted in Stigler (1980a), vol. 2.)

Shaw, G. B. (1914). *Plays: pleasant and unpleasant*. Brentano's, New York.

Smith, H. W. (1947). Plato and Clementine. *New York Academy of Medicine*, **23**, 352–77.

Steinbach, M. (1964). The normal in cardiovascular diseases. *The Lancet*, **2**, 1116–18.

Stigler, S. M. (1978). Mathematical statistics in the early states. *Annals of Statistics*, **6**, 239–65. (Reprinted in Stigler (1980a), vol. 1.)

Stigler, S. M. (ed.) (1980a). *American contributions to mathematical statistics in the nineteenth century*. Arno Press, New York.

Stigler, S. M. (1980b). Stigler's law of eponymy. *Transactions of the New York Academy of Sciences*, 2nd Series, **39**, 147–57.

Stigler, S. M. (1982). A modest proposal: a new standard for the normal. *American Statistician*, **36**, (2), 137–8.

Stigler, S. M. (1986a). *The history of statistics: the measurement of uncertainty before 1900*. Harvard University Press, Cambridge, MA.

Stigler, S. M. (1986b). Laplace's 1774 memoir on inverse probability. *Statistical Science*, **1**, 359–78.

Tacitus, C. (*c.* AD 100). *The histories*. (Published 1931 with facing English translation by C. H. Moore as part of the *Loeb Classical Library*. Harvard University Press, Cambridge, Mass.

Tiles, M. (1993). The normal and pathological: the concept of a scientific medicine. *British Journal of the Philosophy of Science*, **44**, 729–42.

Treloar, A. E. (1940). Normal blood pressure. *Archives of Internal Medicine*, **66**, 848–50.

van der Waerden, B. (1977). Über die Methode der kleinsten Quadrate. *Nachrichten der Akademie der Wissenschaften in Göttingen, Math,-Phys. Klasse*, 75–87.

van Eys, J. (1979). *The normally sick child*. University Park Press, Baltimore.

Venn, J. (1888). *Logic of chance*, 3rd edn. Macmillan, London.

Venn, J. (1889). Cambridge anthropometry. *Journal of the Anthropological Institute*, **18**, 140–54.

von Helfert, J. A. F. (1860). *Die Gründung der Österreichischen Volksschule durch Maria Theresia.* Tempskh, Prague. (Volume 1 of a series of historical works under the editorship of von Helfert.)

Wallis, W. A. and Roberts, H. V. (1956). *Statistics: a new approach.* The Free Press, Glencoe.

Williams, G. Z., *et al.* (1978). Individual character of variation in time-series studies of healthy people II. Differences in values for clinical chemical analytes in serum among demographic groups, by age and sex. *Clinical Chemistry,* **24/2**, 313–20.

Wright, T. W. (1884). *A treatise on the adjustment of observations with applications to geodetic work and other measures of precision.* Van Nostrand, New York.

Youden, W. J. (1984). *Experimentation and measurement,* NBS Special Publication 672. US Department of Commerce, Washington, DC.

Zarkovich, S. (1990). The beginning of statistics in Yugoslavia. *International Statistical Review,* **58**, 19–28.

Part II
Data collection

6 Statistics in Washington, 1935–1945[1]

W. ALLEN WALLIS

Three considerations led me to accept the invitation to join you tonight. First, it is an honor that I would not want to forego. Second, I anticipated, correctly, that it would be an opportunity to renew old friendships and acquaintances and to make new ones. Third, I was given the impression that all that would be expected of me would be rambling reminiscences about statistics in Washington 50 to 60 years ago. With that subject the risk is only epsilon that inacuracies will be detected by more than a tiny number of the audience, so I thought it was an easy subject.

I am a midwesterner, a Minnesotan. My first visit to Washington was in 1927, as a sightseer. That 1927 visit worried my parents. They worried about my safety. The dangers that worried them were not gunshots but disease – not AIDS, but infection from primitive, unsanitary conditions, specifically typhoid fever. That was symptomatic of our attitude in Minnesota about 'the East' – backward and not fully civilized. So before I set out for Washington I had to have three typhoid inoculations; the second one made me sicker than I have been at any other time in what is, I hope, on the way to becoming a long life.

I have done statistical work in Washington twice, first from 1935 to 1937, then again from 1942 to 1945. I have worked also as an economist in Washington twice, 1959 to 1961 and 1982 to 1989, but I will talk tonight only about the statistics episodes. All four periods, of course, included some contamination of the primary field by the other.

In May 1935, as I was ending my second year of graduate study in economics at the University of Chicago and planning to go to Columbia University in October to study statistics with Harold Hotelling, I received a telegram. (I wonder how many of you are old enough to have received serious business messages by Western Union or its competitors Postal Telegraph and RCA?) It was from Hildegarde Kneeland, offering me a summer job. I was happy to accept. Nineteen thirty-five was not the bottom of the Great Depression, but jobs were still scarce – except for economists, statisticians, social workers, and other bureaucrats, thanks to Roosevelt's 'New Deal'.

So one morning in May 1935 I climbed down from an upper berth in a Pullman car of the Pennsylvania Railroad's Liberty Limited (or maybe it was the Baltimore and Ohio's Capitol Limited) that had arrived at Union Station in the early

1. Address to the Washington Statistical Society, 15 June 1994. This chapter first appeared as an article in *Chance*, Vol. 7, No. 4 (1994).

morning hours. (Incidentally, from Chicago at that time there were overnight airplanes to New York and Washington that offered berths; uppers were preferable on planes because the lowers were on the floor, which transmitted sound and other vibrations.)

Washington as a city in 1935 differed as much from Washington today as its statistics did. The most conspicuous difference was the Washington Monument. It had been completed less than 50 years earlier, and it was black, or at least dark gray. Buildings were heated and railroads were powered by coal, which, the oldest of you will remember, pours black smoke and soot out of chimneys. As a makework project, the Monument was cleaned about that time, thereby revealing the line – still visible – at which it had stood half finished for 50 years in the mid-nineteenth century.

There was not much air conditioning in 1935, except downtown in the main movie theaters and the ground floors of department stores, and most of what there was cooled but increased humidity. So in those days Congress went home before summer. The Jefferson Memorial had not been built, and the Lincoln Memorial was not much over 10 years old. There were far fewer cherry trees. Rock Creek Drive had fords, not bridges, across the Creek – and wet brakes did little to stop a car. The Department of Labor had a splendid new building on Constitution Avenue at Fourteenth Street – long since outgrown and turned over to others. Jackson Place, west of La fayette Park, had a miscellaneous collection of buildings, including a handsome new one (now gone) for the Brookings Institution. Almost all taxicabs were Plymouths, the basic fare was 20 cents, and drivers were happy to accept tips of 25 per cent – as they still are. Standard equipment in a government office included a wash basin, a towel that was changed weekly for each person, and a cuspidor that was replaced daily. I used to take a short cut to the Treasury by walking through the portico at the entrance to the White House. The Old Executive Office Building housed the State, War, and Navy Departments. The Mall had many temporary structures built during World War I, most of which were torn down just before we entered World War II.

The job to which I reported in May 1935 was with an agency established not by Congress but by Presidential Decree called the National Resources Planning Board. Later it was called the National Resources Committee. Originally it had been called the National Planning Board. Its goal was to establish comprehensive national economic planning on the Harold Laski model, the sort of planning adopted in the 1940s and 1950s by India and most of the former colonies in Africa. Rexford Guy Tugwell, a professor then at Columbia, later at Chicago, was one of its guiding lights.

In the spring of 1935, shortly before I went to Washington, Hildegarde Kneeland, my boss, had been involved in a highly publicized brouhaha that centered around Tugwell's ideas, or at least ideas attributed to him. Superintendent Wirt of the Gary, Indiana schools reported that at a dinner party in Washington the discussion had involved extensive quotations, highly approving, from Tugwell's writings, and that the ideas were radical and un-American. People who had been at the dinner, including Kneeland, testified before Congress that nothing of the sort had happened and that Superintendent Wirt was a boor and a fool.

The Wirt incident called public and congressional attention to the enthusiasm of many in the administration for national economic planning, and the word 'planning' soon disappeared. Although Congress made repeated attempts to abolish the agency, which was headed by the president's uncle, the administration simply established a new name, transferred to it all the personnel and files, and things proceeded without interruption. Eventually, during World War II, Congress worked its will by impounding all the files, which wiped out the organization. It left behind some worthwhile achievements, notably the work of Kneeland's group on consumer incomes and expenditures and some excellent work on water resources by Abel Wolman, Gilbert White, and their colleagues.

My work, to which I returned for a year after the year at Columbia, involved helping to plan a large-scale survey of consumer incomes and expenditures. Planning for such a survey had begun in 1929 under the aegis of the Social Science Research Council and led by William F. Ogburn, but the plans had not been carried out. They included an interesting suggestion that intrigued us but that ultimately we rejected. This suggestion was that in tables the boundaries of class intervals should be in geometric rather than arithmetic progressions; for example, the interval 100 to 110 would be followed not by 110 to 120 but by 110 to 121, then 121 to 133.1, and so forth.

The 'New Deal' offered the perfect opportunity to complete the plans and to carry them out, and the opportunity was seized by a consortium of three agencies: the Bureau of Labor Statistics to do the field work in urban areas, the Bureau of Home Economics in rural areas, and the National Resources Committee to do overall planning and coordination and the comprehensive reports and analyses.

All three of the groups carrying out the work were headed by women, Faith Williams at BLS, Day Monroe at BHE, and Kneeland at NRC. It was not until the so-called 'women's movement' 40 years later that it occurred to me that there was anything remarkable about this or about my first boss being a woman.

The Study of Consumer Purchases, according to Joe Duncan and Bill Shelton in the excellent history of 50 years of government statistics that they published in 1978, 'far exceeded any previous study of its kind in size and complexity. A double sampling procedure was followed: (1) a systematic and hopefully random sample was used to obtain income and other basic information for classification of families; (2) a predetermined number of families was selected at random within each cell . . .' The guiding genius of the statistical planning was Milton Friedman – who several decades later was to be elected President of the American Economic Association and still later to receive the Nobel Prize in Economics, with emphasis on his contributions to the economics of consumption. He wrote his important paper on analysis of variance using ranks to overcome a technical problem encountered in analyzing data on income and expenditure that, because of heteroscedasticity, were not suitable for the standard Fisherian analysis of variance.

The fundamental purpose of the Consumer Purchases Study was to make jobs for the unemployed. A certain sum had been appropriated by Congress, and a certain number of people to be employed was specified by the administration. The Work-Progress Administration divided the amount of money by the number of people and decreed that it would approve only projects that created one man-year of employment for every expenditure of the magic quotient. The first proposals accepted failed to meet the requirement, however, so the amount of employment required per thousand dollars was raised for later proposals. This happened repeatedly, and each revision made it necessary for us to revise our plans. The revisions took time and we came close to losing out completely as the funds neared exhaustion. Finally, our project was included among a dozen or so to be submitted to the president. By then the president had boarded a naval vessel at San Diego, so the Director of the Bureau of the Budget flew to san Diego and went aboard the ship. The story we heard was that the president asked. 'Are there any doorbell-ringing projects here?' and was told, 'Not that I know of, Sir.' So the president approved all the projects including ours, which was then the largest doorbell-ringing project in American history, except for the decennial censuses.

Doorbell-ringing projects were a touchy political subject at the time. The Administration was accused of excessive and intrusive invasions of privacy. The wife of Secretary of Commerce Roper publicly criticized the Consumer Purchases Study for inquiring about such intimate matters as expenditures on corsets, girdles, and brassieres. As I recall, we cleaned up our language by asking about 'foundation garments' and allowing the interviewers to elucidate.

Sampling was by no means generally acceptable when the Consumer Purchases Study was made. Duncan and Shelton relate that

A somewhat comic, though not necessarily typical reaction to the use of sampling by a Federal agency occurred in 1938 when the National Resources Planning Board published its report *Consumer Incomes in the United States*, based mainly on the Study of Consumer Purchases. It showed a highly skewed distribution of income, with the top 10 per cent of the families and single individuals receiving 36 per cent of the income. Estimates of this type had been published before by the National Bureau of Economic Research, Brookings Institution, and others, but this was the first time that a Federal agency had published such data, and it was based on a sample. The U.S. Chamber of Commerce issued a blast against this report, which it considered to be socialistic propaganda. It said that the estimates were based on 'less than a 1 per cent sample, and a random sample at that!'

The Chamber of Commerce was not alone in objecting to conclusions based on samples. In the Census Bureau, similar sentiments were held strongly by senior officials. Early in our project I was delegated to call on Leon Truesdell, head of the Population Division at the Census, to discuss our plans. Truesdell was a fine gentleman, most considerate even though I was only 22 years old and looked much younger, and he explained patiently that samples are worse than worthless because they can mislead seriously. He gave me an example that I used 20 years later in the statistics textbook that Harry Roberts and I published in 1956. Here is the example, quoted from the book:

After the 1930 census, it was stated on the basis of tabulations of one-half of the states, that the divorce rate had apparently fallen from 1920 to 1930. When all the results were tabulated, it was found that the divorce rate had not changed.

That summarizes Truesdell's illustration of a 50 per cent sample going wrong. What follows in the book is my *obiter dictum*:

The error was due to the fact that the first states reporting were the less-populous agricultural, lower-divorce-rate states. These states should have been compared with the same states in 1920, instead of with the whole country in 1920, though even then the result could have been interpreted only as applying to these states, not the whole country.

Although the Census was a stodgy organization in 1935, there were in Washington then many lively, energetic, and capable young statisticians, including several at the Census. By the time of the 1940 census, the Bureau was second in competence to no other statistical agency in the world.

In defense of the Census's stodginess in 1935, it must be admitted that at that time statistics in the United States was a stodgy subject. The Fisherian revolution, though well under way in the United Kingdom, was only about to begin here, mostly (but by no means exclusively) through Hotelling and his students, especially Sam Wilks and, in turn, his students. Statistics courses in universities centered on such topics as Pearson frequency curves and fitting them by the method of moments. Few statisticians had heard of degrees of freedom, analysis of variance, or even *t* tests.

During the last half of the 1930s, there were spectacular developments in the field of statistics, both in theory and in practice, in both governmental and academic institutions. Statistics is the rare field in which government agencies and universities are far in advance of private business. The only field of business in which the best statistical practices even approximate the best in government is market research.

At that time, the morale of the Washington statistical community was exuberant. A central role was played by Ed Deming through the Department of Agriculture Graduate School. This brought together most of the people who were excited by the developments that were bubbling so vigorously. Moreover, through lectures, seminars, and informal functions Deming introduced R. A. Fisher, Jerzy Neyman, Walter Shewhart, and other pioneers and innovators. Through Deming, Washington learned to appreciate Neyman well ahead of the academic world. Deming also was an ingenious and active innovator himself, at both the Budget Bureau and the Census, collaborating with Morris Hanson, Fred Stephan, Bill Hurwitz, Bill Madow, Abe Girshick, Phil Hauser, and many others. The years 1935 to 1945 may have been the most exciting decade in the history of American statistics.

One subject on which my interests in economics and statistics intersected was the fate of the NRA (the National Recovery Administration) and the AAA (the Agricultural Adjustment Administration). These two major components of the Roosevelt economic program were declared by the Supreme Court to be unconstitutional, the NRA unanimously, the AAA by six votes to three.

The administration's legal tactics were widely criticized on the assumption that they had delayed the decision as long as they could, presumably in the belief that the two programs would become integrated into the economic life of the country so successfully that the Court would not upset them. The critics argued that the programs should have been put before the Court as speedily as possible, during the first years of the 'New Deal' when a high pitch of enthusiasm and confidence approached the hysteria of World War I.

It occurred to me that the administration might have had a different strategy. They might have expected that at least three or four justices would support them and hoped that if they could delay the decision for a few years, they would be able to appoint a justice or two. So I wondered about the probability that in three years there would not be any vacancies, as, in fact, there had not been.

While I studied with Hotelling in 1935–6, I learned about the Poisson distribution and the classic example (due to von Bortkiewicz in 1898) of the number of Prussian cavalry officers killed by horses' kicks. In a paper for Hotelling I showed that the Poisson distribution fitted Supreme Court justices as well as Prussian cavalry officers. My paper was published in the *Journal of the American Statistical Association* in 1936, and a third of a century later a political scientist sent me an article in which he said that my paper had opened a new field of study, the rate of circulation of elites; he cited several references.

During World War II, I organized and headed the Statistical Research Group at Columbia University, which was a project of the Office of Scientific Research and Development working with the Army (which then included the Air Force), the Navy, other OSRD projects, and a few manufacturers. Some of you may have read the ASA Presidentially Invited Address on this subject that I gave in 1978 (published in *JASA* in 1980). The 18 principal members of SRG included a surprising number who were to be leaders in statistics and economics during the rest of the century – two Nobel laureates, a president of the American Association for the Advancement of Science, about 10 presidents of major professional associations, at least as many chairmen of university statistics departments, presidents of three important universities, and authors of innumerable articles, monographs, and books.

The things that won us respect from the armed forces, however, often were unimpressive to our professional colleagues. At one Air Force base, statisticians, not in our group but a related group, had studied the characteristics of a slot machine in the Officers Club. There was strong serial correlation between successive spins. They constructed a circular nomogram from which they made surprisingly reliable predictions after each spin of what the next spin would produce. For a week, until the owner of the machine made his rounds to collect, the club management was kept busy refilling the machine with coins. The machine was taken away, but not the prestige of statistics.

Someone discovered that when silver dollars of certain common vintages are given a vigorous, long-lasting spin on a hard smooth surface, usually a bar, they almost always fall heads up. At Eglin Field I once spun 20 consecutive heads. The observers reacted the way Mark Twain reported that the knights of King Arthur's court reacted to the *Connecticut Yankee*'s solar eclipse; so did a mathematical statistician who had not heard of the phenomenon.

Through Hotelling we learned of a thesis in the Columbia library on the length of the distended penis in males from 6 to 60, which did much to enhance our appreciation by the military.

When I entered statistics, Comptometers were being displaced for calculating by Monroe calculators, whose hand cranks eventually gave way to electric motors. Monroes were supplemented by Marchants, and later Fridens entered the market. Some elementary mechanical programming was added to these machines by the time of World War II. During the war the most reliable means of large-scale computations – for example, preparing ballistic tables for new artillery – was done with large assemblies of telephone relay switches such as constituted those central telephone exchanges that were modern enough for dial telephones. They were slow but totally reliable 24 hours a day, so in practice they were the fastest means of accomplishing such jobs.

During the war, electronic computers began to enter into service. Milton Friedman, who was a member of the Statistical Research Group, used one at Harvard in metallurgical research relating to the turbine blades in jet engines. He calculated a multiple regression function involving, if I recall correctly, 14 independent variables, which at the time was amazing. Near the end of the war the Harvard computer people visited us, knowing that several of us were economists, to ask whether we could think of any possible civilian uses for large electronic computers. We sent them to the National Bureau of Economic Research, and after the war, Millard Hastay of our staff joined the Bureau to help in its extensive business cycle computations, seasonal adjustments, and time series analyses.

In conclusion, I am reminded of a story Mike Nichols told at a University of Rochester commencement, perhaps 20 or 25 years ago. He said that he and Fellini had sat up late one night in Rome bemoaning the evils of the world – pollution, poverty, war, racism, movie critics. Then as they separated one of them exclaimed, 'There never was a better time to be alive!'

In my opinion there never was a better time for a statistician to be alive than the last 60 years. Not yet anyway. But perhaps 'the best is yet to come'.

7 Periodic and rolling samples and censuses

LESLIE KISH

MAJOR DESIGNS OF NATIONAL SURVEYS

Table 1 lists the major types of population surveys now conducted in the USA and in many industrialized countries. Some of these are conducted even more widely, and decennial censuses cover most countries today. I refer here to population surveys of persons, families, households, and dwellings, also to characteristics and variables based on them. As for surveys of other populations – of agriculture, industry, commerce – we shall mention them in the next section, as well as other types of surveys. The surveys listed here are mostly repeated and periodic, and mostly done by the government; in the USA mostly by the US Bureau of Census (USBC). They are mostly national surveys, though others may be regional or even local in scope; or cover only some subpopulation.

Table 1 Major designs of major surveys

1. Decennial census of *basic* data for *small areas* (blocks)
2. Decennial socio-economic data; census samples, long form
3. Annual basic data; mini-census; quinquennial census?
4. Annual socio-economic surveys of diverse objectives
5. Monthly or quarterly labor force surveys
6. Monthly or quarterly demographic surveys
7. Vehicle for diverse socio-economic surveys
8. Individual level data tracked over time, i.e. panel studies and longitudinal surveys
9. Randomized experimental data, to better ascertain cause and effect

Decennial censuses have been the first and foremost system for survey data in the USA and the world. They have been collected in the USA decennially since 1790, but historical instances may be found as far back as AD 2 in China. Their principal aim is to count the population elements in geographical-administrative detail. The principal population elements are persons, families, households, and dwellings; at times they have been potential soldiers, taxpayers, or workers. The basis of geographic detail is association of persons (who are mobile) with 'usual places of residence' which are relatively stable, that is with dwellings, villages, counties, blocks, towns, and cities. From these census data we can derive statistics down in the finest geographic/administrative detail on numbers of persons by sex/age classes; also dwellings, families, and households.

In addition to those basic census data, there arose over decades increasing requests for socio-economic data of many varieties, to be also collected along with the basic data by the census enumerators. It seems cost-effective to use the census machinery to collect other data also with great geographic detail. But collecting these added data increased the cost of censuses, and solutions were found in the last five censuses by resorting to sampling the census households. These 'Census samples' (my word for designs in different countries) are usually 5, 10, or 20 per cent of the complete census; but they may be 1 per cent or less and still be much larger, hence provide more resolution, than almost any national sample. They are used in the USA and in many other countries. Typically the complete census has the 'short form' with few questions, and the 'long form' with many questions is reserved for the census sample. A sample of households may be assigned to all the enumerators, or a sample of special areas may be assigned to special enumerators trained in the complex long form.

However, decennial censuses fail to meet the need for current statistics. Long ago the 'Bureau of the Census has devised a plan for the conduct of a sample census of the population taken on an annual basis [lines 3 and 4 in Table 1] of small areas scattered through the country.' (Hauser 1942). This plan has never been adopted in the USA and few countries have an annual sample census (Canada had a 'quinquennial' in 1991 and again in 1996; the US has one on the books but has never funded it). The cost poses formidable obstacles: a 10 per cent census may cost half as much as a complete census. These may consist of the brief and few basic data (line 3 in table 1) or they may have the greater breadth of social-economic survey data (line 4).

Entirely different in scope are the monthly Current Population Surveys (USBC 1978) of the USA and its many monthly and quarterly equivalents in other countries (lines 5, 6). Their scope and aims have been separated from those of the censuses (but I shall link them in the section on rolling samples). With sampling fractions near 1/1000 it has fewer than 100 000 households monthly, and these are 'overlapping' and clustered. They are designed and used to yield monthly and quarterly estimates of national statistics, also for regions and for large units and subclasses. However, they are neither designed nor used for small area statistics, nor for other small subdivisions of the population or *domains*. Originally designed in 1943 for employment/unemployment and other labor force surveys (line 5), they have also been used for general population and socio-economic statistics (line 6) (Hansen *et al.* 1953, section 12B; Kish 1965, section 10.4). An even more frequently conducted survey is the National Health Interview Survey (NHIS) conducted by the National Center for Health Statistics (1958). It is a weekly sample of 1000 households; note that with some modification, the data collected on their 2500 occupants can be cumulated to 52 000 households, more than 100 000 persons yearly.

An advantage of these kinds of repeated surveys is the opportunity to study group-level changes. Even better measures of change can be obtained through panel studies or longitudinal surveys which track the same individual over time (line 8; see Boruch and Pearson 1988). These permit stronger analyses of cause and effect, although the strongest method is randomized experimentation (line 9; Moses and Mosteller, Chapter 12 this volume).

The sampling frames and resources needed for these periodic statistics have also been used as resources and vehicles for other statistical needs (line 7); for example, annual surveys of statistics of education, income, and crime victimization. Also *ad hoc* one time cross section surveys have been collected on many topics.

There is a great gap between the complete focus of decennial censuses on geographic/administrative and other domain details with the sacrifice of timeliness, and, contrariwise, on the complete focus of monthly samples on timeliness, sacrificing domain details. Many statistical needs could be better filled with a compromise of annual large samples, which are now missing. Cumulation and rolling samples are proposed to fill this gap (p. 130, below).

These numbers and these descriptions are only approximate for the USA in 1994. They have been evolving over time in the USA, and elsewhere. Thus aims, scopes, methods, and resources vary between countries, and within the USA in the past and into the future. Generally these are samples of domiciles (dwellings), and the families, households, and persons who live there. The methods involve interviews in the homes, and increasingly in the USA and a dozen countries by telephone. But complete reliance cannot yet be placed on telephones, and therefore area segments are used for sampling frames or as supplements.

HOW ARE SURVEY NEEDS BEING MET?

Without even mentioning other statistical needs, we shall describe briefly other survey needs and how they are now being met in the USA. Three different avenues will be mentioned: first the great variety of surveys beyond household surveys of the population that are conducted by the government; second, the even greater variety conducted by non-governmental organizations; third, surveys that are not but can be and should be conducted. The various surveys each have strengths and weaknesses, which we discuss case by case. We also present a table summarizing the criteria.

First the government conducts a variety of surveys in addition to the population surveys described. There are surveys of industry, commerce, retail stores, schools, hospitals, prisons, and so on, too numerous and varied even to mention or classify here. Some of these involve interviews, some written forms, some measurements, and some abstracting and copying records. Some may involve complete censuses, some continuous record keeping; others may involve sampling, and the principles of survey sampling can be transferred here also. These surveys are common in most of the industrialized world, and also spreading in the Less Developed Countries (LDCs).

Second, there is even more variety in the USA of the kinds of surveys done by organizations outside the government. Six large examples are the Institute for Social Research at the University of Michigan, National Opinion Research Center at the University of Chicago, Westat Inc. in Rockville, MD, Research Triangle Institute in Research Triangle Park, NC, Audits and Surveys of New York City, and A. C. Nielsen Co. of Chicago. I picked two large, famous examples each from universities, non-profit researchers, and market researchers from scores of other organizations, most of them smaller. There is some division of labor, and the first four abstain from market research for private brands. However, there is also great deal of overlap and competition, and any of those six may bid on some government grants. The sources of grants for surveys may be grants from a government department (federal, state, or local) or foundation (NSF, NRC, NIH), or a private foundation, or a firm, sometimes from outside the USA. Probably the majority of surveys are local rather than national in scope. Probably most are not based on strict probability sampling, and may use questionable methods. Many are done by small, informal organizations, or individual professors. Telephone sampling and interviewing are easier, and have allowed many new players into the survey game.

Third, improvements can and should be introduced into the methods now used for population surveys, noted earlier. Instead of vague generalities I present in later sections a few specific examples on cumulated and rolling samples, on asymmetrical cumulation and a split-panel design (SPD) for periodic surveys. This SPD would be a means of introducing a panel study into the population surveys. Panels of population elements (the same persons, families, households) are necessary for studying the individual (micro) changes over time in periodic surveys. The lack of panels in population surveys is often deplored. These methods are all personal suggestions and these terms should be in quotation marks. They are also controversial, and by suggesting changes they imply criticism of methods now used by the USBC and other excellent statistical offices. My conscious motivation is not self-advancement or a desire for mere change, but a belief, however personal, that they represent sensible improvements over present methods.

SURVEYS, CENSUSES, AND REGISTERS: EIGHT CRITERIA

Surveys, censuses, and registers have different relative strengths. To compare them, I will use the eight criteria indicated in Table 2. These are my personal choices, because there are no objective criteria for choosing criteria. I prefer them to the common practice of arbitrarily choosing one data source and then justifying it with a single criterion. One director (statistical or political) may say 'We must have a census for full geographic detail', and another can counter with 'Sampling is so much cheaper than a census.' Both statements carry weight, but each is incomplete, because all eight criteria should be considered for each situation.

In Table 2 the asterisks mark the relative advantages, I propose, of each source in most situations, though not in all. The relative advantages of samples and censuses are complementary: samples appear stronger for five criteria, but censuses for the other three.

Sample surveys have been designed and operated to obtain rich and deep variables, and for complex statistics. The procedures of measurement and data collection can be designed for the specific needs of the research, and directed toward specific policy decisions. For example, a survey of incomes can devote pages and scores of questions to that topic and interview the head of each economic unit in the household. 'Rich' here stands for breadth and depth in measuring variables and their relations. The observations and other survey procedures can be directed to obtain data and statistics that are relevant and pertinent for the study objectives, and often reasonably accurate (not biased) for the specified objectives. Furthermore, the population contents of survey samples can also be chosen and directed toward those objectives. The population may consist of only adults or only children or only of a specified economic, social, ethnic, or age class. Such tailored directions are not feasible for complete censuses (and even less for administrative registers), because the census aims to cover the entire population, and accepts responses from 'any responsible adult' to reduce the cost of enumeration.

Table 2 Eight criteria for comparing three sources of data

Criteria	Samples	Census	Administrative registers
Rich, complex, diverse, flexible	***		
Accurate, relevant, pertinent	*		?
Inexpensive	**		***
Timely, opportune, seasonal	***		*
Precise (large and complex)		*	*
Detailed for small domains		**	*
Inclusive (coverage), credible, P.R.		*	?
Population content	***	*	

Samples are inexpensive compared with censuses because they are hundreds or thousands times smaller. These factors easily overwhelm the factors of two to five by which the unit cost of census enumeration per household can be cheaper than for a good survey. Above all, here we emphasize that samples are much more *timely* than decennial censuses. Census statistics can be anywhere from 1 to 16 years old, because some of the data of the census of year t may be released in year $t + 6$ and used until year $t + 16$. Consider a typical release (*New York Times*, 6 March 1994) of 'several unexpected findings from a computer analysis of fresh detail from the 1990 Census. Though the Census was conducted in 1990, the trends it brought to light have largely been corroborated by more recent studies . . .' For rapidly changing or fluctuating variables, timeliness can more than compensate for their small sizes; for example, consider epidemics, economic changes, and seasonal crops. But even for population counts of a large city or metropolitan area or a state (province) most of us would favor the results of current samples of 10 per cent over a 10-year-old complete count. Thus timeliness provides the chief motivation for rolling samples: to provide quarterly and yearly statistics for the nation and for its large domains.

On the other hand, complete censuses yield detailed data decennially for small domains and especially for small local areas, which samples fail to provide; this precision of detail may be their chief justification. However, this precision is fixed to a specific moment in time, and it is lost for changing populations and fluctuating variables. Survey samplers have many unhappy experiences when they use obsolete 'measures of size' for blocks and tracts in area sampling designs. These result sometimes in 'surprises' when the actual numbers of dwellings have increased by factors of 10 or 50! (Kish 1965, sections 9.4C, 12.6C).

Censuses seem to obtain often more complete, more inclusive coverage than sample surveys (but not necessarily, not always). First, it is less difficult to check sample coverage in censuses than in samples. Second, censuses also benefit often from public relations campaigns which can improve coverage. The 'ceremony' connected to the decennial censuses may even contribute to the 'social cohesion' of the nation. But in some countries and years censuses have been hurt by political or ethnic conflicts. Consider China's successful censuses of 1982 and 1991, conducted by over five million enumerators, and the Turkish census, which still requires people to be at home for the census day. On the other hand, some censuses of India, Nigeria, and Germany all suffered from harmful protests that resulted in postponement or cancellation.

The great disadvantages of decennial complete censuses are their high total cost, due to their size, and the US Census of 1990 did cost about $2.6 billion. (Yet this can also be viewed as costing 'only' about $10 for 10 years per capita for the 260 million population, which is less than an hour's median wage. And this measure of decennial effort per capita seems constant between countries.) Their cost is the main reason for not doing them more often, and with greater richness and depth of data. Also, it is difficult to marshall the large body of good enumerators and clerks needed for the decennial effort; another reason for lack of depth and accuracy of the data. Temporary employees with short training can hardly be expected to gather data of high quality and great depth. Although the large size of the census yields high detail and 'precision', its 'accuracy' may be low due to large biases caused by relatively unskilled enumerators. These biases must be added to the biases due to obsolescence. Furthermore, beyond costs and strains on resources, we should also consider the social burdens on the time of the respondents. On the other hand, the decennial attention may have educational values for the citizenry.

Administrative registers for a great variety of purposes exist in a bewildering variety of quality, and we cannot discuss them here. What is most important and most common to all of them is that they are inexpensive (because some other purpose pays for them) and that they contain only few data, which are often not most relevant to the survey objectives. The population registers of the four Nordic countries, plus some north European and a few other countries are so accurate and complete that decennial censuses of basic counts may be superfluous, because these can hardly be much better than the registers. Their incompleteness may not be greater than the undercounts in the good censuses of the USA and Canada, but they may be (Moser and Kalton 1971, pp. 160–5). They can be timely, detailed, and available. But this is not always so, and in case of doubt pilot tests are advisable.

Probably more and better registers will be conducted in the future and become available in more countries. The replacement of decennial census counts by administrative registers is not argued here, but it has been proposed and will be in the future (Scheuren *et al.* 1990; Redfern, Chapter 6 this volume). However, the data will always be few and thin. Thus they may displace the basic complete count of the decennial censuses, but not the 'long forms' of richer socio-economic data so much needed by a modern society. Registers cannot give us data that are rich in variables, and also timely and detailed. For these the rolling samples and censuses will be needed.

CONCEPTS OF AVERAGING AND SNAPSHOTS

There are large variations between the strategies for representing variations in the two dimensions of space and of time. For representing spatial variations we try to use either probability selections for survey samples, or the complete coverage censuses. But for representing variations in time it is still customary to resort to judgmental selections in some aspects, though not all. The traditional 'census day' designates one arbitrary day out of 3652 days for residence, and one arbitrary census year from 10 for income. Our monthly CPS surveys choose an arbitrary week to represent employment/unemployment for the month. This inconsistency between representing space and time is due partly to the happenstance of the great traditions of censuses since 1790 and of labor force surveys since the 1950s. However, we may also acknowledge real practical differences in collecting and presenting data between the two dimensions. Nevertheless, we should make an effort to overcome the methodological (philosophical) deficiencies in representing the time dimension.

Significant variations in the spatial distributions of survey variables are well recognized today. Survey sampling studies the differences between large domains for stratification, and especially the 'design effects' due to differences between small areas, which are found to be large for many variables. Furthermore, it is generally agreed that mathematical models to banish those differences do not take us very far; hence also that, in order to represent populations, we must randomize the sample selections over them. In other words, population statistics are generally averages of multidomain statistics or multipopulation statistics, based on probability selections (Kish 1994). We like to examine domain statistics and analyze domain differences, yet insist on using the population averages to describe them. However, lower standards have been used for representing the temporal aspects of populations, where purposive selection still prevails.

Temporal changes in populations and in their variables may be of three kinds: 'secular trends', which are more or less smooth and monotonic like population growth, and which are monitored by decennial censuses; periodic or cyclical changes, such as seasonal variations, which are sometimes 'adjusted'; and irregular variations, which are difficult to describe and often treated as 'random'. Random fluctuations often occur combined and confounded with one or both the cyclical and secular trends. Temporal variations may be less irregular than spatial aspects, hence less difficult to model, for example demographic trends between and beyond censuses; seasonal adjustments may also be less difficult, but not for epidemics, plagues, wars, economic trends, etc. Furthermore, temporal variations are unidimensional, whereas the spatial aspects have two (or three) dimensions.

Designs for cumulating and averaging over temporal variations face psychological blocks, whereas we now accept them for spatial variations; but those blocks can be countered with both theoretical and pragmatic arguments (Kish 1987, section 6.1B). Averaging varying periods is preferable in most situations to accepting an arbitrarily chosen period, just as averaging spatial domains is better than a purposive choice.

ILLUSTRATION AND PRECEDENTS OF AVERAGING

It is commonplace to *cumulate* data from periodic surveys. For example, the National Health Household Interview Surveys are designed to yield annual samples of 52 000 different households by cumulating 52 weekly samples of 1000 households each (NCHS 1958). Although it is possible to cumulate the 60 000 households of the monthly Current Population Surveys, these are rotation samples having overlaps of 7/8, with 60 000/8 = 7500 new households monthly; and cumulating overlaps is a difficulty we must avoid here. We return to this issue in a later section.

Continuous measurements are approximated by administrative registers; also with retrospective studies (for example 'children ever borne'); also rarely with contiguous reference periods of periodic studies ('multiround surveys'). More often we find systematic periodic 'snapshots' that must be filled with models (Kish 1987, section 6.1). For example, monthly labor force surveys often rely on a single week of the month. The decennial censuses take systematic time samples of every tenth year for incomes, and one day in every 3652 for residences. Smoothing between the systematic samples is mostly implicit, and would not do for many variables, either natural (for example temperatures) or social (for example stock prices).

The main problem in temporal averaging comes from confusion between reference periods and reporting periods; this is a general problem, and most important for rolling samples. For example, many of us believe that three monthly reference periods of the labor force survey should be combined into single quarterly reporting periods, because monthly reports are unstable in structure. 'The job market improved further in February' but 'Unusually severe winter weather and statistical quirks again muddied the results' is a recent typical report (*New York Times*, 5 March 1994). Even better would be the cumulated results of 13 weekly reference periods; but perhaps even better a rolling sample of 13 weekly reports.

ROLLING SAMPLES

The bold motivation for rolling sample designs comes from the desire to provide one vehicle for all five major needs outlined in the first two sections:

1. Periodic samples for current statistics: for quarterly, monthly, even weekly data for national statistics and major domains.

2. Annual statistics for minor domains, such as states, cities, and metropolitan areas in the USA, not now available generally in the USA, nor in most other countries, cumulated from the periodic samples.

3. Small-area statistics cumulated for quinquennial sample censuses, and with the richness of the 'long form' of census samples.

4. Decennial sample census or complete census; either rich or only basic data.

5. Panels of elements, but only as needed additions with a 'split-panel design' (described later).

Rolling samples are special cumulated samples. Rolling samples should be based on periodic (weekly, monthly, quarterly) samples, hence their relation to existing periodic samples for estimating changes over time must be discussed. For this question to be meaningful the two kinds of survey endeavors must be potentially similar in four respects: methods of measurement, data collection, the population covered, and sample size and design. Labor force surveys typically interview one 'responsible adult' in each sample household; many of their questions involve basic demographic, economic, and social data, and these have much in common with the contents of the 'long forms' of samples based on censuses. Many countries now conduct similar large periodic surveys of the labor force. I have raised the question of rolling samples in the USA, China, and Canada (Kish 1981, 1990), but it should be raised in other countries also.

The Current Population Surveys of the USA collect about 60 000 monthly household interviews, and 120 of these would cumulate to 7 200 000 decennially. This would be a decennial rolling sample of about 7.2 per cent from the US population of about 100 000 000 households, and a quinquennial rolling sample of 3.6 per cent. This would be adequate for some purposes, but perhaps not for others. Along the way, the rolling samples of 720 000 would yield yearly samples of 0.72 per cent. In Canada the Monthly Labor Force Surveys of about 80 000 households would cumulate to about 1000 000 yearly and to 10 000 000 decennially. These would yield for the population of 10 000 000 households complete coverage decennially, and 10 per cent samples annually. Most countries have a smaller population than Canada, and only two are now larger than the USA. Formidable obstacles impede the uses of these labor force surveys for rolling samples. First, they are based on overlapping samples, and redesigning them to remove the overlap would increase the cost somewhat and also decrease the precision of estimates of change over time (see later for further discussion). Second, rolling samples need to be spread over the population, whereas labor force surveys are typically confined to primary sampling units (for example counties). Hence in the thinly populated rural areas the rolling samples would become somewhat more expensive. Actually, however, this greater travel confinement concerns only about one-quarter or one-third of the samples in the USA and Canada, because most of the samples come from 'self-representing' (metropolitan) areas, where the primary sampling units (PSUs) cover the entire stratum. In these the rolling samples need be only slightly more expensive.

In the Nordic countries, and in a few others, the situation is a little better, because good population registers can supply adequate basic counts of the population. There the pressures for complete counts from the rolling samples should be less, and perhaps the annual rolling samples will become the most important.

Among both the industrialized and the developing countries there are examples of periodic surveys being operated with reasonable success. Any of these can be converted to rolling samples and some probably will be in the future. These can then serve as examples to others.

Rolling samples can be cumulated from periodic samples when these are explicitly *designed* to cover the entire population. For example, 12 monthly or 52 weekly samples with sampling rates of $1/F$ each can be rolled into annual samples of $12/F$ or $52/F$. The cumulated NCHS samples are confined into primary and secondary sampling units, and hence miss the definition of rolling samples.

Rolling censuses denote special cases of rolling samples. Rolling censuses denote a combined (joint) design of F separate (non-overlapping) periodic samples, each a probability sample with a fraction of $f = 1/F$ over the entire population, so designed that the cumulation of F periods yields a detailed census of the whole (changing) population with $f = F/F = 1$. Because the population is changing and moving, the census is defined as the mean over the F periods. The design should also ensure that intermediate cumulations of $k < F$ periods should yield rolling samples with $f = k/F$ and with (geographical, administrative) details intermediate between those based on 1 or F periods.

A good example is a monthly sample with $1/F = 1/120$ cumulated in 10 years to decennial rolling censuses. Twelve consecutive samples would yield a 1/10 annual rolling sample and this would compare with census samples of 1/10; and 60 would yield quinquennial samples of $f = 1/2$. Quarterly rolling samples of $3/120 = 1/40$ would also be useful.

Perhaps even better than monthly samples would be weekly samples of 1/520 which would combine to $13/520 = 1/40$ quarterly samples, to $52/520 = 1/10$ annual rolling samples and complete decennial rolling censuses.

The names rolling samples and censuses were mine, and I prefer them, and they have gained modest acceptance. A specific application may be adapted by the US Bureau of Census for 2000 and beyond, as 'continuous measurements' (Alexander 1993).

Rolling samples facilitate joint satisfaction of three criteria: spatial representation, temporal representation, and richness of data. Good administrative registers, where available, can yield spatial and temporal representation, but not rich data. Annual sample censuses (micro censuses) would also have these features, but they would be too expensive. Decennial censuses have census samples (5, 10, or 20 per cent) for relatively low additional cost for richer data, but they lack timeliness. Monthly surveys, such as the CPS in the USA, must sacrifice spatial detail. Rolling samples can yield annual data (and other periods in which those three criteria are compromised flexibly) with richer data and much spatial detail. The flexibility can be further increased with asymmetrical cumulations (p. 134).

Strategies for variations over time and space

1. Sampling of time for census of space: decennial census

2. Sampling of space for census (?) of time: labor force surveys, NHIS

3. Sampling and cumulating over both time and space: rolling census averaging: rolling censuses

4. Administrative registers with census of both space and time, but only for basic data. Nordic countries

Fritz Scheuren wrote for rolling censuses that 'In fact, Kish seems to be advocating what might be called a *paradigm shift* in census-taking' (Kish 1990). These generous remarks may be correct, because the concepts of averaging variations over time, though often used in practice, are unfamiliar in theory. Philosophically the justification for temporal aggregation resembles that for spatial aggregation. The obstacles are psychological, rooted in familiarity and tradition. People, including many statisticians, *imagine* that they know how to project census data for a day or a year forward for 10 to 15 years of their use. Actually those projections may have huge errors; for example, much greater than those due to the famous 'undercoverage' of censuses (Panel on Small-Area Estimates of Population and Income 1980). Similarly, people, including statisticians and economists, accept the results of a 'typical' week to represent a month, but month after month they must apologize for some vagaries due to weather, or a holiday, or some other hazard.

Pragmatically, we accept and use successfully many cumulative data. Among retrospective data are the 'children ever borne' over fertile spans of 30 years; also they are used for data on serious diseases, education, marital history, etc. Interviews of sample surveys and censuses also aggregate yearly farm production, income, purchases of large durable goods, etc. Also, cumulating rare items and rare elements from periodic surveys is useful (Kish 1965, 11.4). The National Health Interview Surveys (NCHS 1958) may be the best known example of cumulations from periodic samples, consisting of weekly samples of about 1000 households, cumulating into yearly samples of 52 000 households many diverse diseases, each of which is relatively rare. For some rare diseases several years can also be cumulated. These surveys are not 'rolling samples', because they are confined to one set of sampling units (counties etc.). The earliest cumulation I found is for samples of California in 1952 (Mooney 1956), and it was also used later (Kish *et al.* 1961) and then proposed as a method (Kish 1965, section 12.5D].

SAMPLE OVERLAPS

As noted earlier, a formidable obstacle impeding the use of labor force surveys for rolling samples is that they are based on large proportions of overlapping samples;

for example in the USA only 1/8 of the sample is brand new each month; in Canada only 1/6. These large overlaps are used partly because they reduce the variances for comparisons across periods. These comparisons are (arbitrarily) prespecified in the design; these are for monthly and yearly comparisons in the USA, quarterly in others, and only yearly in some. The gains in variances differ between statistics and are mostly modest, and many of these statistical advantages can also be had with much smaller overlaps (say 1/4), especially with weighted estimators (Kish 1965, section 12.4). Furthermore, the gains depend on correlations between periods for the variables, and the correlations for (un)employment are low, whereas the large correlations for some variables (members of the labor force, education), are not very meaningful. However, there is a second and more important advantage to overlaps: the interview in the first wave (month) is more expensive than the later waves. The re-interviews are cheaper, because the identification and the cooperation of the household has already been gained in the first interview. The reduction in cost may be considerable when re-interviews are by telephone, but the first contacts need personal visits.

To understand these advantages more fully, the reader may consult the large though scattered literature on periodic and repeated surveys and some basic treatments (Cochran 1977, sections 12.9–12.12; Kish 1965, sections 12.4–12.6, 1987, Ch. 6]. Nevertheless a few words may be useful here. The labor force surveys typically use partially overlapping area segments. In the USA the CPS uses a complex rotation in which only 1/8 of the segments are new, and $P = 7/8$ are reinterviews (with nearest months and years). In other countries the overlaps may be 3/4 or 1/2, but not smaller. The overlaps reduce the variances of estimates of net changes $(\bar{y}_{t+1} - \bar{y}_t)$ roughly by the factor $1 - PR$, where P is the proportion overlap and R the correlation between the two periods for the variable. This factor varies from a value of 1 for no overlap of $P = 0$, to $1 - R$ for complete overlap of $P = 1$, which is not used for periodic samples, though it has been used for two periods. 'Optimal' weighting formulae can yield considerably greater reductions of the variances and such gains can be had with overlaps as low as 1/3 or 1/4. Surprisingly, with proper weighting it is also possible to reduce the variances of 'current' means $\bar{y}_t$. The tradeoff is that for *sums* of two statistics across periods the variances are increased, by $1 + PR$ for two periods and by $1 + (J - 1) PR$ for the mean of J periods; but these increases can be reduced also by proper weighting (Kish 1965; Cochran 1977).

However, all these reductions for differences (and increases for cumulations) depend on the size of the correlations (mostly positive) R between periods, but these vary greatly between variables, and often they are small. R may be high for variables like education, occupation, and income for salaried employees, but not for unemployment between months, quarters, and years, nor for infectious diseases, etc. Furthermore the correlations are reduced by interviewing errors, by movers from/into segments in overlapping designs. For panels of individuals the values of R are higher, but panels also have other formidable advantages; and a panel can be combined with a nonoverlapping sample in a 'split-panel design' (SPD; see p. 135). Table 3 summarizes the discussion in this section.

Table 3 Purposes and designs for periodic samples (Kish 1987, Table 6.2)

Purpose	Designs	Rotation scheme
A. Current levels	A. Partial overlaps $0 < P < 1$	$abd - cde - efg^1$
B. Cumulations	B. Non-overlaps $P = 0$	$aaa - bbb - ccc$
C. Net changes (means)	C. Complete overlaps $P = 1$	$aaa - aaa - aad^2$
D. Gross changes (individual)	D. Panels	Same elements
E. Multipurpose, time series	E. Combinations, SPD	
	F. Master frames	

[1] In the scheme depicted, one-third of the sampling units (e.g. housing units), stay in the sample for two consecutive periods.

[2] Here there is complete sample overlap of sampling units (e.g. housing units) but not necessarily of elements (e.g. people).

ASYMMETRICAL CUMULATIONS

This topic may serve to best distinguish the rational statistical designs that rolling samples can offer, from the traditional designs that pass for 'common sense'. However, I want to emphasize that asymmetrical cumulation (AC) does not depend on rolling samples, and can be applied to other sample designs, and I proposed AC in Australia separately from it (Kish 1986). I refer mainly to the strategy of balancing of the biases of obsolescent data due to temporal changes against sampling errors. Take for example the justly famous Current Population Surveys of the USA, with monthly samples of about 60 000 households, and twice as many adult persons. Many judge that sample too large because its sampling precision is swamped by structural, temporal, non-sampling errors, due to the vagaries of the weather, or the calendar, or other haphazard factors that appear in its monthly news releases. On the contrary, for the statistics of important small domains the sampling variability is much too great for reliable statistics. Small domains may be either geographical/administrative, such as a state, or 'cross-classes', such as the Black teenage girls and boys in the labor force. Sampling variability of the statistics for these small domains is even greater for the many differences between domain statistics, which are most commonly needed. This is a general problem with applications in many countries and in many subjects (Kish 1986).

The same periodic surveys must serve both for overall (national) statistics and for domain statistics. Asymmetrical cumulations can best satisfy both needs: frequent (monthly) statistics for the total (national) statistics, but less frequent (quarterly or annual) statistics for smaller domains (such as states and large cities), and still less frequent statistics for smaller domains (for example smaller cities). And for these multipurpose aims, rolling samples serve best.

Three main reasons should lead to asymmetrical cumulations: (1) The principal divisions of most countries tend to vary greatly in size, with ranges of 50 or even 100 to 1; for example the states of the USA and Australia, the provinces of Canada and China. Similar variations also exist for other social organizations like firms, universities, and hospitals. (2) Below the level of the principal divisions, statistics are also wanted for their subdivisions, for example counties, districts, etc. which are much smaller and more numerous. (3) Cumulations are often needed for rare items which can be of three kinds (Kish 1965, 11.4).

This topic needs exploration with models that specify the factors of variation due to temporal and spatial and domain sources. The models would serve best if accompanied with the parameters of specific empirical situations. I feel confident that technical articles on these topics will appear in the future.

I need to explain the terms and concepts of *domains*, for those who may not be familiar with them, because they are basic to survey statistics (Kish 1987, section 2.3). *Subclasses* in samples represent *domains*, which are subdivisions of the population. These subdivisions may be *design domains*, especially geographical/ administrative regions, also states and counties, for which separate samples have been planned, designed, and selected. On the other hand, they may be *crossclasses* that cut across the sample designs, across strata, and across sampling units; the sample sizes of these crossclasses depend on random selections and become variable. Most subclasses tend to be of this kind: age, sex, socioeconomic classes, behaviors, attitudes, etc. (Kish 1987, section 2.3). The design-domain/ crossclass dichotomy must also be cross cut by a division due to size, because not all 'subnational' samples can be treated similarly in practice. Most samples yield useful statistics for major domains, such as major regions, but not always for minor domains, such as the 50 states of the USA. And data for 'mini domains' such as the 3000 counties of the USA are beyond the reach of most surveys.

PANELS, SPLIT PANEL DESIGNS (SPD) AND OTHER MODIFICATIONS OF ROLLING SAMPLES

Panels have nothing to do with censuses, but a great deal with the use of overlapping samples for periodic surveys. Panels denote samples in which the same elements (persons, families, households) are measured on two or more occasions for the purpose of obtaining *individual* changes. From the mean of these individual changes the net, mean population change can be estimated. However, from the net changes of means we cannot estimate (directly) the gross change of individuals. This contrast of population/element changes has been variously denoted by individual/mean, or gross/net, or micro/macro, or internal/external changes.

Only panels can reveal the gross changes behind the net change generally (exceptions can be found with strong models or with cross-sectional surveys that obtain accurate retrospective data) (Kish 1987, sections 6.2D, 6.4, 6.5). Many reasons are known and discussed frequently concerning the need of panel data in government statistics (Boruch and Pearson 1988; Kasperzyk *et al.* 1989). The periodic labor force surveys fail to yield it, because the samples are rotated, and also because households and people change and move from the overlapping segments. There is no serious attempt made to recognize and find the sampled individuals between periods.

'*Split panel designs*' (SPD) may be added to rolling samples, as I have proposed (Kish 1987, 1990). This would displace partial overlaps with two samples, a panel *p* plus independent rolling samples *a, b, c, d* . . . Thus the combined sample will consist of *pa–pb–pc–pd* etc. This SPD has two critical advantages over the classical partial overlaps. First, it provides true *panels* of elements (for example persons or households), which are missing for the moving elements of mere overlaps, but panels involve following the movers. They uniquely yield most valuable statistics, which mere overlapping samples of sampling units (for example segments, PSUs) fail to yield. Efforts to convert overlapping segments into panels have not been found practically feasible. Second, in SPD the correlations are present for all periods, not only for the pairs designed (arbitrarily) in the classical symmetrical designs. Often the most desirable comparisons are not foreseen in the design, hence the benefits of correlations are absent for them.

Possible modifications of rolling samples

1. Overlaps between samples. Separated from rolling samples?

2. SPD (Split panel design). Panels and overlaps for all periods

3. Oversampling some small domains

4. Undersampling some expensive domains

5. Weighting, for example moving averages to favor recent data

6. Over (under) sampling for some periods

7. Synthetic estimation for small areas and periods (Platek *et al.* 1987)

ON THE FUTURE OF CENSUSES

Decennial complete censuses of the population have been a great invention, which have made great advances in this century, and especially since 1943, and in several dimensions: (1) They have been adopted by almost all countries, under the guidance of The United Nations Statistical Office. (2) The quantity and depth of census data have been greatly enriched, especially with the use of 'census samples'. (3) The quality of census data has been improved, sometimes with the use of quality checks (census validation surveys). (4) Modern computers have facilitated the efficiency, speed, and variety of computations and presentations of data.

These advances have been obscured by the avalanche of bad news in the media: (1) In some countries, some decennial censuses have been hindered, and even canceled in a few cases, by opposition from ethnic and social groups (see Chapter 8). (2) Increasing mobility of the population, 'not-at-home'-ness, willful non-compliance and refusals, 'anomie' of individuals have contributed both to lower coverages and to higher costs of census taking. (3) Higher labor costs surprisingly seem to have overcome the efficiencies of new machines and methods.

Meanwhile there have been increasing demands on the censuses of many countries for data as bases for distribution of resources, for the allocation of federal funds to states (provinces) and even to counties (districts). Furthermore, there are increasing needs and demands for greater timeliness than the decennial censuses can provide. These needs should lead to future uses of population registers for simple population counts for those countries, such as the Nordic countries, that can provide them. For other purposes and other countries, rolling samples and especially annual samples seem to me the best answer. This is a personal statement and prediction.

Permit me to quote sadly from a recent *Royal Statistical Society Editorial* 'Coverage of the Great Britain Census of Population and Housing'. 'One might expect current official population estimates for Scotland and for England and Wales to be based on the 1991 census. This is not the case: a population age and sex structure based on updating the 1981 census is used instead. This unprecedented decision is due to large deficits in 1991 census output which are concentrated in specific subgroups, but not precisely quantifiable, . . . updating the 1981 census with estimates of subsequent births, deaths and international migration was far more likely to reflect the true population than the figures derived from the census, imputation and the CVS: thus the lamentable but justified substitution . . . Perhaps the most important direct use of population estimates in Britain is in the distribution of resources to subnational areas . . . A single accepted set of population estimates for areas smaller than local authority and health districts has not yet been achieved.' (Royal Statistical Society 1994).

I am not a specialist, and especially not a legal expert on the Census of the US. The US Constitution's Article 1 Section 3 states: 'The actual enumeration shall be made . . . within every subsequent term of ten years, in such a manner as they (the Congress) shall by law direct.' Some believe that this mandates a decennial complete count of persons every ten years; some don't, and some don't know – including myself. Speaking statistically rather than legally, I believe that the obsolescence and other deficiencies of our censuses should lead in the near future to registers for simple counts and to rolling samples and annual reports for most other reeds.

FUTURE NEEDS AND DIRECTIONS

This will necessarily be a personal, subjective statement, which may justify the personal references that reflect my own interests.

1. *Periodic surveys* and censuses have been traditional in official, government statistics, but only lately are they becoming more widespread in academic and even commercial research. Recognition of the worth of periodic survey data facilitates obtaining from agencies and foundations the much greater financial support that periodic surveys need. However, appropriate methods of statistical analyses need to be further developed, because the methods of survey sampling deal largely with single cross-sectional surveys plus some useful extensions to the differences of two surveys. There exists also econometric literature for time series, but these are

mostly for complete populations rather than survey samples, with a few notable exceptions.

2. *Cumulations* of survey data from rolling samples should become a stimulating subject for the statistical analysis of survey data. In a sense, most survey data represent cumulations; for example annual income cumulates variable income over 52 weeks for many; 'children ever borne' a lifetime of fertility; and all national averages cumulate over diverse regions and districts and over diverse domains (Kish 1994). However, these simple aggregations have not dealt with the problems of cumulating over populations that are changing, especially over a 10-year period. The optimal final estimates for $\bar{y}_{t+k}$, when this is based on k periods will present interesting problems that are functions of sample sizes and also of population parameters.

3. *Small-area (domain) statistics* have received much deserved attention since 1970, when I first became interested (Purcell and Kish 1979; Platek *et al.* 1987). This, of course, is of the utmost interest, because the purpose of both rolling samples and of decennial censuses is to provide better statistics for small domains, since even moderate sized samples are usually adequate for national and large domain estimates.

4. *Multipurpose design* needs and is bound to attract much more attention in the future. Now a wide gap exists between survey sampling methods focused on single estimators and actual practice in most surveys that must serve many diverse objectives to be useful and efficient (Kish 1988).

5. *Multipopulation and multinational survey designs* need targeted attention and methodological development. They are becoming increasingly recognized as both important and feasible. Aggregating such spatially separated samples presents problems that somewhat resemble in some aspects those of combining rolling samples from separate periods (Kish 1994).

In making these lists I may have committed some mistakes by including problems for which adequate selections are now available; or contrariwise, problems for which no reasonable solutions are feasible. Even more likely, I must have omitted to list other interesting problems for which adequate solutions are both needed and feasible.

REFERENCES

Alexander, C. H. (1993). A continuous measurement alternative for the U.S. Census, *Report to USBC* (also presented to the 1993 meeting of the American Statistical Association).

Boruch, R. F. and Pearson, R. W. (1988) Assessing the quality of longitudinal surveys. *Evaluation Review*, **12**, 3–58.

Cochran, W. G. (1977) *Sampling techniques*, 3rd ed. Wiley, New York.

Farley, R. (1995) *State of the Union: America in the '80s*. Russell Sage, New York.

Hansen, M. and Hurwitz, W. N. (1946). Sampling methods applied to census work. In *U.S. Bureau of the Census, the history, operations and organization of the Bureau of Census*, pp. 83–94. Government Printing Office, Washington, DC.

Hansen, M. H., Hurwitz, W. N., and Madow, W. G. (1953). *Sample survey methods and theory*, vol. I. Wiley, New York.

Hauser, P. M. (1942). Proposed annual census of the population. *Journal of the American Statistical Association*, **37**, 81–8.

Kasperzyk, D., Duncan, G., Kalton, G., and Singh, M.P. (ed.) (1989) *Panel surveys*. Wiley, New York.

Kish, L. (1965). *Survey sampling*. Wiley, New York.

Kish, L. (1979*a*). Samples and censuses. *International Statistical Review*, **47**, 99–109.

Kish, L. (1979*b*). Rotating samples instead of censuses. *Asian and Pacific Census Forum*, **6**, 1–2, 12–13.

Kish, L. (1981). *Using cumulated rolling samples*, publication 80–52810. US Government Printing Office, Washington, DC 52810; 78 pages.

Kish, L. (1983). Data collection for details over space and time. In *Statistical methods and the improvement of data quality*, (ed. T. Wright), pp. 73–84. Academic, New York.

Kish, L. (1986). Timing of surveys for public policy. *Australian Journal of Statistics* 1–12.

Kish, L. (1987). *Statistical research design*, Ch. 6. Wiley, New York.

Kish, L. (1988) Multipurpose sample design. *Survey Methodology*, **14**, 19–32.

Kish, L. (1990). Rolling samples and censuses. *Survey Methodology*, **16**, 63–79.

Kish, L. (1994). Multipurpose survey design. *International Statistical Review*, **62**, 167–186.

Kish, L. and Verma, V. (1983). Censuses plus samples: combined uses and designs. *Bulletin of the International Statistical Institute*, **50**, 66–82.

Kish, L., Lovejoy, W., and Rackow, P. (1961). A multistage probability sample for continuous traffic surveys. *Proceedings of the Social Statistics Section, American Statistical Association*, 227–30.

Mooney, H. W. (1956). *Methodology in two California health surveys*, US Public Health Monograph No. 70.

Moser, C. A. and Kalton, G. (1971). *Survey methods in social investigation*. Heinemann Educational, London.

National Center for Health Statistics (NCHS) (1958). Statistical design of the Health Household Interview Survey. *Public Health Services*, 584–A2, 15–18.

Panel on Small-Area Estimates of Population and Income (1980) *Estimating population and income of small areas*. National Academy Press, Washington DC.

Platek, R., Rao, J. N. K., Sarndal, C. E., and Singh, M. P. (1987). *Small area statistics*. Wiley, New York.

Purcell, N. and Kish, L. (1979). Estimation for small domains. *Biometrics*, **35**, 365–84.

Royal Statistical Society (1994). Editorial. *Journal of the Royal Statistical Society A*, **157**, 313–16.

Scheuren, F., Alvey, W., and Kilss, B. (1990). Paradigm shifts: the integration of administrative records and surveys. *Proceedings of the Survey Research Section of the American Statistical Association*.

US Bureau of Census (USBC) (1978). *The Current Population Survey: design and methodology*, technical paper 40.

8 Numbering the people: issues of accuracy, privacy and open government

PHILIP REDFERN

INTRODUCTION

The title 'Numbering the people' may be interpreted in two ways. It could mean counting the people by taking a census; alternatively it could mean assigning to each citizen a personal number to distinguish him or her from other citizens – the citizens' names and their numbers would be listed in a register held by the number-issuing authority. In this century personal names have increasingly been supplemented by personal numbers in order to correct for the imprecision and unreliability of names. These two interpretations of my title are closely related and I shall examine both of them.

Many census historians start from the Biblical censuses, and I shall follow their lead. In *Today's English Version* of the Bible, the Book of Numbers begins:

On the first day of the second month in the second year after the people of Israel left Egypt, the LORD spoke to Moses . . . He said 'You and Aaron are to take a census of the people of Israel by clans and families. List the names of all the men twenty years old or older who are fit for military service' . . . Moses and Aaron called together the whole community on the first day of the second month and registered all the people by clans and families. The names of all the men twenty years old or older were recorded and counted, as the LORD had commanded.

Thus, the Biblical census embodied many of the basic ideas underlying both today's censuses and population registers. Note that the time taken to prepare the Biblical census was measured in hours, not the years needed for a census today!

My own interest in these topics began in the late 1960s when, as a civil servant, I worked on a study into the case for issuing a *single* personal number – a Multi-purpose Personal Number – to each citizen of the United Kingdom. The single number would replace the confusing variety of personal numbers employed in different administrative programs, whose use was patchy because the citizen had difficulty in recalling the different numbers. The study ended abruptly by Ministerial decree on the morning of December 3, 1969, to enable the Lord Chancellor to announce that same afternoon (in reply to a question) that no study was being made! That was the first of four occasions that I recall when the government machine (Whitehall) stifled open discussion of this topic.

I gained a new perspective in the 1970s and early 1980s when I was involved in the design and implementation of UK censuses of population. It was during that period, in the summer of 1979, that we at the Office of Population Censuses and Surveys in London had the good fortune of a sabbatical visit from Richard Savage. He brought to our discussions his own experiences gained as a member of the National Research Council's committee that had advised the Bureau of the Census.

Later, I made a study on behalf of the European Community into the different census methodologies adopted by 15 countries in Europe and North America (Redfern 1987). The study showed that conventional censuses have important merits but, increasingly, demerits concerning cost, doubts on public acceptability, undercount and obsolescence of the results. Undercount may be symptom of a malaise in society, and overt hostility to the census certainly is: they may reflect alienation of some sections of the community, or perhaps the citizenry's doubts about the government's motives and openness. To my mind, less than whole-hearted public participation in the conventional census is the greatest threat to its future, and indeed led The Netherlands to totally abandon this instrument.

My study of the Nordic countries introduced me to the Administrative Record Census, or register-based census, most fully developed in Denmark. In this method, the details of an individual conventionally entered on a census questionnaire are replaced by equivalent data extracted from administrative registers, the data being linked together through a multipurpose personal number. That approach would be feasible, it seemed, only in a country with the appropriate administrative infrastructure: namely, personal numbers held in a population register that also recorded each person's current address (place of residence). (Here and in the remainder of this chapter I use the term 'personal number' to mean a multipurpose personal number.) The administrative record census avoids most of the serious demerits of the conventional census, but has its own weaknesses including the fact that some 'census topics' do not appear in any register. The Nordic system of personal numbers and population registers has other statistical merits: more accurate and up-to-date statistics of local populations and an enhanced tool for longitudinal and epidemiological studies.

The basic design of censuses in the United States and Canada has remained conventional. But both countries have been at the forefront in developing new census methodologies and in studying undercount. They have also developed record linkage techniques and applied them widely for both administrative and statistical purposes, though not as yet in order to attempt an administrative record census. The linkage mechanism used has often been the Social Security Number (SSN) in the US or the Social Insurance Number (SIN) in Canada. These numbers serve as *de facto* multipurpose personal numbers despite official denials of any such purpose. But, unlike the systems in the Nordic and Benelux countries, the registers that record the issue of the SSN/SIN do not hold current addresses.

In my study for the European Community I considered whether the demerits of the conventional census might become so grave that more countries would adopt the administrative record census. Experience of conventional censuses in the years since the study was published have not been reassuring. Thus, costs continue to escalate amid Treasury concerns. There was substantial public opposition to the census in the Federal Republic of Germany planned for 1983 but taken in 1987. Public response has been worse than before in the US 1990 census and the UK 1991 census. And demand persists for more up-to-date local statistics than a decennial (or quinquennial) census can provide. But what can a country do to harness its administrative records for census purposes if it has no well-oiled system of personal numbers (to link the records reliably) and current addresses (to provide accurate geographical analysis)?

In my tours of Europe and North America, I had been particularly impressed by the statistical possibilities offered by personal numbers. But of course the discipline of supplying the number on request is accepted by the public – one might say suffered by the public – because the number serves important administrative tasks like tax and healthcare and in some cases is used in the private sector too. The statistical uses of personal numbers are a spin-off from a system serving administrative ends; statistical needs alone could not possibly justify introducing such a system of numbers. But why is it that, in order to manage their public services, the Nordic and Benelux countries have the infrastructure of personal numbers held in a central register with current addresses, while the United States and Canada use the social security numbers held in a central register *without* current addresses, and yet others like Germany and the UK seem to get by without any (multipurpose) personal numbers whether *de jure* or *de facto*? The explanation is *not* that the different countries provide significantly different ranges of public services.

This led me to examine the administrative case for and against personal numbers and population registers, a topic that had previously been studied in the UK rather intermittently (Mallet 1917; Lindop 1978). In summary, the case 'for' is that a person's name is a *weak* identifier, and that appending the number to the name ensures *precise* identification in administrative records and hence greater record accuracy. Later I give a rough measure of the increase in accuracy. Among the principal dividends from this accuracy are more justice in society and more effective administration. Sweden recognized the potential benefits and became the first country to introduce personal numbers nearly half a century ago in 1947 – before the advent of computers; they were building on a system of population registers that the parish clergy had maintained since the seventeenth century.

The case always made against personal numbers is that they facilitate the creation of dossiers (through record linkage) and give more power to the State at the expense of the individual: Big Brother. The dramatic growth in computer capabilities seen in recent years underlines the perceived threat. Privacy Commissioners in Canada and Europe warn of the dangers of the 'surveillance society'. However, the facts and arguments seems to me to refute the case made by the privacy lobby for two reasons. First, we have the evidence from countries that have used personal numbers for a quarter of a century or more. Their citizens have not suffered a serious loss of privacy and do not live in a surveillance society. The world would have heard more cries for help if that had happened. The threat to privacy has been greatly exaggerated. Second, rational analysis shows that precise identification through personal numbers *protects* personal privacy. Or, put the other way round, lack of precise identification involves risks to privacy as a result of wrongful administrative action or impersonation, as I shall explain later. This finding confounds the conventional wisdom.

But people do not always act rationally, particularly when they are not given the facts. Nor do governments. People do not like to think of themselves as mere ciphers in government databanks; and politicians like to be seen to be protecting privacy – whether or not eschewing personal numbers does in reality do that. There is need for study of all the issues surrounding personal numbers. More openness in government would encourage such studies to proceed, would promote public debate and participation, and at the same time lessen the public's suspicions that personal numbers serve an overbearing State.

The following sections of this chapter develop these themes in more depth.

CENSUSES OF THE CONVENTIONAL KIND

Censuses of population in their modern form go back two centuries to the first US census in 1790 and the first UK census in 1801. The distinctive feature of the census is that it provides statistics for each of the myriad small groups within the country – groups usually defined by geography such as the residents of each community or city block. The statistics are needed for monitoring and planning. In the United States, the decennial census is underpinned by the Constitutional requirement that seats in the House of Representatives be apportioned between the States on the basis of population, and by the need for specified statistics for electoral redistricting within each State. The general case for the census was put succinctly by Savage (1982): 'An open society must have an accurate view of itself.' No one has seriously challenged the need for a census. The question therefore turns to its design. Sample surveys alone are no substitute because of the error margins attaching to estimates for small groups of people.

In the last 50 years the methodology of the conventional census has been greatly improved through techniques like optical reading, sampling (for topics for which sampling error is tolerable) and computer editing. Despite that, the approach is being challenged because of the four demerits listed earlier: cost, doubts on public acceptability, undercount and obsolescence of the results.

Census costs are heavy because of the high labour content, including the peaking of manpower in the census cycle and the resulting burden of training, and the use of sophisticated equipment. In terms of constant 1990 dollars, the US 1960 census cost about $0.5 billion and the 1990 census $2.6 billion, a fivefold increase, while the cost per housing unit rose from $10 to $25 (that is, by a factor of 2.5) (National Research Council 1993, p.9). Rising costs have been a significant factor in European moves to use already existing administrative records as a source of census data in place of questionnaires, so saving the cost of the field enumeration.

Users frequently complain that census statistics are out of date because of the substantial time needed for processing and, more importantly, the infrequency of the conventional census (every tenth year or, in a few countries like Canada, every fifth year). That too is a reason for considering administrative records as a data source, because, in principle, such records can be tapped as often as they are updated.

It is on the two remaining interrelated demerits that I want to concentrate. In my view, a continuing future for the conventional census depends on sustaining the public acceptability of the operation and securing a very high level of valid response. Changes in our political, social and economic environments have had a profound impact on people and their attitudes, and made the census task more difficult. Lifestyles have become more complex, informal, urbanized and mobile – in terms of family and household ties, work patterns (including more self-employment and part-time employment) and residence (including more second homes) – though these trends in society also pose problems for the register-based census. People are more difficult to contact: often absent from home, or secure behind physical or electronic barriers. They are more ready to question or rebuff the census-takers (or the government, seen as the hand behind the census). They may resent the burden of form-filling, see the census as an invasion of privacy, or feel that government already holds data now being demanded afresh. They may wish to rebel against authority or may have reasons for wanting to be excluded from the record (for example, if they are illegal immigrants). Or, as Savage (1982) put it:

An individual has little to gain by being counted or responding accurately in a census. The benefits are primarily to groups, including the entire community.

These are some of the influences that lead to undercount and particularly to differential undercount between various groups within society. The mobile young, ethnic minorities and the under-privileged are among those most likely to be missed from the census. Reports on the 1990 US census speak of deteriorating public cooperation as shown by the decline in the proportion of questionnaires that were mailed back without follow-up, from 78 per cent in 1970 to 65 per cent in 1990 (National Research Council 1993, pp. 7, 9). A report on the 1990 census by the General Accounting Office (1992) has the ominous sub-title '1990 results show need for fundamental reform'; and it records a comment by the Bureau of the Census that society has changed dramatically over the last 20 years (p. 8).

Census agencies therefore face major statistical and public relations problems. The first is to devise programs to maximize census coverage. The second is to measure the undercount (strictly *net* undercount, the difference between gross undercount and gross overcount), with an analysis at least by sex, age, region and ethnic group. The third is to carry the estimates of undercount into the final census results for small areas and small groups ('adjustment') if that is technically and politically feasible.

Because the census enumeration attempts to cover everybody, it is a singularly difficult task to estimate how many people have been missed. In some countries, few checks are made on coverage; the census results may be regarded as virtually unimpeachable. By contrast, intense efforts have been made in North America to measure undercount. The Reverse Record Check developed in Canada seems to me to be one of the most rigorous approaches. The method starts by constructing a sample of individuals who, *prima facie*, might be expected to appear in the current census – let us call this year x. This is done by aggregating three subsamples: a sample of individuals recorded in the previous census in year $(x - 5)$, a sample of births and immigrants in the intercensal quinquennium $(x - 5, x)$ drawn from administrative records, and a sample of individuals *missed* from the census in year $(x - 5)$ as revealed in that year's reverse record check. A current address for each member of the sample is traced from administrative sources wherever practicable; and, if the person is not found in the census records either at that address or at an address noted earlier (for example, the address recorded in the previous census), an attempt is made to trace and interview the person to find out whether he might have been enumerated elsewhere. The result gives a measure of gross undercount. But, as with all 'micro' methods that involve tracing, matching or interviewing, an element of uncertainty attaches to the results because some individuals cannot be traced, matched or interviewed. Gross undercount was estimated to be 2.0 per cent in 1971, 1976 and 1981, increasing to 3.2 per cent in both 1986 and 1991. Gross overcount, estimated at about 0.5 per cent in 1991, has to be deducted. For a country with a highly professional census organization and, I would think, fewer problems of race and inner-city deprivation than the US or UK, these results give pause for thought. Can statisticians be satisfied with an instrument that under the relatively favourable conditions of Canada in 1991 undercounted by 3 per cent overall, and by 8 per cent for men aged 20–24, 7 per cent for men 25–34 and 6 per cent for women 20–24? And will the undercount be held at current levels in the future, or improve, or worsen?

These last questions lead into the basic question: what accuracy is needed from the census? Given a relationship between census cost and accuracy, an answer might, in principle, be given by cost–benefit analysis (see, for example, Spencer 1980). In practice, census agencies have aimed to improve on, or at least maintain, previous levels of undercount or of differential undercount between major population groups.

Both 'micro' and 'macro' methods of measuring undercount have been employed in the United States. The principal micro method, the post-enumeration survey (PES), is a re-survey of a sample of the population – usually people living in a sample of areas – the results of which are matched against the census records. This provides an estimate of the numbers erroneously included in the census (gross overcount) and a basis for estimating numbers missed from the census (gross undercount). For the latter, a count is made of the numbers in the sample population who appear both in the census and the PES (say n_1), in the PES but not the census (n_2), and in the census but not the PES (n_3). Then, on the analogy of the wildlife capture–recapture model, the number in the sample population missed from *both* the census and the PES may be estimated as $n_4 = n_2 \times n_3/n_1$, and the factor for grossing up the census results is $(n_1 + n_2 + n_3 + n_4)/(n_1 + n_3)$, provided certain assumptions are valid. The assumptions are, first, that the probability of being recorded in the census is the same for each person in the population, and likewise the probability of being recorded in the PES is the same for each person in the population (the *homogeneity* assumption); and, second, that the probability of a person being recorded in the PES is *independent* of whether he or she was recorded in the census. In practice the calculations are carried out for strata of persons (defined by geographical location, sex, age, ethnic category, place size and owner/renter status) within which the assumptions might be more tenable. None the less, the existence of a group of people who, because of their residential situation or desire to evade the authorities, are missed both by the census and the PES is seen to undermine the assumptions and to lead to a downward bias in the PES estimate of undercount; this has been called 'correlation bias' (see, for example, Citro and Cohen 1985). Extensive analyses of the PES that followed the 1990 US census (National Research Council 1995, pp.96–8) yielded a figure for net undercount of 1.6 per cent overall, but 4.6 per cent for Blacks and 0.7 per cent for non-hispanic Whites.

In the macro approach to measuring net undercount known as *demographic analysis*, the US census counts at national level are compared, by sex, age and race, with estimates from independent sources – namely, enrolments in Medicare for those aged 65 and over, annual figures of births, deaths and migration, and figures from previous censuses for some age groups under 65 (adjusted for undercount in those censuses). But uncertainties in some of these components, especially the annual figures of migration, cast doubts on the resulting estimates of net undercount. And, in the absence of reliable statistics of internal migration, demographic analysis is useless for estimating undercount at the State or small-area level. A critique of demographic analysis was made by Savage (1980); he questioned a method that involves the *replacement* of the census counts by figures from independent sources rather than the *modification* (that is, adjustment) of those counts. Using demographic analysis, the Bureau of the Census estimates that net undercount was 1.2 per cent in 1980 and 1.8 per cent in 1990; and that in 1990 the differential between the net undercount rates for Blacks and non-Blacks was 4.4 per cent, the highest value recorded since estimates were first made in 1940 (National Research Council 1995, pp.30–5). These results are broadly in line with those from the 1990 PES.

Concerns about undercount in the US census, and about the resulting loss of population-related funding suffered by some cities and States, were reflected in the many law suits that they brought against the Bureau of the Census after the 1970 and 1980 censuses. This led to intense debate in the 1980s on the policy arguments for, and the technical feasibility of, adjustment to correct for net undercount not only at national level but also at State and lower geographical levels. Bias in the PES estimates of undercount was seen as a serious obstacle to achieving this. By spring 1987, the Bureau of the Census had concluded that adjustment of the 1990 census results by means of a PES would be feasible and would lead to results that were generally more accurate. It planned accordingly. But the professionals lost control of events when, first, politicians and then the courts intervened.

In the fall of 1987, the Secretary of Commerce, responsible for the Bureau of the Census, rejected the Bureau's recommendation and decided that no adjustment should be made to the 1990 census results. He cited weaknesses and uncertainties in the adjustment process, and added:

If we change the counts by a computerized, statistical process, we abandon a two hundred year tradition of how we actually count people.

His decision was twice challenged in the courts, in 1988 and 1991. The plaintiffs were a number of cities and States, including New York City and New York State.

The United States District Court concluded that the plaintiffs had made a powerful case in favor of adjustment. But it ruled that the Secretary's decision not to adjust was not 'so beyond the pale of reason as to be arbitary or capricious', and that the decision should therefore stand. In 1994 the case went to the United States Court of Appeals. It concluded that the differential undercount in the census between racial and ethnic groups jeopardized the citizen's fundamental right to equal protection; it dismissed the lower court's findings because the arbitrary-and-capricious criterion that had been used was inappropriate in this situation; and it held that a decision not to adjust could not be upheld unless shown to be essential to the achievement of a legitimate governmental objective. The story continues.

This chequered history illustrates the uncertainties and dangers when statistics become entangled with politics and the law. I know of no instance where that kind of case has been taken to law in the UK. Nor am I aware of any instance in which UK politicians have rejected professional advice in an area which is so obviously the domain of the professional statistician (but then such instances might not come to my or public notice because open government has hardly reached the UK's shores!). Later, I give another example – from Germany – of the wide-ranging impact that the law can have on statistics.

Currently, the debate on the design of the US census in 2000 focuses on the notion that virtually all the census results should integrate the counts, imputations and statistical estimates (in particular of undercount), that is, they would *include* what hitherto has been described as adjustment. This is the 'single-number census'. For further discussion see Bureau of the Census (1992), Mulry and Spencer (1993), Zaslavsky (1993) and National Research Council (1994, pp. 21–3, 105–28; 1995, pp. 96–101).

In the UK the principal method of measuring undercount in post-war censuses up to 1981 had been the post-enumeration survey. The low figures of net undercount that this yielded – 0.4 per cent in 1981 – led UK statisticians to believe that their censuses missed fewer people than North American censuses did. However, no allowance had been made for the downward bias in the PES. And, in 1991, the census count (plus an allowance for undercount of 0.5 per cent based on a PES) fell so far short of what had been expected (which had been based on the 1981 census results 'rolled forward' to 1991 by reference to subsequent births, deaths and migration) that a change had to be made in the method of measuring undercount: demographic analysis took the place of the PES. The official estimate of net undercount in the 1991 census is 2.2 per cent. But I believe this figure needs to be reviewed because it is based on the 1981 PES results and on questionable estimates of migration in the decennium 1981–91.

There was little overt public opposition to the 1991 census in the UK, but it is widely surmised that many people tried to evade the census because they believed – wrongly in fact – that names recorded in the census would be carried into the registers used for collecting the Community Charge (or 'Poll Tax'), an unpopular personal tax rescinded in 1993. Discounting this special factor, the upward trend in the level of undercount in the UK census raises doubts in my mind about the long-term viability of the conventional census mechanism.

There is an even more worrying feature of censuses than the levels of undercount experienced in North America and the UK. The census impinges on every household at a particular point in time once every five or ten years. William Kruskal has described it as a 'national ceremony', and, providing the census organisers can catch such a patriotic mood, I would be among the last to decry it. But if a sizeable minority of the people is antagonistic towards the census – possibly as a way of expressing general opposition to the government – the census may face disaster. And the media can be relied on to publicize resistance to the census, both at home and worldwide.

Something like that happened to the most recent census in the Federal Republic of Germany. Two months before it was due to be taken in April 1983, a strident boycott campaign erupted in the press and television. The protests centred on privacy and confidentiality, including the use of census data to correct the local population registers (a practice followed in previous censuses and explained on the census form); but for some people the protests were simply anti-authority. The census was postponed by the Federal Constitutional Court after a case had been brought by private individuals who claimed that the census violated their constitutional rights.

In December 1983 the Court made rulings that have wide implications for the census and for all federal statistics in Germany. The rulings deserve to be summarized here because they illustrate how law which is aimed at data protection can have a severe impact on statistical practice. The Court recognized the individual's right to exercise control over the disclosure and use of information relating to himself or herself. It expressed strong reservations on a 'combined survey' (such as the planned 1983 census) which would collect information to serve both statistical and administrative ends. These objectives tended to be incompatible and 'highly disconcerting for the individual citizen'; and so, the Court argued, separate collection instruments should be employed. The Court laid down the principle that the methods used to collect information should represent the least burden on respondents and the least intrusion into their privacy. Thus, a sample survey was more acceptable than a 100 per cent survey, and voluntary response to a survey was more acceptable than obligatory response. Failure to have regard to this could invalidate a survey. The Court accepted the case for a compulsory census of conventional design after examining whether there was a more acceptable alternative. It rejected a register-based census along Danish lines which, the Court claimed, would mean that 'the individual citizen's entire personality would be registered and catalogued' (see Werner and Südfeld 1986). One might question whether the Court had over-emphasized the impact on privacy of properly conducted statistical operations, at the expense of other societal values served by statistics.

The census in Germany was finally taken in May 1987 with stricter rules on confidentiality – in particular census data could not be used to correct population registers. Despite this unpromising background, the non-response rate was less than 1 per cent according to the Federal Statistical Office. Overt refusals were fewer than non-contacts; and in some cases data taken from local population registers provided a substitute for missing demographic data.

More than a decade before this unnerving experience, the Dutch census of 1971 had run into difficulties. There was then no general law on data protection in The

Netherlands, and the period leading up to census day was marked by public debate on automation, registers and privacy. Action groups opposed to the census sprang up, and their case was helped by the fact that the questionnaire took the form of punched cards in which, for technical reasons, serial numbers had been pre-punched. Some 2.5 per cent of the population did not cooperate in the census and there were many open refusals especially in the big cities. Following a poor response to a voluntary pilot test in 1979, the Dutch census of 1981 was cancelled, and no further population census is planned. The resulting gap in statistical information is being partially filled by demographic data from the municipal population registers and by enhanced sample surveys; but statistics for small areas on topics like economic activity are no longer available (Vliegen and Van de Stadt 1988).

We face future uncertainties about social cohesion and the relationship between State and citizen, of which the experiences in Germany and The Netherlands are illustrations. Future censuses of a conventional kind may therefore face not just an undercount at levels previously experienced but the risk of disaster. Who would have foreseen the German débâcle?

THE ADMINISTRATIVE RECORD CENSUS

The administrative record census, or register-based census, draws its data not from questionnaires completed by the public but from the personal records held by various administrative agencies. A necessary condition is that each person in the records is precisely identified, so that all the records relating to a particular person can be linked. This is achieved in the Nordic countries (Denmark, Finland, Iceland, Norway and Sweden) by use of a multipurpose personal number. I shall now outline the Nordic system of administrative records and describe how it can be harnessed to statistical ends. I shall postpone until the next section a discussion of the wider arguments for and against setting up such a system. That order of treatment corresponds with my personal odyssey.

The essentials of the Nordic system are as follows:

1. Each person, at birth or immigration, is given a unique and unchanging personal number, which he or she uses, with name, in dealings with public agencies. Each person then has a precise written identity: the *multipurpose personal number*, also called a Universal Personal Identifier or a Personal Identification Number (PIN). It embodies a check digit or digits.

2. The set of personal numbers is held in a *central population register* which also contains each person's name, date of birth, sex, current address (place of residence) and minimal additional content. The register might possibly include a person's place of birth, marital status and nationality. Local population registers are also maintained; these are simply extracts from the central population register.

3. The citizen has a duty to report changes to the registry, in particular changes of permanent address. Much of the other updating information comes from registration of births, marriages and deaths.

4. A public agency can access the population register to check the written identities (including personal numbers) of its clients and potential clients, and to obtain details of changes of name or address, deaths, etc.

Two features of the system must be underlined. First, the agencies dealing with different functions like personal tax and healthcare maintain their own separate systems of personal records, though they rely on the central population register for checking the identifying data and addresses of all their clients. Second, the quality of the population register is high both because of the checks made by public agencies and because citizens are prompt to notify the registry of any changes (they have no need to notify other agencies). Comparison with conventional census enumerations have shown error levels in the register (that is, persons missed or registered at the wrong address, and emigrants not deleted) of a fraction of 1 per cent (Redfern 1989, section 2.2). This quality of the central population register in turn ensures that the identifying information and addresses in the records of public agencies are accurate – to a degree which could not possibly be achieved if the different agencies' records were 'free-standing', that is, wholly uncoordinated.

Though the primary objectives of this Nordic infrastructure are administrative, its statistical merits are well recognized. The presence of the personal numbers as identifiers in agencies' records facilitates the linkages needed for longitudinal and epidemiological studies. The central population register itself yields statistics of local populations analysed by the few factors recorded in the register. Thus, Johansson (1987) reported that the Swedish end-of-year population statistics analysed by sex, age and region were available in the fifth week of the new year with error levels 'normally far below 1 per 1,000'. That is a far cry from the situation in the UK and US. There, because of the weakness of statistics of migration (both external and internal), rather little confidence can be placed in the statistics of local populations except at census time – and even then the statistics are slow to emerge and have to be qualified because of undercount.

It was the Danes who in 1981 took the bold step of an administrative record census to replace a conventional census enumeration. Finland took the same step in 1990. The Danish census draws its data not only from registers holding personal data but also from other registers constructed mainly for administrative purposes, including the central register of buildings and dwellings and the central register of enterprises and establishments (Thygesen 1983). The new approach avoids most of the serious objections to the conventional census but, instead, introduces its own problems. Let us start with the problems avoided. First, the register-based census costs less than a conventional census because it substitutes for the field enumeration the very much cheaper task of extracting data from existing registers. This merit is blunted if, as sometimes happens, a register has to be created solely for statistical purposes, for example a register of each person's educational achievements. Second, the register-based census can be taken frequently, say every year.

Third, because the coverage of the register-based census is defined by the central population register, undercount/overcount is a fraction of that of a conventional census. Fourth, there is no form-filling on Census Day, and so no national ceremony either to participate in or to rebel against.

The main technical limitation of the register-based census concerns the range of topics which can be included and their definitions. For some topics, it may be necessary to make an estimate by combining data from a number of administrative registers; occupation is estimated in this way in the Danish census. Other traditional census topics may not appear in any administrative register and so must be excluded from a register-based census; examples are ethnic origin and mode of travel to work. To add questions to an administrative form in order to meet solely statistical needs is unpopular both with administrators and respondents, and creates serious difficulty in maintaining the quality of response. For topics that do appear in registers, the definitions and the points of time to which the data relate will be those that are required for administration rather than statistics. Thus, income – not an easy topic in any survey – will conform to the definitions laid down for tax purposes, and these are liable to change abruptly.

Linking the records of the individuals who together form a household may also present problems in a register-based census – particularly if the household is defined as a group of people sharing common housekeeping. Moreover the statistician becomes dependent on the administrators' processing timetable. A criticism of a quite different kind is that the register-based census is carried out in secret by the government 'over the heads of the citizens'. Strong criticism on privacy grounds was made by the German Constitutional Court.

Sweden has essentially the same infrastructure of personal numbers as Denmark and might, like Denmark, have switched to a wholly register-based census in the early 1980s. The possibility was considered then, but rejected. It was only in 1995 that the decision was taken to set up a wholly register-based census in 2001, and, meanwhile, to abandon the usual quinquennial census in 1995.

However, a partial switch has already been made. Thus, every census in Sweden from 1970 through 1990 retained a questionnaire, but this asked only about topics not well covered by the registers. The questionnaires were mailed out to the names and addresses in the central population register, and the responses were linked to register data on other topics by means of the personal numbers which were pre-printed on the questionnaires. The 1990 questionnaire asked about aspects of economic activity, education, household composition and housing. In a technical sense, the Swedes chose the best of both worlds, maximizing the use of administrative data but still questioning the public on some topics. But they had another reason for adopting this approach: they were diffident about taking a census without public involvement. Sten Johansson (1987), then Director-General of Statistics, Sweden, put the point as follows:

. . . a population census has a ritual aspect in the life of a nation. . . . A population census is best achieved when participation is a well-understood and widely accepted civic duty. To be counted in the census is then a manifestation of citizenship, of being one in and of the nation. Everyone's participation is desired, rich or poor, regardless of any other merit than being.

No one is counted for more than anyone else. This, of course, is part of the rhetoric of the official statistician. If it is only empty rhetoric to the citizens at large, if it cannot be said and understood at least implicitly, because of apathy, cynicism, distrust or fear among the citizenry, then the census is in trouble. A nation that cannot carry out a census for these reasons is a nation in trouble in other ways as well.

There are echoes here of the census problems that struck in The Netherlands and Germany.

The Nordic-style administrative record census relies on the infrastructure of personal numbers in a central population register that also holds current addresses. Some countries, like the UK and Germany, lack this infrastructure. Canada and the United States are at a half-way point: they have a *de facto* personal number, the social security number, but there is considerable room for improvement in the number's integrity. Thus, the SSN/SIN has generally not been issued at birth (though issue at birth is now becoming the norm in the US), and duplicates have crept into the system. Moreover the registers that record the issue of the SSN/SIN do not hold current addresses. Addresses are of course held by various agencies, but they may not be up to date and in some cases may be mailing addresses.

Despite the limitations in the materials at their disposal, statisticians in North America have been attracted to the concept of an administrative record census. An early study in the US was made by Alvey and Scheuren (1982). More recently, Sailer *et al.* (1993) made a provisional estimate of the 1990 US population by sex and age-group, using only a wide range of Internal Revenue Service records 'unduplicated' by means of the SSN. Their estimate represented 96 per cent of the 1990 census-based count (which included an adjustment of 4 million for census undercount), with most of the 4 per cent difference concentrated in the under-25 age-groups.

The Bureau of the Census has ruled out the feasibility of conducting the 2000 census by using only administrative records. But it sees administrative records as an under-utilised resource in conventional census-taking, which could give more operational support; could extend coverage by, for example, providing some data for persons not responding to, or missed from, the conventional enumeration; and could help in coverage evaluation. For these purposes, matching capabilities need to be developed using the SSN, name, address or other keys. The possibility is being studied of setting up a continuously-updated register of residential addresses for use in the Bureau's censuses and surveys. Looking beyond the 2000 census, a Panel from the National Research Council's Committee on National Statistics (1994, pp. 148–159) has argued that the Census Bureau should treat the possibility of a 2010 administrative record census as a live option, to be explored and evaluated during the current decennial census cycle through tests in selected areas. Further, and rather less encouraging, discussion on the feasibility of an administrative record census and of a national register appears in the report of a parallel Panel from the National Research Council's Committee on National Statistics (1995, pp. 59–68).

Work on generating small area statistics from administrative sources has proceeded rather further in Statistics Canada. An annual Taxfiler Family File has been constructed for years from 1982, comprising taxfilers and their dependents linked into families using the SIN as the main linking mechanism. The aim has been to follow census definitions for family structure and family income. For the year 1992 the file covered 96 per cent of the Canadian population (the latter estimated from the 1991 census with adjustment for undercount) – only marginally less than the 97 per cent coverage of the census itself (Leyes and Eisl-Culkin 1994). Using data from successive annual Taxfiler Family Files, Statistics Canada is also creating a longitudinal file in respect of a 1 per cent sample of individual taxfilers.

The Canadian work has demonstrated how data systems based on administrative sources are vulnerable to changes in legislation. Thus, from 1993, the family allowances and tax credits previously available for all child dependents have been replaced by Child Tax Benefits directed at lower income families. Consequently, the tax system no longer provides information on the dependent children of higher income families. The intention is to impute these missing children by linking the Taxfiler Family File with birth records.

Statistics Canada recognizes that the Taxfiler Family File is weak in topic content compared with the long-form census questionnaire. A study made in 1983 (Statistics Canada 1983) reached conclusions that still guide policy:

Administrative records represent a data resource complementary to the Census of Population and not a replacement for it . . . A high priority of many federal departments is cross-classified data involving various combinations of occupation, industry, income and education. There is currently no administrative source that can supply this range of data.

Statistics Canada has, indeed, adopted a more negative attitude to an administrative record census than some outside observers. Thus, the authors of the report 'Private lives and public policies' wrote (National Research Council and Social Science Research Council 1993):

Statistics Canada has an active and successful program to produce current demographic data from administrative sources, and it is possible that this system may at some time take the place of the more traditional kind of population census.

PERSONAL NUMBERS

The preceding section has shown that a system of names, personal numbers and current addresses held in a central population register yields major statistical dividends, one of which is the possibility of an administrative record census. But, both in countries that have this system and in those still without it, there are strongly articulated concerns that personal privacy is threatened by automation and record linkage. These concerns disabled the conventional censuses in The Netherlands and Germany. In 1986, a sociological and longitudinal research project at the University of Stockholm, involving a cohort of 15000 children born in 1953 hit the newspaper headlines, and the furore led to a temporary increase in non-response to Statistics Sweden's sample surveys (Statistics Sweden 1987). Public reactions of these kinds are an obstacle to introducing an infrastructure of personal numbers where none exists, as in the UK and Germany, or to upgrading an existing structure. In the Federal Republic of Germany proposals for personal numbers were put before Parliament in 1971, but lapsed following criticisms that the numbers would threaten privacy and might infringe constitutional rights. To consider the privacy issue we have to ask why personal numbers are introduced and what purposes they serve.

I begin by going back in time to consider the development of personal names. Throughout history an individual has been identified primarily by name. In England until the Norman Conquest in 1066, first names like Richard or Philip usually sufficed, but during the eleventh to sixteenth centuries hereditary surnames were appended by most families. Wealthier families did this to denote their hereditary entitlement to property, and lesser families to help distinguish one person from another. Society has been comfortable with this method of naming and it met the needs for hundreds of years. But does it still meet the needs, or do we have to move to a 'Stage 3'?

In fact, name is a weak identifier because many names are replicated in a population; moreover a person's name may change, for example at marriage or through usage, quite apart from instances of deception. The fact that a person's name is meaningful and can be spoken can result in many mutations of the name. Thus Christopher Richards Davis may record his name, or be recorded, as Christopher Richard Davies or Chris Davis or many other variants. The weakness becomes more serious as schemes of administration expand from the local community to the whole nation, and can be only partially resolved by supplementing names with items like date of birth.

Supplementing a name with a personal number which is invariant and unique to the individual brings precision to their written identity. It is an almost inevitable Stage 3, swept along by information technology and the demands of management science. A personal number is purely functional; it lacks meaning (unless designed to indicate, for example, date of birth); and it cannot be spoken. The number is indeed colourless, cold and clinical – qualities that are needed to resist the temptation to change and embroider. The individual has no incentive to give a wrong personal number unless he intends to deceive, though errors will of course occur. A quoted number is either right or wrong and, unlike a name, cannot be 'perhaps right'. Moreover, most people have little difficulty in recalling a single personal number.

The positive value of a personal number in promoting accuracy is not often recognized by privacy advocates. But Alan Westin (1970), in his seminal book 'Privacy and freedom' which warned of the threat to privacy from unregulated data processing, wrote:

If data collection and data processing of information about individuals is to be truly accurate and extended into new areas, it is essential that every person in the country have one distinctive identifying number. Unless this is so, errors will be made . . .

At this point the statistician must try to put some quantitative measure on the gains in accuracy when a Nordic-style infrastructure of personal numbers is introduced: that is, gains in terms of more precise identification in agencies' records and more up-to-date addresses. That is no easy task. Lack of precision in the records takes several forms: as duplication of some people through a failure to match items of data relating to the same person; as records that are garbled when data relating to two different people are improperly matched; as a failure to capture some records; as out-of-date or inaccurate names and addresses; and as a failure to remove records of people who have died or emigrated. In the context of a census of population, these imprecisions may be gauged by the levels of under-count and overcount. In an electoral register they may be gauged by the number of people entitled to vote who have been missed, and by the extent of 'deadwood' in the register, such as people who have moved out of the district or died.

Actual figures to put on these kinds of imprecision are elusive. I have already discussed measures of undercount and overcount in censuses of population in North America and Europe. There are figures of undercoverage in the electoral registers for a few countries in Europe. Overcoverage in the UK's National Health Service Central Register is a sizeable 5 per cent. In the United States, the Congress's Office of Technology Assessment (OTA) asked a wide range of agencies about the completeness and accuracy of their record systems, but reported that very few agencies made any measurement (OTA 1986, pp. 5, 26, 105). From this limited evidence I conclude that, when records are unsupported by Nordic-style personal numbers, coverage errors of undercount and overcount (which I take as a proxy measure of imprecision) are several percentage points, typically 2 to 5 per cent. In the Nordic countries, on the other hand, coverage errors are a fraction of 1 per cent, rarely as much as 0.5 per cent (Redfern 1989), that is, of the order of a fifth or a tenth of the level found in countries that lack the Nordic system.

This striking difference reflects the fact that in the Nordic system there is little opportunity for creating false identities or false addresses, and no possibility of restricting notification of a change of name or address to just one or two selected agencies. Because all public agencies check their clients' identities and addresses against the population register, only the complete outlaw who avoids contact with all public agencies is able to evade the notice of the population registry. The quality of the central population register is mirrored in the quality of the agencies' records so far as personal identification and addresses are concerned. Moreover, agencies' records of some variables like income will be improved to the extent that precise identification is a deterrent to evasion and misreporting. But the levels of accuracy obtaining in the Nordic countries' registers may not be achievable in countries with a different political or social culture.

The benefits from a Nordic-style infrastructure of personal numbers fall under two main headings. First, the greater accuracy of public agencies' records helps to promote justice (or at least compliance with the law) by ensuring that burdens laid on citizens by law (such as taxes) are not evaded, and that rights (such as social security benefits) are exercised only by those entitled to them. Thus the system acts as a brake on crime and fraud. In addition, the system can give positive support to citizens by helping to trace and contact those who are (or seem to be) entitled to benefits (Thygesen 1989). Second, the greater accuracy of public agencies' records makes public administration more cost-effective: it reduces costs of administration; it increases the yield of taxes and reduces the overpayment of benefits; it helps in tracing patients due for a health check-up and people who are evading payments to support children and former spouses; it helps to curb illegal immigration; and so on. Better statistics are a by-product.

In the United States and Canada similar objectives underly the wide use of the social security number (the SSN and SIN). Thus, matching is a well established practice in the United States with the aim of detecting fraud, waste and abuse, and many examples are reported by the OTA (1986, pp. 38–46, 58–60, 67–77). The use of the SSN to curb illegal immigration has been argued by the General Accounting Office (1988). But the usefulness of the SSN/SIN for both administrative and statistical purposes is hampered by the weaknesses already referred to: in particular the registers that record the issue of the numbers do not hold continuously updated residential addresses. No doubt many would argue that an obligation to register every change of address is foreign to American culture – and indeed to British culture. But, without up-to-date addresses, how can agencies effectively administer programs, whether national or local?

This is perhaps the place to mention the French system of personal numbers, the social security numbers. They are issued at birth and are held in a central population register which does not carry current addresses; so the system's structure has similarities to the SSN/SIN systems. However, uses of the French numbers are rather severely circumscribed by the opinions delivered by the Commission Nationale de l'Informatique et des Libertés (CNIL), the body that advises the executive on data protection matters.

To set against the benefits of a system of personal numbers – with or without up-to-date addresses – are the concerns about personal privacy. The privacy lobby and the media speak of the threats from unregulated matching, dossiers and Orwell's *1984*. Privacy Commissioners have vigorously publicized the dangers and have been influential in limiting the uses of personal numbers; see, for example, the report of the Canadian Parliament's Standing Committee on Justice and Solicitor General (1987).

When I first started to write about personal numbers and population registers (for example Redfern 1989), I recognized the widespread worries about privacy but did not properly analyse the arguments deployed. However, after examining some of the statements made by Privacy Commissioners, I have come to feel that their warnings about '1984' have been built more on a tide of public emotion than on any study of the facts. Let me give two examples of their line. The Canadian Privacy Commissioner (1986), John Grace, wrote:

Computer-matching turns the traditional presumption of innocence into a presumption of guilt. In matching, even when there is no indication of wrongdoing, individuals are subject to high technology search and seizure. Once the principle of matching is accepted, a social force of unyielding and pervasive magnitude is put in place . . . Uncontrolled and general use of the Social Insurance Number establishes a *de facto* national identifier with all its ominous and de-humanizing implications.

David Flaherty, now Information and Privacy Commissioner in British Columbia, wrote (1989):

'Having a Personal Identification Number makes it almost impossible for anyone to escape total surveillance.'

To my mind, terms like 'total surveillance' and 'the surveillance society' are misused; they should more properly be applied to the activities of the former Nazi and Communist régimes.

The first rejoinder to the kind of rhetoric cited is that several countries have 25 years' experience of the Nordic system of personal numbers – Sweden nearly 50 years. Other countries have gone a considerable way in that direction, including the Benelux group, Canada and the United States. Some mistakes have been made by public agencies leading to limited 'privacy disasters' – for example, the much publicized case in the State of Massachusetts in 1982 (House Committee on Government Operations 1988). But there is little hard evidence that a 'surveillance society' has been instituted in any of these countries, thanks to legislation on data protection and freedom of information, to the responsible action of public agencies, and to a vigilant public.

That is not to deny that a vague unease is felt (and fanned) by sections of the community. But we should be wary of equating lobbyists' utterances with the general public's views. As a Panel of the National Research Council's Committee on Statistics says (1994, p. 144):

'The views expressed by data providers and the public in surveys do not always coincide with those of privacy advocates as reflected in congressional testimony, panel reports, and other public venues.'

The second rejoinder rests on the proposition that certain qualities go hand in hand: namely, precision of identities, accuracy in personal records, protection of data, and privacy. Personal privacy is best protected by a high level of accuracy in agencies' records and, in particular, accurate identification. For the citizen's privacy would be jeopardized if, as a result of weak identification, his healthcare or police record were to be incomplete (that is, not fully collated) or inaccessible, or were to be confounded with someone else's record; that could lead to wrongful administrative action – perhaps a wrong clinical decision or a wrong police action. Indeed, wrongful action, taken on the basis of inaccuracies in the data that an agency legitimately holds, is a *greater* invasion of privacy than the previous communication of those data to the agency. Again, a system of precise identification with its in-built checking facilities helps to protect against the risks of impersonation and the loss of privacy that that entails (examples of which are given by the UK Government (1988)).

The point can be put in other ways. The ability to match, far from being an insidious threat to privacy as claimed, is a necessary condition for assuring the integrity of a personal record when, as is usually the case, the record has been collated from source documents prepared at different times and places. The distinguished Canadian statistician Howard Newcombe (1981) gave the apt example of how, in his country, the SIN was essential for piecing together an individual's record in the National Dose Registry. Matching is also a powerful tool for detecting errors and inconsistencies in data.

The demand that personal data shall be 'adequate, accurate and, where necessary, kept up to date' is one of the basic principles for data protection, enshrined in legislation in many countries (Council of Europe 1981). The United States Privacy Act of 1974 requires agencies to 'maintain all records which are used by the agency in making any determination about any individual with such accuracy, relevance, timeliness, and completeness as is reasonably necessary to assure fairness to the individual in the determination'. Through this provision 'Congress has recognized the importance of record quality both to management efficiency and to the protection of individual rights' (OTA 1986, p.110). So how do Privacy Commissioners reconcile their duty to uphold such basic principles with their denunciation of a necessary instrument for their implementation, namely precise identification? – a question I put to the 1993 International Conference of Data Protection and Privacy Commissioners (Redfern 1994). I detected no clear response.

My conclusion is that protection of personal privacy requires the capability to match accurately and economically, which in turn demands a personal number and associated population register. I see that as a verity, supported both by rational analysis and empirical evidence – and indeed statistical measurement. But that is not to condone unregulated matching. Matching should be strictly regulated.

CONCLUDING REMARKS

The quest for accuracy has been a theme throughout this chapter: how to measure undercount/overcount in the census and, if practicable, adjust the census counts accordingly; and how to maximize the precision of personal identification and, in turn, the quality of public agencies' records.

A second theme has been privacy, and the relationship between citizen and State as reflected in the public's attitude to the census and to personal numbers. The citizens' worries about the census are essentially of the same kind as their worries about personal numbers. Are the government's holdings of personal data excessive? What are the intended uses of the data? Is the government able to protect the confidentiality of the data? In most European countries all these matters are, in principle, regulated by data protection legislation. The citizens' worries may range more widely. What are the government's motives for collecting and holding the data? Can the government be trusted? I shall return to this point in a moment.

There is one data protection principle that citizens *ought* to be worrying about, at least if the data serve administrative ends, but it does not feature in the privacy lobby's rhetoric. This is the principle that personal data held by agencies shall be accurate and, where necessary, kept up to date. Accuracy – in particular precise identification – should be demanded by the individual to ensure the integrity of his personal records; and thus to ensure that his privacy is not jeopardized by a wrongful administrative action stemming from faulty data, or by impersonation that better identity checks could prevent. And accuracy should be demanded by the bureaucracy in order to promote effective administration and provide reliable statistics. I gave a broad estimate to show how the accuracy of agencies' records in terms of identities and addresses is so markedly better in countries that identify each individual through a personal number than in countries that do not.

In addition, the bureaucracy should think hard about the vulnerability of its record systems (including the census) to damage from sections of the community who are apathetic or alienated, from those who promote campaigns of non-cooperation for whatever reason, and from those who engage in crime, fraud and impersonation. Here too a system of precise identification offers some remedy. The point may be put in a different way. If we reject precise identification through a personal number, we are supporting, or at least condoning, an 'à la carte society': a society in which a significant proportion (perhaps a few per cent) of the population are enabled to escape duties laid on them by law – such as the duty to report income for tax purposes, the duty to register as an elector and the duty to be counted in a census. Adherence to the rule of law is a touchstone of a mature democratic society; the à la carte society is a step towards anarchy.

If the benefits of precise identification, in terms of privacy and other societal values, are to be realized, the public will need to be better informed. Governments should give a lead here; and so should Privacy Commissioners to whom the public looks for independent advice. Sadly, neither are doing so. The spectre they see of '1984' has swept aside rational analysis, and their advice damages both privacy and the wider interests of the community.

If a system of personal numbers or a conventional census is to succeed – that is, work smoothly with minimum non-compliance and maximum accuracy – the citizenry needs confidence in the executive and assurance that there is no hidden agenda. Verhoef and Van de Kaa (1987) wrote that an effective register system 'requires a constructive, coherent and stable social and political climate'. Earlier I quoted Johansson's remarks in a similar vein in the context of a census. To secure the public's confidence, the executive must be accountable. It must display certain qualities: openness, encouraged perhaps by legislation on freedom of information; a willingness to listen, to discuss with other interests and to respond to their concerns; and a willingness to devolve and distribute power. The antithesis of this is the unaccountable government that is secretive, that acts without proper consultation and research, and that centralizes power. That model still flourishes today.

ACKNOWLEDGEMENTS

My analysis rests on information given me over the past decade from colleagues in many countries, to whom I express my thanks. In particular I am grateful to Joseph Knott of the US Bureau of the Census and John Leyes of Statistics Canada for up-to-date information on the North American scene.

REFERENCES

Alvey, W. and Scheuren, F. (1982). Background for an administrative record census. In *Proceedings of the 1982 meeting of the American Statistical Association, Social Statistics Section*, pp. 137–46.

Bureau of the Census (1992). *Assessment of accuracy of adjusted versus unadjusted 1990 census base for use in intercensal estimates*, Report of the Committee on Adjustment of Postcensal Estimates, 7 August 1992. Bureau of the Census, Washington DC.

Canadian Parliament's Standing Committee on Justice and Solicitor General (1987). *Open and shut: Enhancing the right to know and the right to privacy*, Report on the review of the Access to Information Act and the Privacy Act, esp. pp.44–6. Ottawa.

Canadian Privacy Commissioner (1986). *Annual report for 1985–6*, pp.7, 9. Ottawa.

Citro, C. F. and Cohen, M. L. (ed.) (1985). *The bicentennial census: new directions for methodology in 1990*, pp.139 *et seq*. National Academy Press, Washington DC.

Council of Europe (1981). *Convention for the protection of individuals with regard to automatic processing of personal data*. Council of Europe, Strasbourg.

Flaherty, D. H. (1989). *Protecting privacy in surveillance societies: the Federal Republic of Germany, Sweden, France, Canada and the United States*, p.406. University of North Carolina Press, Chapel Hill.

General Accounting Office (1988). *Immigration control: a new role for the social security card*. General Accounting Office, Washington DC.

General Accounting Office (1992). *Decennial census: 1990 results show need for fundamental reform*. General Accounting Office, Washington DC.

House Committee on Government Operations (1988). *Computer Matching and Privacy Protection Act of 1988*, Report 100–802, p. 6. Washington.

Johansson, S. (1987). Statistics based on administrative records as a substitute or valid alternative to a population census. Paper presented to the 1987 session of the International Statistical Institute, Tokyo.

Leyes, J. and Eisl-Culkin, J. (1994). Administrative social data in Canada: some results and some implications. *Proceedings of the 1994 meeting of the American Statistical Association*.

Lindop, Sir N. (chairman) (1978). *Report of the Committee on Data Protection*, Cmd. 7341, ch. 29. Her Majesty's Stationery Office, London.

Mallet, Sir B. (1917). The organisation of registration in its bearing on vital statistics. *Journal of the Royal Statistical Society*, **80**, 1–30.

Mulry, M. H. and Spencer, B. D. (1993). Accuracy of the 1990 census and undercount adjustments. *Journal of the American Statistical Association*, **88**, 1080–91.

National Research Council's Committee on National Statistics (1993). *Planning the decennial census: interim report of the Panel on Census Requirements in the Year 2000 and Beyond*. National Academy Press, Washington DC.

National Research Council's Committee on National Statistics (1994). *Counting people in the information age: report of the Panel to Evaluate Alternative Census Methods*. National Academy Press, Washington DC.

National Research Council's Committee on National Statistics (1995). *Modernizing the U.S. Census: report of the Panel on Census Requirements in the Year 2000 and Beyond*. National Academy Press, Washington DC.

National Research Council and Social Science Research Council (1993). *Private lives and public policies: report of the Panel on Confidentiality and Data Access*, p.213. National Academy Press, Washington DC.

Newcombe, H. B. (1981). Submission. In *Report of the Privacy Commissioner on the use of the Social Insurance Number*, pp. 55–76. Canadian Human Rights Commission, Ottawa.

Office of Technology Assessment (of Congress) (OTA) (1986). *Electronic record systems and individual privacy*. Washington DC.

Redfern, P. (1987). *A study on the future of the census of population: alternative approaches*, Eurostat Theme 3, series C. Office for Official Publications of the European Communities, Luxembourg.

Redfern, P. (1989). Population registers: some administrative and statistical pros and cons. *Journal of the Royal Statistical Society*, A, **152**, 1–41.

Redfern, P. (1994). Precise identification through a multi-purpose personal number protects privacy. *OUP International Journal of Law and Information Technology*, **1**, 305–23.

Sailer, P., Weber, M., and Yau, E. (1993). How well can IRS count the population? *Proceedings of the 1993 meeting of the American Statistical Association, Government Statistics Section*, pp. 138–42.

Savage, I. R. (1980). Modifying census counts. *Proceedings of the conference on census undercount, July 1980, Arlington, VA*, pp. 62–75. Bureau of the Census, Washington DC.

Savage, I. R. (1982). Who counts? *The American Statistician*, **36**, (3), part 1, 195–200.

Spencer, B. D. (1980) Benefit-cost analysis of data used to allocate funds. Springer, New York.

Statistics Canada (1983). *The use of administrative files as sources of statistical data in relation to the need for a census of population, March 9 1983*. Statistics Canada, Ottawa.

Statistics Sweden (1987). *Statistics and privacy: future access to data for official statistics – cooperation or distrust? Report from a conference in Stockholm, 24–26 June 1987*, esp. pp.i, 11–12. Statistics Sweden, Stockholm.

Thygesen, L. (1983). Methodological problems connected with a socio-demographic statistical system based on administrative records. Paper presented to the 1983 session of the International Statistical Institute in Madrid.

Thygesen, L. (1989). Contribution to the discussion on Redfern (1989). *Journal of the Royal Statistical Society*, A, **152**, 37.

UK Government (1988). *Registration: a modern service*, Cm. 531, para.6.17. Her Majesty's Stationery Office, London.

Verhoef, R. and Van de Kaa, D. J. (1987). Population registers and population statistics. *Population Index*, **53**, 633–42.

Vliegen, M. and Van de Stadt, H. (1988). Is a census still necessary? Experience and alternatives. *Netherlands Official Statistics*, **3**, (4), 27–34.

Werner, J. and Südfeld, E. (1986). Protection of privacy, automatic data processing and progress in statistical documentation in the Federal Republic of Germany. In *Protection of privacy, automatic data processing and progress in statistical documentation*, Eurostat Theme 9, series C, pp. 99–132. Office for Official Publications of the European Communities, Luxembourg.

Westin, A. F. (1970). *Privacy and freedom*, p.304. The Bodley Head, London.

Zaslavsky, A. M. (1993). Combining census, dual-system, and evaluation study data to estimate population shares. *Journal of the American Statistical Association*, **88**, 1092–105.

9 Surveying individuals with disabilities[1]

ALLAN R. SAMPSON

INTRODUCTION

Implementing, monitoring and funding national and local disability programs and legal mandates require meaningful and accurate statistics concerning individuals with disabilities. The 1990 Americans with Disabilities Act (ADA) which extended certain civil rights protections to individuals with disabilities was justified, in part, by disability data demonstrating substantial economic disadvantages towards individuals with disabilities. As McNeil (1991b) noted, 'national surveys consistently showed that two-thirds of the population with a work disability were without a job' and many of these individuals wanted employment. To monitor, now and in the future, the success, compliance, and costs of the ADA, we need disability data of the highest quality. Equally compelling as the ADA data needs, are the disability data requirements for the Social Security Administration, particularly the Disability Insurance Program and Medicaid; for the Veterans' Administration; and for state-level vocational rehabilitation programs. A broader description of programs that depend on disability data is given by Levine et al. (1990).

Clearly the primary disability statistic is the percentage of the US population with a disability. An examination of recent studies indicates a variety of estimates of this basic value. Based upon the 1990–1 panel from the Survey of Income and Program Participation (SIPP), McNeil (1993b) reports 19.4 per cent of the total 251.8 million US population have a disability, and 23.5 per cent of the 195.7 Americans aged 15 or older as having a disability. From the 1990 census data, we find that 12.0 per cent of the total 186.9 million population aged 16 or older, report a disability or limitation (McNeil 1993a). Pope and Tarlov (1991) in their report to the Institute of Medicine note 14 per cent of the entire US population as having a disabling condition affecting activities of daily living. As a comparison, the 1991 Statistics Canada Health and Activity Limitation Survey shows 15.5 per cent of the entire Canadian population with some level of disability, while among those aged 15 or older, the disability rate is 17.8 per cent (Statistics Canada 1992). Haber (1990) in reviewing earlier US data, reports various sources providing work disability rates ranging from 8.5 per cent to 17 per cent. The Appendix provides a schematic of some of these survey results.

1. Research supported by National Security Agency Grant #MDA904–95–H–1011.

Two important observations are in order. Firstly, the proportion of Americans with a disability is substantial. And secondly, the largest estimate is nearly twice as large as the smallest estimate for comparable age groupings.

The needs and uses for data on individuals with disabilities are clearly summarized by McNeil (1993*a*). He writes '. . . the primary purpose of a disability statistics program should be to monitor the extent to which all aspects of society are accessible to all members of society. The process of monitoring means we want to be able to document the current situation regarding accessibility, and to be able to describe, in the future, how the system has changed.' These thoughts are echoed by LaPlante (1991) who writes that proper disability data are 'crucial for services assessment and social planning'.

In this chapter we consider some selected issues concerning surveys about disability, beginning with a brief history. Dealing with the way in which surveyed disability rates seem to vary as they do, we are led to consider frameworks for disability concepts. We next focus on a number of important methodological facets concerning surveys for disability, and conclude with brief recommendations for further steps.

BRIEF HISTORY OF DISABILITY SURVEYS

Beginning with the 1970 Decennial Census, the US Bureau of the Census has included on their 'long forms', questions concerning disability. These forms are completed by approximately one out of every six individuals aged 16 or older. The two 1990 questions each consisted of two parts. These questions are given in the Appendix and a reproduction of the actual 1990 Census questions appears in McNeil (1993*a*, Attachment 1). A recent and more extensive survey was the 1990 and 1991 panels of the Survey of Income and Program Participation (SIPP) which included numerous questions concerning disability. Analyses of these data are presented by McNeil (1993*b*) in *Americans with Disabilities: 1991–92*. McNeil (1993*b*, Appendix C) provides a complete copy of these SIPP questions about disability. The previous such SIPP study was conducted in 1984 and summarized by the United States Bureau of the Census (1986). After the 1980 Census, a follow-up survey concerning individuals with disabilities was planned by the Census Bureau. The survey was pretested in Richmond, Virginia in 1979, but the complete survey was never funded.

The National Center for Health Statistics (NCHS) collects disability data in its National Health Interview Survey (NHIS), which is a long-running survey covering in excess of 100 000 people. Analyses of various years of the NHIS are given by LaPlante (1988, 1991) and in the chapter 'Magnitude and dimensions of disability' in *Disability in America* a volume edited by Pope and Tarlov (1991) for the Institute of Medicine. The NCHS also conducted the 1987 National Medical Expenditure Survey which included a variety of questions concerning disability. In addition, both the Social Security Administration and the Veteran's Administration conducted a number of disability surveys in the 1970s and 1980s.

The National Science Foundation conducts a biennial survey entitled the 'National Survey of Natural and Social Scientists and Engineers' which includes several multipart questions on disability. The most recent summary of these data is for 1991 (National Science Foundation 1992), with projected new analyses to be issued shortly.

Statistics Canada has been aggressively involved, since the early 1980s, in building a Canadian national database on disability. This involvement was directed by a 1981 report of the Special Parliamentary Committee on the Disabled and the Handicapped. Their first major disability survey was the Canadian Health and Disability Survey (CHDS) conducted in 1983–4, utilizing some of the material from the US Census disability pretest of 1979. The CHDS results are reported by Statistics Canada (1986). Subsequently, Statistics Canada has conducted two major Health and Activity Limitation Surveys (HALS), one in 1986 (see *Highlights: disabled persons in Canada*) and one in 1991 (see *Health activity limitations survey – 1991 user's guide*). Unfortunately, Statistics Canada is currently planning to reduce its disability data collection owing to fiscal constraints.

Two widely cited in-depth surveys were privately conducted by Louis Harris and Associates. One, for the International Center for the Disabled, dealt with self-perceptions and experiences in everyday life activities of individuals with disabilities (Louis Harris and Associates 1986). The second, conducted for the National Organization on Disability, dealt with what was needed to bring individuals with disabilities into the mainstream of political participation (Louis Harris and Associates 1987).

Further details concerning some of these surveys are provided in the Appendix. More complete histories of disability surveys are provided by Haber (1990), Pope and Tarlov (1991, Chapter 2), and Sampson *et al.* (1991).

FRAMEWORKS FOR CONCEPTUALIZING DISABILITY

To measure and survey disability, we obviously want to begin by understanding what is meant by disability. There is, however, no universal definition of disability, or its allied notions. Moreover, as Haber (1990) notes, 'it is not clear what a "universal" definition of disability is expected to be used for or what it is expected to include'.

Several paths have been taken towards formulations of definitions or, more generally, frameworks for conceptualizing disability. Two major approaches utilized to develop frameworks and classification schemes are the conceptual functional limitation framework (Nagi 1979) popular in the US, and the International Classification of Impairments, Disabilities and Handicaps (ICIDH) classification scheme developed by the World Health Organization (1980). A different type of approach is to use legislative definitions that are employed in federal programs. For instance, the Social Security Disability Insurance (SSDI) program considers a person to be disabled if they 'are unable to do any kind of work for which [they] are suited and [their] disability is expected to last for at least a year or to result in death'. The ADA uses a broader definition and considers an individual to have a disability if 'the person has (a) a physical or mental impairment that substantially limits one or more major life activities; (b) has a record of such an impairment; or (c) is regarded as having such an impairment'. Researchers allow themselves further freedoms in definitions of disability. For instance, Elkind (1990) argues that individuals with 'severely limited literacy' (about 7 per cent of the US adult population) should be considered as having a disability.

One of the substantial difficulties with programmatic or legislative definitions is their being subject to administrative and possibly judicial changes in definitions. On the one hand, there is social pressure to liberalize criteria to allow more individuals to be eligible for SSDI, and on the other hand, there is fiscal pressure to tighten criteria due to financial concerns about projected SSDI trust fund deficits. The ADA definition of disability will be refined by the courts. For example, under the ADA and its 'definition' of disability, the Civil Rights Division of the Department of Justice has protected against denial of dental treatment to people with HIV or AIDS, and has challenged state medical and bar licensing criteria that involve 'overly broad inquiries into psychological history' (Patrick 1994).

We mention two notions that should be considered in evaluating any framework or definition. One is to be aware that definitions used in long-running surveys or studies can subtly change in mid-course for a variety of reasons, several of which were considered above. The obvious goal is to maintain consistency of long-itudinal information. The second is to be cognizant of the human issues resulting from any definition concerning disability, in particular the sociological impact and ramifications that naming or labeling has upon individuals with a disability (Zola 1991). Zola argues that improper choices of definitions and survey wording can lead to stereotyping of individuals with disabilities and also to harmful internalization of such definitions by disabled persons. 'Disabled' and even 'differently abled' have socially replaced for good reason 'handicapped' or 'crippled'.

One of the two main approaches to a conceptual model concerning disability is given by Nagi (1979), about which McNeil (1993b, p.1) writes is 'perhaps the most important work in the area of a conceptual framework for disability'. Nagi (1979) separates the notions of pathology, impairment, limitations in function or capacity, and disability (see also Pope and Tarlov 1991, p.5). Pathology is a condition in which normal biological processes (Nagi is apparently using 'normal' in the second sense described by Kruskal and Stigler, Chapter 5 this volume) are disrupted and there is a mobilization of defenses. Pathology may result from many sources, for example trauma or degenerative disease processes. Impairment indicates a biological loss or abnormality. Impairments may be concurrent with pathologies and resultant of pathologies, or not necessarily related to pathology, for example a congenital defect. Not all impairments necessarily lead to functional limitations. For instance, certain muscle groups can compensate for particular muscle loss. An impairment-caused limitation in functional activity might be, for example, an inability to lift objects of moderate weight because of a lower back condition, or lack of visual acuity in certain lighting situations, due to some vision loss. Nagi (1979) then defines disability as 'a form of inability or limitation in performing roles and tasks expected of an individual within a social environment'. A warehouse worker might be viewed as disabled due to a functional limitation of not being able to lift as a result of impaired lower back function caused by a trauma.

Nagi's conceptualization lacks one further element and that is the interplay of the environment and the disability. The previously noted warehouse worker with an adaptive power assist device may be able to continue to satisfactorily perform the job.

Another conceptualization of disability is the ICIDH, which is more widely used internationally. The ICIDH uses a three-tiered classification approach: (1) impairment, (2) disability, and (3) handicap. Impairment is a loss or abnormality of function; disability is a restriction in normal activities due to impairment; and handicap is an individual's disadvantage as a result of a disability. In parallel to some standard disease classifications, the ICIDH permits up to four-digit codes for each of impairment, disability, and handicap. As with Nagi's framework, the issue of the role of the environment in providing obstacles, or on the other side support, is not discussed in the current version of the ICIDH. As a result of an international meeting in Canada in 1987, one possible revision of ICIDH's definition of handicap is: 'a handicap is the disruption of an individual's performance of life habits, taking into account age, sex, socio-cultural identity, resulting, on the one hand, from impairment or disabilities, and on the other, from obstacles attribu- table to environmental factors', (see *ICIDH International Network* 1989; Chamie 1990; and McNeil 1991*a*).

A recent blend of the Nagi and ICIDH frameworks was developed by the Committee on a National Agenda for the Prevention of Disabilities – a committee constituted by the Institute of Medicine of the National Academy of Sciences (see Pope and Tarlov 1991).

We conclude this section with several observations. The passage of the 1990 ADA recognizes the importance of environmental factors upon persons with disabilities and provides legal remedies. It is in this setting that it is natural to now re-examine the definitions of disability and handicap to account for environ- mental barriers. One provocative step in this direction is a suggestion by McNeil (1991*b*) towards a disability classification scheme that also allows for environ- mental barriers. The current classification schemes explicitly connect all notions of disability to the individual; McNeil's proposal, while having functional limitations tied to the individual, would have social and environmental barriers identified for their contributions towards creating a disability. Another concern is the fact that the US uses one scheme to approach measuring disability, and that a different scheme, the ICIDH, is broadly used internationally; this causes some incompar- ability in disability data between the US and elsewhere. This issue was addressed at the 1989 National Research Council (NRC) Workshop on Disability Statistics, where it was 'agreed that the ICIDH should be studied further [in the US] if only because of its great popularity abroad' (Levine *et al.* 1990). What becomes clear is that to develop meaningful statistical data for US and worldwide policy usage, we must further develop a well understood common language concerning disability, including its interplay with the environment.

ISSUES CONCERNING SURVEYING INDIVIDUALS ABOUT DISABILITY

Reliability and validity of responses to disability questions

As in all surveys, the provided response depends on many items, including the phraseology of the question, who is providing the responses for the surveyed individual, and the survey's purpose in so far as the purpose affects the respondent's attitude, or question construction, or sampling exclusions. These issues seem particularly germane in surveys concerning disability. Because the language of disability is complex, unless questions are highly specific, questionnaire items may have reliability and validity difficulties, even when the respondent is the target individual. The problem is made more difficult when others respond, for example for institutionalized individuals, children, or for those whose disability does not allow them to answer for themselves.

Haber (1990), in noting that '[work] disability prevalence . . . estimates range from a high of 17 per cent for the 1966 and 1978 SSA studies to a low of 8.5 per cent in the 1980 census' concludes that '[t]he data suggest that these variations . . . [are] closely related to the purposes for which the studies were done or the auspices under which they were conducted'. Data collected under the auspices of federal programs which provide economic and social support to individuals with disabilities need to be considered in that light. Survey results may be affected according to whether the program is of the type which benefits those who are unemployed or is of the type which provides encouragement to obtain employment.

Even for surveys for non-economic purposes, the rate of response concerning disability appears to depend on the context and purpose of the survey. One particular consideration is whether disability questions are asked in a general social survey or in a more focused health-related survey. In the context of the usage by Statistics Canada of screening questions based upon Activities of Daily Living (ADLs) and several general questions, Binder and Morin (1988) report evidence based upon four surveys that prevalence rates were higher for surveys when the screening questions only were asked, as compared to surveys that are '"loaded" in the sense there was a follow-up [health] survey conducted by the same interviewer who conducted the screen'. Binder and Morin also report that in the 1979 US Census pretest in Richmond, a lower prevalence of ADL limitations occurred when a following detailed questionnaire was given by the same interviewer immediately, as opposed to a detailed questionnaire being given later by another interviewer. It has been suggested by Furrie (1995) that the cause of this phenomenon is that individuals who are aware that answering positively to a screening question will cause an additional extensive health interview, will reply negatively to questions which are marginally true.

Based upon consideration of data about work disability, Haber (1990) notes a different phenomenon, in that 'one could reason that marginally disabled people are encouraged to identify themselves as disabled by more extensive questions'. He bases his speculation on the observation that 8.3 per cent of individuals aged 16–64 identify themselves in the 1980 Census as work disabled versus 11.1 per cent who so identify on the more in-depth 1980 post-censal Content Reinterview Survey (CRS). Utilizing what appears to be the corresponding type of data in McNeil (1993a, Attachment 7), we note (see Table 1(c)) the same phenomena in 1990, where the corresponding work disability rates are 7.7 per cent (Census) and 9.7 per cent (CRS). (We note that the 1990 Census work disability rates are based only upon those individuals also reinterviewed for the CRS, as is apparently the case for Haber's observations for 1980.) Although the CRS does contain disability questions in a more extensive questionnaire setting, the respondent's 'no' responses to disability questions will not shorten the survey completion time, as a 'no' response would do in the surveys considered by Binder and Morin. Thus, Haber's observations do not apparently contradict Binder and Morin's. We can perhaps explain Haber's observations as follows. The Census long form is typically completed by one member of the household replying for the others. On the other hand, the CRS is very often completed by the targeted individual. One might now speculate that the individual responding in the CRS might more often consider themselves as having a work disability than did the sole respondent for the household long form. The generalizability of this type of speculation is limited, in that the opposite phenomena occurs for the self-care limitation question. Examining again Attachment 7 from McNeil (1993a), we see that the Census/ CRS matched case data (see Table 1(b)) showed that 2.9 per cent of individuals aged 16–64 reported self-care restrictions in the 1990 Census and 1.3 per cent reported such on the CRS. For this question, the reported rates are higher under the Census than under further detailed CRS questioning. These observations, although preliminary in nature, suggest the need to understand which types of questions can cause relatively higher response rates in screening, and which can cause lower. We need also to consider this understanding in the context of household surveys, individual surveys, and surveys which go into more extensive questioning based upon earlier responses. Further research in these connections is clearly required.

Now let us consider the disability information from the CRS in further depth. As noted in the Appendix, there are two questions, 18 and 19, on the 1990 Census long form. Question 18 deals with work disability and Question 19 deals with mobility limitation and self-care limitations.

Shortly after each Census, the CRS, which contains the long-form questions, and others, is administered to a sample of households. In 1990 the CRS was primarily a computer generated telephone survey. In distinction to the long form where the head of household completes the survey, the CRS attempts to interview each individual covered in the long form. In 1990, approximately 90 per cent of the individuals in the CRS sample of households gave responses for themselves. The data from individuals in these sampled households is then matched to the Census long-form data, resulting in matched data in 1990 for approximately 18 000 people, aged 16 years and older. McNeil (1993a, Attachment 7) summarizes these 1990 matched pair data for mobility limitation, self-care limitation and work disability (Table 1).

Table 1 (a) Mobility limitation (ages 16–64) (McNeil 1993*a*)

		CRS		
		Yes	No	Total
1990	Yes	146	152	298
		(49.0%)	(51.0%)	
Census	No	155	14 194	14 349
		(1.1%)	(98.9%)	
	Total	301	14 346	14 647

Table 1 (b) Self-care limitation (Ages 16–64) (McNeil 1993*a*)

		CRS		
		Yes	No	Total
1990	Yes	69	346	415
		(16.6%)	(83.4%)	
Census	No	120	13 856	13 976
		(0.9%)	(99.1%)	
	Total	189	14 202	14 391

Table 1 (c) Work disability (ages 16–64) (McNeil 1993*a*)

		CRS		
		Yes	No	Total
1990	Yes	778	366	1144
		(68.0%)	(32.0%)	
Census	No	650	12 988	13 638
		(4.8%)	(95.2%)	
	Total	1428	13 354	14 782

First we note that the marginal rates of Table 1 are the values we used in the preceding discussion of why apparently different observations were made by Binder and Morin, and by Haber.

McNeil (1993*a*) focuses on the implications of the data of Table 1 upon reliability issues of the Census long-form disability questions. Complete reliability would be indicated by the off-diagonal elements being zero. In any survey/resurvey setting we clearly expect some off-diagonal entries. McNeil (1993*a*) expresses the most concern about the reliability of the self-care item noting that 'the number of persons who report "yes" in the census and "no" in the CRS is much larger than the number who reported "yes" in both the Census and CRS'. Additionally note that for this question, the proportion replying positively on the Census is much larger than the proportion on the CRS. This may be indicative of something more than reliability difficulties, in that the question may not be validly measuring the true degree of self-care limitation. Again, this must be seen in the likely context that the head of household completed the long form, and the individual the CRS. We also express some concern about the reliability of the mobility limitation question where either off-diagonal is slightly larger then the number reporting yes in both surveys.

Similar questions about the reliability and validity of questions concerning disability can be inferred from examination of some of the preliminary results of the 1991 Canadian HALS, where this survey design is a two-stage one. On the 1991 general Canadian census long form (given to approximately 20 per cent of the population) there are two multipart questions concerning activity limitations (see *HALS – 1991 Users Guide*, p. 9, or Table 2). Two groups are defined by their responses to these questions: the 'yes' group are those who respond positively to any of the questions, and the 'no' group who respond negatively to all the questions. For the second stage of HALS, Statistics Canada chooses random samples from each of the 'yes' group and from the 'no' group. Criteria based on the extensive questions of the HALS can categorize an individual as having or not having a disability. Approximate results from the 1991 HALS (*HALS – 1991 User's Guide*, p. 10) are given in Table 1. (The only first-stage results to which we have access currently are those for the 1986 HALS, where approximately 10 per cent of the 25.6 million Canadian population were in the 'yes' group (Denis *et al.* 1993).

Thus, approximately 20 per cent of the sampled respondents who replied yes to any of the four census questions were classified by HALS as not having a disability based upon an extensive set of disability questions. It is obviously not possible to compare these data directly with the Census/CRS results because of the differences in questions. The closest Census/CRS value to the HALS 20 per cent is for the work disability data (Table 1(c)), where among those replying yes to the Census, 32 per cent replied no on the CRS. The corresponding results for the mobility and self-care questions are harder to compare with HALS.

The other observation from Table 2 is that about 5 per cent of those who replied 'No' to all four questions on the Canadian census were subsequently classified by HALS as having a disability. This is quite comparable to the corresponding 5 per cent figure for work disability on the Census/CRS data (Table 1(c)) and higher than the approximately 1 per cent observed for mobility and self-care limitations in Tables 1(a) and 1(b).

These issues about reliability and validity of the disability questions on both the US and Canadian census long forms indicate why estimating rates of disabilities just from these questions can be problematic. Issues about the reliability and validity of the long-form questions were discussed prior to the 1990 US Census by a subgroup of the 1988 Workshop on the Demography of Scientists and Engineers with Disabilities. This subgroup expressed concern about the effects of forcing the responses to the disability questions to be 'yes' or 'no' (see Sampson *et al.* 1991, Section 3). Also it is

Table 2   HALS—1991 results (approx.)
(Household Survey only) (from HALS 1991 User's Guide)

		HALS disability criteria		
		Yes	No	
	'Yes' Group	28 000	7 000	35 000
		(80.0%)	(20.0%)	
Census	'No' Group	5 600	107 400	113 000
		(5.0%)	(95.0%)	

obvious that the awareness of reliability and validity problems motivated Statistics Canada to design HALS as a two-stage procedure (Dolson *et al.*).

Disability in the context of rare populations

In a national social survey, as we have noted a broad definition of disability yields typically a 10–15 per cent positive response. However, in more focused settings, where we are surveying, for instance, scientists and engineers with disabilities, disabled individuals in the province of Newfoundland, or individuals using wheelchairs, the target population can be viewed as a rare population. Kalton and Anderson (1986) and Sudman and Kalton (1986) discuss some general statistical issues concerning sampling for rare populations.

Kalton and Sudman (1991) note that lacking a pre-specified 'special list' which would include a high percentage of the target population, screening of the entire population on a large scale is most likely needed. As the reliability discussion of the preceding subsection indicates, in-depth questions of only those screened onto the list can be insufficient, and we also need to question some of the individuals screened out. The two-stage HALS is a good example of how to implement such an approach which will, in fact, yield estimates at the provincial level (*HALS 1991 – back-up tables, Provinces and Territories*). In the 1991 HALS, Statistics Canada sampled about 1.5 per cent of those screened into the 'Yes' group by the general Census, and sampled about 0.5 per cent of those not screened in, i.e. those in the 'No' group. In the 1986 HALS, of the estimated 3.2 million Canadians with disabilities, 2.0 million of the estimate is derived from the 'Yes' group sample, while 1.2 million of the estimate is derived from the 'No' group sample. The large-scale application of screening and follow-up of 'yes' and 'no' respondents is apparently fairly recent. Dolson *et al.* (1987) note the 1986 HALS was 'the first post-censal survey of its size in Canada'.

One of the goals of the National Science Foundation (NSF) is to develop strategies to attract individuals into the sciences and engineering professions and also to retain individuals working as scientists and engineers. One of NSF's views is that traditionally under-represented populations must be increasingly involved in these professions. In a 1992 NSF report, it is noted that '[t]he lack of reliable data on . . . disabled scientists and engineers makes it difficult to accurately compare their participation in these professions with their representation in the general work force'. It is thought that individuals with disabilities are, in fact, under-represented in science and engineering professions. However, little information is available to understand why such under-representation occurs and how to change it. Sampson *et al.* (1991) describe six recommendations arising from the Workshop on the Demography of Scientists and Engineers with Disabilities for the further study about individuals with disabilities and their roles in the sciences and engineering. For instance, one of these recommendations is to develop statistical models for examining why individuals with disabilities enter and leave the educational process for the sciences, and employment for the sciences.

There is one longitudinal NSF survey of 50 000–70 000 scientists and engineers that includes several short questions on disabilities. Kalton and Sudman (1991) note the difficulties with obtaining detailed disability data from this general survey which is limited in questionnaire size. To obtain further detailed information concerning individuals with disabilities in order to better meet NSF's goals, Kalton and Sudman (1991) recommend an approach like the HALS where this longitudinal survey and other related surveys could be used as screening surveys for a more in-depth follow-up survey.

Sudman (1991) has suggested another approach for obtaining data on scientists and engineers with disabilities by utilizing network sampling procedures. Network sampling, in general, requires that respondents, besides replying about themselves, to identify others in a specified *network*, for example social circle or colleagues, who have the surveyed characteristic. By utilizing estimates of the network size for each respondent, overall weighted estimates can be obtained. Two relatively recent papers discussing network sampling in rare populations are by Czaja *et al.* (1986) and Sudman *et al.* (1988). Birnbaum and Sirken (1965) were among the originators of network sampling. Sudman suggests a possible network sampling scheme for NSF which would require sampled scientists and engineers to identify those in their work group who are disabled. Besides the standard network sampling problem of obtaining for each respondent a reasonable estimate of the number of other scientists in their group or network, we are confronted with the difficult issue of not only what disability means, but now what is it in the eyes of a beholder. Additionally, we face the problems of hidden disabilities which can include such disabilities as epilepsy and diabetes.

Another singular population of concern in national surveys are disabled individuals living in institutions. These individuals can be administratively excluded from a survey, for instance, the US Survey of Income and Program Participation is a household survey; or can be the focus in a specialized survey, for instance, the HALS Institutions Survey. Haber (1990) discusses the difficulties involved in surveying institutionalized populations using administrative records for sampling or as data sources.

Self-identification of disability

Related to reliability and validity issues, but of importance in their own right, are issues involved with an individual's self-identification as having a disability. Internal perceptions of disability may differ from the intended survey disability definition. In addition, there is the concern by the respondent of possible future discrimination.

The degree to which an individual's internally held perception of their disability agrees with their understanding of the surveyed disability question is too complex an issue to discuss here in any detail. Zola (1991) considers the psychological effects of word choices about disability on a questionnaire and writes 'this is clearly a loaded issue . . . as we structure questionnaires where we require respondents to identify themselves in terms of their disabilities and their consequences'. In addition to having questionnaires provide reliable responses, Zola is concerned with broader sociological consequences of labeling disabilities. Asking an individual who had polio in their youth to self-identify as a polio 'victim' clearly has a potential for negative impact.

Even with the passage of the ADA, individuals with disabilities are concerned with potential discrimination or being stigmatized. These concerns are, perhaps, more pronounced in surveys where confidentiality is perceived to be problematic. We might anticipate in a large corporation's employee survey, an individual with a disability may choose to not self-identify. We can easily imagine the perceived stigma of certain disabilities and the motivation to not respond. With a less than visible, or hidden disability, there may be even more motivation to not respond. For instance, individuals with a particular syndrome or disease such as epilepsy or diabetes may have it under good control with medication and none of their co-workers may be aware of the individual's situation.

Other issues

We now briefly mention some other issues concerning the surveying for disability. For certain disability conditions which ebb and flow, such as multiple sclerosis, there can be a time-varying nature of the disability. We suspect that the current severity of a person's condition can affect strongly their responses to surveys. Equally important is an understanding of disability concepts as related to respondents' ages. Obviously there is a natural change in performance during aging. The interaction of disability notions and the aging process requires much more clarity. In a related context, McNeil (1993a) notes that New York and Seattle have the same prevalence of work disability, whereas the prevalence of mobility limitation is far less in Seattle. We speculate that the *excess* mobility limitations experienced by New Yorkers is due, in part, to the architecture and physical setting of the city, and also due to winter weather conditions. From this we infer that responses to certain disability questions can be affected by the season in which the survey is done.

Another issue that can confound disability surveys is that an individual's disability can dictate the method of response. Visual impairments obviously require different presentations of a written questionnaire, as do auditory impairments for a telephone survey. Quadriplegia has its own requirements. Cognitive disorders of a severe enough nature may require others to respond. The 1991

HALS was a phone survey; some individuals in the 'yes' sample, for example those with an auditory disability, were able to request a personal interview. Only telephone interviews were used for the 'no' sample.

DISCUSSION

The concerns and problems with conducting a survey involving disability items are manifold. We have highlighted some of the major issues, dealing with several of these in depth. Some of the current and contemplated innovative approaches to these issues have been presented.

We would like to conclude with a description of a few of the next steps that need to be taken to further the collection and use of disability statistics.

Definitions need to be clarified. They should reflect the current thinking about the ICIDH and the impact of environmental barriers. The formulation of definitions should reflect the ability to construct valid and reliable questionnaires to assess these definitions.

The CRS and HALS provide insight into reliability and validity issues of questions. There is a need for further work in this general area. Some have suggested a variety of small controlled experiments specifically designed to assess validity and reliability of various question constructs, and to better understand what survey and respondent factors affect the degree of reliability.

More methodological research needs to be done for surveying rare populations defined by disability. The post-censal survey, for example HALS, is relatively new and requires further development (Dolson et al. 1987). Other forms of screening, or other techniques may also prove to be useful.

The 1986 and 1991 HALS conducted by Statistics Canada have been extensively discussed by us in the context of statistics and public policy. But we must note this is Canadian public policy. A strong argument has been made by the US Bureau of the Census that the US undertakes its own post-censal disability survey. Scientific issues concerning such a survey have been discussed in a number of meetings. It is time for the US Congress to provide the political and financial support to undertake this survey.

There are other compelling needs that we have not discussed herein, such as requiring more longitudinal data and having better coordination of disability surveys among US governmental agencies. For more extensive presentations of issues that need still to be addressed concerning disability statistics, the reader is referred to the writings of John M. McNeil (Bureau of the Census), Haber (1990), Pope and Tarlov (1991), Sampson et al. (1991) and Levine et al. (1990).

We conclude with a statement by Levine et al. (1990). They note that without meaningful disability data, 'policy will be based solely on guesswork, with results that are not likely to meet the needs of persons with disabilities or policy makers' objectives'. Our collective challenge is to work towards obtaining disability data that will meet these needs.

APPENDIX

Some recent surveys and reported disability rates

1990 Census 'long form' (McNeil 1993*a*)

(self-administered)

---

18. Does this person have a physical, mental, or other health condition that has lasted for 6 or more months and which—
a. Limits the kind or amount of work this person can do at a job?
   [ ] Yes   [ ]No
b. Prevents this person from working at a job?
   [ ] Yes   [ ] No
19. Because of a health condition that has lasted for 6 or more months, does this person have any difficulty—
a. Going outside the home alone, for example, to shop or visit a doctor's office?
   [ ] Yes   [ ] No
b. Taking care of his or her own personal needs, such as bathing, dressing, or getting around inside the home?
   [ ] Yes   [ ] No

Results
Percentage of US population aged 16 or older with a disability or limitation, work, mobility or self-care:

$$\frac{22\,351\,129}{186\,887\,433} = 11.96\%$$

1990/91 Survey of Income and Program Participation (SIPP) (McNeil 1993*a*)

(interviewer administered)

Part D—Functional limitations and disability

28 questions including types of disabilities, activities of daily living and work limitations

---

Results
Percentage of US population aged 15 or order with a disability:

$$\frac{46\,023\,000}{195\,729\,000} = 23.51\%$$

(With severe disability: 12.05%. With not a severe disability: 11.46%)

Percentage of US population of all ages with a disability:

$$\frac{48\,936\,000}{251\,796\,000} = 19.43\%$$

(With severe disability: 9.57%. With not a severe disability: 9.86%)

1985 National Health Interview Survey (NHIS) (LaPlante 1988)

(interviewer administered)

21-page questionnaire with 10 groupings of questions including limitations of activities, restricted activities, and condition lists.

Results

Percentage of US population aged 18 or older with any degree of activity limitation due to chronic conditions:

$$\frac{29\,347\,000}{168\,899\,000} = 17.38\%$$

Percentage of US population of all ages with any degree of activity limitation due to chronic condition:

$$\frac{32\,540\,000}{231\,549\,000} = 14.05\%$$

1991 Canadian census of population 'long census form' (Denis *et al.* 1993)

(self-administered)

ACTIVITY LIMITATIONS	
18. Is this person limited in the kind or amount of activity that he/she can do because of a long-term physical condition, mental condition or health problem:	At home? [ ] No, not limited [ ] Yes, limited
	At school or at work? [ ] No not limited [ ] Yes, limited [ ] Not applicable
	In other activities, e.g., transportation to or from work, leisure time activities? [ ] No, not limited [ ] Yes, limited
19. Does this person have any long-term disabilities or handicaps?	[ ] No [ ] Yes

Results

Percentage of Canadian population of all ages who responded positively to at least one of these questions in *1986*:

$$\frac{2\,400\,000}{25\,600\,000} = 9.38\%$$

1991 Canadian Health and Activity Limitation Survey (HALS) (Statistics Canada 1992)

(interviewer-administered)

53-page survey with 9 groupings of questions including activities of daily living, employment, transportation, and accommodation.

Results

Percentage of Canadian population aged 15 or older with a disability:

$$\frac{3\,795\,000}{21\,320\,000} = 17.80\%$$

Percentage of Canadian population of all ages with a disability:

$$\frac{4\,185\,000}{27\,000\,000} = 15.50\%$$

ACKNOWLEDGEMENTS

Throughout I have enormously benefited from interactions with John ('Jack') McNeil, who graciously shared his thoughts and writings. Graham Kalton has also been very helpful in bringing various materials to my attention. Jean-Pierre Morin provided much information on Statistics Canada's activities, and Henry Woltman concerning the Content Reinterview Survey.

REFERENCES

Binder, D. A. and Morin, J.-P. (1988). Use of questions on activities of daily living to screen for disabled persons in a household survey. *Canadian Journal of Statistics*, **16**, Supplement, 143–56.

Birnbaum, Z. W. and Sirken, M. G. (1965). Design of sample surveys to estimate the prevalence of rare diseases: three unbiased estimates. *Vital and health statistics*, PHS Publication No. 1000 – Series 2-#11. US Government Printing Office, Washington DC.

Chamie, M. (1990). The status and use of the International Classification of Impairments, Disabilities and Handicaps (ICIDH). *World Health Statistics Quarterly*, **43**.

Czaja, R. F., Snowden, C. B., and Casady, R. J. (1986). Reporting bias and sampling errors in a survey of a rare population using multiplicity counting rules. *Journal of the American Statistical Association*, **81**, 411–19.

Denis, D. J., Grondin, C., Lavigne, M., Lynch, J., and Morin, J. -P. (1993). Methodology: Health and Activity Limitation Survey 1991 household component. *Report*, Statistics Canada.

Dolson, D., McClean, K., Morin, J. -P., and Théberge, A. (1987). Sample design for the Health and Activity Limitation Survey. *Survey Methodology*, **13**, 93–108.

Elkind, J. (1990). The incidence of disabilities in the United States. *Human Factors*, **32**, 397–405.

Furrie, A. D. (1995). Private communication.

Haber, L. D. (1990). Issues in the definition of disability and the use of disability survey data. In *Disability statistics: an assessment* (ed. D. Levine, M. Zitter, and L. Ingram). National Academy Press, Washington DC.

Louis Harris and Associates (1986). *The ICO survey of disabled Americans: bringing disabled Americans into the mainstream. A nationwide survey of 1000 disabled people*, Study No. 854009. Louis Harris and Associates, Inc., New York.

Louis Harris and Associates (1987). *Participation, voting and elections by disabled americans*, Study No. 874008. Louis Harris and Associates, Inc., New York.

Health and Activity Limitations (HALS) Survey – 1991 User's Guide, non-catalogued Publication. The Health and Activity Limitation Survey, Statistics Canada, Ottawa.

Health and Activity Limitations (HALS) Survey 1991: back-up tables, Provinces and Territories, Report 10/29/92, Statistics Canada, Ottawa.

Highlights: disabled persons in Canada, Catalogue #82–602, Statistics Canada, Ottawa.

ICIDH International Network, Vol. 2, No. 1, (1989). Proposal for revision of the third level of the ICIDH: the handicap, Quebec.

Kalton, G. and Anderson, D. W. (1986). Sampling rare populations. *Journal of the Royal Statistical Society*, A, **149**, 65–82.

Kalton. G. and Sudman, S. (1991). Sampling scientists and engineers with disabilities: perspectives. In *Agenda for Access: Scientists and Engineers with Disabilities*, (ed. A. Sampson, V. Stern, and R. Spoeri). AAAS, Washington DC.

LaPlante, M. P. (1988). *Data on disability from the National Health Interview Survey, 1983–85*, an InfoUse report. US National Institute on Disability and Rehabilitation Research, Washington DC.

LaPlante, M. P. (1991). Disability in basic life activities across the life span. *Disability Statistics Report* 1. National Institute on Disability and Rehabilitation Research, Washington DC.

Levine, D. B., Zitter, M., and Ingram, L. (1990). *Disability statistics: an assessment*. Committee on National Statistics, Commission on Behavioral and Social Sciences and Education, National Academy Press, Washington DC.

McNeil, J. (1991*a*). A review of the US disability surveys based on the recommendations of the Council of Europe's Committee on Experts. Presentation at the 1991 annual meeting of the Society for Disability Studies.

McNeil, J. (1991*b*). Measuring disability and environmental barriers. Presentation at the 1991 annual meeting of the American Statistical Association.

McNeil, J. (1993*a*). Census Bureau data on persons with disabilities: new results and old questions about validity and reliability. Presentation at the 1993 annual meeting of the Society for Disability Studies.

McNeil, J. M. (1993*b*). *Americans with disabilities: 1991–92*, US Bureau of the Census current population reports, p. 70–33. US Government Printing Office, Washington DC.

Nagi, S. Z. (1979). The concept and measurement of disability. In *Disability policies and government programs*, (ed. E. D., Berkowitz), pp. 1–15. Praeger, New York.

National Science Foundation (1992). *Women and minorities in science and engineering: 1992 update*, NSF Report 92–303. National Science Foundation, Washington DC.

Patrick, D. L. (1994). Remarks of Deval L. Patrick, Assistant Attorney General for Civil Rights. Speech to Disability Rights Education and Defense Fund, 10 November 1994.

Pope, A. M. and Tarlov, A. R. (1991). *Disability in America: toward a national agenda for prevention*. National Academy Press, Washington DC.

Sampson, A. R., Stern, V., and Spoeri, R. (ed.) (1991). *Agenda for access: scientists and engineers with disabilities* (with the collaboration of G. Kalton, I. R. Savage, S. Sudman, and I. Zola), Report, Project on Science, Technology and Disability, American Association for the Advancement of Science AAAS, Washington DC.

Statistics Canada (1986). *Report of the Canadian Health and Disability Survey 1983–1984*, Report Catalogue 82–555E. Health Division, Statistics Canada, Ottawa.

Statistics Canada (1992). 1991 Health and Activity Limitation Survey. *The Daily*, 13 October 1992. Statistics Canada, Ottawa.

Sudman, S. (1991). Sampling of scientists and engineers with disabilities: a methodological approach. In *Agenda for access: scientists and engineers with disabilities*, (ed.) A. Sampson, V. Stern, and R. Spoeri. AAAS. Washington, DC.

Sudman, S. and Kalton, G. (1986). New developments in the sampling of special populations. *Annual Review of Sociology*, **12**, 401–29.

Sudman, S., Sirken, M. G., and Cowan, C. D. (1988). Sampling rare and elusive populations. *Science*, **240**, 991–5.

United States Bureau of the Census (1986). *Disability, functional limitation and health insurance coverage; 1984/85*, Current Population Reports, P70–8. US Government Printing Office, Washington DC.

World Health Organization (1980). *International classification of impairments, disabilities and handicaps – a manual of classifications relating to the consequences of diseases*. United Nations, Geneva.

Zola, I. K. (1991). The naming question: reflections on the language of disability. In *Agenda for access: scientists and engineers with disabilities*, (ed). A. Sampson, V. Stern and R. Spoeri. AAAS, Washington DC.

10 Constructed social networks in the study of diffusion[1]

JAMES S. COLEMAN

INTRODUCTION

The aim of population sampling is to choose a sample from a population of independent individuals to provide a good estimate of the distribution (or of some parameters of the distribution) of characteristics of the individuals. The unit of observation is the individual (from whom data are typically obtained by interview or questionnaire), and the unit being described is the set of individuals, each of whom is regarded as an independent element of the set.

It can reasonably be said, then, that sampling theory is not intended to make use of relations that may exist among individuals. The existence of these relations is not ignored in sampling theory; rather, samples are designed to overcome any effects of these relations on estimates of population parameters. Typically, a population sample based on personal interviews will be a multistage sample, the first stage being a primary sampling unit (PSU), the second being a sample of enumeration districts (ED) within the PSU, the third being a sample of blocks within an ED, the fourth being a sample of dwelling units (DU) within the block, and the fifth being an individual within the DU. Several dwelling units are often selected within the block, several blocks within the ED, and several EDs within the PSU. The principal reason for such clustering is to reduce cost, and the principal deterrent is the increase in variances of the estimates as compared with a simple random sample.

The increase in variance arises because persons in the same block, ED, or PSU are in general more alike in the characteristics under study than are persons selected at random from the population. This similarity may arise because they know each other, or because they are subjected to common environmental stimuli, or for another reason. Regardless of the cause, this similarity is a problem, and much of the effort in sampling is an attempt to overcome this problem.

The purpose of this chapter is to initiate an approach that subverts this goal. Subversion of this goal becomes necessary whenever the aims of a sample survey include the aim of making use of the relations that exist among individuals. This principle is recognized in some survey work. 'Snowball sampling' is a method of sampling which proceeds in two or more stages, with the relations between persons being used in the second and any subsequent stage (see Goodman 1961). The

---

1. I am indebted to William McPhee for ideas about sampling relationships.

respondent in the first stage is asked to identify one or more individuals to whom he has a certain relation, and the second stage sample is drawn from these identified individuals. The procedure may be repeated at the second and subsequent stages.

Another form of sampling in which relations between individuals are explicitly taken into account is 'dense sampling' within some well-defined social unit. This is two-stage or multistage sampling, with the clusters in the final stage being large relative to the size of the unit. An example is sampling of students in school, as has been carried out in a series of studies initiated by the US Department of Education. In one of the studies, *High school and beyond*, carried out in 1980, 1015 high schools were selected in the first stage, and 36 sophomores and 36 seniors were sampled in the second stage. Students were asked names of their closest friends. In the smaller schools, all or nearly all students in the sophomore and senior classes of the school were sampled, and many friends were within the sample. In larger schools, a smaller fraction of friends were within the sample, but some were. For all cases in which friends were within the sample, it is possible to capture and make use of the relations. Beyond that, it is possible, for all the schools, to capture something about the effect of the relations through aggregation of individual responses of the 35 fellow-students of each of the 36 sampled students, to obtain a measure of social context surrounding each student.

Snowball sampling and dense sampling within social units are two examples of sampling carried out in such a way as to make use of relations among individuals. They do not exhaust the possible modes of sampling that attempt to capture some aspect of social structure. Sampling of specific roles in formal organizations makes it possible to capture information about role relations from both sides of the relation, and sampling of departments that stand in a particular relation to one another makes it possible to capture interdepartmental relations. Once the general principle of sampling relations, or of capturing information about a sample of relations, becomes clear, the principle can be applied in a variety of settings.

The matter can become complex, however, because once the idea of sampling elements of social structure is introduced, then the theory of sampling is called into question in a more fundamental way than indicated above. For some purposes, the aim of sampling relations is not merely to obtain a sample of relations, each regarded as independent of the others, but to characterize structural units larger than the individual. These may be cliques, networks, or other structures tied together by relations. When the study of these larger units is of interest, then relations become merely stepping stones to the characterization and study of supra-individual structures. If relations are sampled without regard to the nodes (individuals) they share, then the sample is one of pair relations, but of no structure beyond the pair. Two-stage snowball samples exemplify this.

Yet it is not clear just how sampling theory should, and could, be developed when data are to be collected at the level of individuals, information is to be obtained from them about their relations to other individuals, and this information is to be used to re-create the larger structures within which these individuals find themselves. The theory is poorly developed, and would undoubtedly benefit from sustained effort toward its development. That development in turn can be expected to stimulate the quantitative study of social structure – an activity that is central to scientific sociology, but not abundant in sociological research.

One point that seems evident in this development is that sampling theory will necessarily become much more dependent upon knowledge and theory about social structure, as it comes to be used in the study of social structure. Another is that sampling theory will necessarily have greater diversity, with the particular branch depending upon the particular kinds of processes or structures under study. It is toward the study of one of these processes, diffusion, that the work discussed in the present chapter is directed.

DIFFUSION

One social process that is important in a variety of substantive areas is diffusion. The item being diffused may be an item of information, a contagious disease, a belief, a value, or something still different. The mechanism of transmission will be different for different items, and will depend on the kind of relation that exists between a person who has the item and a person who does not. Thus if diffusion through a social structure is to be studied, data must be obtained on the kind of relation through which transmission takes place. To consider an extreme case, diffusion of the AIDS virus is transmitted primarily through very specific kinds of sexual relations.

The process to which the present work is directed is the diffusion of sexually transmitted diseases (STDs) in a sexually interacting population. This is likely to be of growing interest, quite apart from the current AIDS epidemic, because the essential constraint on this diffusion process, that is monogamy in sexual relations, is decreasingly characteristic of sexually active persons. Sexual monogamy, if universal, would create a sexual structure of disconnected pairs, among which a diffusion process could not operate. Multiplicity of sexual partners can create very diverse and complex structures within which diffusion can take place, with the number of paths increasing as the number of partners of the average person increases. For the study of diffusion in a structure the links of which are identified only at the time of data collection, it is not possible to sample the structure in a systematic way, although some steps may be taken that increase the probability of obtaining information about the structure. These steps include stratification with oversampling in strata that have portions of the structure which are important in the transmission process (for example, young single males in urban areas), sampling of sites at which links in the structure are created, such as singles bars or gay bars, combined with dense sampling within sites. All of these modifications of standard population sampling can aid the process of sampling social structure for the study of diffusion, yet they do not carry matters very far. In this chapter, I will describe a different approach, apart from, or in addition to, the sampling modifications mentioned above, that can be used for the study of diffusion processes.

A PSEUDO-SOCIAL NETWORK

The general strategy to be examined here is the use of information from interview or observation of the individual to create pseudo-relations among members of the sample. The end result is a constructed, hypothetical network that approximates in some ways the true network in the population from which these individuals were drawn. In contrast to the sampling procedures mentioned earlier, which are designed to capture relations in the actual structure, this procedure is designed to create a structure that simulates, in ways relevant to the process being studied, the true structure.

Before describing the methods proposed for creating the simulated structure, I will sketch the way that structure is intended to be used. That will give some idea of just what aspects of the structure it is most important to reproduce accurately, if the process is to be modeled accurately.

THE DIFFUSION PROCESS, AND GOALS OF MODELING

The questions to which answers are desired in the study of STDs are questions of how large a segment of the population will be invaded by the disease, and what parts of the population. The inhomogeneous character of any network, dense in some places and weakly connected in other places, means that any item being diffused through these networks may show a very uneven diffusion process. When there are weakly connected components, then a cumulative curve of diffusion might look like that of Fig. 1. The points of rapid growth shown in the curve are periods following an entry of the item into a densely connected portion of the network where it can diffuse rapidly. The periods of slow growth represent periods following the exhaustion of a densely connected segment, during which the item diffuses slowly along the weakly connected paths toward another densely connected segment.

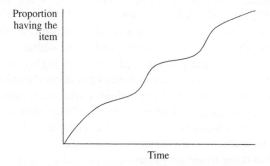

Proportion having the item

Time

Fig.1

But nearly all diffusion processes involve items with a limited period of diffusibility. This is clearest in the case of infectious diseases. For a given disease there is a period following the time at which an individual becomes infected during which the disease may be transmitted. There is sometimes a latency period as well, following the infection and preceding the period of infectivity. In the case of items of information, the interest of an individual receiving the information may fade after a period of time, with the result that this individual stops transmitting the information to others. In some cases, the period of saliency (and thus transmission attempts) may begin from a single starting point, rather than from the time at which the individual receives the item. For example, in a study of the introduction of a new broad-spectrum antibiotic into medicine in the United States in 1954, the period of saliency began with the drug's introduction, rather than beginning anew for each physician who adopted it into practice (see Coleman *et al.* 1966).

The combination of a time-limited period of diffusion (whether from the start of an individual's reception of the idea, or from the start of diffusion) with inhomogeneity in the social structure means that the spread of an item between weakly connected parts of the network is problematic. In Fig. 1, the diffusion might have died during either of the periods of slow growth. In order to have any predictability of when the diffusion will die out, and which segments of the structure it will invade before doing so, it is necessary both to have a model of the process (probability of transmission given contact as a function of the time since receiving the item and time since start of diffusion), and a model of the structure of contacts through which the item is diffused. The combination of these two parts of an overall model of the diffusion process can be seen by assuming full information about both its components and developing the mathematical structure for modelling the process if that full information existed. Then it is possible to see how the mathematics would be modified if information were limited in one way or another. Parenthetically it should be stated that there has been extensive modelling of diffusion processes in which the social structure is assumed homogeneous. Bartholomew (1982, Chapters 9, 10) gives a comprehensive description of this work. There has been much less work on models which assume inhomogeneity of structure. This work has taken two forms. One is to assume a small number of mutually exclusive groups or strata within which there is one frequency of contact and between which there is a smaller frequency of contact. A second form, begun by Hagerstrand (1967) assumes that frequency of contact is determined by distance between two persons. Models for both directions of work are discussed by Bartholomew (1982, pp. 259–63 for the first, pp. 272–82, 296–9 for the second).

The principal reason that work has been so much more fully developed on the process side than on the structure side seems to be that deductions can be carried much farther by modelling the process explicitly with highly simplified assumptions about the structure than without those assumptions. Needless to say, this is not a very creditable reason for disregarding structure if one's goal is, as I indicated, to answer the questions of what parts of a population an item being diffused will invade, and when it will do so. Nevertheless, the fact remains that rather extensive information on the structure is necessary if the questions are to be answered without making those simple assumptions about structure. The present chapter is directed to finding ways of retaining the complexity of structure without full information about it, but with information from a sample of members of the population.

To model the process with complete information, we can first define these quantities:

1. $p_k(t, \tau)$ = probability of transmission of the item from an actor who has the item to an actor who does not, given a contact of type k, at time t from the beginning of diffusion and time τ from the time at which the actor having the item received it. It is assumed that $p_k(t, \tau)$ is independent of the actor who has the item and the actor with whom that actor has contact, but depends on the type of contact, k, on the time from start of diffusion (t), and on the length of time the actor who has the item has had it (τ).

2. c_{kij} = frequency of contact of type k between actors i and j in time period Δt. (The time period Δt is taken to be very small, so that the probability of more than one contact in Δt is negligible. Thus c_{kij} can be interpreted as a probability of contact in time period Δt.) Note that although it may be most natural to think of c_{kij} being symmetric for i and j, the model does not require the assumption that c_{kij} is symmetric. However, the assumption is made that c_{kij} is independent of i's or j's possession of the item.

3. $r_i(t)$ = probability that actor i has the item at time t.

If we know $r_i(0)$, and know $p_k(t,\tau)$ for all types of contact and all times from the start of diffusion and from the start of an actor's possession, and know the frequencies c_{kij} for all persons i and j, for all types of contact k, then it is possible to predict the spread of the item through a structure. The initial vector $r(0)$ has elements $r_i(0)$ that are either 0 or 1 if the state of each actor is known; if only the probability that an actor possesses the item is known, then $r_i(0)$ may take on values between 0 and 1.

The generating equation for the transmission of the item is composed in this way: $p_k(t,\tau) c_{kij}$ = probability that j got the item from i in the time period $(t, t + \Delta t)$ via contact type k, given that i has the item.

Then if contacts are independent and the transmission events are independent the probability that j did not get the item from any person in this period through contact type k is s_{kj}, where s_{kj} is given by

$$s_{kj} = \prod_{j=1}^{n} [1 - p_k(t,\tau) c_{kij} r_i(t)]$$

and the probability that j did not get the item from any kind of contact with another person is the product of s_{kj} over the m types of contact

$$s_j = \prod_{k=1}^{m} s_{kj}.$$

Then the probability that j did acquire the item from someone, through some contact, and did not have it before, is $(1 - s_j)[1 - r_j(t)]$, and the probability that j has the item at time $t + \Delta t$ is

$$r_j(t + \Delta t) = r_j(t) + (1 - s_j)[1 - r_j(t)] = 1 - s_j[1 - r_j(t)].$$

This may be expressed in terms of the change in $r_j(t)$, or

$$\Delta r_j(t) = r_j(t + \Delta t) - r_j(t) = (1-s_j)[1-r_j(t)]. \tag{1}$$

When taken to the limit, this difference equation becomes:

$$\frac{dr_j(t)}{dt} = [1-r_j(t)]\sum_k \sum_i p_k(t, \tau) c_{kij} r_i(t).$$

Equation (1) could be used to calculate the spread of the item from a known initial vector, if $p(t,\tau)$ and c_{kij} were known. The first of the quantities, $p_k(t,\tau)$, is characteristic of the item being spread. In the case of infectious diseases, the disease has a characteristic latency period and period of infectivity, so that p as a function of τ is known. It is often assumed that p is not a function of τ, that is, the probability of transmission or virulence of the disease does not change over the period of diffusion. In diffusion of cognitive or affective items, such an assumption is ordinarily not warranted.

The social structural information is contained in the quantities c_{kij}. It is this information that cannot be obtained for a large population at reasonable cost. Thus it is this information for which some kind of approximation can be sought.

CONSTRUCTION OF A NETWORK

Suppose that a survey of a community is carried out to obtain the measures c_{kij}. All members of the community are interviewed, with the result that there are no sampling problems. If information is obtained from each about his contacts, then it is possible to reconstruct the network from this information, and to determine the values of c_{kij}. If there are reporting errors, then accounts will not balance. As in any double-entry book-keeping system, there is redundancy for every entry: i's report and j's report should match. It will be necessary to establish conventions to resolve reporting discrepancies (for example, discrepancies could always be resolved in favor of the person who reported a contact with another who did not report the contact, or in favor of the person who reported the higher frequency of contact, when both reported some contact). Another source of error lies in the method of reporting contacts. The frequency of contact is subject to random variation, so that the report by a respondent for 'the past month', for example, may vary from month to month.

There are two circumstances which introduce additional problems in reconstructing the network from data of the sort obtainable in a survey. One of these is that it is often not possible to obtain information on the identity of the person to whom the respondent has a connection, but only on certain characteristics. The second is that the survey does not cover the whole population, but only a fraction of the population. The sampling fraction may be the same for all, or it may differ for different strata in the population. I will address these two problems in order.

THE FIRST PROBLEM: INFORMATION ON ONLY CHARACTERISTICS OF PARTNER, NOT IDENTITY

Suppose information is obtained from members of the sample on their own characteristics (m in number) and the same m characteristics of the persons with whom they have contact, though not their identities. These persons are unlikely to be in the sample anyway. Suppose this information is used to specify values of m categorical variables, $x_{i1}, . . ., x_{im}$ characterizing the ith respondent and analogous values $y_{ij1}, . . ., y_{ijm}$ for the jth person with whom respondent i is in contact. These characteristics are ordered in importance, with x_{i1} and y_{ij1} the most important. What is necessary then is an algorithm to fill in the entries c_{kij} in the three-dimensional matrix of contact. One such algorithm, which treats the respondents $1, . . ., n$ in sequential order, and the variables $x_{i1}, . . ., x_{im}$, in sequential order, is as follows:

1. For the first survey respondent, find the set of survey respondents indexed by h such that $x_{h1} = y_{111}$. That is, these are the members of the sample who have the same value on variable 1 as does the first contact of respondent 1 (as reported by respondent 1).

2. From this set of respondents, find the subset, indexed by k, such that $x_{11} = y_{kj1}$ for some j. This is the subset, within the set of persons who match respondent 1's reported contact in the first variable, who report a contact that matches respondent 1 on this variable.

3. Beginning with the subset resulting from step 2, repeat steps 1 and 2 for variables $2, . . ., m$, stopping when the subset of matching individuals is empty, if this occurs before all m variables are compared.

4. Go back to the last preceding subset before the empty subset, having say, n_{11} members. Select one from this set with probability $1/n_{11}$. This creates relation number 1 for person number 1 in the constructed network.

5. Continue with the second respondent, and through the remaining members of the sample.

6. Continue steps 1–5 through the list of respondents until all contacts are exhausted.

7. If at any stage a respondent who is selected as a contact has been used through a match with an earlier respondent, then choose the next best match.

8. Some procedure for allocating unmatched contacts among members of the population is necessary.

We can ask what kinds of systematic biases exist in the constructed network relative to the true network. Two kinds of systematic bias involve what I will call 'closure' of a network. A network is m-closed or contains an m-cycle if exactly m connections beginning with some person i leads back to i. For example, a network i–j–k–i is a 3-cycle, and a network i–j–k–h–i is a 4-cycle. A network of n persons is open if there are no m-closed cycles within it, for all $m < n$.

One kind of bias can be seen by recognizing that if in this constructed network, i is connected to j, j to h, and h to some person in a subset of which i is a member, the constructed network does not give any higher probability for the connection of h to i than for the connection of h to any other member of that subset. In true networks, this probability will often be higher. Thus the networks will often be more open, or the cycles larger, in the constructed network than in the true network.

THE SECOND PROBLEM: SAMPLE SIZE AND POPULATION SIZE

There is also a bias, but in the other direction, induced by the second problem. The source of this bias can be seen by recognizing that the sample is much smaller than the population, and therefore the networks close up, creating cycles that, *ceteris paribus*, are smaller than the cycles in the true network. For example, consider an extreme: there are three persons in the sample, each with only two relations, and only one set of classifications. Respondent 2 meets the criteria for respondent 1, as follows: $x_{21} = y_{111}$ and $x_{11} = y_{211}$. Respondent 3 meets the criteria for respondent 2, as follows: $x_{31} = y_{221}$ and $x_{21} = y_{311}$. Respondent 1 meets the criteria for respondent 3, as follows: $x_{11} = y_{321}$ and $x_{31} = y_{121}$.

This would lead us to create links between all three, that is, for contact of type k (assumed here) $c_{k12} = c_{k21} = 1$, $c_{k23} = c_{k32} = 1$, and $c_{k13} = c_{k31} = 1$. Thus the diffusion would go from person 1 to 2 to 3 and then back to 1, never proceeding beyond these three persons. The cycle is smaller, the network more likely to be closed than in the true network. In the true network, the larger number of persons means that a chain could (and ordinarily would) go much longer before it turned in on itself and completed a cycle. The sample network would give quite different results for a diffusion process than would the true network.

This second problem, due to the difference between sample size and population size, might be addressed by duplicating the number of records for each person, with the number of duplicates for each member of the sample determined as the inverse of the sampling probability. This leaves, however, the first kind of bias due to the tendency of networks to close in upon themselves, creating smaller cycles than would occur in random networks. Later, I suggest a means, by use of estimates from a snowball sample, of addressing both kinds of bias simultaneously (see the section entitled 'Sampling chains').

It is possible to see just how these two circumstances (information only about certain characteristics of a person's contacts, and a sample rather than a census) combine by imagining a sample drawn from a population of identical twins, with a sampling fraction of 1/2, exactly one member of each pair of twins falling into the sample. From each person in the sample information is obtained concerning contacts, as before. Information is not obtained on the identity of the person with whom the contact occurred, but only on which pair of twins the person contacted was a member of. We can now index the pairs rather than the individuals by h, i, and j, with the sample of size n and the population of size $2n$. Consider three sets of twins h, i, and j, with h_1, i_1, and j_1, drawn in the sample. Suppose i_1 in the sample reports a contact with j. This contact may be with j_1 (in the sample) or j_2 (not in the sample). If it is not with j_1, and j_1 did not have a contact with i_2, then j_1 will not report a contact with i, resulting in what appears to be a reporting error, although it is not. (If the number of identical i's and j's increases beyond 2 to a larger number, the proportion of such apparent errors will decrease so that this is not a serious source of error.) Suppose however, that i_1's contact is with j_1. Then j_1 will report a contact with i. If we use this as a 'confirmation' of i_1's report, we may establish that c_{kij} is not zero, its value depending on the frequency of contact. Now suppose j_1 reports in addition a contact with h, and h_1 confirms this by reporting a contact with j. Finally, suppose that h_1 reports a contact with i, and i_1 confirms this by reporting a contact with h. If there were only one i, j, and h, we would have a 3-cycle as shown in Fig. 2, with h, i, and j, linked together.

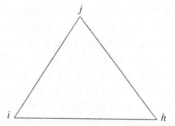

Fig. 2

But consider two types of structures. In a structure of type 1, 'the friends of my friends are my friends'. That is, if an i has a relation with a j and that j has a relation with an h, then the h will have a relation with the i. If the social structure from which the sample was drawn were of this sort, and if the j connected to i_1 is j_1, then the h to which j_1 is connected is a friend of i_1's friend. Connecting h and i as in the graph is justified if h_1 names an i as his friend, because in this kind of structure, the h to which the j who is a friend of i_1 is connected will be the same h who is a friend of i_1. If the j connected to i_1 is not j_1, but j_2 instead, then if j_1 names an h, the h will ordinarily not be i_1's friend, but i_2's. In all these cases, it is correct to establish the triad as shown in Fig. 2.

But the social structure may be of type 2, one in which the friends of my friends are no more likely to be my friends than is someone who is unconnected to a friend of mine. In that case, the probability is only $1/2$ that the h connected to the j that is connected to i_1 is connected to i_1. That h has an equal probability of being connected to i_2, resulting in a network like that of Fig. 3.

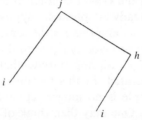

Fig. 3

The empirical difficulty is this: in a situation like that described, with two persons in each identifiable class ('identical twins'), from which a sample is drawn by selecting one person randomly from each pair, and with information from each sampled individual about the class of the individuals to which he is connected, it is not possible to distinguish structures like Fig. 2 from structures like Fig. 3. More generally, if the class sizes are n_h, n_i, and n_j for classes h, i, and j, respectively, the two extremes are:

(1) for structures of type 1, i–j, j–h, and h–i connections imply Fig. 2 with certainty; and

(2) for structures of type 2, i–j, j–h connections imply Fig. 2 with probability $1/n_i$, and Fig. 3 with probability $(n_i-1)/n_i$.

An empirical structure lies somewhere between these two extremes, but the data give no information about where. The importance of knowing is, of course, evident: if the structure is like that of Fig. 2, then diffusion that begins with i_1 does not spread beyond the triad; if the structure is like that of Fig. 3, diffusion that begins with i_1 continues to spread, with $n_i/2 + n_j/2 + n_h/2$ as the expected number having the item before diffusion is stopped by a completed cycle.

At this point, I see no way to determine, for an empirical structure, just where it lies between type 1 and type 2, except through obtaining information from a snowball sample on the identities of the persons they are connected to. This information could then he used to obtain a probability that a given triad, i,j,k, was closed like Fig. 2 rather than being open like Fig. 3. Similarly, snowball-sample information could be used to determine the probability that a tetrad, that is, i,j,h,k,i, closed in on itself rather than remaining open.

SAMPLING CHAINS

With information about the probability that a triad in which i is connected to j and j to k is closed (via a connection between k and i), or a tetrad, in which i is connected to j, j to k, and k to h is closed (via a connection between h and i), and assuming that the tendency toward closure was exhausted beyond the tetrad, it becomes possible to construct a pseudo-social network using sample data that mimics the true network. In the algorithm described earlier, this would be achieved by choosing with the relevant closure probability a j to complete the i–j relation who is identical to k, where the k–h–i relation (for a triad) or the k–g–h–i relation (for a tetrad) was clearly already established. Suppose, however, there is only one j who fits the matching criteria, and this j is the same person as the k to which i is indirectly linked. Then with probability equal to the probability that the triad or tetrad is not closed, a new j with appropriate characteristics but not indirectly connected to i will be generated. In this fashion, new sample members will be generated, so that the sample is no longer representative of individuals, but is instead a sample of chains. One may then think of the data from individuals as merely providing the information from which the sample of chains can be created. There remain a number of questions. Three of these are:

1. How should individuals be drawn in the initial sample to maximize sample efficiency? (For example, persons with large numbers of relations should be sampled with a higher probability than those with a small number of relations. Should the probability be proportional to $n_i - 1$, where n_i is the number of relations individual i has?)

2. If we conceive of the chains as the elements of the finally constructed sample, how is the sampling probability for each chain calculated?[2]

3. How can the structure created in the way described above be tested for its similarity to the true structure?

APPLICATION OF THE MODEL TO SIMULATION OF AN AIDS EPIDEMIC

In application to the AIDS epidemic,[3] there are two kinds of transmission structures. One is heterosexual transmission, with each individual having two or more partners. In such a network, all m-cycles must consist of an even number of persons (for example, $M_1 - F_1 - M_2 - F_2 - M_1$, or $M_1 - F_1 - M_2 - F_2 - M_3 - F_3 - M_1$). The second is a homosexual, bisexual, or needle-sharing network. In such a network, cycles can occur with an odd or even number of individuals (for example, $H_1 - H_2 - H_3 - H_1$, or $H_1 - H_2 - H_3 - H_4 - H_1$). In any given chain, both kinds of structures may occur.

In application, the creation of the sample of chains allows construction of the three-dimensional C matrix with entries c_{kij} as discussed earlier in the chapter. This matrix may then be used to project forward an actual vector $r(t)$ of possession of the AIDS virus, or to project a hypothetical vector. The latter simulation would be used to answer questions of the form: 'If the AIDS epidemic had a particular distribution in the population at time t, how far could we expect the epidemic to reach?' Or 'For a particular distribution at a given time, what would we expect the distribution to be like two years later?' Note, however, that for this second question, information beyond that discussed here, concerning the probability of establishing new contacts, would be necessary.

CONCLUSION

In this chapter I have sketched how one might go about creating a constructed social network from a sample of a population, in order to study processes utilizing that network. One such process is diffusion of an infectious disease or a belief or an item of information, and I have indicated how the model might be used in

---

2. Spencer and Foran (1991) present methods for estimating the sampling probabilities for aggregations of individuals. An approach similar to theirs might be used to estimate one sampling probability of a chain.

3. See Castillo-Chavez (1989) for other models of AIDS transmission

simulating a diffusion process, including a specific application to the diffusion of AIDS through a population.

There remain a number of different problems in the creation and use of such constructed networks. Nevertheless, the potential value seems sufficiently great to warrant further work.

ACKNOWLEDGEMENT

In his work, Richard Savage has consistently shown an interest in and ability to apply statistics to real problems, and to develop statistical methods that can address real problems. I will describe just how I benefitted from this talent at a very early stage of my career. In 1955–6, having just completed my Ph.D. at Columbia, I was a Fellow at the Center for Advanced Study in the Behavioral Sciences. I was working on mathematical models for the study of attitude or behavioral change, a problem area into which Paul Lazarsfeld had initiated me. With the use of data from two-wave or multiwave panel data, discrete-time Markov chains had been applied to the study of attitude change, by Ted Anderson and others, but these models had one implication that I could not accept. This was that the time point at which change was assumed to occur was the time at which the panel was observed or interviewed. Reality, as I saw it, was quite different. Change between states could occur at any time between observation points, masquerading as either no change at all (if, for example, the change were from state i to state j and then back to i) or as a single change (if the change were from i to j to k).

I was attempting to develop a model to capture this independence of change in state from time of observation. Richard Savage was that year the statistical adviser to the Center's Fellows. He saw the problem and guided me in just the right direction, that is to continuous-time Markov processes, of which I had not previously known. These processes, elaborated in several ways, came to form the core of my *Introduction to Mathematical Sociology* (1964) and then of much subsequent work in the application of mathematical models in sociology. Today, these models are widely used, not only with panel data, but also with continuous-observation data and cross-sectional data. Had it not been for the fortunate circumstance that it was Richard Savage who was the statistical adviser at the Center in 1955–6, this development might have taken place only years later.

The topic of this chapter does not deal with these models, making it especially important to point out this early impact that Richard Savage had on my work.

REFERENCES

Bartholomew, D. J. (1982). *Stochastic models for social processes*. Wiley, New York.

Castillo-Chavez, C. (1989). *Mathematical and statistical approaches to AIDS epidemiology*. Springer, New York.

Coleman, J. S. (1964). *Introduction to mathematical sociology*. The Free Press of Glencoe, New York.

Coleman, J. S., Katz, E., and Menzel, H. (1966). *Medical innovation.* Bobbs-Merrill, Indianapolis.

Goodman, L. (1961). Snowball sampling. *Annals of Mathematical Statistics,* **32,** 148–70.

Hagerstrand, T. (1967). *Innovation diffusion as a spatial process.* University of Chicago Press.

Spencer, B. D. and Foran, W. (1991). Sampling probabilities for aggregations, with applications to NELS: 88 and other educational longitudinal surveys. *Journal of Educational Statistics,* **16,** 21–34.

Part III
Uses of statistics for policy analysis

Part III
Uses of statistics for policy analysis

11 Why forecasts fail and policies are often frustrated[1]

NATHAN KEYFITZ

A nation can be ruined by cleverly crafted short-term solutions to its long-term problems. Some people are homeless. They can't afford privately available housing? Rent hotel space for them, or quickly build low-rent apartments in a scheme of so-called urban renewal. Single girls have carelessly become pregnant? Provide them with a temporary income provided there is no man in sight to support them. Crime is increasing? Mandate longer sentences and build more jails. And even more obvious, the treasury is empty? A painless answer: borrow the money.

Subsequent unsatisfactory experience has told us something about longer-term effects. The low-rent public housing, far from contributing to renewal, gave rise over a very few decades to eyesores; they were vandalized, abandoned by their legitimate tenants, became hideouts for criminals. Single girls deliberately become pregnant to claim the government income to which they are entitled. Similarly in regard to the building of jails — the sequel to the initial building was the need for more jails, and now we seem capable of filling all the jails that can be built. Borrowing that provided short-term solutions is responsible for the huge debts that governments have now piled up.

Real life examples, unfortunately, can be listed indefinitely. When there was a run on banks in the early 1930s, the government issued a guarantee to depositors; the guarantee was successful in immediately restoring confidence in the banking system. But the longer-run effect was less happy: depositors no longer had to be concerned about the management of their funds, so allowing the managers, especially of savings and loans companies, to take risks of a kind that were unknown earlier.

A large literature has grown up over half a century, both in the United States and in France, on unintended and unanticipated consequences. In many examples it is at least possible to see after the event just why the consequences were not foreseen. But there are many other cases, as we will see, in which it is not really possible to say after the event, 'We should have thought of that.'

Strategic planning was devised a few years back to reconcile short- and long-term objectives; that we hear less about it now is not because the need is less but

---

1. This chapter is due above all to Fred Mosteller, who made me think. He is not responsible for the results of my thinking, though I have incorporated a number of specific suggestions.

because the social science knowledge required to do it effectively proved lacking. In some instances a perfectly logical short-term solution turned out in the longer run to worsen the situation it aimed to alleviate, in other instances the solution created wholly new and unanticipated problems.

Some policies have been more durably successful. The Federal Reserve Bank seems to be able, at least so far, to balance on the knife edge of low inflation and low unemployment. Raising margin requirements on the stock market has checked the spread of panic when the market falls – at least there has been no serious repeat of ever-widening repercussions of a fall such as those of 1929–32. Canada's Family Allowances did not succeed in raising the birth rate, but they did something equally important: they put money into the hands of all mothers (avoiding the dismal effects of providing help to single mothers only that is too well known in the United States) gave child raising more dignity, raised the stature of women. But if we cannot tell in advance whether a proposed measure will be successful, installing one short-term plan after another in the hope that we will hit it lucky this time is an expensive way to proceed.

It is the weakness of forecasting that puts policy analysts in this difficult position. The accuracy of forecasts in some fields – astronomers forecast an eclipse of the sun 10 years ahead to within one second – contrasts with its persistent errors in others – weather, earthquakes, plus virtually all those where human behavior is an element.

The difference in predictability is partly a difference in time scales. The general proposition of this chapter is that while short-term forecasts based on linear models are satisfactorily accurate; major difficulties affect long-term forecasts. For eclipses of the sun the short term is thousands of years; for the weather it is one or two or three days; for the economy it is a year or two. A well-behaved function can be extrapolated reasonably well for a short period ahead using the linear term of its Taylor expansion, so that we can calculate the future even in ignorance of the shape of the function, sometimes using as few as two preceding values; with more values we can hope to go further into the future, but in the absence of knowledge of the true shape of the function the distant future is necessarily uncertain.

If one could only forecast the concrete outcome if policy A is adopted, and the outcome if policy B is adopted, then the choice would be simple, at least in the numerous cases where the objective (lowering unemployment, choosing students who will graduate) is non-controversial. When choosing a policy by forecasting outcomes is too difficult resort is made to a partial forecast – if everything else remains the same while we reduce tariffs then incomes and employment will rise. If everything else remains the same then more severe sentencing will reduce crime. Yet every such partial forecast depends on a model, and if empirical data cannot be brought to test such models against alternatives then their use is risky.

I go on to list some of the models that are currently used in forecasting and policy analysis in the several social sciences, and show how, when several of the sciences are focused on one event, they vary greatly in the way it is understood.

THE CENTRALITY OF DISCIPLINES

Note that most of the difficulties of this chapter, that aspires to be interdisciplinary, do not appear to the practitioners of any single discipline. When Thomas C. Schelling, recent President of the American Economic Association, in an elegant paper, takes up the matter of policies that have patently failed, he runs through a list much longer than mine, and incisively demonstrates that they were bound to fail. The general principle they disregarded is that (Schelling 1981):

Almost any compensatory program directed toward a condition over which people have any kind of control . . . provides some incentive to get into that condition. It reduces the incentive to stay out of it.

No one can deny this. Disaster relief for the victims of floods encourages building too close to rivers that occasionally go on a rampage, so causing the undesired condition – loss of one's home – that it was designed to compensate. Notice that in the short term the objective of the relief is met perfectly; it will take time for new buildings to go up on similar sites and so increase the hazard. Whatever the shortcomings of the reward–punishment scheme, that scheme has enough applicability to guarantee the validity of Schelling's assertion, though one has to wait a few years before the incentive to build in dangerous places can be implemented.

The question then becomes not so much why a policy failed, as why it was ever legislated to begin with. The answer, both Schelling and I say, is politics. The difference is that he, speaking in his capacity as an economist, is free of further responsibility, while I, foolhardy, have undertaken to worry about elements of situations irrespective of which science deals with them. I cannot lay claim to knowledge that stands above the several disciplines. Practically all of the worthwhile knowledge of the world, social or physical, has been attained in one or another of the sciences, and in respect of policy a large part of it is in economics. But political scientists, psychologists, sociologists, anthropologists, historians and others also have much to say, and when their perspectives are figured in the result is indeterminacy.

INTERPRETATION IS CENTRAL

As an example of the way that a discipline can provide satisfactory short-term answers that fail in the long term, consider the standard reward and punishment model, that economics and many other disciplines rely on. I give two examples of its incompleteness.

Legislated policy on crime interprets acts in the framework of one culture, while many of the actors interpret it in terms of another. Legislators are middle-class citizens for whom going to jail is a terrible humiliation, so they confidently enact laws that will ensure that more criminals are apprehended, and that those who are guilty spend longer periods in jail. But suppose drug peddlers and other criminals interpret jail as a part of their initiation into a profession which, if not honorable in the larger society, is at least highly profitable without being particularly dishonorable in their smaller society. With this interpretation jail is still not to be sought, but it is by no means punishment severe enough to cause peddlers to give up their profession. In fact they can help advance their professional careers by the contacts they make in prison, just as a politician advances his by contacts on the golf course.

Thus I suggest that jail has different meanings for different people, and those whom it is meant to scare into obedience to the law may be the ones who are least afraid of it. But in the short run, jail can reduce street crime insofar as potential criminals are kept off the streets.

The contrast of interpretation that with some hyperbole I suggested for criminals *vis-à-vis* the corrections system applies to parents *vis-à-vis* their children. Every parent has to face it. When the child behaves in a way that is to be encouraged the parent naturally praises it (reward) and when it fails to behave the parent scolds (punishment). But this requires that the child interpret the parental praise and scolding as intended. If it interprets the scolding merely as a sign that affection is lacking and accordingly turns sullen and still fails to behave in the way expected by the parent, and the parent thinks that the inadequate response is because the scolding was not severe enough, and proceeds to beating, then things will get worse and worse between them. That example shows how feedback, starting from a trifling initial incident, can harden into unfortunate traits of character of both participants. Neither one is forming the other; both are being formed by the process. More will be said on this reciprocal interaction later.

Most of what I have said so far falls under the head of variability of interpretation, and how difficult that makes it to anticipate a reaction that would be obvious if only rewards and punishments, money incentives, jail sentences and parental reprimand meant the same to everybody and under all circumstances, if everyone had access to full information, especially of the intentions of others.

We go on to another kind of uncertainty in human affairs.

OPEN AND CLOSED LOOPS

The easiest models to work with, to fit to data, to analyze, to use for forecasting and for policy formulation, are those in which A causes B, A→B, and nothing else enters. We call that an open loop, meaning that it is not a loop at all. A can be an elaborate concatenation of elements, but however many those elements, as long as the direction of influence is always in one direction the notion of cause is fully applicable, and if the elements of A are known and controllable, then A can be used to control B. This condition is so much the ideal that the planner is likely to declare it to exist even when events prove that the operative mechanism is more complex.

Feedback

If A and B above occur at the same time, and B can cause A, B→A, as well, then the door is open to difficulties that greatly complicate the work of the analyst. The causal diagram here would be a closed loop, written A→B→A or A↔B. A small amount of A causes a small amount of B, and that in turn increases A, which then increases B, and so on indefinitely. Do we blame A, and cure B by attacking A? Or the converse?

It is not surprising that the several disciplines, particularly economics and psychology, prefer linear open loop models, that fortunately seem all that is needed for many short-term forecasts. Open loops permit unambiguous statements of cause. If besides A causing B it is also true that B causes A, but not immediately, then until this second part of the machinery comes into operation the action of A on B is an adequate description well suited to short-term forecasting.

Such feedbacks are common in social life. As in a similar case mentioned above, parents start by treating their child with that combination of affection and firmness that has been the traditional ideal; the child responds with affection and self-discipline; that makes the affection of parents easier to exercise and demonstrate, and so on in reciprocal fashion, in a beneficial circle. Other parents treat their child with impatience and reveal little affection (though they may actually feel the very strongest affection); the circle can develop in a very different way. Both cases are what engineers call positive feedback; in popular speech they are beneficial and vicious circles respectively.

Magnification of differences

There is plenty of evidence on the effect of praise and scorn on performance. One sociologist (Whyte 1955) in a famous study observing the behavior of Italian boys' gangs saw that when they had a little money they would spend it in a bowling alley, and it turned out that the gang leader always won. It was not that he was a better bowler, but rather that he had the very vocal support of his followers against an outside challenger. In short he was not the leader because he was the best bowler, but the converse; he was the best bowler because he was the leader.

Think of a child that for any reason gives the impression of being just a little stronger than his or her mates – perhaps it wins a children's race just by chance. As a result it is encouraged to go in for sports as a runner; that makes it stronger yet, and so the process continues. The runner who initially is thought weaker is discouraged by bystanders, even laughed at when trying to compete, abandons the competition and is inclined to avoid sport thereafter. Does the first child ultimately come to win medals for accomplishment in sport because of its initial start – a small random variation – or because of better subsequent training and moral support? The question is intrinsically unanswerable if the subsequent training is itself the result of the small initial advantage.

A similar feedback can apply in regard to books and reading. Through some trivial circumstance a child is led to look at a book, finds it somewhat pleasurable, and that makes it seek other books, reading them increases its sensitivity to written matter, so with every book it becomes more receptive to books. Another child, for whatever reason, has a book pushed on it, finds it lacking in material or ideas that correspond to its preoccupations, is put off reading and takes up other matters, and the failure to get in at the starting age for such things, say between ages 5 and 10, is a handicap from which it may never recover.

Many other such feedbacks similarly magnify slight, totally unimportant, initial differences. In a well-run school with disciplined children the devoted teacher is encouraged by the responses of classes to her instruction. Where children's response is even slightly less satisfactory, the teacher's devotion in the exercise of her profession declines, and her losing interest in the job acts back on the pupils, lowers the level of interest and makes teaching less satisfying. At the end of that sequence of successive alternating actions and reactions is a school where no one learns, and the teacher has a merely custodial function, relieved to hear the final bell each day. Who is to blame – the teacher or the pupils?

Feedback can also occur between two variables. Thus a recent UNICEF book finds that education and health are mutually reinforcing. Healthy children will be able to absorb their schooling better, and better educated children will take the measures necessary to keep healthy. This is described as synergy between health and education (UNICEF 1994), and the mutual support makes it largely meaningless to ask how much of the children's mental and physical welfare is due to health and how much to education.

Christopher Jencks comes close to the idea here when he takes account of the 'effects [of genes] on the way that parents, teachers, schools and peers treat a child, as well as on the environment children select for themselves' (Jencks 1992, p.106). That is to say the genes as such do not make much difference between one child and another, but if they make even a small difference on whether the child will choose books or television, they will make a big difference to the way that child grows up.

The feedback between child and parent affects both, though the child much more. Without being described in quite these words, the process is plainly implicit in the literature. Thus we find in Cairns (1979, p.327) that

The interaction out of which the organism develops is not one . . . between heredity and environment. It is between organism and environment. And the organism is different at each different stage of its development.

And again

. . . variance in specific maternal behaviours uniquely predicts a range of specific development outcomes in children.

But that is only part of the story:

The arrow of socialisation is not uniquely one way, mother→baby; infants in their own way also influence mother, i.e. infant→mother, and contribute to their own development: infant→mother→infant. (Bornstein, 1991)

I find many feedbacks in the social science literature, usually implied rather than expounded as such and ranging over a wide expanse of subject matter. For instance Jerome Kagan (1994, p.120):

If the culture has a small number of impoverished citizens, it will appear to many that it is possible to eliminate poverty; and charity toward the poor will be promoted. However if there are too many disenfranchised, as in India or Tibet, success will seem unattainable, and concern for the poor is likely to be replaced with . . . a mood of detachment.

Transporting that idea to the United States, it is possible that the present unwillingness to redistribute income, expressed as hostility to taxes, is the cumulative outcome of a closed loop process that could translate Kagan's words as more poor→more indifference→more poor yet→more indifference . . .

The general principle is that when A, the person, influences the relevant environment B by the choices he or she makes, and the environment chosen in turn influences the person, and the reciprocal influence continues indefinitely, then the very notion of causality, as familiar to common sense as it is to science, simply loses its meaning. In symbols A can be the cause of B, i.e. A→B, but if B is also the cause of A, i.e. A↔B, then naming B as the cause is every bit as convincing as naming A. When a small inheritable difference between two individuals is magnified by their selecting different environments, and the end is a large difference between them, then attributing the cause to either genes or environment is arbitrary.

It is valuable to know when a question cannot be meaningfully answered, so that time can be saved from investigating it.

FEEDBACKS AND GENDER

The point is carried further in respect of gender differentiation. It was suggested that students' and teachers' constructions of gender and science affect student outcomes – the attitudes of girls as well as their participation in science (Kahle *et al.* 1994). The basic underlying point is that students, like other people, want to do whatever they will do well enough to excite admiration, and to avoid activities on which they will turn out to be inadequate. For some trifling reason a girl fails the first test in arithmetic, so she decides that mathematics is too difficult for her. At that point she could easily be convinced that she really should not give up, that in fact arithmetic can be grasped by a person of her capacities, but no one comes along to persuade her of this. The result is a cumulation of such events and a hardening of her sense of inadequacy in mathematics with each passing year; as she stays away from mathematics what she hears of it makes it seem increasingly arcane and out of her reach. To convince her otherwise, fortunately, is always possible, but the younger she is when a skilled teacher takes her in hand the more satisfactory the outcome will be.

The collective effect of this goes further and constitutes a self-imposed gender bias. Females, it is said, are just 'not good at mathematics', and that excuses each girl from even starting to try. Thus not only individually but collectively the casually repeated phrase 'not good at mathematics' makes itself true even for girls who do not have that initial adverse experience. Spread of the slogan 'What one person can do another can' as the women's movement has gathered strength over the past two or three decades has proven that on all important matters the immemorial male bias was an artificial social construction. And changes in attitudes of Blacks have been occurring along similar lines and have had positive results in the same direction as for females.

Imprinting of labels on a child can start very young. As the well-known economist Ester Boserup (1987) says:

Much female aptitude for routine and precision work, unsuitability for leadership and unwillingness to take responsibility results from family socialization in the first years of life. Most often the schools continue in the same vein.

The acceptance of the label by the child is needed if its effect is to be as strong as historical experience shows.

The superposition of multiple feedback mechanisms in climate offers no less awkwardness for long-term prediction than it does to social science trying to say what the next generation will be like. On global warming, we hear disputes among experts on whether or not it is occurring now, on whether it will occur in the future, and if it does by how much. That will serve as an example from physical science of multiple feedbacks and the uncertainty they create.

FEEDBACKS IN GLOBAL WARMING

Four of the mechanisms involved in global warming can be listed briefly to illustrate how such feedbacks compete with one another and interact in a physical application.

One is the effect of water vapor (*New Scientist* 1992):

a warmer atmosphere can hold more water vapor . . . and . . . this is itself a greenhouse gas.

Thus warming increases the water vapor content of the atmosphere and more water vapor acts the way that carbon dioxide does, so further increases warming – a positive feedback.

Another instance of positive feedback involves the capacity of the oceans to hold carbon dioxide:

As the oceans warm, they are less able to absorb carbon dioxide from the atmosphere.

Less carbon dioxide in the water leaves more in the atmosphere, and more in the atmosphere warms it and the oceans so the carbon dioxide in the oceans diminishes further and that in the air increases.

And another positive feedback

is the possible release of greenhouse gases such as methane, currently frozen into the tundra of the far north. If the frozen ground melts enough to release the gases, they could rise through the atmosphere and lead to further warming.

On the other hand one kind of negative feedback – that would be stabilizing – would exist if clouds were increased by warming; one writer refers to

the formation of certain types of clouds that reflect more solar radiation back into space as the world warms. Less radiation from the Sun means that the Earth becomes cooler than it otherwise would.

The *New Scientist* summarizes this last:

Many GCMs [climate models] also include the effects of clouds . . . The IPCC reserved judgment on whether clouds will produce net positive or negative feedback in a warming world.

This is hardly a complete inventory – there could be dozens of other feedbacks – but it shows how any one of the feedbacks can interact with others in a circular process. Thus warming due to melting of the polar ice caps will also help to melt the frozen tundra of Canada and Siberia, that will release methane, and this will melt the polar ice cap further. And further advance of science could well reveal many forces other than feedbacks. Most of the global stock of carbon dioxide and methane is contained in the deep oceans, so a small change in the appetite of the oceans for these gases could override the several surface forces listed.

I go on to a further level of complexity in the social world, rarely included among the assumptions of social science.

OVERCOMING A HANDICAP

Fred Mosteller points to a mechanism that is the opposite of that described above and on which he cites reliable testimony. The child that has a disadvantage and is jeered at by schoolmates has a stimulus to overcome the disadvantage, and this stimulus can in some individuals act so strongly that the child not only draws equal to its classmates, but far outdoes them.

That is in the sharpest contrast to the mechanism described above, in which the child starts a little ahead in some activity, and parlays that into something big through successive encouragement of others. In a way that makes things too easy: it seems to say that all the child needs is continuous praise and it will do better and better. We should know that matters are not so simple.

There are many real life cases of the person being handicapped in some way, and through determination coming up from behind. A child recovering from polio becomes a swimming champion or a champion runner. I have a nephew who is dyslexic, and who has become a successful print designer. The statistician Sir Ronald Fisher had very poor eyesight all his life, which seemed to preclude a research career, especially one involving mathematics that ordinarily demands so much pencil and paper work. He responded by developing a unique capacity to visualize multidimensional figures, and with this capacity he could simply write down new algebraic results, leaving it to Harald Cramer and others laboriously to prove them formally.

Mosteller's point applies not only to individuals but in Toynbee (1954) to the rise and fall of nations. It can be taken as falling under our heading of interpretation above: just as jail or parental punishment has a different effect depending on how it is interpreted, so a handicap can be interpreted by the one that suffers it as a condemnation to a subordinate place, or as a challenge to be overcome. The interpretation can be by a single individual, or can be built into the culture of a whole society.

What if social life is such that both models apply, and whether in a particular case the handicap is a condemnation or a challenge depends on the individual and the circumstances? So stated that would make forecasting impossible, unless special knowledge of the case gave us a hint of which road would be chosen. Toynbee thinks he gives an indication of whether challenge and response is going to work: the challenge must be difficult but not overwhelming – but other historians find his case less than convincing.

The possibly favorable effect of challenge is thus to be contrasted with the effect of praise. Apparently either one can go either way: the challenge may be discouraging or energizing, the praise can lead to more achievement or only to more self-satisfaction without achievement.

Thus in listing the repertory of social influence on an individual we have at least three types: reward–punishment, praise, and challenge. The three act differently on different individuals, and applied to the group they suggest radically different policies. In real individuals all of them can be operative, and the difficulty resides in establishing with what weights or proportions.

That list of three influences on human behavior, among its other shortcomings, fails to take account of competing sources of information.

ACCESS TO INFORMATION: THE CAR WITH TWO DRIVERS

Aside from all the difficulties of prediction and control suggested above, there is another problem to be faced by the one who would steer society towards an idyllic crime-free world. Suppose a vehicle that has a second steering wheel, independently steered, so that two drivers are both able to influence direction. The vehicle would then be outside the control of either of the two drivers. In application to upbringing, instead of the child being exposed to fairly consistent influences of parents and teachers and protected by them when under age from outside alternatives, its environment has now come to include a wholly independent and competing force: the electronic media. It is exposed almost from its earliest days to two sets of information, and two contrasting and competing moralities.

The child faces the TV screen for a considerable length of time each week, with an intensity of attention that more than matches that in the classroom, so that a new non-school component of education provides its own daily lessons, not five but seven days a week. The lessons of television concern behavior as much as those of the home and the classroom, but the substance of what is taught is radically different. Insofar as education by parents and teachers on the one side steers the child morally in one direction, and the media steer it in a different direction, adult control of the outcome is lost. There have always been inter-generational changes, but now for the first time in history anywhere, parents have lost the monopoly of information that enabled them without interference to impress their values on the child. We now have two drivers with independent steering wheels trying to steer the car.

The resulting break in the sequence of the generations seems to have occurred in the 1960s. It looks like a genuine mutation in the continuity of culture, of a kind and suddenness never before known. Parents did not see the erosion of their authority coming, and when it occurred and they realized what was happening they were helpless to restore their position.

It is true that parents are busy now with activities that keep them away from their children, but the major factor releasing children from the influence of their parents was not so much the labor force preoccupations of the latter (Presser 1989) as the availability of television to fill the gap. At the outset television seemed neutral to parents, a convenient electronic governess. It has turned out to be far from neutral, providing a kind of moral guidance the very opposite of what a traditional governess would provide.

The effect of violence shown on TV has been almost continuously in the news for many years now. As John Condry says, 'Hundreds of studies . . . broadly agree that children who are heavy viewers of television are more aggressive than children who are light viewers' (Condry 1993). As I write this the press carries an account of the researches of Leonard D. Eron, who interviewed children in 1960, 1970, and 1980, and found that 'the best predictor of aggression among boys was . . . the amount of television violence they had watched a decade earlier . . . Such forms of entertainment do not merely mirror what happens on the streets but help provoke it' (Eron 1994). President Clinton, in his 1995 State of the Union message, was emphatic on the 'mindless violence' that goes over the air day and night, and he called on the television industry to do something about it.

Jerome Kagan makes a somewhat different point. Television and films (and, I would add, much of modern writing and indeed of social science) have weakened the transmission of ways of behavior between the generations. He speaks of the recent trend to 'legitimize prostitution and adultery by implying that standards for sexual behavior [are] conventional' (Kagan 1994, p.121). Once prevailing standards become seen as conventional then one is as good as another; even if they always have been conventional the fiction that they are divinely ordained, that they are somehow built into the nature of things, was a means of imprinting them emotionally on the young. When parents could pass that on for at least the child's first few years even those who thought it a fiction had to agree that what came later was unlikely to disturb the emotionally rooted sense that certain behavior was simply wrong. Today at the very youngest ages the voice of TV contradicts and drowns out the voice of the parent and teacher so that emotional attachment to what the latter declare to be right is never attained.

Among other effects of television is to depreciate reading. The association of television with loss of capacity to read effectively is clear, but the direction of causation is contested. Thus a popular writer (Leach 1994) points out that

Many Western parents complain that their children read too little because they watch TV too much. If that is true so is the reverse: children watch TV because they do not read.

Teachers on the one side and television executives on the other choose opposite directions of this causal nexus. Again a feedback – the more children spend time watching TV the less their ability to read and to derive enjoyment from books, and vice versa.

Meanwhile Bernard Sharratt expands the electronic media to include computers, and he draws up a scenario (Sharratt 1994) for some time in the not too distant future

of a generation so enmeshed in electronic information, so tuned in not just to television but to pervasive interactive multimedia, so besotted by on-line data services, as to have grown up barely acquainted with printed books at all.

The picture is that of the computer nerd spoken of by Sheryl Wudunn: 'brilliant, driven, but utterly lost when in human company' (Wudunn 1995).

For the long term, the period of a generation at the end of which we will be replaced by our children, there is no present activity more important than child-raising – in the home, at school, and in the street. How our children will behave as adults depends on how they are brought up now, and so upbringing can be considered a central problem of our times, and at the root of many of the long-term problems spoken of above. Prisons are a short-term solution to crime; the long-term solution is to be found long before, when the prisoner was a child. If only upbringing and subsequent control of crime was a matter of rewards and punishment policy would be easy. Experienced parents, teachers, and legislators now know that the process of child upbringing cannot be governed by what has corresponded to Newton's first law as the basis of the social sciences – pull the child in the desired direction with carrots and push it away from the undesired with sticks.

UNNECESSARY PESSIMISM GENERATED
BY FAILED POLICIES

As little as 30 years ago optimism prevailed and told us that nothing could stop our progress; there were a few problems of course but we showed every determination to deal with them and once certain things were done we would emerge into a problem-free epoch, the end of history. The war on poverty would enable the very poor to rise into the middle class; the war on drugs would get rid of that incubus; a war on crime would check violence. Some schools were below standard and action at the federal level, guided by the 'Education President', as George Bush once called himself, would put the US equal to the best of their foreign competitors. Evidence was presented showing that we were year by year winning those wars, that we were aiding the poor, confiscating drugs, and improving the schools. Every month the news carried reports of victories – a cache of drugs discovered, a major dealer captured. Some individual schools established records for scholarship.

What seems to have happened instead is that we won battles, yet victory in the wars is as far away as ever. And that has had an unfortunate effect: it is taken to mean that we as nations are no longer in control, that we have tried and failed and it is now no longer worth trying. We read that 'The age of using governments to reform the world may be over' (*The Economist* 1995). If that means that nothing can or should be done it could be a wrong interpretation. Yet it could also be the outcome of another mechanism, not taken up here – the interaction between the freeing of national and international markets on the one hand, and the action of governments within any country on the other.

On that view governments are withdrawing from schemes to help their citizens because they have become powerless to help. Where for a long time they could fix the value of their currency and make it stick, now the amount of funds sloshing over national boundaries and available for currency speculation makes that impossible. At one time they could print money and set interest rates to make employment; now they can do that only at great risk. They used to control information, for example by censoring books coming from abroad; now they cannot stop radio and TV signals at the border, and these latter have more popular influence than books. And especially to the point here, they cannot engage in social policies at home without risking their international trade. In a phrase of Daniel Bell that has become famous, 'The nation-state is by now too small for the big problems of life and too big for the small problems' (Bell 1995).

A pair of European scholars speak of the difficulty that national income maintenance programs, social services, and means-tested social assistance have in adapting to the global economy (Rieger and Leibfried 1995). Only by capping welfare state development, pursuing a policy of retrenchment and curtailing social rights could the nation keep its competitive position. The fact that much of Europe is going through essentially the same changes as the United States suggests that governments are withdrawing from social policies as much because they have lost the power to intervene as because they realize that past policies have been short-term successes but long-term failures. That freeing world markets makes national governments powerless was as little taken into account as the effect of the world airline network in spreading AIDS.

Some favorable circumstances lead to more of the same, so the long-term effect is in the same positive direction as the short-term, and carries the latter forward. A recent RAND study (Grissmer 1994) confirms what had been noted earlier: that more Black children are attending high school in the 1990s than in the 1970s, and that a main factor in high school attendance for all children is the attendance of their parents. If that is the dominant force, and high school has the beneficial effect that we see when comparing present high-school graduates with dropouts, then the movement promises that soon substantially all of the population will have high school at least, and the same process will continue through college. College graduates show an increasingly large advantage over non-college, and if this cross-sectional advantage can be held over time, then the whole population will sooner or later have that advantage. There are some qualifications to the logic here. As Bruce Spencer points out to me, perhaps education merely helps individuals to compete against less educated individuals in the labor market;

on the other hand it is possible that education improves productivity absolutely. Yet until the opposite is proved, we have as strong an argument for optimism as the failed policies provide for pessimism.

If linear extrapolations fail as long-term forecasts that is because they need something added to them. The linear of a single discipline may well be the main component and suited to the short term, but as in a Taylor expansion of a function of time the quadratic and other terms difficult to handle come sooner or later to be required and so start what seem like the intractable problems of long-term forecasting and policy.

CONCLUSION

In a feedback model the possibility of forecasting is limited and causation is elusive. That such models represent a component of real world events explains some of the stubbornness that social problems offer to policies that would durably solve them. Adding to the difficulties are the different interpretations of the same signals by human actors.

Those varied difficulties are avoided in the simple linear models leading to equilibrium typically employed in economics and other social sciences. Such models account for short-term changes, show clear-cut causation, and permit planning. The planning works for a while, but in the longer run is often frustrated. This condition, a series of short-term successes leading to long-term failure, tells us that underlying social and even physical phenomena is a tangle of nonlinearities, feedbacks interacting with one another, misunderstandings of signals. These complexities do not typically appear when the several sciences make their analyses separately. But in the long term and in the real world the forces considered by the several sciences operate simultaneously, while the categories used in the sciences are resistant to simultaneous treatment. The forces of economics, politics, and society are inseparable, and in the long run they interfere drastically with one another, however troublesome that may be to our long-run forecasts and policies.

By facing up to the complexities we stand a better chance of prolonging the short run in which projections are worthwhile and policies work.

REFERENCES

Bell, D. (1995). Social science: An imperfect art. *The Toqueville Review*, **16**, 21.

Bornstein, M. H. (1991). *Cultural approaches to parenting*. Lawrence Erlbaum Associates, Hillsdale, NJ.

Boserup, E. (1987). Inequality between the sexes. In *The new Palgrave*. Vol. 2, p.826. Macmillan, London.

Bronars, S. G. and Grogger, J. (1994). The economic consequences of unwed motherhood: using twin births as a natural experiment. *The American Economic Review*, **84**, 5 December, 1141.

Cairns, R. B. (1979). *Social development: the origins and plasticity of interchanges*. W. H. Freeman, San Francisco.

Condry, J. (1993). Television and the American child. *Daedalus*, **122**, (winter), 259–78.

The Economist (1995). 4 March, 78.

The Economist (1995). Deinventing government. 20 May, 16.

Eron, L. D. (1994). *New York Times*, 17 December, 1.

Grissmer, D. W., *et al.* (1994). *Student achievement and the changing American family.* RAND, Santa Monica, CA.

Jencks, C. (1992). *Rethinking social policy: race, poverty, and the underclass.* Harvard University Press, Cambridge, MA.

Kagan, J. (1994). *The nature of the child*, tenth anniversary edition. Basic Books, New York.

Kahle, J. B., *et al.* (1994). Gender differences in science education: building a model. *Educational Psychologist*, **28**, 379–404.

Laslett, P. (1965). *The world we have lost.* Scribner, New York.

Leach, P. (1994). *Children first.* Knopf, New York.

The New Scientist (1992). 2 May, 40–1.

Presser, H. B. (1989). Can we make time for children? The economy, work schedules, and child care. *Demography*, **26**, 523–43. (Valerie Kincade Oppenheimer has also contributed on this point.)

Rieger, E., and Leibfried, S. (1995). *Globalization and the western welfare state: an annotated bibliography.* University of Bremen, Centre for Social Policy Research, working paper no. 1, p. 5.

Rosenblatt, R. (1995). Teaching Johnny to be good. *The New York Times Magazine*, 30 April, 5, 36.

Schelling, T. C. (1981). Economic reasoning and the ethics of policy. *The Public Interest*, **63**, (Spring), 37–61.

Sharratt, B. (1994). Review of *The Guttenberg: The fate of reading in an electronic age. New York Time Book Review Section*, 18 December.

Toynbee, A. J. (1954). *A study of history.* Oxford University Press.

UNICEF (1994). *The state of the world's children 1994.* Oxford University Press.

Whyte, W. F. (1955). *Street corner society.* University of Chicago Press.

Wudunn, S. (1995). *New York Times*, 22 May, 6.

12 Experimentation: just do it!

LINCOLN E. MOSES AND FREDERICK MOSTELLER

INTRODUCTION

Progress in activities like medical care, education and business grows largely from making changes in the way things are done. We will call those 'policy changes'. Their many forms include: decisions to change, abandon, or begin regulatory measures; decisions to invest or divest; decisions to introduce, modify, or curtail services or product lines. The success of policy changes rests in large part on the availability and reliability of the information considered in making the decision. Information sources include sample surveys, administrative records, focus groups, theoretical formulations – and experiments.

In this chapter, we urge wider use of systematic well-conducted experiments as a tool in policy formulation. The experimental method has revolutionized physics, chemistry, and biology, in the modern era. More recently it has brought strength to psychology, medicine, education, pharmacology, and various branches of engineering. We urge expanded use of the method in the policy formation process. We see three main reasons for now emphasizing the use of experiments in policy formation. First, using alternatives to experimentation is, in the nature of things, often disappointing. Second, small improvements are much more likely to be accessible than are large ones; this in turn demands the best of technology to appraise accurately the actual worth of proposed innovations. Third, the feasibility of the experimental method for informing policy appears to be widely underestimated.

Using a collection of past experiences as a basis for forming new policy is a natural feature of the social landscape – but it entails a lot of difficulty and trouble; experience is often hard to interpret. David Byar, a noted cancer researcher, tells (Byar 1991; Green and Byar 1984) of trying to interpret a rich body of clinical data on thyroid cancer patients, some of whom had received radiation treatment and others who had not. The mortality among those who did receive radiation therapy was notably higher than among those who did not. Some of the difference could be explained away by differences in age, severity of disease, etc., but the basic finding still stood: those receiving radiation were dying faster. He and his co-workers concluded that the apparent finding was spurious, probably an outcome of non-comparability (which they could not measure) between the thyroid cancer patients for whom physicians did and did not prescribe radiation therapy. Such stories are not unusual in medicine, nor in other fields as well. Experience can be very hard to interpret!

Disappointing as retrospective interpretation can be, forecasts, formal or informal, may be even more troubled. Consider the story of the Massachusetts gun law. Some years ago, to discourage handguns, the legislature decided that there ought to be a law that anyone carrying such a gun without a permit would definitely go to jail for at least a year. The law was passed with enthusiasm. Years later, even though the streets have handgun killings every week, indeed nearly every day, practically no one has been convicted and jailed under this law even though many are caught with the weapons. Part of the reason is that judges do not like to be told what to do, and so mandatory sentencing, generally speaking, is a failure. Another part of the reason is that this law gives the prosecution a lever for settling cases through plea bargaining at a lesser penalty. Thus a law that clearly seems to say that anyone caught with an unregistered handgun surely goes to jail, does not work out that way at all, though it may have some effect, such as leverage for the prosecution. Clearly in a complicated system like the justice system it is not obvious how a change in the law will work out.

Work of Gilbert *et al.* (1975) illuminates how prior ideas about effective innovations, when put to the test of experimentation, often do not live up to their promise. They reviewed the outcomes of 28 experiments that appeared to be large enough and sufficiently well carried out to reach conclusions. They reviewed studies in education, welfare, criminal justice, medical care, manpower training, surgery, and preventive medicine. They scored the effectiveness of the intervention according to a single five-point scale: + + a great success, + a modest success, 0 not much effect, − a modestly harmful innovation, − − a definitely harmful innovation. Their results were as shown in Table 1.

Table 1 Effectiveness of 28 social and medical interventions. (Reproduced with permission of Academic Press, Inc. from Gilbert *et al.* (1975, p. 114))

Rating	Count	Percentage	
+ +	6	21%	
+	6	21%	
0	13	46%	
−	2	7%	} 57%
− −	1	4%	

Total 28

Table 1 tells us that over half of the interventions failed to have a positive effect on the problem they were designed to solve! Of those that seemed beneficial, half appeared to be highly successful, and half had only small effects. Of course, all the interventions studied had been *expected* to make very positive contributions or they would not have been introduced and studied carefully. Their proposers believed that the interventions were sure winners.

The 28 studies described above were collected from lists of studies and some biases favorable to intervention may have been present. To avoid such bias,

Gilbert and colleagues did a second study (Gilbert *et al.* 1977) in which they collected a sample of 36 well-done randomized trials in surgery and anesthesia for the period 1964–72; that was a more objective sample of all randomized controlled studies in the literature. Their scoring system was close to the earlier one. The + + meant that the innovation was highly preferred to the standard treatment, + meant that the innovation was preferred, and similarly with − and − −. The 0 was divided into two classes, (i) those where the innovation was regarded as a success because it added a treatment for the use of the physician even though its success rate was only approximately equal to that of the standard treatment, or (ii) the innovation performed about equally to the standard but was a disappointment because it did not add a treatment, for various reasons such as high cost or problems of training or equipment. Using essentially the same notation as before they found the results given in Table 2; this shows again that more than half of the innovations failed to be beneficial when tried out.

Table 2 Results for 36 surgical and anesthetic innovations. (Reproduced with permission of Oxford University Press from Gilbert *et al.* (1977, p. 128))

	Rating	Count	Percentage	
Innovation highly preferred	+ +	5	14%	
Innovation preferred	+	7	19%	
Innovation a success	0	4	11%	
Innovation a disappointment	0	10	28%	
Standard preferred	−	6	17%	} 56%
Standard highly preferred	− −	4	11%	
	Total	36		

The analyses given above for the two investigations are qualitative. The second paper, on the medical investigations, also provided a quantitative analysis. It divided the therapies into primary and secondary. Primary trials dealt with treatments intended to prevent death; in secondary trials the treatments were intended to promote recovery from surgery, such as by avoiding infections. In primary trials the measure of gain was the improvement in survival of the innovation group compared with that of the standard treatment group at about the time 50% had died. In the secondary treatment, the measure of gain was the percentage improvement in avoiding the complication being treated (i.e. if the innovative treatment prevented the complication in 60% and the standard in 50%, the gain was 10%). The overall findings were remarkable (Table 3).

Table 3 Average percentage gain attributed to surgical innovation. (Reproduced with permission of Oxford University Press from Gilbert *et al.* (1977, p. 134)

	Estimated mean gain (%)	Estimated standard deviation of gains(%)	Number of studies
Primary therapies	1.3	7.7	19
Secondary therapies	0.4	20.6	17

Thus, Table 3 shows that on the average the gain in survival rate for all the primary treatments tested was 1.3%, and for relief of complications by the secondary treatments 0.4%. Considering the variability of the numbers, the average gains are very close to zero. (A genuine 1.3% improvement in survival rate should be regarded as valuable, but here its uncertainty ranges at least from -14.1% to $+16.7\%$.) Note that the averages 1.3% and 0.4% are not by themselves the improvements that we want to preserve. Those averages are made up of positive (beneficial) and negative (harmful) effects. We wish to preserve the beneficial effects and avoid the harmful ones. And so the ultimate improvements in the instances where beneficial effects are found will be higher than these averages. Even if these averages had been negative, preserving the beneficial treatments and avoiding the harmful ones improves the total system substantially.

Small effects are the rule when innovations are evaluated, and to be found and kept they need to be evaluated carefully. Great ideas bringing great benefits are rather rare, but fortunately, identifying and preserving small benefits improves progress enormously.

In the past generation, therapies have been developed for various forms of leukemia, turning that from a uniformly fatal disease to one that can often be cured. That achievement has involved many trials of many possible innovations; ineffectual (or harmful) ones have been discarded; and beneficial ones retained. Experimentation over decades, finding and retaining modestly better treatments has led to an imposing success.

Even the hard sciences are not able to investigate every important question by means of experiments; astronomy, geology, and many branches of biology attest to this. Naturally, it is true as well that not all policy proposals are amenable to experimental investigation. But we have much scope for more than the present use of this powerful method. In the next sections of this chapter the reader will find accounts of numerous and varied policy-oriented uses of the method, a more systematic consideration of randomized experiments, and remarks about further extending uses of the experimental approach in policy formulation.

SOME EXAMPLES

We offer a number of examples that illustrate the broad variety of operational and policy questions amenable to resolution by the experimental method. Some examples explore ways to execute established functions more effectively; others explore the value of proposed changes in policy. We begin with a few of the first kind, and afterwards turn to some that assess policy changes.

Renewing driver's licenses

Some years ago the California legislature allowed the Department of Motor Vehicles to permit drivers to renew their driving licenses by mail (rather than in person) if their previous four years showed no moving violation and no accident. Opposition to this legislation expressed concern about the absence of a vision test. Those in charge of the Department of Motor Vehicles thought it important to check this out, and so while they allowed the bulk of eligible drivers to renew by mail, they chose a 10% sample, randomly, to renew in the previous manner. The numbers involved were in the hundreds of thousands. The subsequent driving records of the two groups would give a precise indication of differential safety-related problems, if any. No such differences appeared, and the new procedure was retained with confidence.

Checking on the value of an official practice

In the second half of 1980 a manager in a Washington statistical agency noted a small room, always occupied by four clerks using telephones. Inquiry revealed that they were telephoning recipients of questionnaires who were late in responding, to remind recipients of their legal obligation to reply. The clerks were engaged in 'follow-up of non-response'. The manager inquired, 'Why is this done?' She was told, 'To improve the response rate' – but no facts existed about how well it worked. So she (the manager – a statistician) required that half the names on the non-respondent list – chosen with a table of random numbers – not be phoned *at all* that month. Then the timeliness of response in the two groups, called and uncalled, could be compared and the benefits of phone follow-up weighed against costs. The result was surprising. Response was no better in the group receiving telephone follow-up! The four clerks were assigned to more useful work.

This example repays a little reflection. Crucial to its success was the fact that the assignment to 'no follow-up call' was made by a random mechanism. Had the supervisor *chosen* the firms not to be called that would admit doubts of many sorts: did she choose for 'no call' those firms whose previous record showed high probability of filing the report? Had she preferred assigning 'no call' to *small* firms, where absent data would be less harmful? And if so, how would that be related to response rate? The doubts could go on endlessly; but random allocation defeats them all: both those we can think of and those we cannot.

Improving IRS collection of delinquent accounts

Perng (1985) reports a more complicated experiment comparing six ways for the Internal Revenue Service to deal with individuals' delinquent tax accounts. The basic pattern, already in use, involved four successive notices – we call them here A,B,C, and D – with intervals between them of five, three, and four weeks respectively, and a four-week interval after notice D before transferring the account to a field office for other (and much more costly) collection efforts. This basic pattern, identified as 5–3–4–4 was modified in several ways, to produce five new variants. One simply replaced the three-week interval between notices B and C by a 15-week interval; others involved phone contact, an additional interim notice, offers of installment paying, and combinations of these. Delinquent accounts were assigned to one of the six treatments on the basis of the last digits of their social security numbers. This is not quite random assignment, but IRS has experience to show its effectiveness in use, and for samples totaling in the tens of thousands the systematic convenience was a strong consideration. There was a clear winner: the 15 weeks' wait between notices B and C produced the best results, and that with less extra effort and cost than required by most of the other variants.

Agricultural progress and experimentation

The development of greatly increased agricultural productivity in the twentieth century has rested largely on field experiments in which new varieties of crops (and new agriculture practices) are compared with standard ones. So important is this empirical testing to agricultural progress that a large part of modern statistical design of experiments actually grew up in the context of agricultural experimentation. Crop yields depend not only upon the variety of crop raised and on crop-growing methods, but also upon the weather, fertility of the land used, insect population, past use of the land in question, etc. In short, the control of 'all relevant factors' is exceedingly difficult in agricultural research; this recognition led to adoption of the strategy of randomized assignment as a way to prevent extraneous influential factors from producing biased estimates of difference between varieties or of the effectiveness of new agricultural practices.

Licensing new drugs

The Food and Drug Administration controls the licensing of new drugs for marketing in the USA. A key systematic component is demonstrating safety and efficacy – how well the drug works – in at least 'two well-controlled studies in humans'. In practice this usually means at least one randomized control trial (RCT), large enough to have high probability of detecting important short-term favorable or adverse effects if they exist, and additional studies, possibly including some further randomized ones.

Both safety and efficacy are important features of a drug's performance, but they relate to RCT investigations rather differently. A drug that cures a condition in half the patients who receive it may be valuable indeed, and a trial involving a few hundred patients may suffice to show its efficacy. But, that same trial will not be large enough to identify reliably a rare important adverse effect like drug-induced cardiac arrest at a rate of one in a thousand or a slow-to-develop adverse effect like cancer. So, for practical purposes the RCT often resolves the efficacy question while leaving the possibility of rare or slow-developing severe side effects to be further illuminated by surveillance in the post-marketing period.

Our examples thus far have dealt with *routines*: the first three with alterations, including abandonment, of existing routines and the last two with continuing programs of experimentation which have themselves become routinized. Our next examples show experimental approaches to resolving questions about proposed new policy.

The Salk polio vaccine trial

The policy question in 1954 was whether nationwide vaccination with the new Salk polio vaccine should be undertaken. The Salk vaccine trial (Meier 1989) involved nearly 2 000 000 school children, all in first, second, or third grade. In many US states (involving about three-fifths of the total) the study used first and third graders as 'observed controls' to compare polio incidence with those in the second grade who were vaccinated, after their parents gave written consent. In the other states random assignment to vaccine or placebo injection, following parental permission, was used in grades 1, 2, and 3. This latter sub-study randomized about 200 000 children to the placebo and 200 000 to the vaccine. There were 57 confirmed cases of polio among the vaccinated children and 142 cases among the placebo children. This gave a definitive answer to the question.

A surprising side result appeared; the two groups of unvaccinated children, (i) those whose parents had withheld permission and (ii) those with permission-granting parents who had received the placebo, differed significantly in the incidence of polio. The placebo children had a higher incidence of polio (and of paralytic polio) than did their uninjected classmates. This fact displays a flaw in the observed-controls part of the vaccine trial; the observed controls included some children whose parents would have withheld permission while the placebo-injected second-graders did not. And as it turned out, there was more natural polio immunity in families that refused permission. Apparently families of higher socio-economic status (SES) tend more to protect their young children from encountering unsanitary conditions (reducing the likelihood of early exposure to polio virus – and immunity to it), and these families are also more likely to cooperate with official authorities – enrolling their children in the study. Thus, the permission-giving families would, on average, have lower levels of natural immunity.

Scandinavian highway experiments

In 1968 the use of highway speed limits, well established in the USA, was more controversial in parts of Europe. Empirical assessment of their actual value for highway safety was the subject of a large experimental study in Scandinavia

(Haight 1985). All the roads in the European system in Sweden were included, together with some of the principal national main roads. The key idea was that this network was divided into 'segments' – and each segment was subject to a speed limit for a portion of the time of the experiment, and without a speed limit for the rest of the time. This design of the study, plus an ingenious but simple analysis of the data, controlled the interfering effects of variables like weather, traffic volume, and seasonal events.

Minneapolis domestic violence experiment

Misdemeanor domestic assaults can be handled in various ways by the police. Three possible strategies, compared in a randomized field trial in Minneapolis, are mediation, arrest, and ordering one of the parties to leave the premises. The experiment (Sherman and Berk 1985), which lasted for more than a year, required the police officer who was called to the scene to use the method that corresponded to the color of the next (numbered) ticket in his pad of domestic violence tickets. The study utilized about 30 police officers and covered 314 incidents. The findings were that in the six-month follow-up period there was less repeated violence (10% official recidivism) in the arrested group than in the other groups (about 20%).

The experiment presented instructive features. First, acceptance by police officers of arresting, or not, in accordance with the color of the next ticket in their pad of domestic violence reports was a signal event. Second, official acceptance of such a mechanism stands as a demonstration that there are circumstances where random assignment can coexist with the constraints of law enforcement. Finally, Minneapolis thereafter cooperated with yet other randomized experiments in criminology.

The Manhattan bail bond experiment

An organization called the Vera Foundation suggested to the court that arrested persons with close ties to the community will return to the court for trial even if they are not required to put up bail (Botein 1964–5). The arrested who could not put up bail were ordinarily detained in jail until trial. The court expressed interest in trying out the release without bail of community-connected people. Workers for the Foundation developed a scoring system for choosing defendants suitable for release. They split a large number of favorably scoring defendants (about 6400) randomly into two equal-sized groups. For one group they recommended to the court release without bail, and for the other equivalently scoring group they made no recommendation. (Persons arrested for very serious crimes were not entered into this experiment.)

The court followed the recommendations for release without bail in about 50% of the 'recommended' cases, and among the 'no recommendation' cases it released only 16%. In all those released without bail only seven-tenths of 1% failed to show up for trial.

Naturally the court was impressed with this performance and over the years it gradually released more and more of the arrested persons unable to produce bail but who were recommended for release. The experiment produced additional information. Among the 'recommended' group 60% were acquitted or had their case dismissed, whereas in the equivalent 'no recommendation' group only 23% were acquitted or dismissed. Thus the consequences of being released instead of detained in jail are substantial.

When this approach with the same scoring system was tried in Des Moines, Iowa, out of 740 recommended for release without bail, the court released 716, and all but 16 showed up for trial (of the 16, 6 appeared a few days late; the remaining 10 included 7 traffic violators, 2 accused of forgery, and 1 with breaking and entering) (Dunn and George 1964). Having the second demonstration in Iowa rather than Manhattan added substantial generality to the original finding because something that works in large cities might not work in smaller cities, or vice versa.

Not only was it found that arrested people with strong community ties would almost certainly return for trial even without bail, but also the experiment uncovered the huge differential in outcome of the trial depending on being jailed until trial or released. Presumably those released are better off because they continue to earn and have more freedom to arrange their defense.

The Tennessee kindergarten and early grade study of effects of class size

The State of Tennessee decided to carry out a substantial experiment dealing with the class size question for four years starting in 1985 beginning with kindergarten and continuing through the early grades. The classes were to be of three types: small 13–17 pupils; regular 22–25 pupils; and regular with a teacher aide. The small classes averaged 15, down about 35% from the average regular of about 23. Within a school grade pupils and teachers were assigned to classes at random. The state funded the extra teachers and aides required for the experiment.

The first graders took two standardized tests in reading, the Stanford Achievement Test (SAT) for word study skills and reading, and the Tennessee Basic Skills First (BSF) tests for reading, a curriculum-based test. In mathematics first graders took one SAT (standardized) and one BSF (curriculum based) test.

The differences in performance among groups are often given as effect sizes, here defined as the difference between means divided by the standard deviation for individuals in the regular classes. The first line of Table 4 compares the performance of the small classes with that of the regular size class without an aide. The middle line of Table 4 shows the effect sizes for small classes compared with the average of the performance of the regular classes and those with aides. The third line compares regular size classes with and without an aide. For the standardized test (SAT), both reading and math show a benefit of about one-quarter of a standard deviation. For the curriculum oriented tests (BSF) the reading is benefited by about one-fifth of a standard deviation, and for math only one-eighth. When the addition of an aide is compared with the regular class performance, the gain averages about one-twelfth of a standard deviation, for both reading and math.

Table 4 Effect sizes in first grade: differences between averages in units of regular class standard deviation. Table 5 in Finn and Achilles (1990), reproduced with permission of the *American Educational Research Journal*

	Reading		Math	
	SAT	BSF	SAT	BSF
Small minus regular	0.30	0.25	0.32	0.15
Small minus (regular + aide)/2	0.23	0.21	0.27	0.13
Aide minus regular	0.14	0.08	0.10	0.05

Special interest attaches to the effect of class size on the Minorities as compared with the Whites. In small classes compared to regular-size or regular-size with aide the effect size for the Minorities was just about double that of Whites, averaged over the four tests. (Data not shown here.)

Thus, in a very large study (Finn and Achilles 1990), at least in the first grade, class size matters and teaching support does also, though not as much.

This experiment was carried out in kindergarten, first, second, and third grade. Then all children reverted to regular-sized classes. Over the years the improvement for the smaller classes held up well through the grades. The larger gain for minorities did not recur in grades 2 and 3; instead their gain was comparable with that achieved by whites.

In a follow-up survey for grades 4, 5, and 6, after students returned to regular-sized classes, the students who were in the smaller classes during kindergarten and grades 1, 2, and 3 continued to perform better in reading and mathematics than the students who started out in regular-sized classes.

Because this experiment was so large and so well-controlled (randomized teachers, randomized students, scores of schools, thousands of students, with students from urban, inner city, rural, and suburban areas), the results were compelling. The state of Tennessee has introduced the smaller classes in the 17 districts in which students are most at risk of falling behind in their school progress.

RANDOMIZED EXPERIMENTS: THE ESSENTIAL FEATURES

We point to four characteristics of randomized investigations that characterize the method and also account for the strength and reliability of conclusions obtained using it:

- treatments are actively imposed (rather than passively observed)
- random assignment to treatment groups ensures comparability of subjects, thus ruling out a large class of alternative 'explanations' of results
- the effort is protocol-driven
- outcome assessment and other processes that influence the data are applied symmetrically to all study subjects.

The treatments are actively imposed

In any complicated situation, if we want to know what will happen if we change the arrangements, we have to change them and see. Theorizing, guesswork, and calculations are much less to be trusted, though they help us to decide what to look for.

In the Salk trial the dose of vaccine (or placebo) was actually imposed on each subject by injection. But in another large RCT (The Coronary Drug Project Research Group 1980) concerning the drug clofibrate (for cholesterol reduction) the drug doses were only handed to the patient (to take later) – and the amount actually taken was *observed*. In the trial there was no statistically significant evidence of drug effectiveness as measured by extended survival or reduced incidence of cardiovascular events. But then it was found that five-year mortality of clofibrate subjects was much lower among those who actually took more than 80% of their dose than among those who actually took less than 80% (the two death rates were 15.0% and 24.6% respectively). This difference was too large to be explained by random variation; and it seemed at first glance to indicate drug effectiveness. But note, the finding that one larger dose is accompanied by better survival is based on passive observation of subjects treated alike (all were in the clofibrate group). The comparison is between two groups, high- and low-compliers, *constituted by self-selection*, rather than by random assignment. This indication of drug effectiveness, based on passive observation proved to be illusory, as more careful analysis revealed. Among the placebo patients there were also some who took more than 80% of their medication and others who took less; and again the high-compliers had lower five-year mortality than the low-compliers. (The two rates were 15.1% and 28.3%) So the encouraging-looking evidence of drug effectiveness was actually pointing to some longevity difference associated not with clofibrate, but with a propensity to follow a dosage schedule – of whatever drug. This illustrates how inferences from *observed* comparisons are less reliable and therefore less informative than *experimental* comparisons.

Random assignment to treatment groups

Comparing current experience using a new treatment with previous experience using a former treatment is convenient and deceptively attractive. But such use of 'historical controls' suffers from the liability that the two treatments, old and new, are applied to *separately constituted groups*; they may differ in important ways that we do not recognize or understand, and those differences may emerge as apparent treatment effects. The randomized study avoids this problem. The treatment groups are established by randomly dividing a *singly constituted group* of subjects, all meeting the same explicitly stated inclusion and exclusion criteria. The subgroups are as alike as random samples from the same population – not identical, but differing (only!) by 'sampling' error – the very kind of disturbance contemplated and taken into account by tests of statistical significance.

Protocol driven

A randomized study cannot just happen, it is too complex for that; it will be planned. A protocol is a written outcome of the planning: defining treatments, specifying inclusion and exclusion criteria for subject eligibility, prescribing record keeping, tests and measures to be used, quality and accuracy audits to be undertaken, statistical analyses proposed, etc. The protocol is useful in many ways! The intended study is rendered explicit. The writing of the protocol (typically a cooperative process) addresses many potential problems, preventing some and addressing others. The protocol serves also as a procedures manual, and later it largely writes the methods section of resulting publications.

Symmetry of outcome assessment, follow-up, etc.

While random assignment of treatments rules out bias that could otherwise affect the study from the start, bias might creep in later. Processes that affect the data, like assessment of outcomes, follow-up of subjects, must be administered in ways that are quite the same for all treatment groups to forestall bias at later stages. For example, if experimental subjects were followed up more (or less) diligently than controls, the comparison of treatment and controls could be distorted. Thus, suppose that experimental subjects were followed up more assiduously than controls; that would artificially *depress* the apparent benefit of treatment if more intense follow-up tended to reveal additional deaths; in contrast, more intense follow-up of experimental subjects would artificially *raise* the apparent benefit of treatment if extra follow-up tended to locate patients who had dropped from medical contact because they were cured and felt no need to return for check-up. So it is important that treatment and control subjects be followed up in exactly the same ways, to reduce bias in results.

It is especially important that subjective outcomes such as 'improved', 'unchanged', and 'worse', be assessed by persons who do not know which treatment the subject received, to prevent an obvious possible bias from distorting the results.

It is notorious among statisticians that data acquired from separate record systems are liable to be inconsistent. The protocol-driven randomized study addresses this matter squarely, by having a common data collection system for all subjects, whatever treatment group they belong to.

In summary, the practices we have described are intended to bypass resort to the assumption of 'other things being equal' and instead *arrange* that other things be equal.

One might think that we doubt the possibility of learning anything definite in the areas of health, education and the like except by randomized investigations. Such a position would be too strong; it would deny that is possible to learn from experience, whereas that is merely difficult (and often treacherous). Learning from experience can also be a stumbling process – and slow. Consider an example. Earlier we saw how a single large experiment convincingly demonstrated the value of the Salk vaccine in the summer of 1954. In that same year were published seven important studies concerning the connection between lung cancer and smoking;

hundreds of studies, including those, finally led ten years later to the Surgeon General's 1964 finding that cigarette smoking was a cause of lung cancer. The Salk vaccine question could be and was examined experimentally, but the much stronger relation between lung cancer and smoking could not. Since each individual observational study of lung cancer and smoking was liable to *some* source of possible bias, each was somewhat equivocal. Thus, it took a long time and many studies before the accumulating evidence could finally support a compelling conclusion.

EXTENDING BROAD USE OF THE METHOD

Statistics can be defined as a body of methods for learning from experience. Then, considering the soundness and strength of the experimental method when well executed, it is quite natural that a pair of statisticians should be urging broader and more frequent use of randomized studies in resolving unanswered policy questions.

Difficulties

Before proposing some specific measures we will first explore difficulties that must be understood, for they stand in the way of applying the method successfully:

1. An experiment may actually be impossible. The lung cancer and smoking problem is an example. The impracticality of arranging that for a period of decades some chosen persons would not smoke while others, also chosen, would smoke, ruled out the experimental approach for that problem. The National Halothane study (Bunker *et al.* 1969) compared the safety of several anesthetic agents in the 1960s – but non-experimentally. The study was driven to use epidemiological methods because to detect differences of plausible magnitude would have required hundreds of thousands of patients; neither sufficient funds nor trained personnel could have been marshalled to the task. The comparative safety question was instead studied in a retrospective cohort design covering 850 000 surgical procedures. The study provided less definitive answers than an RCT, if feasible, would have offered.

2. Randomized studies are a form of very careful investigation, and like all careful work, they require painstaking attention to a host of details for the whole life of the study. Significant resources may be necessary to support the enterprise; this can raise the problem of securing funding.

3. Where subjects in the randomized study may experience disadvantage by participating, there are ethical questions at hand – and they must be squarely faced, and solved, for the study to be legitimate. Informed consent procedures, Institutional Review Boards, various regulatory measures, and malpractice suits all speak to the reality of this issue.

Counterproposal and critique

Each of the foregoing considerations can be regarded as a 'cost' of doing randomized studies, which need trained personnel and funding, which require unremitting painstaking efforts, and which may entail thorny ethical problems. It is no wonder that one finds advocacy for, instead, employing statistical analysis of data already in hand as an alternative to using experimentation. But such counterproposals face grave difficulties, both in theory and in practice. The hope is to 'make' two groups 'comparable' by statistical adjustment, so that any remaining outcome differences can be attributed to the treatments (for example anesthetic A or anesthetic B).

But, realizing this hoped-for result requires three things: (i) knowledge of which variables must be taken into account, (ii) measuring those variables on each subject, and (iii) using those measurements appropriately to adjust the treatment comparison. Failure is likely on all three counts. We often don't understand what factors cause an individual's disease to progress or not. Even if we knew those factors, we might well find they had not been measured. And if they were, the correct way to use them in adjustment calls for theoretical understanding we seldom have. Each of these three prerequisites for correct adjustment poses deeper questions than the one we began with, 'Does treatment A help more than treatment B?'

Parallel difficulties beset adjustment efforts in non-medical areas, such as education and criminal justice where patterns of causation may be even less well understood, and measurements of relevant variables less well advanced than in medicine. The same considerations apply to such homely activities as delivering the mail or improving traffic safety.

Before leaving the topic of costs associated with randomized trials, let us pause a moment to consider some costs associated with mistaken decisions. When a useless treatment is put into place it has the same badge of honor as a useful one, and unless it is decidedly harmful its lack of value will be slow to be detected. First, whatever problem the device was meant to solve will be believed to have been treated, and that will reduce efforts to find a fresh innovation. Second, applying the treatment is costing money, and that money is now being wasted. Third, it has a constituency, who benefit from its use because they supply materials, equipment, or services, and will be encouraging wider use of the treatment. Fourth, change itself is costly because few treatments stand alone disconnected from other parts of programs. The combination of the constituency and the reluctance to introduce changes once a system is working is difficult to overcome. Consequently bad decisions are likely to remain in place for substantial periods and be doubly costly, once just paying for the useless service and second losing out on the gains a genuine improvement would bring.

Another difficulty

It is not sufficient to have written a protocol; continued adherence to the protocol is also necessary. And this involves human problems. The personnel who conduct the operations must be 'on board'. An early experimental study, the Lanarkshire Milk Experiment (Student 1931), was entirely vitiated by well intentioned 'modifications' imposed on the spot by the teachers – who gave supplemental milk to the children who stood most in need of it, rather than to those randomly assigned. Now two *non*-comparable groups of children received or did not receive, supplemental milk in their rations, and the efficacy of the supplement could not be assessed. Other, analogous, stories abound – with varying degrees of horror.

The Minneapolis Domestic Violence experiment could not have succeeded without the cooperation of arresting officers – and that was ensured by a thorough, long, careful process of interactive education. The investigators (Sherman and Berk 1985) write:

The introduction of an experiment into an organization is a major act of planned change, and should be treated like any other change. Even if only a few people are directly affected, the others will want to know what is going on. Failure to include them in a communications loop, or to give them the opportunity of venting their feelings directly, could result in sabotage.

Some proposals

We turn now to some specific ways to broaden the use of randomized experiments.

Large simple trials

Richard Peto and others have suggested that medicine would be well served if it had more large simple randomized clinical trials (Yusuf *et al*. 1984). The idea of simplicity is to reduce the amount of information being collected from each patient and thus reduce the costs of the trial and the burden on the patient of providing the information. The largeness of the trial is intended not only to get the sample size high, but to include all kinds of patients in the trial. Frequently trials do not include patients who suffer from conditions over and above the disease being treated. For example drugs being planned for use of older people are often tested only in people who have no infirmities beyond that being treated, but the more aged people become, the more likely they are to be suffering from several conditions. Therefore sometimes drugs intended for the oldest old do not get tested on them at all. (The argument favoring that approach says that first one should see if the treatment works under ideal conditions, and only later should we find out whether it works in average or wider conditions.) One intent of Peto's plan is to include all groups in the sample (who have no contraindications) so that the inference for the use of the treatment will directly have wide applicability.

The large samples also have the benefit of more reliability than smaller trials, and thus to some extent avoid the tendency of small trials to be variable in their performance, with the result that those that accidentally have good outcomes are published and disseminated while the ones with accidentally poor outcomes are suppressed because their investigators become discouraged about pursuing them through the publication process, and these poor outcome studies lurk in the 'file drawer'. This source of possible publication bias is often called 'the file drawer problem'. (In medicine, research done on the publication bias question makes it fairly clear that it is not the bias of the editors toward publishing positive results that leads to publication bias, but rather that the authors become discouraged and do not pursue their work through the publication process. This information is somewhat contrary to what one's first thought would be as the reason for publication bias. In some other fields, however, such as psychology, the editors do ordinarily discourage publishing negative findings and so publication bias may come from different sources in different fields of endeavor.)

Firms

Here is an idea to establish a facility for continuously investigating suitably chosen problems within a framework of normal operations (Neuhauser 1989). An institution, such as a hospital, breaks itself into two or more equivalent medical systems called firms. Each firm has the same number of beds, the same number of physicians of each sort, the same number of nurses, and so on. Patients entering the institution for the first time are assigned randomly to one of the firms. Thus, the firms are as equivalent as possible in staff and patients. When the institution wants to test out some new method of treating patients, investigators can assign one method to one firm and another to another one. Then over time they can compare the outcomes of the differing treatments, sometimes using routinely collected observational data.

Naturally it takes a long time to set up such an arrangement, and so relatively few hospitals have firms, but a number do, and interest in the approach seems to be sustained.

One benefit of having lots of firms would be that one has ready-made organizations oriented toward clinical trials. Without such a prepared organization each new study has to be developed especially and physicians and patients recruited for the study. We can appreciate the practical value of prepared organizations by recalling that at the beginning of the century we had no sampling organizations and so trying to carry out a national sample required lengthy organizational work. Today many survey organizations are available and prepared to field a national sample survey in a matter of days. Thus readiness matters and would help even in the more complicated field of medical experimentation.

In addition, because the firms deal with all the patients passing through the system, they are not dealing with a specialized set of patients as sometimes is the situation with clinical trials. This means that generalization to all patients may be made more readily.

Conserving/consolidating experimental findings

Research synthesis

When multiple studies are carried out on the 'same' topic in the 'same' way, the results often differ, usually in magnitude, but sometimes even in conclusions. The sameness is never exact in genuine investigations. Of course, the more numerous the studies become the more information is at hand – crying out to be consolidated.

At the same time the number (if not the proportion) of 'discordant' studies also grows, challenging the analyst to produce a fair summary. Sampling variability alone would cause some variation, but in addition there are actual differences in how treatments are carried out in different studies.

The traditional 'literature review' by an acknowledged expert was always vulnerable to subjective bias. Further, in recent years increasingly massive bodies of literature overwhelm the limit of what single reviewers can do. More recently, new and valuable methods of quantitative research synthesis (or 'meta analysis') have grown up.

The key features of this emerging technology include comprehensive coverage of the relevant studies, objective and systematic devices for reviewing studies in a uniform way, and the use of suitable statistical techniques. Typically such a meta analysis proceeds in accordance with a written protocol, promoting care at all stages of the effort.

Some questions about the methods still await final resolution. How, if at all, should the levels of quality of various studies be numerically taken into account? How shall the practical importance of the 'file drawer problem' be gauged? And then, there is the 'apples and oranges problem' (or pseudo-problem). The idea is this: among studies comparing the efficacy of two modes of chemotherapy A and B for breast cancer, it could be that the outcome in one study is five-year survival, in another two-year survival, in another time to recurrence, etc. Now the issue: the various A versus B comparisons *can* be numerically combined (by means of the effect size, already discussed in the Tennessee schools section above). But does such a summary have meaning? On the one hand, the summary construct is hard to explain, but on the other, if A outperforms B across so many ways of comparison the summary seems to *gain* cogency thereby. Another variant of the same theme arises if different studies use somewhat differing forms of A and B (for example dosage variants).

Most of the criticisms of methods of quantitative research synthesis are criticisms of science as a whole or of the primary scientific papers being used in the study rather than of the method. Were it not for the attempt at synthesis the issues might not have arisen. For example, as long as we talk about single investigations we do not talk about publication bias. But it is more important to appreciate that the synthesis approach offers some ways of attacking these problems that were rarely considered before these synthesis methods came into use. Usually they can be studied only when multiple investigations are available.

The problem of multiple papers on the same topic has always been with us and the differences in outcomes have been substantial in the hard sciences. They can be swept under the rug peremptorily by saying that each outcome is that produced by a specific laboratory by a specific method and that there is no reason to try to combine them. Science then loses a lot of universality.

The main point of this discussion is to note that we have use for multiple experiments and ways of combining information from them. But we cannot carry out such syntheses unless we have the experimental results to combine. It is important therefore that the experiments be carried out and that they be synthesized.

Obstetrics: an example

In the field of obstetrics there has been carried out, over a period of about 15 years, a substantial effort, pulling together all trials of obstetric procedures, both organizing them and analyzing them. A group at Oxford University has undertaken to find all the randomized or approximately randomized trials that have been carried out and then get teams of researchers to review and form a research synthesis for each procedure in a standard way. Finally these results have been published (Chalmers et al. 1989) and made available also in electronic form so that others can reanalyze them. Thus far obstetrics is the only field of medicine where such a substantial job of organizing and analyzing the randomized controlled trial information has been carried out.

The Oxford group has now proposed to carry out this idea on a broad scale for all of medicine under the leadership of Iain Chalmers. Organizations all over the world are planning to join the effort, and so we may have in a decade or so the same complete story of clinical trials in all of medicine that we have now for obstetrics.

The enterprise is called the Cochrane Collaboration. Archie Cochrane was a distinguished clinician with a quantitative bent, and his dream was that all the clinical trials would be gathered together and organized. When this is done his dream will have been realized.

Better current reporting improves future synthesis

To preserve the information obtained in good experimental work, so that it can be used effectively in later research synthesis, journal editors should make sure that the published paper is adequate for future use. Will the facts presented enable it to be used in research synthesis? Many articles describe treatments inadequately and fail to include critical information such as sample sizes, means, and standard errors. For example, merely reporting the F value of an analysis of variance does not tell which treatments performed well, though it may tell us that some performed better than others but not which ones or by how much. This is not the place to provide guidelines for inclusion (Halvorsen 1994; Cook et al. 1995), but the growing use of research synthesis means that important studies will not later carry their appropriate weight if authors have failed to supply critical information or editors have deleted the descriptions or the statistics to save space.

CONCLUSION

The reader now knows that we believe the method of randomized controlled experiments deserves much wider use in designing, testing and choosing policy changes. If we are right in that belief, various tasks fall naturally to statisticians, teachers of policy and teachers of statistics.

The teacher

We should include a careful, even if brief, treatment of randomized experimentation in our survey statistics courses (and introductory public policy courses.) No elementary statistics text (or public policy text) should lack a section on the topic. Curricula for undergraduate and graduate degrees in statistics should contain offerings – possibly required offerings – in the use of experiments in policy formation.

Much important education in statistics occurs in the context of supervised (or apprentice) consultation with clients seeking statistical assistance. Such transactions can offer opportunity for advancing the use of the method.

The teacher who takes up the challenge to treat experiments as an essential topic in the statistics or policy cause he or she teaches will find excellent books, chapters, and survey papers upon which to draw. We name a few sources which may be useful: Hoaglin *et al.* (1982), Boruch and Wothke (1985), Moses (1985), and Light *et al.* (1990).

The change agent

Bringing randomized experimentation into a setting where it is a new idea calls for thoughtful, careful planning. The substantive problem chosen for such an initial effort should be genuinely attractive to the client, likely to yield a successful result (as nearly as can be judged beforehand) and 'small' in both resources needed and time required for completion. Modest beginnings that reach conclusions briskly will encourage use.

Opportunity for useful application of the method may be at hand whenever some new undertaking is to be launched; typically several variant approaches offer themselves and it is less than certain which may be preferable. Such a situation can call for trying two or more approaches in a randomized way.

The process of developing the protocol is likely to be filled with 'teachable moments'. The protocol is not acceptable if it lacks any of these essentials: clear description of alternative treatments; clear specification of eligibility and how it is determined; randomization of subjects (or events or situations) to treatments *after* determination of eligibility; simultaneous use of the various treatments (rather than A for first year and B for the second); when feasible, outcome evaluation that is not informed of which treatment was applied to the subject whose outcome is being measured (blindness).

With the protocol in hand – which may have involved many institutional actors already – there comes the task of preparing participants (and interested on-lookers) for actually doing the experiment. The work of Sherman and Berk (1985) offers guidance here.

Successful application of the method in a new area is likely to open the door to broader use in that area.

Professional societies

We believe that both statisticians and policy wonks can advance the effort that we advocate by pushing their professional societies in various ways: holding sessions on the topic at society meetings; sponsoring single journal issues devoted to policy formation and experimentation; inviting special journal articles or addresses at meetings; informing journalists of the importance of experimentation and the weaknesses of other methods of appraising the merits of changes.

Notice that the experimental method may be most widely applied in the areas of clinical trials and agriculture. (This was not always so. Medicine had relatively few clinical trials early in this century.) Linked to that advancement are both a professional society (The Society for Clinical Trials) and a journal *Controlled Clinical Trials*. These organs began after the activities were already well advanced, but the relation now between clinical trial activity and society-cum-journal is symbiotic, and affords a model we should aspire to.

ACKNOWLEDGMENTS

We appreciate the support in part for the preparation of this manuscript by the Stanford Medical School of Stanford University and by a grant to the Center for Evaluation of the Initiatives for Children of the American Academy of Arts and Sciences from the Andrew W. Mellon Foundation.

REFERENCES

Boruch, R. F. and Wothke, W. (ed.) (1985). *Randomization and field experimentation.* Jossey-Bass, San Francisco.

Botein, B. (1964–5). The Manhattan bail project: its impact on criminology and the criminal law processes. *Texas Law Review,* **43**, 319–31.

Bunker, J. P., Forest, W. H. Jr., Mosteller, F., and Vandam, L. D. (ed.) (1969). *The National Halothane Study: A study of the possible association between halothane anesthesia and post-operative hepatic necrosis,* Report of the Subcommittee on Anesthesia, Division of Medical Sciences, National Academy of Sciences – National Research Council. National Institutes of Health, National Institute of General Medical Sciences. US Government Printing Office, Washington DC.

Byar, D. P. (1991). Problems with using observational data bases to compare treatments. *Statistics in Medicine,* **10**, 663–6.

Chalmers, I., Enkin, M. W., and Keirse, M. J. N. C. (1989). *Effective care in pregnancy and childbirth.* Oxford University Press.

Cook, D. J., Sacket, D. L., and Spitzer, W. O. (1995). Methodologic guidelines for systematic reviews of randomized control trials in health care from the Potsdam Consultation on meta-analysis. *Journal of Clinical Epidemiology,* **48**, 167–71.

The Coronary Drug Project Research Group. (1980). Influence of adherence to treatment and response of cholesterol on mortality in the Coronary Drug Project. *New England Journal of Medicine,* **303**, 1038–41.

Dunn, M. R. and George, T. W. (1964). Des Moines pre-trial release project 1964–65. *Drake Law Review*, **14**, 98–100.

Finn, J. D. and Achilles, C. M. (1990). Answers and questions about class size: a statewide experiment. *American Educational Research Journal*, **27**, 557–77.

Gilbert, J. P., Light, R. J., and Mosteller, F. (1975). Assessing social innovations: an empirical basis for policy. In *Evaluation and experiment*, (ed. C. A. Bennett and A. A. Lumsdaine), pp.39–193. Academic Press, New York.

Gilbert, J. P., McPeek, B., and Mosteller, F. (1977). Progress in surgery and anesthesia: benefits and risks of innovative therapy. In *Costs, risks and benefits of surgery*, (ed. J. P. Bunker, B. A. Barnes, and F. Mosteller), pp.124–69. Oxford University Press, New York.

Green, S. B. and Byar, D. P. (1984). Using observational data from registries to compare treatments: the fallacy of omnimetrics. *Statistics in Medicine*, **3**, 361–70.

Haight, F. A. (1985). Do speed limits reduce traffic accidents? In *Statistics: a guide to the unknown*, (2nd edn), (ed. J. M. Tanur *et al.*), pp.170–7. Wadsworth and Brooks/Cole, Monterey, C. A.

Halvorsen, K. T. (1994). The reporting format. In *The handbook of research synthesis*, (ed. H. Cooper and L. V. Hedges), pp.425–37, especially 428, 431–2. Russell Sage Foundation, New York.

Hoaglin, D. C., Light, R. J., McPeek, B., Mosteller, F., and Stoto, M. A. (1982). *Data for decisions*, Chap. 2,3. Abt Associates, Cambridge, MA.

Light, R. J., Singer, J. B., and Willett, J. D. (1990). *By design: planning research on higher education*. Harvard University Press, Cambridge, MA.

Meier, P. (1989). The biggest public health experiment ever: the 1954 field trial of the Salk poliomyelitis vaccine. In *Statistics: A guide to the unknown*, (3rd edn), (ed. J. M. Tanur *et al.*), pp.3–14. Wadsworth and Brooks/Cole, Pacific Grove, CA.

Moses, L. (1985). Randomized clinical trials. In *Assessing medical technologies*, Committee for Evaluating Medical Technologies in Clinical Use, pp.73–9. National Academy Press, Washington DC.

Neuhauser, D. (1989). The metro firm trials and ongoing patient randomization. In *Statistics: a guide to the unknown*, (3rd edn), (ed. J. M. Tanur *et al.*), pp 25–30. Wadsworth and Brooks/Cole, Pacific Grove, CA.

Perng, S. S. (1985). Accounts receivable treatments study. In *Randomization and field experimentation*, (ed. R. F. Boruch and W. Wothke), Chap. 5, Jossey-Bass, San Francisco.

Sherman, S. W. and Berk, R. A. (1985). The randomization of arrest. In *Randomization and field experimentation*, (ed. R. F. Boruch and W. Wothke), Chap. 2, Jossey-Bass, San Francisco.

'Student' (William Sealy Gossett). (1931). The Lanarkshire milk experiment. *Biometrika*, **23**, 398–406, see esp. p. 399.

Yusuf, S., Collins, R., and Peto, R. (1984). Why do we need some large simple trials? *Statistics in Medicine*, **3**, 409–20.

13 Talents, rewards and professional choice: a general equilibrium analysis

STEPHEN P. DRESCH AND KENNETH R. JANSON

> In dealing with any natural phenomenon – especially one of a vital nature
> . . . – the mathematician has to simplify the conditions until they reach the
> attenuated character which lies within the power of his analysis.
>
> Karl Pearson[1]

INTRODUCTION

Even the most casual observer recognizes that 'talent', however conceived, varies significantly across individuals. Not only are some individuals 'more talented' than others; perhaps more importantly, individuals differ in the fundamental nature of their talents. Thus, one individual may exhibit 'scientific' talent, another 'artistic' talent, another a 'talent' for manipulation of others, etc. Correspondingly, as similarly casual observation reveals, professions or occupations are differentiated by the degree to which individual performance is dependent on specific talents and hence by the extent to which rewards (earnings and other perquisites of employment) reflect the particular configurations of talent brought to bear by individual practitioners. Thus, casual observation gives rise to a quite sophisticated characterization of the role of talent in interacting labor markets.

The sophistication implicit in casual observation contrasts sharply with the naivete of much that passes as 'public policy analysis'. For example, policy actions are frequently justified in terms of claimed 'shortages' of personnel in particular occupations, without consideration for the qualitative capabilities ('talents') demanded in these occupations, the underlying supply of these capabilities, or the opportunity costs of diverting these capabilities from other socially valued uses to policy-preferred activities. In short, public policy is often grounded in a simplistic view of relevant phenomena, ignoring the richness of underlying processes which would be self-evident even to the casual observer, and, in consequence, the results of policy action frequently diverge radically from the intentions.[2]

---

1. As quoted (without citation) by Alfred J. Lotka (1956 (1924), p.300).

2. We would argue that simplistic 'post-Sputnik' claims of a 'shortage' of highly trained US scientists led to policies which had serious unintended consequences. From the late 1950s through the early 1970s public policy contributed to achievement of a three- to four-fold increase in the rate at which young people were attracted to scientific careers. However, as the flow into science accelerated, the capability

Although casual observation is sufficient to raise serious questions concerning the eventual consequences of naive public policies, the demand for the appearance of rationality in the formulation of policy requires something more than casual observation. However, when rigorous economic and statistical science is foiled by the complexities of phenomena, entrepreneurial pseudoscientism triumphs, and superficial and misleading analyses rationalize unwise and ill-considered public policy actions.[3]

But, when reality is 'too complex' for meaningful analysis, what is the statistician or economist to do? If entrepreneurial pseudoscientism strips away important complexities and produces irrelevancy while pretending to analyze the 'real world', one alternative is to identify these important but submerged complexities, capture these in an 'artificial world' in which they are not lost in a sea of second-order complexities, and explicate significant phenomena within the confines of this artificial world.

Here the 'important complexities' concern the process by which talent is allocated in society, but these are shrouded by such second-order complexities as, for example, how 'talents' should be measured, whether meaningful measurements of talent can be obtained for the relevant population, how talents affect performance of individuals, and how these consequences of talent are to be measured. To avoid paralyzing entanglement in these second-order complexities, we simply assume them away in developing a caricature of the world in which rigorous analysis can capture the richness of the process evident even to casual observation.

This caricature incorporates (1) a very parsimonious parametric representation of the distribution of the population in a multidimensional talent space, (2) a similarly parsimonious parametric representation of competing occupational demands for

---

distribution of entrants arguably shifted downward significantly, with the consequence that much of the desired gain in aggregate scientific performance failed to materialize due to the erosion of the competencies of entrants into science.

While expansion of the scale of the scientific enterprise may not have generated a comparable surge in scientific performance, that expansion severely eroded the supply of talent to competing sectors. As a result, performance declined in both scientific and non-scientific sectors. Thus, paradoxically, policies designed to spur scientific advance tended, directly and indirectly, to produce a deceleration of scientific and technological–economic advance, the consequences of which continue to be felt two decades later.

3. That this type of simplistic pseudoscience continues to carry great weight in policy circles is clearly revealed by the widely quoted scientist–engineer 'pipeline' studies of the National Science Foundation's Division of Policy Research and Analysis (1990), which proclaimed a 675 000 cumulative 'shortfall' in the US production of scientists and engineers between 1986 and 2010. After enjoying substantial influence in academic and governmental circles, these studies were subjected to scathing criticisms. Opening an April 1992 hearing of the Subcommittee on Investigations and Oversight of the Committee on Science, Space, and Technology of the US House of Representatives, Chairman Howard Wolpe observed:

... Because of the confusing and interchangeable use of the words 'shortfall', 'shortage', and 'scarcity', and discussions by [National Science] Foundation officials of supply and demand, many members of Congress, academic institutions, the media and the public became convinced fewer degrees meant that a real 'shortage' of workers was looming, and government intervention in the form of increased financial support for science and engineering education was necessary.

From the very beginning, labor economists and statisticians, including those inside the Foundation, scoffed at the methodology as seriously flawed ... (US House of Representatives 1993, pp.3–4).

talent, and (3) a 'market' in which individuals, identified by their talents, are matched to occupations, identified by the rewards which they offer to persons with different configurations of talent. While being quite simple, simulations of this model mimic the realities of heterogeneous markets for heterogeneous labor, permitting the qualitative assessment of the consequences of specific changes in occupational demands, such as those sought through public policy intervention.

Also, these simulations generate precisely the types of observations which can be made in reality, specifically observations of individual talents, occupations elected by individuals and the rewards which these individuals receive. However, the fundamental difference between this mimic of reality and reality itself is that, in this 'artificial' system, we have exact knowledge of the underlying distributions of talents and of the structural relationships between these talents and professional productivity and rewards. This permits us to compare inferences of these relationships which can be made with 'realistically observable' data with the known, 'true' relationships. By implication, systematic discrepancies between inferred and true relationships in this artificial context can be argued to be paralleled by qualitatively similar discrepancies between inferred and true relationships in actually observed markets for heterogeneous labor.

On this basis, our analysis calls into serious question much of the empirical literature concerning the determinants of earnings. Because 'occupation', as employed here, could be defined in terms of educational attainment, these questions concerning the validity of empirical analyses apply not only to those focused on occupational earnings narrowly defined but also to the much broader body of empirical literature concerned with the earnings consequences of (returns to) schooling.

Specifically, when those individual attributes (for example, talent) which enter into the determination of earnings *within* an occupational- or schooling-class of workers also influence the choice of occupational or schooling class, then earnings functions estimated only on the basis of observations of those who have selected a particular occupational or schooling class are likely to be seriously biased. Thus, our analysis provides strong indirect support for those who have argued that empirical estimates of the returns to schooling are severely inflated.[4]

THE MODEL

In order to parallel important aspects of reality, talent must be multidimensional, and (1) the various dimensions of talent must not be perfectly correlated, (2) different occupations must differentially reward different configurations of talent, and (3) within occupations different dimensions of talent must not be perfectly interchangeable. Parsimoniously conjoining these requirements, the model identifies three specific talent dimensions, between two of which a positive correlation is observed, the third being uncorrelated with the first

---

4. Dresch (1983) summarizes the argument that the same factors (notably ability, or 'talent') which influence the returns to schooling are also reflected in higher earnings in the absence of schooling.

two. Nine occupations are identified, exhibiting widely varying demands for particular types of talent.[5] Rewards commanded by an individual within any occupation are stipulated to be logarithmically linear, with independent occupational- and individual-specific random components. Any individual is 'assigned to' (or, chooses) that occupation offering him the highest reward.

INDIVIDUAL TALENTS

For ease of discussion the three dimensions of individual talent identified can be designated 'manipulative talent' (T_1), 'artistic talent' (T_2), and 'scientific talent' (T_3). The distribution of the population over this three-dimensional talent space is stipulated to be multivariate normal:

$$f(T_1, T_2, T_3) \sim N(M, \Sigma)$$

where

$$M = \begin{Bmatrix} \mu_1 \\ \mu_2 \\ \mu_3 \end{Bmatrix}, \; \mu_k = 100, \; k = 1,2,3$$

$$\Sigma = \begin{Bmatrix} \sigma_1^2 & \sigma_{1,2} & 0 \\ \sigma_{2,1} & \sigma_2^2 & 0 \\ 0 & 0 & \sigma_3^2 \end{Bmatrix} = \begin{Bmatrix} 400 & 200 & 0 \\ 200 & 400 & 0 \\ 0 & 0 & 400 \end{Bmatrix}, \; \sigma_{k,\,k'} \equiv \sigma_{k',\,k}, \; k \neq k'$$

i.e.

$$\sigma_k^2 = 400 \text{ or } \sigma_k = 20, \; k = 1,2,3$$
$$\sigma_{1,2} = 200$$
$$\sigma_{1,3} = \sigma_{2,3} = 0.$$

Noting that the correlation between talents k and k' is

$$\rho_{k,k'} = \frac{\sigma_{k,k'}}{\sigma_k \, \sigma_{k'}}$$

the variance–covariance matrix Σ implies that

$$\rho_{1,2} = 0.5$$
$$\rho_{1,3} = \rho_{2,3} = 0.$$

---

5. Two occupations identical apart from relative size are included as a test of the internal consistency of the model and for purposes of possible future analyses of the effects of entry barriers (occupational licensure).

i.e. scientific talent (T_3) is stipulated to be uncorrelated with manipulative and artistic talents $(T_1, T_2,$ respectively), while between manipulative and artistic talents a correlation of 0.5 is stipulated.[6]

For the purposes of interpretation, the marginal distribution in each of the talent dimensions is similar to that generally stipulated for intelligence (IQ) and related test scores, i.e. talent in each dimension is distributed normally with mean 100 and standard deviation 20,[7] although we do not mean to suggest that the multi-dimensional 'talent' postulated here is substantively equivalent to IQ, its components or surrogates, however conceived or measured.

Professional rewards

Any individual i, with known talents $< T_{1,i}, T_{2,i}, T_{3,i} >$, confronts a spectrum of alternative possible occupations j $(= 1,. . .,9)$, each of which offers particular rewards to talent. The reward functions have the general form:

$$R_{j,i} = \exp[\beta_{j,0} + \beta_{j,1} T_{1,i} + \beta_{j,2} T_{2,i} + \beta_{j,3} T_{3,i} + \beta_{j,4} P_j + w_j S_{j,i} + (1-w_j) S_i]$$

where

P_j = proportion of labor force in occupation j,
$$0 \leqslant w_j \leqslant 1,$$
$$S_{j,i} \sim N (0, \sigma_j^2),$$

an occupation-specific random term,

$$S_i \sim N (0, \sigma_I^2), \sigma_I = 0.3,$$

---

6. As implemented, the model accepts any specified degree of correlation between two of the talents, with the third then specified as independent of the first and second, permitting analyses of the conceptually interesting range of alternative inter-talent relationships. However, our substantive application here was guided by Karol I. Pelc's argument that correlations between specific dimensions of talent should be anticipated and reflected in the model. Specifically, Pelc suggested that it was plausible to assume a positive correlation between manipulative talent (which we were then characterizing as a 'talent for lying, cheating and stealing') and artistic talent, in that both involve the capacity to 'create' (and to convince others of the existence of) a non-existent 'reality'; the former falsifies reality for self-aggrandizing purposes, the latter for esthetic purposes. As reinforcement for his argument, Pelc subsequently pointed out, first, Serge Lang's (1988) identification of 'interpretive creativity' with the purveyance of 'misinformation' and 'falsification of history', and second, Pablo Picasso's dictum that '[a]rt is a lie that makes us realize the truth' (cited by Alvin P. Sanoff in a review of James Simpson, *Simpson's contemporary quotations: the most notable quotes since 1950* in *US News & World Report*, 6 June 1988, p.53). Interestingly, given the specific professional reward-*cum*-assignment functions which we specify, the stipulation of a positive correlation between manipulative and artistic talents, both of which are uncorrelated with scientific talent, leads to a stable solution of the model, whereas the specification of a positive correlation between artistic and scientific talents, both uncorrelated with manipulative talent, results in relatively unstable solutions (with some occupations assigned no members of the labor force and with extreme sensitivity of the occupational assignments to minor changes in the reward-function parameters).

7. The specific functional form is identical to that employed for a single talent by Dresch and Janson (1987) and is taken from Price (1963, p.52), drawing on Harmon's (1963) analysis of US Armed Forces Qualifying Test scores of scientists.

an individual-specific random term (stipulated to be independent of the occupation-specific random term).[8]

In this general (fundamentally dynamic) form, individuals arrive sequentially at the point of professional choice and evaluate the opportunities offered by competing professions; each is then assigned to (elects) that occupation offering him the highest rewards, i.e. $\max_j [R_{j,i}]$. The individual's professional selection is a function of the specific labor force distribution (vector of values P_j) which he confronts; however, his election of one profession over others modifies this distribution, altering the vector P_j. Accordingly, *ceteris paribus*, the next arrival confronts a slightly different opportunity set. Thus, as in the world it is intended to reflect, the model offers different opportunities to otherwise identical individuals, discriminating between individual entrants on the basis of their relative temporal positions in the aspirant queue.

The relative elasticity of demand for the services of a particular occupational group is captured by the influence of the occupation's proportionate share of the labor force, P_j, on the prospective rewards of the marginal entrant,[9] the coefficient of which ($\beta_{j,4}$) is plausibly non-positive and can be interpreted as a 'quasielasticity' (percentage change in prospective rewards associated with a one percentage point change in the occupation's share of the labor force).[10] Because talent in each dimension has a mean of 100, the talent coefficients $\beta_{j,k}$, $K = 1, 2, 3$, (multiplied by 100) can also be interpreted as 'quasielasticities', i.e. percentage variations in an individual's rewards associated with one percentage point variations from the talent mean.

The non-deterministic nature of these rewards is reflected in the two independent random terms, one of which ($S_{j,i}$) is occupation-specific (with a variance of σ^2_j), the other of which (S_i) is individual specific (with a variance of σ^2_I). For a given individual, the individual-specific random term (S_i) is drawn once and thus is identical across occupations. In contrast, the occupation-specific random terms ($S_{j,i}$, $j = 1, \ldots, 9$) are independently determined for each occupation and individual.

---

8. In principle, the reward functions, although unidimensional, can be interpreted implicitly to embrace all aspects of the occupation entering into the individual utility function, i.e. non-pecuniary as well as pecuniary rewards. Systematic differences between occupations which enter into all individuals' utility functions would be captured by the coefficients of the reward function (especially the intercept term), while individually idiosyncratic occupational utilities would be reflected in the individual-specific random term. In addition to aspects of professions directly entering the individual utility function, the reward functions reflect factors which influence the professional success of the individual, explicitly in the case of talents and implicitly in the case of individual diligence and effort. With reference to the latter, congenital 'loafers' would be distinguished by large negative values of the individual-specific random term, while occupation-specific disinclinations of the individual would be reflected in his occupation-specific random term. An interesting extension of the study would involve explicit investigation of relationships between talents and effort in various professional groups.

9. Specifically, the elasticity of demand, defined as the ratio of the relative rate of variation in quantity (P_j) to the relative rate of variation in price (R_j), is

$$\varepsilon_j = \frac{-dP_jR_j}{dR_jP_j} = -(\beta_{j,4}P_j)^{-1}.$$

Thus, the elasticity of demand is an inverse function of the coefficient of the occupation's share of the labor force in the reward function.

10. In contrast to the *elasticity* of rewards with respect to the occupation's proportionate share of the labor force, which can be interpreted as the ratio of the percentage variation in rewards to the percentage variation in labor force share, the *quasielasticity* can be interpreted as the percentage variation in rewards associated with a *one percentage point* variation in labor force share.

Further, individual occupations differ in the relative weights $[W_j, (1 - W_j)]$ attached to these respective random terms. Thus, in some occupations the variance in rewards across individuals, *ceteris paribus*, is largely attributable to unobserved differences between individuals (with $1 - W_j$ close to unity), while in others the variance in earnings is endemic to the occupation (with W_j close to unity). In the former case (variance attributable to unobserved individual differences) the intraoccupational variance in rewards will have no effect on occupational choice, while in the second (variance endemic to the occupation) the intraoccupational variance will have potentially significant impacts on occupational choice.[11]

The stipulated coefficients of the specific reward functions employed in this analysis are presented in Table 1. Because, for n occupations, there are only $n - 1$ independent occupational proportions P_j, for one occupation, the Lumpen Proletariat, the coefficient of that occupation's proportion of the labor force (P_1) is set equal to zero. Given the coefficients specified for the reward function of Lumpen Proletarians, the median reward offered in this occupation (unity) can be interpreted as a numeraire; rewards in other occupations have meaning only relative to the rewards offered Lumpen Proletarians. As can be readily observed, the system is homogeneous of degree zero in the absolute level of rewards, i.e. occupational assignments would be unaffected by equiproportionate scaling (equal changes in the intercepts of the logarithms of rewards) of all occupational reward functions.

Table 1 Occupational reward functions

Occupation	$\beta_{j,0}$	$\beta_{j,1}$	$\beta_{j,2}$	$\beta_{j,3}$	$\beta_{j,4}$	σ_j	w_j	$\sigma_{j,1}$ for $\sigma_I = 0.3$**
1 Lumpen Proletariat	0	0	0	0	0	0.2	1.0	0.200
2 Crafts and Trades	−1.849	0.001	0.010	0.010	−1	0.3	0.5	0.212
3 Management	−1.754	0.005	0	0.015	−3	0.4	0.5	0.250
4 Finance and Sales	−5.536	0.050	0	0.002	−5	0.5	0.8	0.404
5 Bureaucracy	−5.352	0.050	0	0	−4	0.1	0.8	0.100
6 Technocracy	−3.062	0	0	0.030	−3	0.3	0.5	0.212
7 Literate Professions I*	−6.062	0.020	0.020	0.020	−9	0.4	0.5	0.250
8 Scholarly Elite	−8.750	0.005	0.025	0.050	−9	0.4	0.5	0.250
9 Literate Professions II*	−6.062	0.020	0.020	0.020	−13.8	0.4	0.5	0.250

* Two variants of Literate Professions are identical apart from scale $(\beta_{j,4})$ and are equivalent to a single Literate Profession with $\beta_{j4} = -5.238$.

** Consolidating occupation- and individual-specific random terms, the conditional variance of rewards for occupation j is $\sigma_{j,1}^2 = w_j^2 \sigma_j^2 + (1 - w_j)^2 \sigma_I^2$.

11. An individual's calculated opportunity set (vector of rewards, inclusive of occupation- and individual-specific random components) can be interpreted as an expectation (with the actual reward received in any elected occupation then subject to further random variation, although any further random component must be independent of the already specified occupational- and individual-specific random terms). Under this interpretation, our occupational assignment rule (assignment to that occupation offering the highest expected reward) implicitly requires the assumption of risk neutrality. Alternatively, if perfect foresight (knowledge) is assumed, then assignment to the occupation offering the highest reward entails no implicit assumption concerning individual attitudes toward risk.

The final parameter of the model, the standard deviation of the individual-specific random term (σ_I) is stipulated to be 0.3. Conjoining the independent (uncorrelated) variances of the occupational- and individual-specific random terms, it is possible to derive the conditional variance of rewards for each occupation,[12] $\sigma_{j,I}^2$:

$$\sigma_{j,I}^2 = w_j^2 \sigma_j^2 + (1-w_j)^2 \sigma_I^2.$$

The consolidated conditional standard deviations $(\sigma_{j,I})$ are also reported in Table 1. The stipulated values of the variances of the individual- and occupational-specific random terms were selected to result in a distribution of consolidated standard deviations comparable with that observed for the conditional standard deviations of logarithms of occupational earnings in the US economy (Dresch 1986).

The consolidation of the occupation- and individual-specific variances is necessary for the purposes of obtaining conditional expectations of rewards. Specifically, because the normally distributed random terms are associated with the logarithm of rewards, the conditional distribution of rewards, given values for all other reward-determining variables (T_1, T_2, T_3, P_j), will be lognormal, for which the expectation (mean) is

$$
\begin{aligned}
R_j(T_1, T_2, T_3, P_j) &= E[R_j(T_1, T_2, T_3, P_j)] \\
&= \exp(\beta_{j,0} + \beta_{j,1}T_1 + \beta_{j,2}T_2 + \beta_{j,3}T_3 + \beta_{j,4}P_j + 0.5\,\sigma_{j,I}^2)
\end{aligned}
$$

If the final term in this expression, $0.5\,\sigma_{j,I}^2$, were excluded, one would have the conditional *median* rather than *mean* reward.[13]

STATIC SIMULATION OF THE MODEL

To obtain a basic solution of the model, occupational rewards and assignments were simulated for a labor force of 10 000 individuals, drawing from the appropriate normal distributions to obtain talents and occupation- and individual-specific random terms for each simulated individual. Restricting the model to a static solution, the occupational distribution of the labor force (vector of values P_j) was externally stipulated and was thus identical for each simulated individual. With appropriate specification of the intercepts $(\beta_{j,\,0})$ and coefficients of the occupational shares of the labor force $(\beta_{j,\,4})$, the resultant distribution of the simulated labor force of 10 000 is identical to the exogenously specified labor force distribution used to determine each simulated individual's opportunity set (vector of rewards).[14]

---

12. These variances are conditional on the values of the variables entering into the reward function (talents and the occupations' proportions of the labor force).

13. See Aitchison and Brown (1957, p.8).

14. Operationally, obtaining this static solution involved setting all values of $\beta_{j,4}$ (coefficients of the occupational proportions P_j) equal to zero and stipulating a 'provisional' set of constant terms $(\beta_{j,0}^p)$ which produced acceptable occupational proportions (P_j) for our hypothetical labor force of 10 000 individuals (with the meaning of the term 'acceptable' discussed further below). Then, using the previously stipulated values of $\beta_{j,4}$ (Table 1), it was possible to determine values of $\beta_{j,\,0}$, from the relationship $\beta_{j,\,0} = \beta_{j,0}^p - \beta_{j,4}P_j$. The only divergence from this procedure involved the second of the two Literate Professions: having determined $\beta_{7,\,0}$ for the first of these (occupation seven), for the second (occupation 9) it was stipulated that $\beta_{9,0} = \beta_{7,0}$, and the value of $\beta_{9,4}$ was obtained as $\beta_{9,4} = (\beta_{9,0}^p - \beta_{9,0})/P_9$.

Table 2 Static simulation of a labor force of 10 000

Occupation (j)	P_j	$\overline{R}_j$	Mean (T_k)	Standard deviation (T_k)	Skewness (T_k)	Kurtosis (T_k)
1 Lumpen Prol.	0.301	1.12				
T_1			90	15.1	−0.44	2.92
T_2			91	17.5	−0.11	2.80
T_3			88	16.3	−0.25	2.87
2 Crafts and Trades	0.202	1.32				
T_1			95	13.6	−0.59	3.19
T_2			107	14.6	−0.06	2.96
T_3			98	14.5	−0.28	2.74
3 Management	0.108	1.36				
T_1			96	13.7	−0.39	2.90
T_2			90	14.8	−0.21	2.95
T_3			107	12.8	−0.23	3.11
4 Fin and Sales	0.091	2.69				
T_1			123	11.5	0.54	3.56
T_2			107	17.1	0.00	2.98
T_3			95	17.7	−0.13	3.08
5 Bureaucracy	0.083	2.50				
T_1			128	10.4	0.86	4.15
T_2			109	16.0	−0.02	3.03
T_3			90	17.0	0.02	2.91
6 Technocracy	0.094	1.76				
T_1			87	16.7	−0.11	2.61
T_2			85	15.7	−0.23	2.87
T_3			125	11.1	0.13	2.92
7 Lit. Prof.	0.047	2.37				
T_1			117	10.9	0.27	3.32
T_2			123	13.6	0.12	2.66
T_3			111	13.0	−0.17	2.89
8 Schol. Elite	0.041	3.63				
T_1			105	15.3	−0.09	3.00
T_2			117	14.5	0.30	3.18
T_3			134	10.8	0.25	3.36
9 Lit. Prof.	0.033	2.38				
T_1			117	10.9	−0.05	2.90
T_2			124	14.5	0.11	3.09
T_3			110	12.6	−0.36	3.09

This static solution is summarized in Table 2, which indicates the occupational distribution of the labor force (P_j), and, for assignees to each occupation, mean rewards $(\overline{R}_j)$ and the mean, standard deviation, skewness and kurtosis of each of the three talent variables. By comparison with the talent distributions of assignees, it will be recalled that, for the population as a whole, each dimension of talent (the first two of which exhibit a positive correlation of 0.5) is distributed normally with mean 100 and standard deviation 20, implying skewness of zero and kurtosis of 3.

The results of the simulation reported in Table 2 are generally self-explanatory and plausible. The reward functions were purposely designed to result in the assignment of approximately one-half of the labor force to the Lumpen Proletariat and Crafts and Trades, permitting attention to focus on the remaining seven occupations, four of which (Management, Finance and Sales, Bureaucracy, Technocracy) are of similar relative size, with the Literate Professions (two variants) and the Scholarly Elite constituting smaller, selective groups. Mean rewards range from 3.63 (Scholarly Elite)[15] to the vicinity of 2.5 (Finance and Sales, Bureaucracy, Literate Professions), 1.76 (Technocracy), about 1.35 (Management and Crafts and Trades), and, finally, 1.12 (Lumpen Proletariat).[16]

Mean talents vary significantly across occupations, reflecting differences across occupations in the marginal rewards to specific talents. Manipulative talent (T_1) is extremely high (mean greater than 120) in Finance and Sales and Bureaucracy, high (117) in the Literate Professions, and exceeds the population mean (105 versus 100) for the Scholarly Elite; in all other occupations the manipulative mean is well below the population mean, with a low of 87 in Technocracy. Artistic talent (T_2) is highest for the Literate Professions (mean of 123 or 124) and is high (117) for the Scholarly Elite; due to the positive correlation between manipulative and artistic talent, artistic talent is as high (107) in Finance and Sales (for which there is no return to artistic talent but a high return to manipulative talent) as in Crafts and Trades (for which artistic talent is relatively highly rewarded but manipulative talent is of no benefit). The lowest level of artistic talent (85) is exhibited by Technocracy. Scientific talent (T_3) is highest for the Scholarly Elite (134) and Technocracy (125), and is moderately high (110 or 111) in the Literate Professions. Comparing Finance and Sales, with a slight return to scientific talent, to Bureaucracy, for which there is no reward for scientific talent, mean scientific talent is

---

15. Clearly, any 'realistic' interpretation of the high rewards claimed by the Scholarly Elite requires that rewards be conceived to include non-pecuniary benefits of incumbency in at least that profession.

16. The effect of occupationally endemic variance (i.e. w_j at or close to unity) on occupational assignment/choice is clearly revealed by the mean reward received by Lumpen Proletarians. Were the entire population to be assigned to the Lumpen Proletariat $(P_1 = 1)$, mean rewards in that occupation would be only 1.02 $(= \exp{(0.5\, \sigma_{j,1}^2)} = \exp{[0.5(0.2^2)]})$, in contrast to the observed mean of 1.12. Clearly, many of those for whom the occupational-specific random term for the Lumpen Proletariat is negative are being assigned (correctly) to other occupations, while many who would have been expected to enter other occupations are being assigned to the Lumpen Proletariat as a result of occupation-specific random terms which are positive for the Lumpen Proletariat and/or negative for the otherwise expected occupation. Together, these effects serve to raise the mean reward of Lumpen Proletarians by approximately 10 per cent above that which would be expected on the basis of the Lumpen Proletarian reward function in isolation.

higher in the former than in the latter (95 versus 90). Scientific talent is lowest (88) among Lumpen Proletarians.

In all cases the within-occupation standard deviations of talent (ranging from 10 to 18) are less, often substantially less (with 14 of the 27 falling in the range 10 to 15), than the standard deviations for the entire population (definitionally 20). The lowest standard deviations (10 to 12) are observed in those occupations with markedly high returns to particular talents (the Scholarly Elite and Technocracy in the case of scientific talent; Bureaucracy, Finance and Sales and the Literate Professions in the case of manipulative talent).

For the Lumpen Proletariat, Crafts and Trades, and Management, the distributions of manipulative and scientific talent (T_1, T_3 respectively) are distinctly negatively skewed. Artistic talent (T_2) is similarly negatively skewed for Management and Technocracy. Marked positive skewness of manipulative talent (T_1) is observed in Finance and Sales and Bureaucracy. Finally, the Scholarly Elite exhibits positive skewness of both artistic and scientific talent (T_2, T_3 respectively). While positive skewness tends to reflect strong positive returns to the specific talent in the occupation, negative skewness is generally indicative of relatively low returns in comparison with closely competing occupations.

Marked divergence of kurtosis from the normal (mesokurtic) value of three is observed only in the case of manipulative talent (T_1) in Finance and Sales and Bureaucracy, for which high values are indicative of thick upper tails (due to concomitant positive skewness), reflecting the extremely high relative return to this type of talent in these occupations by comparison to all others.

OCCUPATIONAL PARTITIONING OF THE TALENT SPACE

Effectively, the individual occupational assignments determined by the application of the occupational assignment rule $^{\max}_j[R_{j,i}]$ result in a partitioning of the talent space $<T_1, T_2, T_3>$. Because of the presence of occupation-specific error terms, this partitioning is 'fuzzy', as persons exhibiting identical configurations of talent are assigned to different occupations due to stochastic differences in rewards. However, each occupation will tend to command a particular region of the talent space, with the density of the overlaps determined by the magnitudes of the variances of the occupation-specific random terms.

Expectations of rewards can be utilized to obtain a non-fuzzy, deterministic and thus more easily represented occupational partitioning of the talent space; interpretively, this distinct partitioning would be observed if assignments to occupations were based on (risk-neutral) expectations rather than knowledge of occupational- and individual-specific random terms. Thus, Figs. 1(a) to 1(h) identify for each point in the $<T_3, T_2>$ plane (holding constant the value of T_1) that occupation j for which

$$^{\max}_j \{E[R_j(T_1, T_2, T_3, P_j)]\} = \exp(\beta_{j,0} + \beta_{j,1}T_1 + \beta_{j,2}T_2 + \beta_{j,3}T_3 + \beta_{j,4}P_j + 0.5\sigma^2_{j,1})\}.$$

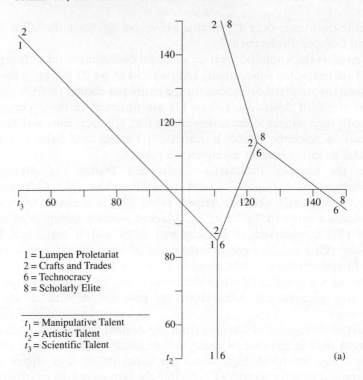

1 = Lumpen Proletariat
2 = Crafts and Trades
6 = Technocracy
8 = Scholarly Elite

t_1 = Manipulative Talent
t_2 = Artistic Talent
t_3 = Scientific Talent

(a)

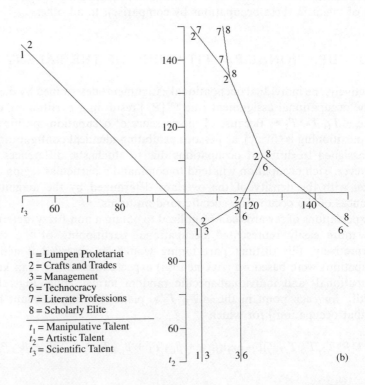

1 = Lumpen Proletariat
2 = Crafts and Trades
3 = Management
6 = Technocracy
7 = Literate Professions
8 = Scholarly Elite

t_1 = Manipulative Talent
t_2 = Artistic Talent
t_3 = Scientific Talent

(b)

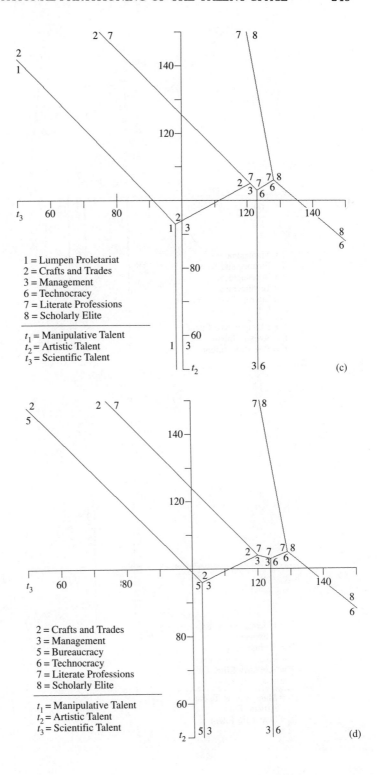

1 = Lumpen Proletariat
2 = Crafts and Trades
3 = Management
6 = Technocracy
7 = Literate Professions
8 = Scholarly Elite

t_1 = Manipulative Talent
t_2 = Artistic Talent
t_3 = Scientific Talent

(c)

2 = Crafts and Trades
3 = Management
5 = Bureaucracy
6 = Technocracy
7 = Literate Professions
8 = Scholarly Elite

t_1 = Manipulative Talent
t_2 = Artistic Talent
t_3 = Scientific Talent

(d)

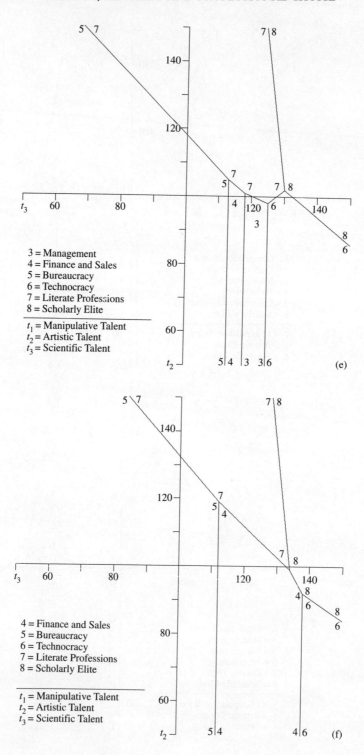

3 = Management
4 = Finance and Sales
5 = Bureaucracy
6 = Technocracy
7 = Literate Professions
8 = Scholarly Elite

t_1 = Manipulative Talent
t_2 = Artistic Talent
t_3 = Scientific Talent

(e)

4 = Finance and Sales
5 = Bureaucracy
6 = Technocracy
7 = Literate Professions
8 = Scholarly Elite

t_1 = Manipulative Talent
t_2 = Artistic Talent
t_3 = Scientific Talent

(f)

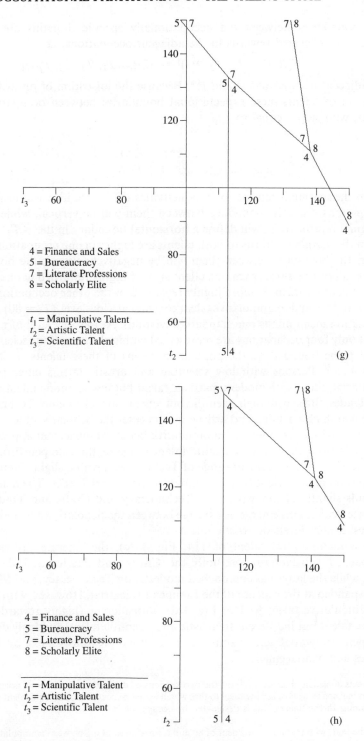

Fig.1 Professional partitions for $t_1 = 80$ (a), 100 (b), 114 (c), 115 (d), 120 (e), 130 (f), 140 (g), 150 (h).

The boundaries between the occupationally specific domains are defined by equality of expected rewards in the adjacent occupations, i.e.

$$E[R_{j^*}(T_1, T_2, T_3, P_{j^*})] = E[R_{j^{**}}(T_1, T_2, T_3, P_{j^{**}})]$$

for adjacent occupations j^* and j^{**}. Because the logarithm of rewards is a linear function of talent, these expectational boundaries between occupations will be linear, with slopes equal to

$$-\frac{\beta_{j^{**},3} - \beta_{j^*,3}}{\beta_{j^{**},2} - \beta_{j^*,2}}.$$

When the marginal returns to (productivities of) T_2 are identical in the adjacent occupations, then the boundary between them will be vertical, while equality of marginal returns to T_3 will define a horizontal boundary in the $< T_3, T_2 >$ plane. When the marginal returns to both talents are higher in one occupation than in the other, the boundary between them will be negatively sloped; the boundary will exhibit a positive slope when one talent is more highly rewarded in one occupation while the other talent is more highly rewarded in the other occupation.[17]

Figure 1(a) holds manipulative talent constant at a low level, $(T_1 = 80)$ (equal to the population mean minus one standard deviation). At this low level of manipulative talent only four occupations are represented within the area of the scientific–artistic talent plane bounded by the population means of these talents $\pm$ 2.5 standard deviations.[18] Persons with low scientific and artistic talents enter the Lumpen Proletariat, those with moderate artistic talent but low scientific talent enter Crafts and Trades, those with high scientific but low artistic talent enter Technocracy, and those with high scientific and artistic talents enter the Scholarly Elite.

In Fig. 1(b), at the mean of manipulative talent, Management appears, drawing primarily from the higher scientific talent range of the Lumpen Proletariat and from the low scientific talent range of Technocracy, with a slight claim on the low artistic and higher scientific talent range of Crafts and Trades. The Scholarly Elite expands slightly at the expense of Technocracy and Crafts and Trades, but the Literate Professions emerge as a wedge between the Scholarly Elite and Crafts and Trades at high levels of artistic talent.

At a manipulative talent of 114, Fig. 1 (c), the Literate Professions have encroached substantially on both the Crafts and Trades and the Scholarly Elite, while the latter has encroached modestly on Technocracy, and Management has expanded at the expense of the Lumpen Proletariat. However, with an increase in manipulative talent to 115, Fig. 1(d), Bureaucracy (highly rewarding manipulative talent but indifferent to artistic and scientific talent) suddenly displaces the Lumpen Proletariat and claims some territory previously held by Crafts and Trades and Management.

---

17. In this quasideterministic analysis, the two versions of the Literate Professions necessarily occupy the same subspace, a subspace identical to that which would be occupied by an equivalent single Literate Professions. In the figures, this is designated by occupation 7.

18. Note that, with manipulative talent of 80 and a correlation of 0.5 between manipulative talent and artistic talent, in Fig. 1(a) the expected value (conditional mean) of artistic talent is 90.

With manipulative talent at one standard deviation above the mean (i.e. 120), Fig. 1(e), Bureaucracy and the Literate Professions have fully occupied the territory previously claimed by Crafts and Trades, Bureaucracy has expanded at the expense of Management, the latter of which has lost even more territory with the appearance of Finance and Sales (which, unlike Bureaucracy, provides a marginal reward to scientific talent). At a manipulative talent of 130, Fig. 1(f), Finance and Sales has completely displaced Management and has encroached on Technocracy, the Scholarly Elite and the Literate Professions, the latter of which has claimed territory allocated to the Scholarly Elite at lower levels of manipulative talent while losing some of its own territory to Bureaucracy.

As manipulative talent increases further to 140 and 150, Figs. 1(g) and 1(h), Finance and Sales completely displaces Technocracy and encroaches substantially on the territory of the Scholarly Elite, while both Finance and Sales and Bureaucracy expand at the expense of the Literate Professions.

Clearly, persons with talent configurations near the boundaries of the occupational partitions have greater 'freedom' of occupational choice than persons with talent combinations well within the domain of a single occupation. Thus, for example, in Fig. 1(e) an individual exhibiting manipulative and scientific talents approximately one standard deviation above the respective means, with mean artistic talent, faces roughly equal rewards in five occupations (Bureaucracy, Finance and Sales, Management, Technocracy, Scholarly Elite, Literate Professions). In contrast, with low levels of scientific and artistic talent, an individual with a manipulative talent of 114 or 115 (Figs. 1(c) and 1(d)) has as effective choices only the Lumpen Proletariat and Bureaucracy; with higher or lower manipulative talent even this choice disappears. In general, the number of effective occupational options (the number of intersecting or relatively near occupational boundaries) is greatest for those with relatively high scientific talent, reflecting the fact that scientific talent is relatively highly rewarded in a relatively large number of occupations.[19]

OBSERVED OCCUPATIONAL ASSIGNMENTS AND STATISTICALLY INFERRED REWARD FUNCTIONS

In light of the efforts devoted to the empirical estimation of earnings functions[20] and of the significance attributed to the findings of these analyses,[21] the present analysis can make a significant contribution by addressing the issue of statistical inference: when individuals select from among alternative available opportunities on the basis of rewards which depend, at least in part, on observable individual

---

19. Thus, the quasielasticity of rewards with respect to scientific talent is one or greater in five of the eight distinct occupations (counting Literate Professions only once), while the quasielasticities with respect to manipulative and artistic talent are one or greater for only three of the eight occupations.

20. See, for example, Dresch (1986) for one of the more exhaustive (and, arguably, exhausting) of the empirical exercises, and Blaug (1976) for a dated but still substantively accurate characterization of this literature.

21. With reference to the putative implications of the earnings function literature for public policy, especially with reference to education, see Tinbergen (1975).

characteristics, what statistical inferences concerning the determinants of rewards can be drawn from observations of individual characteristics and rewards received?

Imagine that a Hypothetical Census Bureau decides to obtain information on the occupations, occupational rewards (earnings) and talents of a sample drawn from our imaginary labor force,[22] and that a Hypothetical Economist then analyzes these data in order to identify the effects of talents on occupational rewards.[23] In only two respects does the Hypothetical Census Bureau enjoy a significant advantage over any actual census bureau: (1) it has available instruments which permit it to measure manipulative, artistic and scientific talents without error;[24] and (2) it is able to obtain accurate reports of actual occupational rewards received by individuals.[25] In all other respects, this Hypothetical Census Bureau operates subject to the same constraints which confront any real census bureau. In particular, it is able to observe only the observable; specifically, it can observe rewards actually received by an individual in his selected occupation, but it is incapable of observing the rewards which would have been received in any occupation other than the one elected.

However, as the agents of the Hypothetical Census Bureau fan out through the labor force, administering talent tests and collecting information on actual occupations and rewards received therein, they are shadowed by agents of an Omniscient Census Bureau, who supplement the Hypothetical Census Bureau's data with information concerning the rewards which individuals would have received in occupations other than those which they in fact entered. As the Hypothetical Economist analyzes the 'real' data collected by the Hypothetical Census Bureau, an Omniscient Economist analyzes the data as supplemented by the Omniscient Census Bureau.

The occupational reward functions estimated by the Hypothetical and Omniscient Economists are presented in Table 3, as are the 'true' coefficients (stipulated in the model generating the labor force observations). The functions provided by the Hypothetical Economist are identified as estimated from 'assignee samples' (consisting of persons who were assigned to, or elected, the specific occupation), while the Omniscient Economist's estimates are based upon a 'random sample' (with information on rewards which would have been received by an individual in each occupation, whether or not that occupation was elected).

---

22. To ease its computational burdens (and remain within the operational constraints of its micro-computer-based statistical software), the Hypothetical Census Bureau does not sample all occupations at equal rates. Rather, it selects a random sample of 500 from each occupation with more than 500 incumbents and collects a 100 per cent sample of each occupation with 500 or fewer incumbents.

23. The Hypothetical Census Bureau and Economist are assumed to confront no divisive debates concerning the nature of talents, biases in their measurement, 'nature' versus 'nurture' in the determination of talents (calling into question, on sociopolitical grounds, even the recognition of individual differences in talent), etc.

24. Alternatively, errors in the measurement of talent can be assumed to underlie the individual-specific error terms in the occupational reward functions.

25. Thus, the Hypothetical Census Bureau has surmounted the difficulties encountered in actual surveys as a result of incomplete, erroneous reporting of earnings, of non-pecuniary components of rewards, etc.

Table 3 Talent correlations and statistically estimated (OLS) reward functions

Occupation (j)	Assignee talent correlations			Reward functions		
	T_1	T_2		Assignee sample	Random sample (total labor force)	True
1 Lumpen Prol.			R^2	0.124	0.002	
T_2	0.307		s	0.176	0.206	0.2
T_3	-0.003	-0.091				
			β_0^P	-0.4683	0.0573	0
$n = 500$				(0.0739)	(0.0726)	
				[-6.3]	[0.8]	
			β_1	0.0008	0.0000	0
				(0.0006)	(0.0005)	
				[1.4]	[0.1]	
			β_2	0.0019	-0.0004	0
				(0.0005)	(0.0006)	
				[3.9]	[-0.7]	
			β_3	0.0037	-0.0002	0
				(0.0005)	(0.0005)	
				[7.2]	[-0.5]	
2 Crafts and Trades			R^2	0.458	0.660	
T_2	0.292		s	0.176	0.208	0.212
T_3	-0.017	-0.081				
			β_0^P	-1.5601	-2.1075	-2.051
$n = 500$				(0.0916)	(0.0735)	
				[-17.0]	[-28.7]	
			β_1	0.0023	0.0013	0.001
				(0.0006)	(0.0005)	
				[3.8]	[2.5]	
			β_2	0.0069	0.0100	0.01
				(0.0006)	(0.0005)	
				[11.9]	[17.8]	
			β_3	0.0086	0.0102	0.01
				(0.0005)	(0.0005)	
				[15.9]	[21.2]	

Table 3   (continued)

Occupation (j)	Assignee talent correlations		Reward functions		
	T_1	T_2	Assignee sample	Random sample (total labor force)	True
3 Management			R^2 0.471	0.629	
T_2	0.330		s 0.180	0.241	0.25
T_3	0.071	0.015			
			β_0^P −1.5298	−2.0746	−2.077
$n = 500$			(0.0908)	(0.0849)	
			[−16.8]	[−24.4]	
			β_1 0.0047	0.0042	0.005
			(0.0006)	(0.0006)	
			[7.5]	[6.7]	
			β_2 0.0015	0.0004	0
			(0.0006)	(0.0006)	
			[2.7]	[0.6]	
			β_3 0.0115	0.0155	0.015
			(0.0006)	(0.0006)	
			[18.2]	[27.7]	
4 Fin. and Sales			R^2 0.762	0.869	
T_2	0.372		s 0.256	0.394	0.404
T_3	0.151	−0.068	β_0^P −4.4081	−6.1791	−5.990
$n = 500$			(0.1366)	(0.1390)	
			[32.3]	[−44.5]	
			β_1 0.0383	0.0509	0.05
			(0.0011)	(0.0010)	
			[34.4]	[49.5]	
			β_2 0.0018	0.0009	0
			(0.0007)	(0.0011)	
			[2.5]	[0.8]	
			β_3 0.0034	0.0021	0.002
			(0.0007)	(0.0009)	
			[5.1]	[2.4]	

Table 3 (continued)

Occupation (j)	Assignee talent correlations			Reward functions		
	T_1	T_2		Assignee sample	Random sample (total labor force)	True
5 Bureaucracy			R^2	0.964	0.991	
T_2	0.435		s	0.101	0.096	0.1
T_3	0.190	−0.186				
			β_0^P	−5.5655	−5.6804	−5.686
$n = 500$				(0.0581)	(0.0339)	
				[−95.8]	[−167.5]	
			β_1	0.0483	0.0501	0.05
				(0.0005)	(0.0003)	
				[97.3]	[199.5]	
			β_2	0.0008	−0.0002	0
				(0.0003)	(0.0003)	
				[2.4]	[−0.6]	
			β_3	0.0004	0.0000	0
				(0.0003)	(0.0002)	
				[1.3]	[0.0]	
6 Technocracy			R^2	0.685	0.894	
T_2	0.337		s	0.183	0.203	0.212
T_3	0.076	0.024				
			β_0^P	−2.7094	−3.4755	−3.344
$n = 500$				(0.1036)	(0.0716)	
				[−26.1]	[−48.5]	
			β_1	0.0014	0.0000	0
				(0.0005)	(0.0005)	
				[2.7]	[0.1]	
			β_2	0.0015	0.0009	0
				(0.0005)	(0.0005)	
				[2.9]	[1.6]	
			β_3	0.0236	0.0304	0.03
				(0.0007)	(0.0005)	
				[32.1]	[64.6]	

Table 3 (continued)

Occupation (j)	Assignee talent correlations			Reward functions		
	T_1	T_2		Assignee sample	Random sample (total labor force)	True
7 Lit. Prof.			R^2	0.755	0.913	
T_2	0.259		s	0.210	0.242	0.25
T_3	0.115	−0.268				
			β_0^P	−4.9978	−6.5703	−6.480
				(0.1546)	(0.0887)	
	$n = 472$			[−32.3]	[−74.01]	
			β_1	0.0197	0.0190	0.02
				(0.0009)	(0.0006)	
				[21.1]	[29.4]	
			β_2	0.0141	0.0213	0.02
				(0.0008)	(0.0007)	
				[18.4]	[32.1]	
			β_3	0.0157	0.0204	0.02
				(0.0008)	(0.0006)	
				[19.6]	[34.9]	
8 Schol. Elite			R^2	0.798	0.954	
T_2	0.176		s	0.229	0.244	0.25
T_3	0.101	−0.392				
			β_0^P	−7.3968	−9.2549	−9.121
$n = 414$				(0.2143)	(0.0966)	
				[−34.5]	[−95.8]	
			β_1	0.0064	0.0050	0.005
				(0.0008)	(0.0007)	
				[8.5]	[7.0]	
			β_2	0.0205	0.0254	0.025
				(0.0009)	(0.0007)	
				[23.6]	[35.4]	
			β_3	0.0408	0.0509	0.05
				(0.0012)	(0.0006)	
				[35.0]	[80.6]	

Table 3 (concluded)

Occupation (j)	Assignee talent correlations		Reward functions		
	T_1	T_2	Assignee sample	Random sample (total labor force)	True
9 Lit. Prof.			R^2 0.795	0.895	
T_2	0.301		s 0.209	0.261	0.25
T_3	0.214	−0.292			
$n = 335$			β_0^P −5.2608 (0.1738) [−30.3]	−6.4653 (0.1161) [−55.7]	−6.523
			β_1 0.0202 (0.0011) [18.2]	0.0200 (0.0008) [24.2]	0.02
			β_2 0.0146 (0.0009) [16.2]	0.0196 (0.0009) [22.5]	0.02
			β_3 0.0168 (0.001) [16.9]	0.0200 (0.0008) [25.9]	0.02

Exhibit:
Talent correlations for total labor force
T_2	0.5	
T_3	0	0

(. . .): standard error of estimated coefficient.
[. . .]: t-ratio of estimated coefficient.
s: standard error of estimated equation.
n: sample size.

The results of the Hypothetical Economist's analysis can be very quickly summarized. The proportion of the variance of rewards explained by his reward functions exceeds 0.75 in five of the nine occupations, and for only one occupation (Lumpen Proletariat) is the R^2 distinctly low (0.124); for cross-sectional analyses, in which an R^2 of 0.25 or higher is commonly considered very good, these results are indeed impressive. Of the 27 talent coefficients (three dimensions of talent for each of nine occupations) estimated by the Hypothetical Economist, only two are not significantly different from zero by commonly accepted statistical standards; indeed, t-statistics in excess of ten are found for 14 of these coefficients, and in one case the astonishing value of 95 is observed. Finally, standard errors of the estimated equations are modest, approximately 0.25 or less in all cases, and less than 0.2 in five of the nine cases.[26]

---

26. In interpreting the standard errors, it might be noted, since the reward functions are log linear, the antilogarithm of the standard error, $\exp(s_j)$, expresses the standard error as a proportion of the predicted value. For small values of s_j, $\exp(s_j) \approx s_j$

The Omniscient Economist's review of these findings by the Hypothetical Economist can also be succinctly summarized:

1. First, the Omniscient Economist pointed out that, while the Hypothetical Economist had self-deprecatingly noted the low explanatory power of the estimated reward function for Lumpen Proletarians, his reported R^2 is nonetheless significantly greater than zero, while the true R^2 for Lumpen Proletarians is in fact zero.

2. Second, while only two of the talent coefficients estimated by the Hypothetical Economist are not significantly different from zero, the Omniscient Economist pointed out that nine of the true coefficients (one-third of the 27) are, in fact, zero; thus, the Hypothetical Economist has reported statistically significant (positive) coefficients in seven cases in which the true coefficients are zero.

3. Third, and related to the second, only six of the 27 talent coefficients estimated by the Hypothetical Economist do not differ significantly from the true values, i.e. 21 of these 27 coefficients are significantly different from true values.

4. Fourth, of the Hypothetical Economist's nine estimated constant terms of the reward functions, only one does not differ significantly from the true value.

5. Finally, while the Hypothetical Economist had taken pride in the low standard errors of his estimated reward functions, eight of the nine estimated standard errors are less than the true values, and in one case the estimated standard error is only 60 per cent of its true value. Thus, what the Hypothetical Economist has claimed as a strength of his analysis, the discovery of only a relatively small random component in rewards, is actually a weakness, in that the random component is, in fact, substantially larger than his naive analysis indicates.

That the errors in the reward functions estimated by the Hypothetical Economist result from systematic selection into occupations is clearly revealed by the talent correlations computed for the nine assignee samples, as also reported in Table 3. Thus, while the true (population) correlation between manipulative and artistic talent, $\rho_{1, 2}$, is 0.5, the assignee correlations are all less than 0.44, and in three cases these are less than 0.3. Similarly, in contrast to the population correlation of zero between manipulative and scientific talent ($\rho_{1, 3}$), five of the assignee correlations are greater than 0.1. Finally, while the true correlation between artistic and scientific talent ($\rho_{2, 3}$) is also zero, four of the assignee correlations are less than -0.18, and one (scholarly elite) is as low as -0.4. Essentially, the specific patterns of occupational rewards to talent determine occupational selections for which interrelationships between talents within the cadre of occupational assignees differ significantly from those which characterize the population at large.

In short, the Omniscient Economist concluded, the results reported by the Hypothetical Economist are systematically biased. Because these biases result from systematic self-selection of occupation in a multioccupation context and from the influence of the random errors of rewards on occupational choice, their probable presence should have been recognized by the Hypothetical Economist.

While the foregoing is concerned with biases in the estimation of talent coefficients in reward functions for an artificial population, this artificial population is, we would argue, a close analog to true populations. Moreover, our conclusions with reference to talent coefficients estimated for this artificial population provide strong grounds for viewing skeptically the results of ordinary least-squares estimates of the effects of *any* individual characteristics for *any* subpopulation whenever these individual characteristics can be anticipated to be differentially valued in different subpopulations and thus can be anticipated to influence subpopulation membership.[27]

COMPARATIVE STATICS: VARIATIONS IN DEMAND FOR THE SCHOLARLY ELITE

The issue of comparative statics constitutes the final focus of this analysis, with an examination of the effects on the interoccupational distribution of the labor force and on intraoccupational labor force characteristics of variations in relative occupational demands. Because of recurrent public-policy attention and intervention focused on the cadre of fundamental scientists,[28] we focus this analysis on variations in the relative demand for the Scholarly Elite.[29]

A spectrum of five comparative static equilibria is described in Table 4. These equilibria were obtained by varying the consolidated intercept term ($\beta^P_{8.0} = \beta_{8.0} + P_8\beta_{8.4}$) in the reward function of the Scholarly Elite from -9.521 to -8.721 (in increments of 0.2). Because these coefficient changes have the effect of altering the equilibrium values of all nine occupational proportions (P_j) when the talent coefficients are held fixed, this method involves the implicit modification of all true intercept terms ($\beta_{j.o}, j = 1, \ldots, 9$), holding constant the coefficients of the occupational proportions ($\beta_{j.4}$). Thus, as the consolidated intercept of the Scholarly Elite is increased (from -9.521 to -8.721, holding the consolidated intercept terms constant for all other professions), the true intercept for this profession increases even more substantially (from -9.443 to -7.668), compensating for the increase in the proportion of the labor force attracted to the Scholarly Elite.

---

27. The artificial population simulated here would provide an ideal focus for examination of the properties of alternative statistical estimators (for example, instrumental-variables generalized least-squares techniques) designed to deal with the problems identified in the Hypothetical Economist's OLS estimates.

28. For the present purposes we will not attempt a rigorous definition of the term 'fundamental science'. Operationally, as developed by de Solla Price (1977), fundamental science is distinguished from 'other science' (i.e. from extra- or quasi-scientific activities of scientists) by the capacity of a purchaser to 'order' the latter, while this is impossible in the case of the former. Suffice it to say that fundamental science embraces much of what is classified by the National Science Foundation as 'basic research', probably includes a large fraction of 'applied research', and constitutes an important fraction of the activities even of many of the scientifically trained who are ostensibly devoted to 'development'.

29. If fundamental scientists comprise between one-third and one-half of the Scholarly Elite, then this analysis is consistent (in the range of labor force proportions attracted to the Scholarly Elite and to fundamental science) with our own earlier analysis using a simple two-sector (science, non-science) model (Dresch and Janson 1987).

Table 4 Comparative static simulations of a labor force of 10 000. (Variations in demand for Scholarly Elite, $\beta_{8,0}^{P}$)

Occupation (j)	$\beta_{8,0}^{P}$	$\beta_{j,0}$	P_j	$\overline{R}_j$	T_1	T_2	T_3
1 Lumpen Prol.	−9.521	0	0.301	1.12	90	91	88
	−9.321	0	0.301	1.12	90	91	88
	−9.121	0	0.301	1.12	90	91	88
	−8.921	0	0.300	1.12	89	91	87
	−8.721	0	0.299	1.12	89	91	87
2 Crafts and Trades	−9.521	−1.844	0.207	1.33	95	107	99
	−9.321	−1.845	0.206	1.32	95	107	99
	−9.121	−1.849	0.202	1.32	95	107	98
	−8.921	−1.856	0.195	1.30	95	107	98
	−8.721	−1.866	0.185	1.29	95	106	97
3 Management	−9.521	−1.746	0.110	1.37	96	90	108
	−9.321	−1.747	0.110	1.37	96	90	107
	−9.121	−1.754	0.108	1.36	96	90	107
	−8.921	−1.761	0.105	1.35	96	89	107
	−8.721	−1.775	0.101	1.33	95	89	106
4 Fin. and Sales	−9.521	−5.534	0.091	2.69	123	107	96
	−9.321	−5.535	0.091	2.69	123	107	95
	−9.121	−5.536	0.091	2.69	123	107	95
	−8.921	−5.542	0.090	2.69	123	107	95
	−8.721	−5.552	0.088	2.69	123	107	94
5 Bureaucracy	−9.521	−5.352	0.084	2.50	128	109	90
	−9.321	−5.352	0.084	2.50	128	109	90
	−9.121	−5.352	0.083	2.50	128	109	90
	−8.921	−5.353	0.083	2.50	128	109	90
	−8.721	−5.356	0.083	2.50	128	109	90
6 Technocracy	−9.521	−3.030	0.105	1.81	88	87	126
	−9.321	−3.041	0.101	1.79	87	86	126
	−9.121	−3.062	0.094	1.76	87	85	125
	−8.921	−3.091	0.084	1.70	86	83	124
	−8.721	−3.130	0.071	1.65	84	81	123
7 Lit. Prof. I	−9.521	−5.992	0.054	2.51	117	123	114
	−9.321	−6.021	0.051	2.48	117	123	113
	−9.121	−6.062	0.047	2.37	117	123	111
	−8.921	−6.122	0.040	2.32	117	124	109
	−8.721	−6.192	0.032	2.24	117	124	106
8 Schol. Elite	−9.521	−9.443	0.009	3.94	103	120	141
	−9.321	−9.139	0.020	3.78	106	119	137
	−9.121	−8.750	0.041	3.63	105	117	134
	−8.921	−8.265	0.073	3.57	105	115	131
	−8.721	−7.668	0.117	3.58	104	113	128
9 Lit. Prof. II	−9.521	−5.989	0.039	2.47	117	124	113
	−9.321	−6.022	0.036	2.40	117	124	111
	−9.121	−6.062	0.033	2.38	117	124	110
	−8.921	−6.113	0.030	2.36	118	124	108
	−8.721	−6.181	0.025	2.35	118	124	106

Correspondingly, the true intercept terms for other professions decline to compensate for the reduced labor force claims of these occupations. In general, the declines in the true intercepts are marginal, especially for Finance and Sales and Bureaucracy, which reward very different talents than does the Scholarly Elite, although the declines for Technocracy (by 0.1 over the range of equilibria) and for the Literate Professions (by 0.2) are non-trivial, reflecting the competing demands of Technocracy, the Literate Professions and the Scholarly Elite for high scientific talent.

Ceteris paribus (specifically, holding talents constant), each of these successive 0.2 increases in $\beta^P_{8,0}$ implies a 22 per cent [$= 100 (e^{0.2} - 1)$] increase in rewards to incumbency in the Scholarly Elite. Further, holding constant the configuration of talents and the Scholarly Elite's share of the labor force, rewards would increase by 35, 48, 62 and 82 per cent with each of the successive increases in demand, as indicated by the increases in the true intercepts ($\beta_{8,0}$). However, 'all else' (specifically, the configuration of incumbents' talents and the occupational proportions) is not held constant, and, as a result, actual mean rewards of members of the Scholarly Elite generally *decline* as demand increases; thus, as revealed by Table 4, the 22 per cent *ceteris paribus* increase in rewards of the Scholarly Elite implied by each increment in the consolidated intercept contrasts sharply with observed 4 per cent declines in actual mean rewards occasioned by the two initial increases in demand (as mean rewards of the Scholarly Elite decline from 3.94 to 3.78 and 3.63) and with the 1.7 per cent decline and 0.2 per cent increase implied by the two subsequent demand increases (as mean rewards of the Scholarly Elite decline further to 3.57 and then rise slightly to 3.58).

These declines in mean rewards reflect the fact that increases in relative demand induce increases in the Scholarly Elite's equilibrium share of the labor force (from 0.9 per cent to 2.0, 4.1, 7.3 and 11.7 per cent respectively), increases which can be achieved only by drawing less talented individuals into the Scholarly Elite. Thus, mean artistic and scientific talents decline substantially. For example, mean scientific talent declines from 141 when the Scholarly Elite's share of the labor force is 0.9 per cent to 128 when this share is increased to 11.7 per cent, a decline greater than one intraoccupational standard deviation (or two-thirds of a population standard deviation), while artistic talent declines from 120 to 113, or by more than one-half of an intraoccupational standard deviation (one-third of a population standard deviation).[30] Interestingly, the mean levels of scientific talent of the Scholarly Elite are consistent with Harmon's (1963) estimates of the modal IQ scores of recipients of science doctorates, noting that, with a positively skewed distribution, the mean will exceed the mode. Moreover, the orders of magnitude of the declines associated with expansion of the Scholarly Elite are consistent with the declines simulated by Dresch and Janson (1987) for roughly comparable relative increases in the size of the cadre of fundamental scientists.

Comparing the extreme equilibria, the 10.8 percentage point (more than tenfold) expansion of the Scholarly Elite is accomplished primarily by drawing

---

30. Intraoccupational standard deviations of talent differ only slightly across comparative static equilibria and are approximately equal to those indicated in Table 2 for the basic static solution.

personnel from professions demanding similar talents, notably Technocracy (which suffers a 3.4 percentage point decline in labor force share), the two Literate Professions (which together lose 3.6 percentage points), Crafts and Trades (declining by 2.2 percentage points) and Management (contracting by 0.9 percentage points); in contrast, the slight contractions in Bureaucracy (by 0.1 percentage points), the Lumpen Proletariat (0.2 percentage points) and Finance and Sales (0.3 percentage points) reflect the trivial or non-existent demand for scientific talent in these occupations.

In the Literate Professions a substantial decline in mean scientific talent (from 114 to 106) is observed, although mean manipulative and artistic talents rise very slightly as those with the highest scientific talent (but mediocre manipulative and artistic talents) are attracted to the Scholarly Elite. In Technocracy a modest three-point erosion of scientific talent is conjoined with more substantial six- and four-point declines in manipulative and artistic talents, because, holding constant scientific talent, those with the highest manipulative and artistic talents will be most likely to depart for the Scholarly Elite. As a result of the combined effect of (1) the reduction in demand (intercept terms) and (2) the erosion of talent, mean rewards decline in all occupations other than the Lumpen Proletariat, Finance and Sales and Bureaucracy; however, with the exception of Technocracy and the Literate Professions, in which rewards decline by about 10 per cent, the erosion of rewards is generally marginal.

Conclusion

In this chapter we have presented a rather simple stochastic model of individual characteristics ('talents'), of differential demands for these characteristics in a range of available occupations and of occupational assignment/choice. Although highly parsimonious, this model provides an interesting and, we would argue, descriptive mimic of reality. Specifically, it has permitted us to address within its artificial environment issues of statistical inference which are encountered but commonly ignored in the analysis of actual information concerning the determinants of earnings and occupational choice and to examine the direct and indirect consequences of increases in the relative size of the scientific cadre.

However, this application does not exhaust the potential usefulness of the model. In developing the model we were particularly interested in the consequences of occupational licensure and of concomitant constraints on intraoccupational competition for the talent configurations and rewards of occupational incumbents, but other obvious foci include the dynamic adaptation of differentiated labor markets to non-uniform growth of occupational demands and labor supply, the implications of non-neutral technological change, and the consequences of endogeneity of instrumental talents. Thus, we anticipate that models of this type will permit the illumination of a variety of fundamental issues confronted in the analysis of actual labor markets but ignored because of their complexity.

ACKNOWLEDGMENTS

This paper has examined the economic and statistical implications of a model developed by the authors in 'Recruitment and accomplishment in fundamental science: a generalization of the "giants, pygmies" model,' *Technological Forecasting and Social Change*, **37**, no. 1 (1990), extending a more specialized model analyzed in 'Giants, pygmies and the social costs of fundamental research, or, Price revisited', *Technological Forecasting and Social Change*, **32**, no. 4 (1987), and acknowledgements in those papers apply here as well. I. Richard Savage, Wen-he Lu, and Karol I. Pelc provided invaluable advice and criticism. The contributions of seminar participants at Northwestern University's School of Education and Social Policy and at the Institute of Economics and Forecasting of Scientific and Technological Progress of the Academy of Sciences of the (then) USSR, Moscow, are also acknowledged.

REFERENCES

Aitchison, J. and Brown, J. A. C. (1957). *The lognormal distribution*. Cambridge University Press, London.

Blaug, M. (1976). The empirical status of human capital theory: a slightly jaundiced survey. *Journal of Economic Literature* (September).

Dresch, S. P. (1983). Education and lifetime earnings: the Census Bureau's misguided misrepresentation. *Review of Public Data Use* (December).

Dresch, S. P. (1986). *Occupational earnings, 1967–1981: returns to occupational choice, schooling, and physician specialization*. JAI Press, Greenwich, CT.

Dresch, S. P. and Janson, K. R. (1987). Giants, pygmies and the social costs of fundamental research, or, Price revisited. *Technological Forecasting and Social Change*, **32**, no. 4.

Dresch, S. P. and Janson, K. R. (1990). Recruitment and accomplishment in fundamental science: a generalization of the 'Giants, pygmies' model. *Technological Forecasting and Social Change*, **37**, no. 1.

Harmon, L. R. (1963). The high school backgrounds of science doctorates. *Science*, **133**, 679.

Lang, S. (1988). Academic, journalistic, and political problems. *The Chronicle of Higher Education* (3 February) B4.

Lotka, A. J. (1956). *Elements of mathematical biology*. Dover Publications, New York. (Originally published as *Elements of physical biology*, 1924.)

National Science Foundation, Division of Policy Research and Analysis (1990). *The state of academic science and engineering*. National Science Foundation, Washington DC.

Price, D. J. de S. (1963). *Little science, big science*. Columbia University Press, New York (Republished, with additional papers, as *Little science, big science . . . and beyond*. Columbia University Press, New York, 1986.]

Price, D. J. de S. (1977). An extrinsic value theory for basic and 'Applied' research. In *Science and technology policy* (ed. J. Haberer). Lexington Books, Lexington, MA.

Tinbergen, J. (1975). *Income distribution: analyses and policies*. North Holland, Amsterdam.

US House of Representatives, Committee on Science, Space, and Technology, Subcommittee on Investigations and Oversight (1993). *Projecting science and engineering personnel requirements for the 1990s: How good are the numbers?* [Hearing, April 8, 1992]. US Government Printing Office, Washington DC.

14 Statistical analysis for the masses

SAM L SAVAGE

Several years ago I came to the conclusion that many graduates of basic statistics courses don't understand the Central Limit Theorem. I was wrong. They don't even understand the concept of a probability distribution! I will present evidence for this bad news, but also suggest that good news may be on the way.

THE BAD NEWS

The sample population

My evidence for bad news is based on experience with those who have attended my seminar on 'Management Science in Spreadsheets' which has been offered throughout the United States since 1990. The brochure states that:

This introductory seminar is designed for managers, accountants, engineers, and other professionals involved in forecasting, profit maximization, cost minimization, evaluation of risk, and decision-making under uncertainty. Formal training in management science or statistics is not required.

Thus this group is self-selected to have a practical need for dealing with uncertainty. Few have had extensive training in probability or statistics, but by a show of hands, virtually all have had at least an introductory course in statistics. The typical class size is between 15 and 40 with a total of over 1000 attendees.

During my lectures I use a lap-top computer and projection system to present live models in spreadsheets such as 1–2–3 or Excel. In this environment I pose questions to the audience concerning chance phenomena which, after some discussion, I answer experimentally on the spot using Monte Carlo simulation. This process has revealed some surprising misconceptions concerning uncertainty.

The experiments

I have repeatedly performed three experiments within this group, at first informally, then with somewhat more care, with consistent results.

Problem 1 – averages of random variables

I begin my seminar with a discussion of random variables.

Random variables I define a random variable as 'a number you don't know yet'. As a simple example, I introduce the spinner shown in Fig. 1, and point out that the result of a spin is modeled by the RAND function found in all spreadsheets. To provide motivation, I ask the participants to imagine that God will determine the profit of their company next year (in millions) by giving such a spinner a good whack. To provide even more motivation, I tell them that if profit is less than $200 000 they're fired.

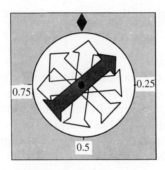

Simulation of a spin

- I simulate profit in millions, by placing the RAND function in a blank spreadsheet and running a Monte Carlo simulation of several hundred trials.
- Before showing the results, I ask what the average is likely to be. The predominant answer is $500 000 (so far so good).
- I then display a 5-bin histogram of the outcomes of RAND as shown below.
- I also display the cumulative graph showing that the probability of getting fired ($x < 0.2$) is 20%.

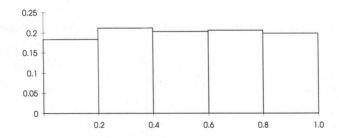

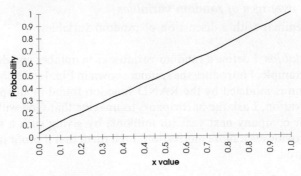

For the first two years of giving these seminars, I would then perform the following experiment.

The average of two spins

- I admit to the class that the above model of profit is naive, and that actually God whacks the spinner twice and averages the results.
- When asked what the average profit will be now, the consensus is still $500 000.
- Next I ask the class to draw a 5-bin histogram of the results. Virtually everyone draws something like Fig. 2 or Fig. 3. The proportion of each varies from group to group, but is roughly evenly divided.

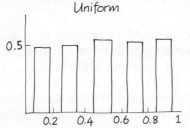

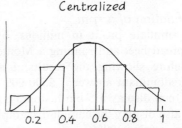

Fig. 2 Uniform distribution. Note that in this example the probability sums to 2.5.

Fig. 3. Centralized distribution. Bins, continuous lines, or as in this case both, are sometimes drawn.

- Next I simulate (RAND + RAND)/2 and display the resulting histogram below.

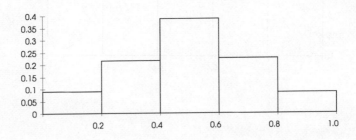

Theoretically this is a triangular distribution as can be appreciated intuitively by thinking about the outcome of rolling one and two dice.

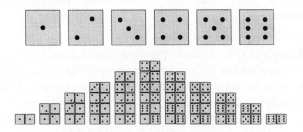

Only a handful out of 1000 subjects have drawn a clearly triangular distribution, and such people are probably better suited to being statisticians than managers. In short, *it's dumb to be too smart*. As far as I am concerned the correct practical answer to the question:

What does the distribution of the average of two spins look like?
is
It goes up in the center and down on the ends

It is far more important to be aware of the economic implications of diversification than to know the exact shape of any particular distribution.

- With this in mind I continue my demonstration by displaying the cumulative distribution which shows that the probability of getting fired is now under 10%, less than half of what it was with one spin.

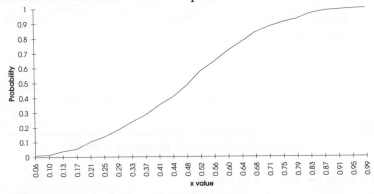

- After the correct answer has been presented, I ask how many have heard of the Central Limit Theorem. By a show of hands, virtually *all* have, although apparently few have developed a mature relationship with the subject. I also ask for the term by which their stockbroker refers to this concept. The word I am looking for and occasionally get is *diversification*. I also suggest that whenever they are faced with an important 'number they don't know yet' they should try to visualize its *shape* as approximated by a histogram.

The unjustified conclusion For two years I concluded that since roughly half the subjects drew something like Fig. 3, that they understood that the distribution would centralize in going from one to two spins. The following experiment indicated otherwise.

Problem 2 – probability distributions

The distribution of one spin In about the third year of giving these seminars, I asked the participants in one session to draw the histogram of the outcome of the *single* spin before showing them the results of the Monte Carlo experiment. I was surprised to find the same results I had been getting for the average of two spins; that is roughly 50% each of Fig. 2 and 3. I went on with the lecture and as usual asked for the average of two spins, again finding similar results. Since then, I have always asked them to draw the histograms for both one and two spins with consistent results.

I have never let my education interfere with my learning: Mark Twain In a classic case of the phenomenon referred to by Mark Twain, these graduates of a basic statistics course have learned that the maximum likelihood answer to a statistics 'picture' question is a 'bell-shaped curve'. I suspect that if the one-spin test were administered to those with no formal training in probability or statistics, that the percentage of correct answers would go up.

The joint distribution Once people have seen the correct results for a single spin their opinions have no doubt been biased concerning the result for the average of two spins. None the less it is interesting to observe the joint distribution of the two responses over the two cases (one spin, two spins).

1. *Seminar participants*: The results for 43 participants at a recent seminar are shown below.

Average of 2 Spins / 1 Spin	Correct*	Incorrect
Correct	11	12
Incorrect	9	11

The joint distribution for 43 seminar attendees.

*I count as correct any centralized distribution.

Note the roughly uniform distribution over the four possibilities. They are, clockwise from the upper left, correct for one and two spins, correct only for one spin, incorrect for both, and correct only for two spins.

2. *A more sophisticated population*: Admittedly, the backgrounds of those attending seminars vary widely, and most have been out of school for decades. Therefore I was particularly surprised when I tried this with eight masters level students in operations research at Stanford University. These

students had all recently taken courses beyond basic statistics and some were taking graduate level statistics concurrently. The results below show that five out of the eight thought that the distribution of a single spin was non-uniform!

Average of 2 Spins / 1 Spin	Correct*	Incorrect
Correct	3	
Incorrect	3	2

The joint distribution for 8 masters students in operations research.

*I count as correct any centralized distribution.

Problem 3 – functions of a random variable

Although the concepts of the central limit theorem and the diversification of risk are important, there is an even more important lesson that seems to have slipped by most graduates of a statistics course. It concerns functions of a random variable.

A stochastic cost model A supply firm carries a piece of equipment for which demand is random with a monthly average of five units. The firm stocks five units of inventory to satisfy this demand.

The cost of maintaining the inventory has two components:

1. If the demand is less than the number stocked, a $50 storage cost is incurred for every unit stocked in excess of demand.

2. If the demand is greater than the number stocked, an air freight cost of $150 per unit is incurred for the shortfall.

This situation is reflected in the spreadsheet model shown below (the formulae are shown in cells C5, C6 and C8).

	A	B	C	D	E	F
1	Demand		Amt Stocked			
2		5		5		
3						
4	Costs	Per Unit	Total			
5	Storage Cost	$50.00	IF(Amt_Stocked>Demand,+(Amt_Stocked-Demand)*S_COST,0)			
6	Air Freight	$150.00	IF(Amt_Stocked<Demand,+(Demand-Amt_Stocked)*F_COST,0)			
7						
8	Overall Cost		C5+C6			

The average overall cost

- I plug the *average* demand of five into cell A2, and neither storage nor freight costs are incurred, yielding an overall cost in C8 of zero. Therefore I say: 'the *average* overall cost is zero, right?'

At this point many eyes have glazed over, but those who understand the question generally nod their heads approvingly. Rarely does someone object or give any indication that this is in error.

- Simulation of overall cost quickly shows what's going on. I replace demand (A2) by a Poisson random variable with mean of 5, and run 50 or so iterations, yielding an average cost of around $200, not 0. Of course, I explain, since this experiment was run with random numbers, one would not expect exactly 0 even if this were the theoretical result.

- By inspecting the histogram of outcomes (below), it is clear that since there are no negative costs to cancel out the positive ones that a mean of 0 is out of the question.

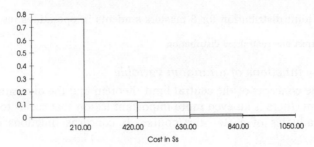

Three perspectives of what went wrong. I consider this to be such an important lesson that I repeat what went wrong in three ways, one of which hopefully hits home.

1. *Average inputs (demand) don't necessarily yield average outputs (cost).* I explain that if the model happens to be linear, then average inputs *do* yield average outputs. But when I ask by a show of hands how many know what linear means only a small percentage respond. Therefore it is safer to assume that you *don't* get average outputs.

2. $E(F(X)) \neq F(E(X))$ unless F is linear. I explain that this is the way it is expressed (and for the most part left to languish) in text books.

3. *A sobering example.* Finally I impress on the class that this can have serious consequences. Consider a drunk[1] wandering back and forth across a busy highway whose position is denoted by X. Assume that his average position, $E(X)$, is on the center line, and let $F(X)$ represent the state of the drunk. Then

$$F(E(X)) = \text{alive}$$

whereas

$$E(F(X)) = \text{dead}.$$

Average position of drunk, $E(X)$
is centre line

The tip of the iceberg

And what have others learned about errors in judgment under uncertainty? I recommend *Judgment under uncertainty: heuristics and biases* edited by Kahneman *et al.* (1982). This contains a wide variety of well documented and consistent errors in judgment, even among 'experts' who have had substantial statistical training.

If the statistics courses are not providing basic statistical intuition, it is not necessarily because they failed to cover the material, but perhaps just the opposite. That is, by covering so *many* topics, they may yield a poor signal to noise ratio when it comes to the basics.

And if the graduates of statistics courses don't know what a probability distribution is, how about the tens of millions of users of electronic spreadsheets who have had no statistics whatever. After all, 100% of them have numbers in their spreadsheet models about which they are uncertain. One can only guess at the economic impact of tens of millions of average values being plugged into potentially nonlinear models upon which business and government decisions are being based.

THE GOOD NEWS

A goal

In the preface to *Judgment under uncertainty: Heuristics and biases* it is stated that two earlier investigators, J. Bruner and H. Simon, were 'concerned with strategies of simplification that reduced the complexity of judgment tasks, to make them tractable for the kind of mind that people happen to have'.

I believe a similarly worthy goal is to 'design strategies of simplification that reduce the complexity of judgment tasks, to make them tractable for the kind of mind *and computer* that people happen to have'. And the good news is that the kind of computer people have today is the size of a book and contains more raw computing power than the entire United States at the time Bruner and Simon initiated their work in the mid 1950s.

Consumer stochastics

I refer to the fulfillment of this goal as 'consumer stochastics' (part of a larger trend that I call 'consumer analytics'). This differs from the overall field of statistics, only in its target audience. Whereas statistics has aided scientists and engineers in almost every discipline since long before electronic computing, consumer stochastics is aimed at non-scientists and non-engineers, who face uncertainty on a regular basis, that is, most professionals. This will not be the first time that a technology has moved from a highly trained audience to a more general one.

Picking up groceries with an internal combustion engine

The first internal combustion engines, for example, were employed solely by 'engineers' for turning drive belts in factories and other industrial settings. No one would have thought of using one of these noisy, dangerous and tremendously heavy pieces of equipment for picking up groceries. Today of course, the internal combustion engine is the method of choice for picking up groceries even among non-engineers, thanks to power steering, automatic transmissions, and oil pressure warning lights.

Similarly, the benefits of statistical analysis are now spreading beyond the realm of the statistically trained. Come to think of it, the oil pressure warning light embodies a statistical test for predicting engine failure with clear penalties for both type 1 and type 2 errors.

Examples

Things I would classify as consumer stochastics fall into three categories which I will call sublimated statistics, institutionalized statistics, and general tools for thought.

Sublimated statistics

Today we are surrounded by mechanical and electronic devices like the warning light above, which continually perform statistical tests. Some of these are quite complex. For example, headphones which generate anti-noise, and video cameras which electronically correct images for vibrations. The key to sublimated statistics is that if it performs correctly we don't know it's there.

Institutionalized statistics

There are also narrow contexts in which traditional statistical measures have been adopted by non-statisticians. For example, in the 1950s, Harry Markowitz (1959) pioneered the use of variance as a risk measure for stock portfolios. Derivations of this approach, which assumes a multivariate normal distribution of returns, are alive and well today in the finance community. In fact, in an attempt to establish industry benchmarks (and perhaps preempt additional banking regulation), J. P. Morgan & Co. now publishes its in-house risk measurement techniques which are based on the Markowitz approach (see the *Wall Street Journal*, 11 October 1994). This includes daily estimates of the covariance of numerous market factors.

Although an institutionalized measure, as in this case, can have a tremendous social impact, it may nonetheless be difficult to generalize. For example, when the underlying distributions are highly asymmetric, as with certain derivative financial instruments, the Markowitz risk measure is no longer appropriate. This may partially explain the reluctance of some investors to use derivatives: it is not that they are necessarily riskier, but merely that a method for measuring their risk has not yet been institutionalized.

Risk detectors Given the increased use of derivative investment instruments, and a series of recent fiascoes such as Orange County and Barings Bank, the financial community is currently aware that it needs good standardized indicators of risk beyond the original Markowitz model. A measure known as Value at Risk (VAR) has now been proposed which is applicable in situations with asymmetric risk (Beckstrom *et al.* 1994). In addition, the SEC, for example, is trying to devise 'yardsticks' for mutual fund risk (the *Wall Street Journal*, March 29, 1995). I call such institutionalized constructs *risk detectors*, and believe they will become increasingly important in the area of finance.

General tools for thought
Perhaps the most remarkable aspect of consumer stochastics is the recent proliferation of general analytical tools to tackle problems of uncertainty. Many of these are available as enhancements to electronic spreadsheets.

Monte Carlo simulation: killing cockroaches with steamrollers The most widespread among these is the brute force application of the Monte Carlo simulation. Although suggested as an analytical tool for business as early as 30 years ago (Hertz 1979), one often heard the sentiment that this technique was akin to killing cockroaches with a steamroller. I like that analogy, because had steamrollers kept technological pace with computers, they would cost pennies today, fit in your wallet, travel hundreds of miles per hour, and be the weapon of choice against the cockroach.

Currently there are several widely available commercial packages which bring Monte Carlo capability to spreadsheets: @RISK, Crystal Ball, Savage (1993) and Savage (1997). If these products do nothing else, they provide first-hand intuition into the concept of probability distributions, which may put them slightly ahead of most statistics courses.

But the users of Monte Carlo simulations won't know what distributions to use, you say. I used to feel that way too until I fully comprehended the gravity of approximating random values by their averages (remember what happened to the drunk in the highway). I am now convinced that modeling every distribution in the world as triangular, specified by a minimum, maximum, and most likely value, would be a significant improvement over the status quo.

But we can often easily do much better that the triangular distribution. I take the simplistic view (and it had better be simplistic if the masses are going to use it) that every random process has its own distribution which you can get a picture of by executing the histogram function on the historical data in your spreadsheet. The theory of probability has isolated certain idealized classes of these which have been given names (normal, binomial, Poisson, etc.). But the relationship between these idealized distributions and the historical data is analogous to that of Spam and the ham from which it was derived: something is usually lost in the process.

Simulation can be run by directly sampling the historical data itself (the ham), as championed as early as 1969 by economist Julian Simon (see Simon *et al.* 1976). This resampling process is simple, direct, and doesn't require a statistician as an intermediary to estimate distributions. This technique is the basis for the bootstrap method pioneered by Bradley Efron (Efron and Tibshirani 1993) which is now popular even among some professional statisticians. Furthermore, multi-variate data can also be used in this manner without losing the statistical dependence between variables. As both the power of computers and the quantity of digitized information continue to grow, this approach can only become more relevant.

There is a catch to this approach, however. It is only accurate if the future of the random process being modeled behaves like its past, that is, the process is *stationary*. This problem will be addressed below.

Time series analysis: forecasting the future Time series analysis is comprised of statistical techniques to forecast series of random variables such as sales, prices or interest rates which are measured at regular time intervals. Traditionally these routines have been contained in serious statistical analysis software packages like SAS and SPSS, but these hardly qualify as consumer stochastics. Recently, with the aid of expert systems, time series analysis has been automated in moderately priced commercial software packages (see for example Forecast Pro). Automated forecasting packages are in use in a wide variety of industries.

As an example, past monthly sales for some piece of equipment might be fed into a forecasting package, whereupon it yields the expected demand, five for example, for the next month. Then typically this number is plugged into a spreadsheet model to predict profit or cost . . . wait a minute. How many times do I have to go through this? Remember, plugging in averages is foolhardy.

Instead of just spitting out an expected or average demand, the forecasting software can also provide an estimate of the distribution of demand. This *can* often be sensibly plugged into a Monte Carlo simulation such as the spreadsheet inventory model discussed earlier. Perhaps this process of channeling the output of time series analysis directly into Monte Carlo simulation can be automated to include something like an oil pressure light that warns of non-stationarity.

Decision trees: forcing us to assess probabilities There are also currently several commercial packages for formulating decision trees either on their own or coupled to spreadsheets (Data; DPL; Savage 1993). Of course decision trees don't yield correct decisions unless we input correct probabilities for uncertain events, so in most cases what good are they? What they are good for is helping us focus on those issues most relevant to our decision making. And when these issues involve probabilities that are hard to estimate, the software provides graphical sensitivity analysis showing managers the consequences of various levels of uncertainty. All this leads towards improved intuition in decision making under uncertainty, and away from what Efron refers to in jest as the 'time honored tradition' of using averages.

But that's not all Other consumer stochastics tools are also quickly falling into the hands of the masses:

1. *Regression.* Linear regression is included with all spreadsheets. In fact, a recent seminar attendee from the legal analysis department of a large accounting firm told me that some courts now require a regression to be run of total cost against quantity for settling disputes involving fixed and variable costs.

2. *Markov chains.* Markov chains (Savage 1993) are a compelling paradigm in the spreadsheet, in which it is easy to graph the populations in various states over time.

3. *Stochastic optimization.* Stochastic optimization, considered computationally prohibitive only a few years ago, is now becoming popular. Small problems may be solved using built-in spreadsheet solvers, or in auxiliary software coupled to spreadsheets (for example What's *Best!*).

4. *The lunatic fringe.* In less chartered waters, products based on fuzzy logic and neural networks are also gaining acceptance. Seminar attendees from a major bank are using neural nets to predict credit-worthiness in loan applications, for example.

Where do concepts leave off and tools begin?

Some academicians aware of my approach concede that the spreadsheet is a powerful tool, but claim to prefer teaching concepts instead of tools. My response is that one can teach the concept of transferring momentum from a large mass swung on a lever arm to thin iron spikes, forcing them through pieces of wood which are thereby fastened together. I myself prefer a hammer and nails.

Can some of the concepts of statistics be similarly codified into tools as successfully as concepts of physics have been codified into the carpenter's tool box? What would these tools look like? These questions will ultimately be settled through a process of both intellectual and market evolution which has just begun. But one thing is for sure: they will not be widely adopted unless they are extremely easy to use.

The keystroke metric. I measure the complexity of an analytical technique in terms of the number of keystrokes required to apply it. I pick the electronic spreadsheet as my origin (I don't count the number of keystrokes required for using the spreadsheet itself). For example, to run the Monte Carlo simulation of the inventory model of section one required six keystrokes as follows:

(1) Paste Poisson(Mean) function into Demand cell;

(2) Replace Mean with 5;

(3) Click Simulate Run command;

(4) Type in number of iterations;

(5) Click on output cell (total cost);

(6) Click OK.

Icons of uncertainty To get the ball rolling I have listed several potential tools for people with spreadsheet models (worksheets) containing formulae and numbers, some of which they don't know yet. This represents a market of tens of millions. I will assume further that the users have access to historical data on their uncertain numbers (down to a market of merely millions). These tools would augment the current spreadsheet commands and function sets, and be accessed by clicking icons (Table 1). Undoubtedly, once these were tried in practice they would prove to be flawed, but my hope is that they would ultimately evolve into a set of tools which improved the user's ability to deal with uncertainty.

Communicating distributions Once managers start asking themselves 'what is this distribution?' instead of 'what is this number?', they are in a position to use the various tools described above for their own analysis. But there still exists the problem of communicating what they have learned to others. For example, although the forecasting department may know the distribution of demand, the normal channels of business communication are only set up to receive the mean, and perhaps a confidence interval which is generally ignored. What is needed is a convenient way to pass distributions around, perhaps in the form of spreadsheet formulae transmitted across computer networks. These formulae would contain random number generators from the distributions in question, appropriately correlated among themselves as required.

Skepticism, pessimism and hope

Skeptics who think that none of this will work run the risk of those who thought consumers would never figure out how to use internal combustion engines, cathode ray tubes, or computers.

There may be pessimists who are afraid that it just might work, and in the process degrade the traditional fields of probability and statistics. However, as statistical measures gain further acceptance in business, law, medicine, and government it should only increase the demand for high-quality statistical analysis.

Table 1 'Icons of uncertainty'

Icon	Command or function	Action	Syntax
	Histogram	Display histogram of selected data along with mean and standard deviation. Warning message for obvious non-stationarity	Select data. Click icon or perform menu command. Specify number of bins in dialog box.
	Input	Specify data to be resampled for a given cell in the worksheet. This results in the following formula being placed in the cell: $$=\text{INPUT}(\textbf{data–range})$$ where **data–range** is the range containing the data to be resampled during simulation.	Select cell containing uncertain number. Click on icon or perform menu command. Specify range containing data to be resampled.
	Output	Specify that the output distribution of a cell containing a formula depending on input cells be estimated through simulation.	Select cell. Click icon or perform menu command. Specify in dialog box, whether to add cell to or remove cell from list of output cells.
	Forecast	Perform simple time series forecast. Place random number formulas representing future periods in specified cells. For example, if the forecast were performed through linear regression, then the formula in the cell representing future time t would be: $$b + a * t + \text{INPUT}(\textbf{resid})$$ where a and b are the slope and intercept of the regression line, and **resid** is the range in which the residuals of the regression were stored.	Select data. Click icon or perform menu command. Specify locations of residuals and future time periods in dialog box.
Run	*Run*	Run a simulation creating histograms (including cumulative) of output cells.	Click Run icon or perform menu command.

Also, as with nearly all technological advances, there will be those who warn that encouraging those beyond the priesthood to try things on their own will lead to costly mistakes. Of course people will make mistakes with these tools, but none so costly as depriving the masses from more convenient and intuitive ways of dealing with uncertainty.

I prefer to hope that the statistical techniques launched in the twentieth century will lead to widespread benefits in the twenty-first century, in the way that the thermo, fluid and electrodynamics of the nineteenth century led to the transportation systems, electronics, and telecommunication of today.

REFERENCES

@RISK, Palisade Corp., Newfield, NY.

Beckstrom, R. A., Lewis, D., and Roberts C. (1994). VAR: pushing risk management to the statistical limit. *Capital Market Strategies*, No. 3, November IFR Publishing, London.

Crystal Ball, Decisioneering Inc., Boulder, CO.

DATA, Treeage Inc., Boston, MA.

DPL, Applied Decision Analysis, Menlo Park, CA.

Efron, B. and Tibshirani, R. J. (1993). *An introduction to the bootstrap*. Chapman & Hall, New York.

Forecast Pro, Business Forecast Systems, Belmont, MA.

Hertz, D. B. (1979). Risk analysis in capital investment, *Harvard Business Review*, 57, No.5.

Kahneman, D., Slovic, P., and Tversky, A. (1982). *Judgement under uncertainty: Heuristics and biases*. Cambridge University Press.

Markowitz, H. M. (1959). *Portfolio selection, efficient diversification of investments*. Wiley, New York.

Savage, S. L. (1993). *Fundamental analytic spreadsheet tools for quantitative* management. McGraw-Hill, New York.

Savage, S. L. (1997). *INSIGHT business analysis tools for Microsoft Excel*. Duxbury Press, Belmont, CA.

Simon, J. L., Atkinson, D. T., and Shevokas, C. (1976). Probability and statistics: experimental results of a radically different teaching method. *American Mathematical Monthly*, **83**, (9).

Wall Street Journal (1994). Morgan unveils the way it measures market risk (October 11).

Wall Street Journal (1995). SEC seeks aids in devising yardstick for funds' risk (March 29).

What's *Best!*, Lindo Systems Inc., Chicago.

Index